Server-Side **Swift** with **Vapor**

By Tim Condon, Tanner Nelson & Logan Wright

Server-Side Swift with Vapor

By Tim Condon, Tanner Nelson & Logan Wright

Notice of Rights

Notice of Liability

Trademarks

ISBN: 978-1-950325-27-6

About the Authors

Tim Condon is a software engineer who has worked in most areas of the industry, including security, back-end, front-end and mobile! Having previously worked for the BBC, he is now the founder of Broken Hands, specializing in Vapor training and consultancy. Tim joined the Vapor core team in 2020 and divides his time between Broken Hands and maintaining the core Vapor framework and many other packages around it. On Twitter he can be found sporadically tweeting @0xTim. You can find more about him at www.timc.dev.

Logan Wright began his career as an iOS Developer working on many categories of applications from navigation, to customized bluetooth communication protocols. Always a major supporter of OSS, Logan met Tanner through the Vapor project. Eventually, that grew into a full-time position and the community as we know it today.

Tanner Wayne Nelson is an American software engineer. He created Vapor while working and attending New York University in 2016. He eventually left school to focus on the framework full time, overseeing the release of 4 major versions. In late 2020, he stepped down from the Vapor core team to join SpaceX.

About the Editors

Richard Critz did double duty as editor and tech editor for this book. He is the iOS Team Lead at raywenderlich.com and has been doing software professionally for over 40 years, working on products as diverse as CNC machinery, network infrastructure, and operating systems. He discovered the joys of working with iOS beginning with iOS 6. Yes, he dates back to punch cards and paper tape. He's a dinosaur; just ask his kids. On Twitter, while being mainly read-only, he can be found @rcritz. The rest of his professional life can be found at www.rwcfoto.com.

Darren Ferguson is the final pass editor for this book. He's an experienced software developer and works for M.C. Dean, Inc, a systems integration provider from North Virginia. When he's not coding, you'll find him enjoying EPL Football, traveling as much as possible and spending time with his wife and daughter. Find Darren on Twitter at @darren102.

Dedications

"To the Vapor team, thank you for creating the framework — none of this would exist without you! To the Vapor community, thank you for being the best open source community anywhere in the world! To my editors, Richard and Darren, thank you for guiding my writing into something worth publishing. Finally, thank you to Amy, who has put up with endless hours of me writing and being absent but supported me throughout."

— Tim Condon

"To everybody in the open source community that saw value and supported Vapor as we grew. This project wouldn't exist without their continued support. Also, the Ray Wenderlich team for making videos early on and helping us create this book. Tim Condon for being one of our biggest contributors and writing so much great content here. Finally, Jonas and Tanner for being great people to work with and giving so much to Vapor."

— Logan Wright

"To my late grandfather who sparked my love for computers."

— Tanner Wayne Nelson

Table of Contents

Acknowledgements

The *Server-Side Swift with Vapor* team would also like to thank Jonas Schwartz for his work as one of the original authors of this book.

Book License

Before You Begin

This section tells you a few things you need to know before you get started, such as what you'll need for hardware and software, where to find the project files for this book, and more.

What You Need

To follow along with this book, you'll need the following:

- **Swift 5.2**: Vapor 4 requires Swift 5.2 minimum in both Xcode and from the command line.
- **Xcode 11.4 or later**: Xcode is the main development tool for writing code in Swift. You need Xcode 11.4 at a minimum, since that version includes Swift 5.2. You can download the latest version of Xcode for free from the Mac App Store.

If you haven't installed the latest version of Xcode, be sure to do that before continuing with the book. The code covered in this book depends on Swift 5.2 and Xcode 11.4 — you may get lost if you try to work with an older version.

This book provides the building blocks for developers who wish to use Vapor to create server-side Swift applications. It shows you how to take the familiar type-safe, compiler-driven world of Swift you know from iOS and use it on the server.

The only prerequisites for this book are an intermediate understanding of Swift and iOS development. If you've worked through our classic beginner books — *Swift Apprentice* https://www.raywenderlich.com/books/swift-apprentice and *UIKit Apprentice* https://www.raywenderlich.com/books/uikit-apprentice — or have similar development experience, you're ready to read this book.

As you work through the book, you'll develop a server-side app called TIL — Today I Learned — for recording and categorizing acronyms. You'll first build a REST API to support iOS and other client apps. Then, you'll build a web site with direct access to the data and protect it all with authentication.

Book Source Code & Forums

Where to download the materials for this book

The materials for this book can be cloned or downloaded from the GitHub book materials repository:

- https://github.com/raywenderlich/vpr-materials/tree/editions/3.0

Forums

We've also set up an official forum for the book at https://forums.raywenderlich.com/c/books/server-side-swift-vapor. This is a great place to ask questions about the book or to submit any errors you may find.

About the Cover

Server-Side Swift with Vapor

The Mexican salamander, or axolotl, is an especially unique amphibian in that it remains a fully aquatic creature in adulthood and retains its gills instead of growing lungs like most amphibians.

Axolotls are exceptionally easy to breed in captivity, and for this reason are studied extensively in such wide-ranging fields as heart defects and neural tube development. But perhaps the most fascinating feature is their ability to completely regenerate entire limbs, other appendages, and even brain sections when damaged.

Unfortunately, the wild axolotl's habitat is limited to a few lakes in central Mexico, which are under stress due to rapid urban development along with the introduction of non-native predators to their natural habitat. Consequently, the axolotl has earned a categorization of "Critically Endangered" on global conservation lists.

For more information, check out the following great resources:

- http://www.iucnredlist.org/details/1095/0
- http://www.pbs.org/wgbh/nova/next/nature/saving-axolotls/

Section I: Creating a Simple Web API

This section teaches you the beginnings of building Vapor applications, including how to use Swift Package Manager. You'll learn how routing works and how Vapor leverages the power of Swift to make routing type-safe. You'll learn how to create models, set up relationships between them and save them in a database. You'll see how to provide an API to access this data from a REST client. Finally, you'll build an iOS app which leverages this API to allow users to display and interact with the data.

Chapter 1: Introduction

Vapor is an open-source web framework written in Swift. It's built on top of Apple's SwiftNIO library to provide a powerful, asynchronous framework. Vapor allows you to build back-end applications for iOS apps, front-end web sites and stand-alone server applications.

About Vapor

Apple open-sourced Swift in December 2015, thereby enabling developers to create applications for macOS and Linux written in Swift. Almost immediately, a number of web frameworks written in Swift appeared. Tanner Nelson started Vapor in January 2016, and Logan Wright joined him shortly thereafter. Over time, a large and engaged user community has embraced the framework. Vapor has a Swift-like API and makes heavy use of many powerful language features. As a result, it has become the most popular server-side Swift framework on GitHub.

Vapor consists of a number of packages including Leaf — a templating engine for front-end development — and Fluent, a Swift Object Relational Mapping (ORM) framework with native, asynchronous database drivers. One of its biggest strengths is its community. There's a very dedicated following on GitHub and an extremely active chat server on Discord.

How to read this book

The chapters in the first three sections build on each other. If you're new to Vapor, you should read them in sequence. If you're experienced with Vapor, you can skip from chapter to chapter to learn how to use the latest features and treat this book as a reference.

Each chapter provides starter and final projects. The book is *very* code heavy and you should follow along with the code to truly understand it all.

The chapters in Section 4 stand alone and you can read them in any order. Written by the core Vapor team, they provide deeper insight into how best to use Vapor.

The best way to learn about Vapor is to roll up your sleeves and start coding. Enjoy the book!

Update Note

The third edition of this book is a complete rewrite to update it for Vapor 4! This edition also includes a new chapter on how to implement Sign In With Apple.

Chapter 2: Hello, Vapor!

By Tim Condon

Beginning a project using a new technology can be daunting. Vapor makes it easy to get started. It provides a handy command line tool to create a starter project for you.

In this chapter, you'll start by installing the Vapor Toolbox, then use it to build and run your first project. You'll finish by learning about routing, accepting data and returning JSON.

Vapor Toolbox

The Vapor Toolbox is a command line interface (CLI) tool you use when developing Vapor apps. It helps you create a new Vapor project from a template and can add dependencies as needed.

Before you can install the toolbox, you need to ensure your system has Swift installed. On macOS, simply install Xcode from the Mac App Store. On Linux, download it from https://www.swift.org as install as described below.

> Vapor 4 requires Swift 5.2, both in Xcode and from the command line. Xcode 11.4 and 11.5 both provide Swift 5.2.

Installing on macOS

Vapor uses Homebrew to install the Toolbox.

> If you don't have Homebrew installed, visit https://brew.sh and run the installation command.

In **Terminal**, run the following commands:

```
brew install vapor
```

Note: Vapor is now part of Homebrew Core. If you have an old version of the toolbox installed using Vapor's Homebrew tap, you can update to the latest version with the following:

```
brew uninstall vapor && brew untap vapor/tap && brew install
vapor
```

This removes Vapor from the list of Homebrew's taps and installs the latest version of the toolbox from Homebrew Core.

Installing on Linux

This book focuses primarily on using Xcode and macOS for developing your apps. However, everything you build with Vapor will work on versions of Linux that Swift supports. The Vapor Toolbox works in exactly the same way, with the exception that you can't use Xcode on Linux.

Installing Swift

To install Swift on Linux, go to https://swift.org/download/ and download the toolchain for your operating system. Follow the installation to install the toolchain on your machine. When complete, enter the following at a shell prompt:

```
swift --version
```

You should get the correct version of Swift returned:

```
Swift version 5.2.4 (swift-5.2.4-RELEASE)
Target: x86_64-unknown-linux-gnu
```

Installing Vapor

In your console, run the following commands:

```
# 1
git clone https://github.com/vapor/toolbox.git
# 2
cd toolbox
# 3
git checkout 18.0.0
# 4
swift build -c release --disable-sandbox
# 5
mv .build/release/vapor /usr/local/bin
```

Here's what this does:

1. Clone the toolbox from GitHub.
2. Navigate into the toolbox directory that you cloned.
3. Check out version 18.0.0. You can find the latest release of the toolbox on the releases page on GitHub at https://github.com/vapor/toolbox/releases.
4. Build the toolbox in release mode. `--disable-sandbox` allows the toolbox to execute other processes.
5. Move the toolbox into your local path so you can call it from anywhere.

This book uses Ubuntu 20.04 throughout when referring to Linux, but the other supported versions of Linux should work in exactly the same way.

Building your first app

Setting up a Vapor project can seem complicated at first as there are a number of required files and directories. To help with this, the Toolbox can create a new project from a template. The toolbox can generate templates for a simple API, websites and authentication. You can even create your own templates.

First, create a new directory in your home directory or somewhere sensible to work on your Vapor projects. For example, enter the following commands in Terminal:

```
mkdir ~/vapor
cd ~/vapor
```

This creates a new directory in your home folder called **vapor** and navigates you there. Next, create your project with:

```
vapor new HelloVapor
```

The toolbox then asks if you'd like to use Fluent and other packages. For now, type **n** followed by **Enter** for them all. You'll learn about Fluent and other packages later. The toolbox then generates your project for you.

You should see the following:

To build and start your app, run:

```
# 1
cd HelloVapor
# 2
swift run
```

Here's what this does:

1. cd is the "Change Directory" command and takes you into the project directory.
2. This builds and runs the app. It can take some time the first time since it must fetch all the dependencies.

```
HelloVapor — swift run — swift — Run — 80×46
→ HelloVapor git:(master) swift run
Fetching https://github.com/vapor/vapor.git
Fetching https://github.com/apple/swift-nio-extras.git
Fetching https://github.com/vapor/routing-kit.git
Fetching https://github.com/swift-server/async-http-client.git
Fetching https://github.com/vapor/async-kit.git
Fetching https://github.com/apple/swift-log.git
Fetching https://github.com/vapor/websocket-kit.git
Fetching https://github.com/apple/swift-nio-ssl.git
Fetching https://github.com/apple/swift-crypto.git
Fetching https://github.com/apple/swift-metrics.git
Fetching https://github.com/swift-server/swift-backtrace.git
Fetching https://github.com/apple/swift-nio.git
Fetching https://github.com/vapor/console-kit.git
Fetching https://github.com/apple/swift-nio-http2.git
Cloning https://github.com/apple/swift-metrics.git
Resolving https://github.com/apple/swift-metrics.git at 2.0.0
Cloning https://github.com/vapor/console-kit.git
Resolving https://github.com/vapor/console-kit.git at 4.1.1
Cloning https://github.com/apple/swift-crypto.git
Resolving https://github.com/apple/swift-crypto.git at 1.0.2
Cloning https://github.com/apple/swift-nio-ssl.git
Resolving https://github.com/apple/swift-nio-ssl.git at 2.7.5
Cloning https://github.com/vapor/websocket-kit.git
Resolving https://github.com/vapor/websocket-kit.git at 2.1.0
Cloning https://github.com/swift-server/swift-backtrace.git
Resolving https://github.com/swift-server/swift-backtrace.git at 1.2.0
Cloning https://github.com/vapor/routing-kit.git
Resolving https://github.com/vapor/routing-kit.git at 4.1.0
Cloning https://github.com/swift-server/async-http-client.git
Resolving https://github.com/swift-server/async-http-client.git at 1.1.1
Cloning https://github.com/vapor/async-kit.git
Resolving https://github.com/vapor/async-kit.git at 1.1.1
Cloning https://github.com/apple/swift-nio-http2.git
Resolving https://github.com/apple/swift-nio-http2.git at 1.12.2
Cloning https://github.com/vapor/vapor.git
Resolving https://github.com/vapor/vapor.git at 4.10.3
Cloning https://github.com/apple/swift-nio-extras.git
Resolving https://github.com/apple/swift-nio-extras.git at 1.5.1
Cloning https://github.com/apple/swift-nio.git
Resolving https://github.com/apple/swift-nio.git at 2.18.0
Cloning https://github.com/apple/swift-log.git
Resolving https://github.com/apple/swift-log.git at 1.2.0
[1383/1383] Linking Run
[ NOTICE ] Server starting on http://127.0.0.1:8080
```

The template has a predefined route, so open your browser and visit **http://localhost:8080/hello** and see the response!

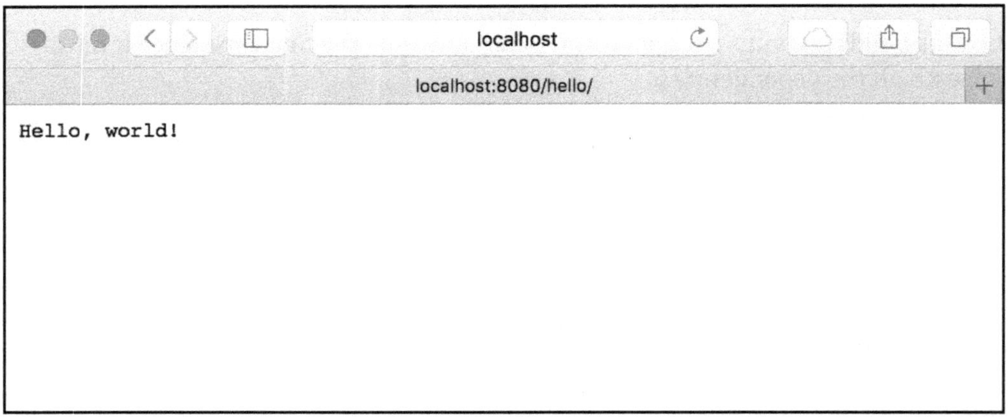

Swift Package Manager

Vapor Toolbox uses Swift Package Manager, or SwiftPM, — a dependency management system similar to CocoaPods on iOS — to configure and build Vapor apps. Open your project directory and look at the structure. On macOS in **Terminal**, enter:

```
open .
```

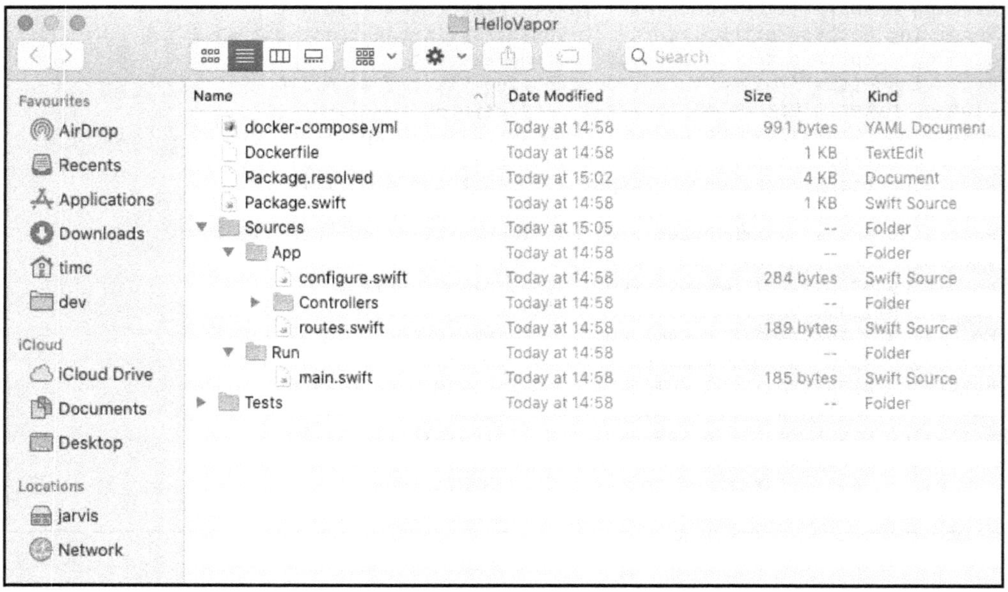

Notice there's no Xcode project in your template even though you've built and run the app. This is deliberate. In fact, the project file is explicitly excluded from source control using the **.gitignore** file. When using SwiftPM, Xcode creates a workspace in a hidden directory called **.swiftpm**.

A SwiftPM project is defined in the **Package.swift** manifest file. It declares targets, dependencies and how they link together. The project layout is also different from a traditional Xcode project. There is a **Tests** directory for tests. There is a **Sources** directory for source files. Each module defined in your manifest has its own directory inside **Sources**. Your sample app has an `App` module and a `Run` module, so **Sources** contains an **App** directory and a **Run** directory.

Inside the **Run** directory, there's a single file: **main.swift.** This is the entry point required by all Swift apps.

> **Note**: On iOS, this is usually synthesized with a `@UIApplicationMain` attribute on the `AppDelegate`.

The template contains everything you need to set up your app and you shouldn't need to change **main.swift** or the `Run` module. Your code lives in `App` or any other modules you define.

Creating your own routes

> **Note**: This section, as does most of the book, uses Xcode. If you're developing on Linux, use your favorite editor, then use **swift run** to build and run your app.

Now that you've made your first app, it's time to see how easy it is to add new routes with Vapor. If the Vapor app is still running, stop it by pressing **Control-C** in Terminal. Next enter:

```
open Package.swift
```

This opens the project in Xcode as a SwiftPM workspace. It will take a couple of minutes for Xcode to download the dependencies. When it's finished, open **routes.swift** in **Sources/App**. You'll see the route you visited above.

To create another route, add the following after the `app.get("hello")` closure:

```
app.get("hello", "vapor") { req -> String in
  return "Hello Vapor!"
}
```

Here's what this does:

- Add a new route to handle a GET request. Each parameter to `app.get` is a path component in the URL. This route is invoked when a user enters **http://localhost:8080/hello/vapor** as the URL.
- Supply a closure to run when this route is invoked. The closure receives a `Request` object; you'll learn more about these later.
- Return a string as the result for this route.

In the Xcode toolbar, select the **HelloVapor** scheme and choose **My Mac** as the device.

Build and run. In your browser, visit **http://localhost:8080/hello/vapor**.

What if you want to say hello to anyone who visits your app? Adding every name in the world would be quite impractical! There must be a better way. There is, and Vapor makes it easy.

Add a new route that says hello to whomever visits. For example, if your name is Tim, you'll visit the app using the URL **http://localhost:8080/hello/Tim** and it says "Hello, Tim!".

Add the following after the code you just entered:

```
// 1
app.get("hello", ":name") { req -> String in
  // 2
  guard let name = req.parameters.get("name") else {
    throw Abort(.internalServerError)
  }
  // 3
  return "Hello, \(name)!"
}
```

Here's the play-by-play:

1. Use `:name` to designate a dynamic parameter.
2. Extract the user's name, which is passed in the `Request` object. If Vapor can't find a parameter called `name`, throw an error.
3. Use the name to return your greeting.

Build and run. In your browser, visit **http://localhost:8080/hello/Tim**. Try replacing **Tim** with some other values.

Accepting data

Most web apps must accept data. A common example is user login. To do this, a client sends a POST request with a JSON body, which the app must decode and process. To learn more about POST requests and how they work, see Chapter 3, "HTTP Basics."

Vapor makes decoding data easy thanks to its strong integration with Swift's `Codable` protocol. You give Vapor a `Codable` struct that matches your expected data, and Vapor does the rest. Create a POST request to see how this works.

> This book uses the RESTed app, available as a free download from the Mac App Store. If you like, you may use another REST client to test your APIs.

Set up the request as follows:

- **URL**: **http://localhost:8080/info**
- **Method**: **POST**
- Add a single parameter called **name**. Use your name as the value.
- Select **JSON-encoded** as the request type. This ensures that the data is sent as JSON and that the `Content-Type` header is set to `application/json`. If you're using a different client, you may need to set this manually.

Your request should look similar to the following:

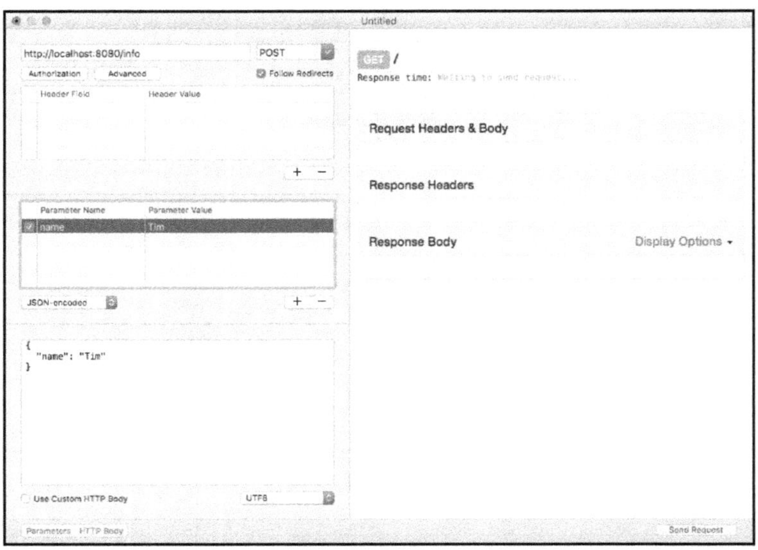

Go back to Xcode, open **routes.swift** and add the following to the end of the file to create a `struct` called `InfoData` to represent this request:

```
struct InfoData: Content {
  let name: String
}
```

This `struct` conforms to `Content` which is Vapor's wrapper around `Codable`. Vapor uses `Content` to extract the request data, whether it's the default JSON-encoded or form URL-encoded. `InfoData` contains the single parameter `name`.

Next, add a new route after the `app.get("hello", "vapor")` closure:

```
// 1
app.post("info") { req -> String in
  let data = try req.content.decode(InfoData.self)
  return "Hello \(data.name)!"
}
```

Here's what this does:

1. Add a new route handler to handle a POST request for the URL **http://localhost:8080/info**. This route handler returns a `String`.
2. Decode the request's body using `InfoData`.
3. Return the string by pulling the name out of the `data` variable.

Build and run the app. Send the request from RESTed and you'll see the response come back:

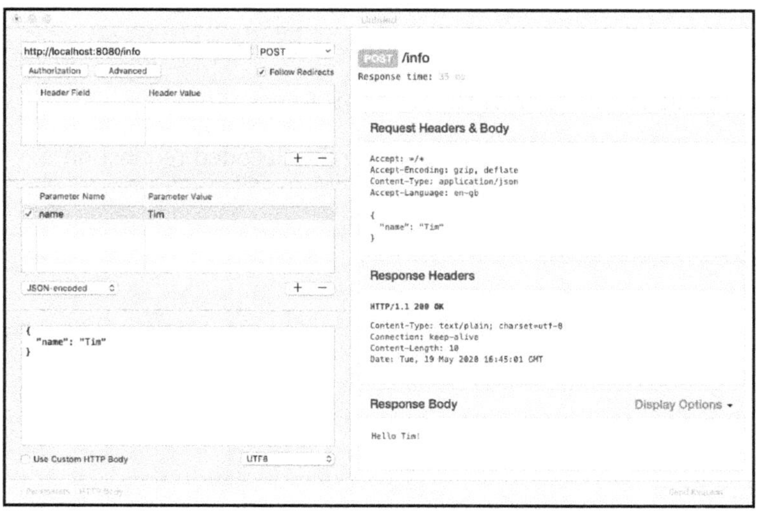

This may seem like a lot of boilerplate to extract a single parameter from JSON. However, `Codable` scales up and allows you to decode complex, nested JSON objects with multiple types in a single line.

Returning JSON

Vapor also makes it easy to return JSON in your route handlers. This is a common need when your app provides an API service. For example, a Vapor app that processes requests from an iOS app needs to send JSON responses. Vapor again uses `Content` to encode the response as JSON.

Open **routes.swift** and add the following struct, called `InfoResponse`, to the end of the file to return the incoming request:

```
struct InfoResponse: Content {
  let request: InfoData
}
```

This `struct` conforms to `Content` and contains a property for the request.

Next, replace `app.post("info")` with the following:

```
// 1
app.post("info") { req -> InfoResponse in
  let data = try req.content.decode(InfoData.self)
  // 2
  return InfoResponse(request: data)
}
```

Here's what changed:

1. The route handler now returns the new `InfoResponse` type.
2. Construct a new `InfoResponse` type using the decoded request data.

Build and run the app. Send the same request from RESTed. You'll see a JSON response containing your original request data:

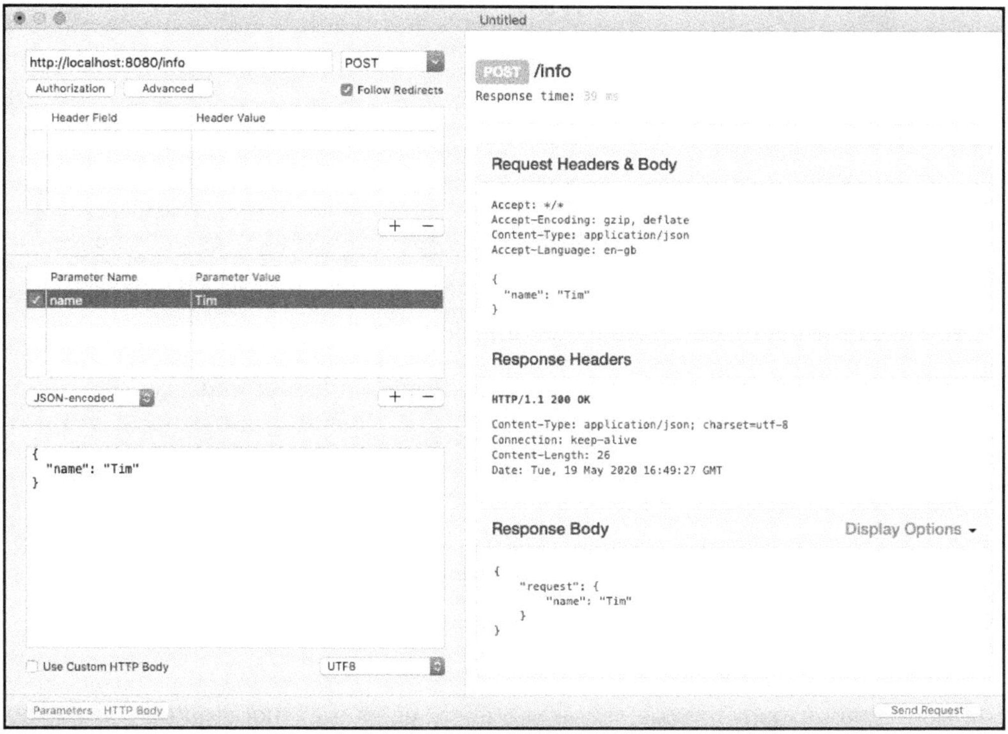

Troubleshooting Vapor

Throughout the course of this book, and in any future Vapor apps, you may encounter errors in your projects. There are a number of steps to take to troubleshoot any issues.

Update your dependencies

Another scenario you may encounter is hitting a bug in Vapor or another dependency you use. Make sure you are on the latest package version of any dependencies to see if the update fixes the issue. In Xcode, choose **File ▸ Swift Packages ▸ Update to Latest Package Versions**. If you're running the app in Terminal, or on Linux, type:

```
swift package update
```

This SwiftPM command pulls down any updates to your dependencies and use the latest releases you support in **Package.swift**. Note that while packages are in the beta or release candidate stages, there may be breaking changes between updates.

Clean and rebuild

Finally, if you are still having issues, you can use the software equivalent of "turn it off and on again". In Xcode, use **Command-Option-Shift-K** to clean the build folder.

You may also need to clear your derived data for the Xcode project as well and the workspace itself. The "nuclear" option involves:

- Remove the **.build** directory to remove any build artifacts from the command line.
- Remove the **.swiftpm** directory to delete the Xcode workspace and any misconfigurations.
- Remove **Package.resolved** to ensure you get the latest dependencies next time you build.
- Remove **DerivedData** to clear extra Xcode build artifacts.

Vapor Discord

The steps above usually fix most issues you might encounter that aren't caused by your code. If all else fails, head to Vapor's Discord server. There you'll find thousands of developers discussing Vapor, its changes and helping people with issues. Click the **Join Chat** button on Vapor's web site: https://vapor.codes.

Where to go from here?

This chapter provides an overview of how to get started with Vapor and how to create basic routes. The first two sections of this book show you how to build a complex app, including an API, a website, and authentication in both parts. As you progress through them, you'll learn how to use core Vapor concepts, such as futures, Fluent and Leaf. By the end of section 2, you'll have a solid foundation on which to build any server-side Swift app in Vapor.

Chapter 3: HTTP Basics

By Tim Condon

Before you begin your journey with Vapor, you'll first review the fundamentals of how the web and HTTP operate.

This chapter explains what you need to know about HTTP, its methods, and its most common response codes. You'll also learn how Vapor can augment your web development experience, its benefits, and what differentiates it from other Swift frameworks.

Powering the web

HyperText Transfer Protocol, or HTTP, is the foundation of the web. Each time you visit a website, your browser sends HTTP requests to and receives responses from the server. Many dedicated apps — ordering coffee from your smartphone, streaming video to your TV, or playing an online game — use HTTP behind the scenes.

At its core, HTTP is simple. There's a client — an iOS application, a web browser or even a simple cURL session — and a server. The client sends an HTTP request to the server which returns an HTTP response.

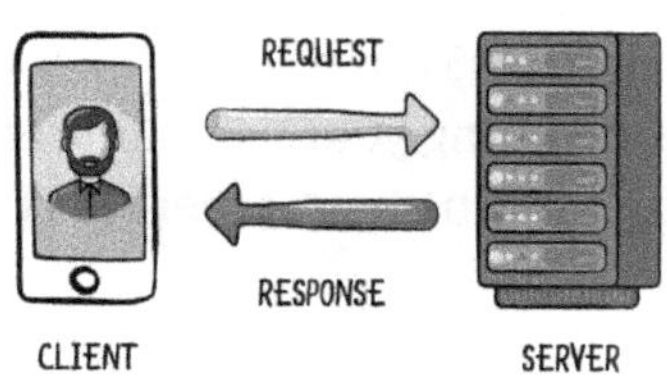

HTTP requests

An HTTP request consists of several parts:

- **The request line**: This specifies the HTTP method to use, the resource requested and the HTTP version. `GET /about.html HTTP/1.1` is one example. You'll learn about HTTP versions later in this chapter.
- **The host**: The name of server to handle the request. This is needed when multiple servers are hosted at the same address.
- **Other request headers** such as Authorization, Accept, Cache-Control, Content-Length, Content-Type etc.
- **Optional request data**, if required by the HTTP method.

The HTTP method specifies the type of operation requested by the client. The HTTP specifications define the following methods:

- GET
- HEAD
- POST
- PUT
- DELETE
- CONNECT
- OPTIONS
- TRACE
- PATCH

The most common HTTP method is `GET`. It allows a client to retrieve a resource from a server. Clicking a link in a browser or tapping a story in a News app both trigger a `GET` request to the server.

Another common HTTP method is `POST`. It allows a client to send data to a server. Clicking the login button after entering your username and password can trigger a `POST` request to the server. You'll learn about other HTTP methods as you work through the book.

Frequently, the server needs more than the resource's name to properly service a request. This additional information is sent in **request headers**. Request headers are nothing more than key-value pairs.

Some common request headers are: `Authorization`, `Cookie`, `Content-Type` and `Accept`. You'll learn in later chapters how Vapor can use some of these to make your server-side apps more robust.

HTTP responses

The server returns an HTTP response when it has processed a request. An HTTP response consists of:

- **The status line**: contains the version, status code and message
- **Response headers**
- **An optional response body**

The **status code** and its associated message indicate the outcome of the request. There are many status codes but you won't use or encounter most of them. They're broken into 5 groups, based on the first digit:

- **1**: informational response. These don't occur frequently.
- **2**: success response. The most common, `200 OK`, means the request was completed successfully.
- **3**: redirection response. These are used frequently.
- **4**: client error. One of the most common is `404 Not Found`. You've probably seen some different and entertaining 404 pages!
- **5**: server error. This frequently indicates an improperly configured server, resource exhaustion or a bug in the server-side app.

There is even an April Fools' joke status code: `418 I'm a teapot`!

The response may include a **response body** such as the HTML content of a page, an image file, or a JSON description of a resource. The response body is optional, however, and some response codes — `204 No Content` for example — won't have one.

Finally, the response may include some **response headers**. These are analogous to the **request headers** described earlier. Some common response headers are: `Set-Cookie`, `WWW-Authenticate`, `Cache-Control` and `Content-Length`.

HTTP in web browsers

When you ask your browser to load a page, it sends an HTTP GET request for that page. The server returns the HTML in the response's body. As the browser parses the HTML, it generates additional HTTP GET requests for any assets — images, JavaScript, CSS — the page references.

A properly formatted HTML page contains both a <head> and a <body> section. When processing a page, the browser waits until it receives all external resources referenced in the <head> section to render the page. The client renders assets referenced in the <body> section as it receives them.

Web browsers use only the GET and POST HTTP methods. The majority of browser requests are GET requests. The browser may use POST to submit form data or upload a file. This will become important in later chapters; you'll learn techniques to address this then. It's also impossible to customize the request headers sent by a browser without using JavaScript.

HTTP in iOS apps

Your iOS apps — this also applies to other HTTP clients, such as Rested, JavaScript, Postman — are far less constrained. These apps are able to use all HTTP methods, add custom request headers and implement custom response handling. This is more work but the flexibility allows you the freedom to develop exactly what you need.

HTTP 2.0

Most web services today use HTTP version 1.1 — released in January 1997 as RFC 2068 (https://tools.ietf.org/html/rfc2068). Everything you've learned so far is part of HTTP/1.1 and, unless otherwise noted, is the version used throughout this book.

HTTP/2 expands the communications between client and server to improve efficiency and reduce latency. Individual requests are identical to those in HTTP/1.1, but they may proceed in parallel. The server can anticipate the client's requests and push data, such as stylesheets and images, to the client before it requests them. Vapor supports HTTP/1.1 and HTTP/2 in both its client and server functions.

REST

REST, or representational state transfer, is an architectural standard closely related to HTTP. Many APIs used by apps are REST APIs and you'll hear the term often. You'll learn more about REST and how it relates to HTTP and CRUD in Chapter 7: "CRUD Database Operations". REST provides a way of defining a common standard for accessing resources from an API. For example, for an acronyms API, you might define the following endpoints:

- **GET /api/acronyms/**: get all acronyms.
- **POST /api/acronyms**: create a new acronym.
- **GET /api/acronyms/1**: get the acronym with ID 1.
- **PUT /api/acronyms/1**: update the acronym with ID 1.
- **DELETE /api/acronyms/1**: delete the acronym with ID 1.

Having a common pattern to access resources from a REST API simplifies the process of building clients.

Why use Vapor?

Server-side app development with Swift and Vapor is a unique experience. In contrast to many traditional server-side languages — for example PHP, JavaScript, Ruby — Swift is strongly- and statically-typed. This characteristic has greatly reduced the number of runtime crashes in iOS apps and your server-side apps will also enjoy this benefit.

Another potential benefit of server-side Swift is improved performance. Because Swift is a compiled language, apps written using Swift are likely to perform better than those written in an interpreted language.

However, the biggest reason to write server-side Swift apps is you get to use Swift! Swift is one of the fastest-growing and most-loved languages, its modern syntax and features combining the best of many languages. If you currently develop for iOS, you probably already know the language well. This means you can start sharing core business logic code and models between your server-side apps and your iOS apps.

Choosing Swift also means you get to use Xcode to develop your server applications! Though Foundation on Linux is a subset of what you'll find on iOS and macOS, you can do the majority of your development in Xcode. This gives you access to powerful debugging capabilities in the IDE, a feature most server-side languages don't have.

Vapor and the server-side Swift ecosystem

Vapor has emerged as the main high-level server-side Swift framework and its developers work closely with the Swift Server Work Group (SSWG). The SSWG is a steering team that promotes the use of Swift on the server. It's made up of engineers from Apple and the community, including the Vapor core team.

The SSWG also has an incubation process for recommended projects built on top of SwiftNIO, such as a PostgreSQL driver and metrics libraries. Because Vapor is also built on top of SwiftNIO, you can use any of these packages with your server-side Swift apps. Many of these projects are already integrated into Vapor!

Finally, Vapor has an amazing active and vibrant community, which you're encouraged to get involved with!

Chapter 4: Async

By Tim Condon

In this chapter, you'll learn about asynchronous and non-blocking architectures. You'll discover Vapor's approach to these architectures and how to use it. Finally, the chapter provides a small overview of SwiftNIO, a core technology used by Vapor.

Async

One of Vapor's most important features is `Async`. It can also be one of the most confusing. Why is it important?

Consider a scenario where your server has only a single thread and four client requests, in order:

1. A request for a stock quote. This results in a call to an API on another server.
2. A request for a static CSS style sheet. The CSS is available immediately without a lookup.
3. A request for a user's profile. The profile must be fetched from a database.
4. A request for some static HTML. The HTML is available immediately without a lookup.

In a synchronous server, the server's sole thread blocks until the stock quote is returned. It then returns the stock quote and the CSS style sheet. It blocks again while the database fetch completes. Only then, after the user's profile is sent, will the server return the static HTML to the client.

On the other hand, in an asynchronous server, the thread initiates the call to fetch the stock quote and puts the request aside until it completes. It then returns the CSS style sheet, starts the database fetch and returns the static HTML. As the requests that were put aside complete, the thread resumes work on them and returns their results to the client.

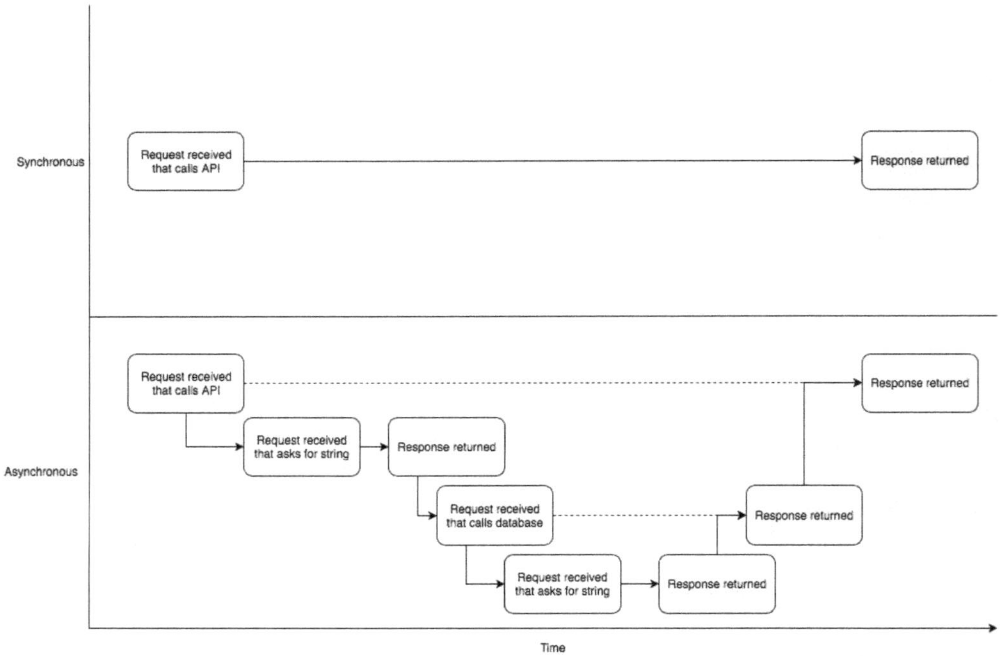

"But, wait!", you say, "Servers have more than one thread." And you're correct. However, there are limits to how many threads a server can have. Creating threads uses resources. Switching context between threads is expensive, and ensuring all your data accesses are thread-safe is time-consuming and error-prone. As a result, trying to solve the problem solely by adding threads is a poor, inefficient solution.

Futures and promises

In order to "put aside" a request while it waits for a response, you must wrap it in a **promise** to resume work on it when you receive the response.

In practice, this means you must change the return type of methods that can be put aside. In a synchronous environment, you might have a method:

```
func getAllUsers() -> [User] {
  // do some database queries
}
```

In an asynchronous environment, this won't work because your database call may not have completed by the time `getAllUsers()` must return. You know you'll be able to return `[User]` in the future but can't do so now. In Vapor, you return the result wrapped in an **EventLoopFuture**. This is a future specific to SwiftNIO's `EventLoop`. You'd write your method as shown below:

```
func getAllUsers() -> EventLoopFuture<[User]> {
  // do some database queries
}
```

Returning `EventLoopFuture<[User]>` allows you to return *something* to the method's caller, even though there may be nothing to return at that point. But the caller knows that the method returns `[User]` at some point in the future. You'll learn more about SwiftNIO at the end of the chapter.

Working with futures

Working with `EventLoopFutures` can be confusing at first but, since Vapor uses them extensively, they'll quickly become second nature. In most cases, when you receive an `EventLoopFuture` from a method, you want to do something with the actual result inside the `EventLoopFuture`. Since the result of the method hasn't actually returned yet, you provide a callback to execute when the `EventLoopFuture` completes.

In the example above, when your program reaches `getAllUsers()`, it makes the database request on the `EventLoop`. An `EventLoop` processes work and in simplistic terms can be thought of as a thread. `getAllUsers()` doesn't return the actual data immediately and returns an `EventLoopFuture` instead. This means the `EventLoop` pauses execution of that code and works on any other code queued up on that `EventLoop`. For example, this could be another part of your code where a different `EventLoopFuture` result has returned. Once the database call returns, the `EventLoop` then executes the callback.

If the callback calls another method that returns an `EventLoopFuture`, you provide another callback inside the original callback to execute when the second `EventLoopFuture` completes. This is why you'll end up chaining or nesting lots of different callbacks. This is the hard part about working with futures. Asynchronous methods require a complete shift in how to think about your code.

Resolving futures

Vapor provides a number of convenience methods for working with futures to avoid the necessity of dealing with them directly. However, there are numerous scenarios where you must wait for the result of a future. To demonstrate, imagine you have a route that returns the HTTP status code **204 No Content**. This route fetches a list of users from a database using a method like the one described above and modifies the first user in the list before returning.

In order to use the result of that call to the database, you must provide a closure to execute when the `EventLoopFuture` has resolved. There are two main methods you'll use to do this:

- **flatMap(_:)**: Executes on a future and returns another future. The callback receives the resolved future and returns another `EventLoopFuture`.
- **map(_:)**: Executes on a future and returns another future. The callback receives the resolved future and returns a type other than `EventLoopFuture`, which `map(_:)` then wraps in an `EventLoopFuture`.

Both choices take a future and produce a different `EventLoopFuture`, usually of a different type. To reiterate, the difference is that if the callback that processes the `EventLoopFuture` result returns an `EventLoopFuture`, use `flatMap(_:)`. If the callback returns a type other than `EventLoopFuture`, use `map(_:)`.

For example:

```
// 1
return database.getAllUsers().flatMap { users in
  // 2
  let user = users[0]
  user.name = "Bob"
  // 3
  return user.save(on: req.db).map { user in
    //4
    return .noContent
  }
}
```

Here's what this does:

1. Fetch all users from the database. As you saw above, `getAllUsers()` returns `EventLoopFuture<[User]>`. Since the result of completing this `EventLoopFuture` is yet another `EventLoopFuture` (see step 3), use `flatMap(_:)` to resolve the result. The closure for `flatMap(_:)` receives the completed future `users` — an array of all the users from the database, type `[User]` — as its parameter. This `.flatMap(_:)` returns `EventLoopFuture<HTTPStatus>`.
2. Update the first user's name.
3. Save the updated user to the database. This returns `EventLoopFuture<User>` but the HTTPStatus value you need to return isn't yet an `EventLoopFuture` so use `map(_:)`.
4. Return the appropriate `HTTPStatus` value.

As you can see, for the top-level promise you use `flatMap(_:)` since the closure you provide returns an `EventLoopFuture`. The inner promise, which returns a non-future `HTTPStatus`, uses `map(_:)`.

Transform

Sometimes you don't care about the result of a future, only that it completed successfully. In the above example, you don't use the resolved result of `save(on:)` and are returning a different type. For this scenario, you can simplify step 3 by using `transform(to:)`:

```
return database.getAllUsers().flatMap { users in
  let user = users[0]
  user.name = "Bob"
  return user
    .save(on: req.db)
    .transform(to: HTTPStatus.noContent)
}
```

This helps reduce the amount of nesting and can make your code easier to read and maintain. You'll see this used throughout the book.

Flatten

There are times when you must wait for a number of futures to complete. One example occurs when you're saving multiple models in a database. In this case, you use `flatten(on:)`. For instance:

```
static func save(_ users: [User], request: Request)
    -> EventLoopFuture<HTTPStatus> {
  // 1
  var userSaveResults: [EventLoopFuture<User>] = []
  // 2
  for user in users {
    userSaveResults.append(user.save(on: request.db))
  }
  // 3
  return userSaveResults
    .flatten(on: request.eventLoop)
    .map { savedUsers in
      // 4
      for user in savedUser {
        print("Saved \(user.username)")
      }
      // 5
      return .created
    }
}
```

In this code, you:

1. Define an array of `EventLoopFuture<User>`, the return type of `save(on:)` in step 2.
2. Loop through each user in `users` and append the return value of `user.save(on:)` to the array.
3. Use `flatten(on:)` to wait for all the futures to complete. This takes an `EventLoop`, essentially the thread that actually performs the work. This is normally retrieved from a `Request` in Vapor, but you'll learn about this later. The closure for `flatten(on:)`, if needed, takes the returned collection as a parameter.
4. Loop through each of the saved users and print out their usernames.
5. Return a **201 Created** status.

`flatten(on:)` waits for all the futures to return as they're executed asynchronously by the same `EventLoop`.

Multiple futures

Occasionally, you need to wait for a number of futures of different types that don't rely on one another. For example, you might encounter this situation when retrieving users from the database and making a request to an external API. SwiftNIO provides a number of methods to allow waiting for different futures together. This helps avoid deeply nested code or confusing chains.

If you have two futures — get all the users from the database and get some information from an external API — you can use `and(_:)` like this:

```
// 1
getAllUsers()
  // 2
  .and(req.client.get("http://localhost:8080/getUserData"))
  // 3
  .flatMap { users, response in
    // 4
    users[0].addData(response).transform(to: .noContent)
}
```

Here's what this does:

1. Call `getAllUsers()` to get the result of the first future.
2. Use `and(_:)` to chain the second future to the first future.
3. Use `flatMap(_:)` to wait for the futures to return. The closure takes the resolved results of the futures as parameters.
4. Call `addData(_:)`, which returns some future result and transform the return to `.noContent`.

If the closure returns a non-future result, you can use `map(_:)` on the chained futures instead:

```
// 1
getAllUsers()
  // 2
  .and(req.client.get("http://localhost:8080/getUserData"))
  // 3
  .map { users, response in
    // 4
    users[0].syncAddData(response)
    // 5
    return .content
}
```

Here's what this does:

1. Call `getAllUsers()` to get the result of the first future.
2. Use `and(_:)` to chain the second future to the first future.
3. Use `map(_:)` to wait for the futures to return. The closure takes the resolved results of the futures as parameters.
4. Call the synchronous `syncAddData(_:)`
5. Return `.noContent`.

Note: You can chain together as many futures as required with `and(_:)` but the `flatMap` or `map` closure returns the resolved futures in tuples. For instance, for three futures:

```
getAllUsers()
  .and(getAllAcronyms())
  .and(getAllCategories()).flatMap { result in
    // Use the different futures
}
```

`result` is of type `(([User], [Acronyms]), [Categories])`. And the more futures you chain with `and(_:)`, the more nested tuples you get. This can get a bit confusing! :]

Creating futures

Sometimes you need to create your own futures. If an `if` statement returns a non-future and the `else` block returns an `EventLoopFuture`, the compiler will complain that these must be the same type. To fix this, you must convert the non-future into an `EventLoopFuture` using `request.eventLoop.future(_:)`. For example:

```
// 1
func createTrackingSession(for request: Request)
    -> EventLoopFuture<TrackingSession> {
  return request.makeNewSession()
}

// 2
func getTrackingSession(for request: Request)
    -> EventLoopFuture<TrackingSession> {
  // 3
  let session: TrackingSession? =
    TrackingSession(id: request.getKey())
  // 4
  guard let createdSession = session else {
```

```
        return createTrackingSession(for: request)
    }
    // 5
    return request.eventLoop.future(createdSession)
}
```

Here's what this does:

1. Define a method that creates a TrackingSession from the request. This returns EventLoopFuture<TrackingSession>.
2. Define a method that gets a tracking session from the request.
3. Attempt to create a tracking session using the request's key. This returns nil if the tracking session could not be created.
4. Ensure the session was created successfully, otherwise create a new tracking session.
5. Create an EventLoopFuture<TrackingSession> from createdSession using request.eventLoop.future(_:). This returns the future on the request's EventLoop.

Since createTrackingSession(for:) returns EventLoopFuture<TrackingSession> you have to use request.eventLoop.future(_:) to turn the createdSession into an EventLoopFuture<TrackingSession> to make the compiler happy.

Dealing with errors

Vapor makes heavy use of Swift's error handling throughout the framework. Many methods either throw or return a failed future, allowing you to handle errors at different levels. You may choose to handle errors inside your route handlers or by using middleware to catch the errors at a higher level, or both. You also need to deal with errors thrown inside the callbacks you provide to flatMap(_:) and map(_:).

Dealing with errors in the callback

The callbacks for map(_:) and flatMap(_:) are both non-throwing. This presents a problem if you call a method inside the closure that throws. When returning a non-future type with a closure that needs to throw, map(_:) has a throwing variant confusingly called flatMapThrowing(_:). To be clear, the callback for flatMapThrowing(_:) returns a **non-future type**.

For example:

```
// 1
req.client.get("http://localhost:8080/users")
  .flatMapThrowing { response in
  // 2
  let users = try response.content.decode([User].self)
  // 3
  return users[0]
}
```

Here's what this example does:

1. Make a request to an external API, which returns `EventLoopFuture<Response>`. You use `flatMapThrowing(_:)` to provide a callback to the future that can throw an error.
2. Decode the response to `[User]`. This can throw an error, which `flatMapThrowing` converts into a failed future.
3. Return the first user — a non-future type.

Things are different when returning a future type in the callback. Consider the case where you need to decode a response and then return a future:

```
// 1
req.client.get("http://localhost:8080/users/1")
  .flatMap { response in
  do {
    // 2
    let user = try response.content.decode(User.self)
    // 3
    return user.save(on: req.db)
  } catch {
    // 4
    return req.eventLoop.makeFailedFuture(error)
  }
}
```

Here's what's happening:

1. Get a user from the external API. Since the closure will return an `EventLoopFuture`, use `flatMap(_:)`.
2. Decode the user from the response. As this throws an error, wrap this in `do/catch` to catch the error
3. Save the user and return the `EventLoopFuture`.
4. Catch the error if one occurs. Return a failed future on the `EventLoop`.

Since the callback for `flatMap(_:)` can't throw, you must catch the error and return a failed future. The API is designed like this because returning something that can both throw synchronously and asynchronously is confusing to work with.

Dealing with future errors

Dealing with errors is a little different in an asynchronous world. You can't use Swift's `do/catch` as you don't know when the promise will execute. SwiftNIO provides a number of methods to help handle these cases. At a basic level, you can chain `whenFailure(_:)` to your future:

```
let futureResult = user.save(on: req)
futureResult.map { user in
  print("User was saved")
}.whenFailure { error in
  print("There was an error saving the user: \(error)")
}
```

If `save(on:)` succeeds, the `.map` block executes with the resolved value of the future as its parameter. If the future fails, it'll execute the `.whenFailure` block, passing in the `Error`.

In Vapor, you must return something when handling requests, even if it's a future. Using the above `map/whenFailure` method won't stop the error happening, but it'll allow you to see what the error is. If `save(on:)` fails and you return `futureResult`, the failure still propagates up the chain. In most circumstances, however, you want to try and rectify the issue.

SwiftNIO provides `flatMapError(_:)` and `flatMapErrorThrowing(_:)` to handle this type of failure. This allows you to handle the error and either fix it or throw a different error. For example:

```
// 1
return saveUser(on: req.db)
```

```
  .flatMapErrorThrowing { error -> User in
    // 2
    print("Error saving the user: \(error)")
    // 3
    return User(name: "Default User")
}
```

Here's what this does:

1. Attempt to save the user. Use `flatMapErrorThrowing(_:)` to handle the error, if one occurs. The closure takes the error as the parameter and must return the type of the resolved future — in this case `User`.
2. Log the error received.
3. Create a default user to return.

Vapor also provides the related `flatMapError(_:)` for when the associated closure returns a future:

```
return user.save(on: req).flatMapError {
  error -> EventLoopFuture<User> in
    print("Error saving the user: \(error)")
    return User(name: "Default User").save(on: req)
}
```

Since `save(on:)` returns a future, you must call `flatMapError(_:)` instead. **Note:** The closure for `flatMapError(_:)` cannot throw an error — you must catch the error and return a new failed future, similar to `flatMap(_:)` above.

`flatMapError` and `flatMapErrorThrowing` only execute their closures on a failure. But what if you want both to handle errors and handle the success case? Simple! Simply chain to the appropriate method!

Chaining futures

Dealing with futures can sometimes seem overwhelming. It's easy to end up with code that's nested multiple levels deep.

Vapor allows you to chain futures together instead of nesting them. For example, consider a snippet that looks like the following:

```
return database
  .getAllUsers()
  .flatMap { users in
    let user = users[0]
    user.name = "Bob"
```

```
      return user.save(on: req.db)
        .map { user in
          return .noContent
    }
}
```

map(_:) and flatMap(_:) can be chained together to avoid nesting like this:

```
return database
  .getAllUsers()
  // 1
  .flatMap { users in
    let user = users[0]
    user.name = "Bob"
    return user.save(on: req.db)
  // 2
  }.map { user in
    return .noContent
  }
```

Changing the return type of flatMap(_:) allows you to chain the map(_:), which receives the EventLoopFuture<User>. The final map(_:) then returns the type you returned originally. Chaining futures allows you to reduce the nesting in your code and may make it easier to reason about, which is especially helpful in an asynchronous world. However, whether you nest or chain is completely personal preference.

Always

Sometimes you want to execute something no matter the outcome of a future. You may need to close connections, trigger a notification or just log that the future has executed. For this, use the always callback.

For example:

```
// 1
let userResult: EventLoopFuture<User> = user.save(on: req.db)
// 2
userResult.always {
  // 3
  print("User save has been attempted")
}
```

Here's what this does:

1. Save a user and save the result in `userResult`. This is of type `EventLoopFuture<User>`.
2. Chain an `always` to the result.
3. Print a string when the app executes the future.

The `always` closure gets executed no matter the result of the future, whether it fails or succeeds. It also has no effect on the future. You can combine this with other chains as well.

Waiting

In certain circumstances, you may want to actually wait for the result to return. To do this, use `wait()`.

> **Note**: There's a large caveat around this: You can't use `wait()` on the main event loop, which means all request handlers and most other circumstances.

However, as you'll see in Chapter 11, "Testing", this can be especially useful in tests, where writing asynchronous tests is difficult. For example:

```
let savedUser = try user.save(on: database).wait()
```

Instead of `savedUser` being an `EventLoopFuture<User>`, because you use `wait()`, `savedUser` is a `User` object. Be aware `wait()` throws an error if executing the promise fails. It's worth saying again: This can only be used off the main event loop!

SwiftNIO

Vapor is built on top of Apple's SwiftNIO library (https://github.com/apple/swift-nio). SwiftNIO is a cross-platform, asynchronous networking library, like Java's Netty. It's open-source, just like Swift itself!

SwiftNIO handles all HTTP communications for Vapor. It's the plumbing that allows Vapor to receive requests and send responses. SwiftNIO manages the connections and the transfer of data.

It also manages all the `EventLoops` for your futures that perform work and execute your promises. Each `EventLoop` has its own thread.

Vapor manages all the interactions with NIO and provides a clean, Swifty API to use. Vapor is responsible for the higher-level aspects of a server, such as routing requests. It provides the features to build great server-side Swift applications. SwiftNIO provides a solid foundation to build on.

Where to go from here?

While it isn't necessary to know all the details about how `EventLoopFutures` and `EventLoops` work under the hood, you can find more information in Vapor's API documentation (https://api.vapor.codes/async-kit/master/AsyncKit/Extensions/EventLoopFuture.html) or SwiftNIO's API documentation (https://apple.github.io/swift-nio/docs/current/NIO/Classes/EventLoopFuture.html). Vapor's documentation site also has a large section (https://docs.vapor.codes/4.0/async/) on async and futures.

Chapter 5: Fluent & Persisting Models

By Tim Condon

In Chapter 2, "Hello, Vapor!", you learned the basics of creating a Vapor app, including how to create routes. This chapter explains how to use Fluent to save data in Vapor applications. You'll need to have Docker installed and running. Visit https://www.docker.com/get-docker and follow the instructions to install it.

Fluent

Fluent is Vapor's ORM or **object relational mapping** tool. It's an abstraction layer between the Vapor application and the database, and it's designed to make working with databases easier. Using an ORM such as Fluent has a number of benefits.

The biggest benefit is you don't have to use the database directly! When you interact directly with a database, you write database queries as strings. These aren't type-safe and can be painful to use from Swift.

Fluent benefits you by allowing you to use any of a number of database engines, even in the same app. Finally, you don't need to know how to write queries since you can interact with your models in a "Swifty" way.

Models are the Swift representation of your data and are used throughout Fluent. Models are the objects, such as user profiles, you save and access in your database. Fluent returns and uses type-safe models when interacting with the database, giving you compile-time safety.

Acronyms

Over the next several chapters, you'll build a complex "Today I Learned" application that can save different acronyms and their meanings. Start by creating a new project, using the Vapor Toolbox. In Terminal, enter the following command:

```
cd ~/vapor
```

This command takes you into a directory called **vapor** inside your home directory and assumes that you completed the steps in Chapter 2, "Hello, Vapor!". Next, enter:

```
vapor new TILApp
```

When asked if you'd like to use Fluent enter **y** and then press **Enter**. Next enter **1** to choose PostgreSQL as the database, followed by **Enter**. When the toolbox asks if you want to use Leaf or other dependencies, enter **n**, followed by **Enter**. This creates a new Vapor project called **TILApp** using the template and configuring PostgreSQL as the database.

The TIL app uses PostgreSQL throughout the book. However, it should work without any modifications with any database supported by Fluent. You'll learn how to configure different databases in Chapter 6, "Configuring a Database".

The template provides example files for models, migrations and controllers. You'll build your own so delete the examples. In Terminal, enter:

```
cd TILApp
rm -rf Sources/App/Models/*
rm -rf Sources/App/Migrations/*
rm -rf Sources/App/Controllers/*
```

If prompted to confirm the deletions, enter **y**. Now, open the project in Xcode:

```
open Package.swift
```

This creates an Xcode project from your Swift package, using Xcode's support for Swift Package Manager. It takes a while to download all the dependencies for the first time. When it's finished, you'll see the dependencies in the sidebar and a **TILApp** scheme available:

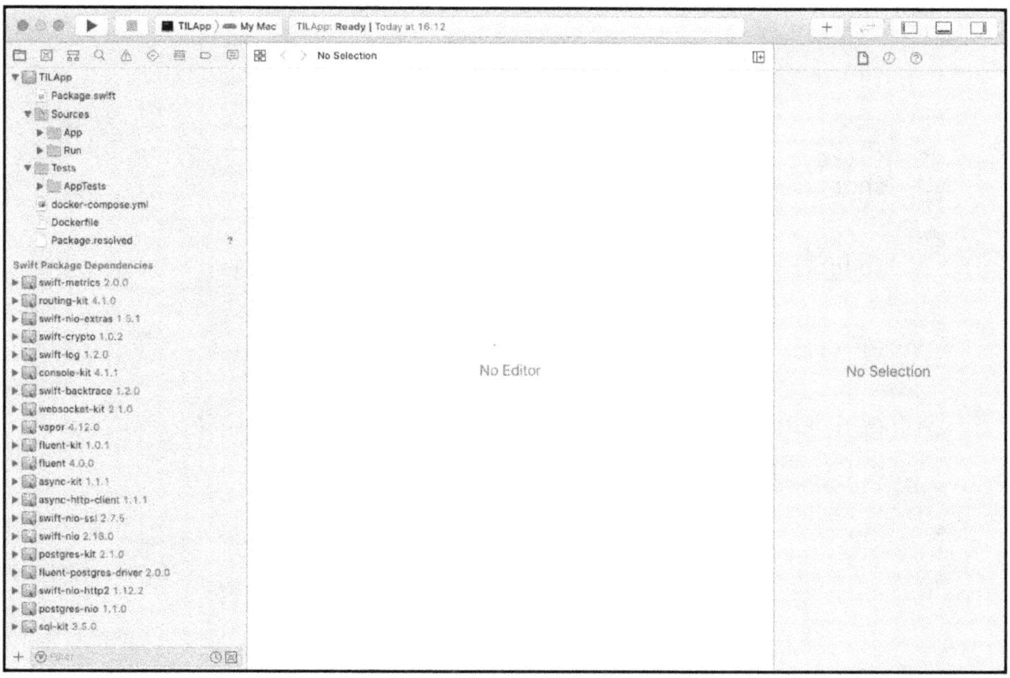

First, open **configure.swift** and delete the following line:

```
app.migrations.add(CreateTodo())
```

Next, open **routes.swift** and delete the following line:

```
try app.register(collection: TodoController())
```

This removes the remaining references to the template's example model migration and controller.

Create a new Swift file in **Sources/App/Models** called **Acronym.swift**. Inside the new file, insert the following:

```
import Vapor
import Fluent

// 1
final class Acronym: Model {
  // 2
  static let schema = "acronyms"

  // 3
  @ID
  var id: UUID?

  // 4
  @Field(key: "short")
  var short: String

  @Field(key: "long")
  var long: String

  // 5
  init() {}

  // 6
  init(id: UUID? = nil, short: String, long: String) {
    self.id = id
    self.short = short
    self.long = long
  }
}
```

Here's what this code is doing:

1. Define a class that conforms to `Model`.
2. Specify the `schema` as required by `Model`. This is the name of the table in the database.
3. Define an optional `id` property that stores the ID of the model, if one has been set. This is annotated with Fluent's `@ID` property wrapper. This tells Fluent what to use to look up the model in the database.
4. Define two `String` properties to hold the acronym and its definition. These use the `@Field` property wrapper to denote a generic database field. The `key` parameter is the name of the column in the database.
5. Provide an empty initializer as required by `Model`. Fluent uses this to initialize models returned from database queries.
6. Provide an initializer to create the model as required.

If you're coming from Fluent 3, this model looks very different. Fluent 4 leverages property wrappers to provide strong and complex database integration. `@ID` marks a property as the ID for that table. Fluent uses this property wrapper to perform queries in the database when finding models. The property wrapper is also used for relationships, which you'll learn about in the next chapters. By default in Fluent, the ID must be a `UUID` and called `id`.

`@Field` marks the property of a model as a generic column in the database. Fluent uses the property wrapper for performing queries with filters. The use of property wrappers allows Fluent to update individual fields in a model, rather than the entire model. You can also select specified fields from the database instead of all fields for a model. Note that you should only use `@Field` with non-optional properties. If you have an optional property in your model you should use `@OptionalField`.

To save the model in the database, you must create a table for it. Fluent does this with a **migration**. Migrations allow you to make reliable, testable, reproducible changes to your database. They are commonly used to create a **database schema**, or table description, for your models. They are also used to seed data into your database or make changes to your models after they've been saved.

Fluent 3 could infer a lot of the table information for you. However this didn't scale to large complex projects, especially when you need to add or remove columns or even rename them. In Xcode, create a new Swift file in **Sources/App/Migrations** called **CreateAcronym.swift**.

Insert the following into the new file:

```
import Fluent

// 1
struct CreateAcronym: Migration {
  // 2
  func prepare(on database: Database) -> EventLoopFuture<Void> {
    // 3
    database.schema("acronyms")
      // 4
      .id()
      // 5
      .field("short", .string, .required)
      .field("long", .string, .required)
      // 6
      .create()
  }

  // 7
  func revert(on database: Database) -> EventLoopFuture<Void> {
    database.schema("acronyms").delete()
  }
}
```

Here's what the migration is doing:

1. Define a new type, `CreateAcronym` that conforms to `Migration`.
2. Implement `prepare(on:)` as required by `Migration`. You call this method when you run your migrations.
3. Define the table name for this model. This must match `schema` from the model.
4. Define the ID column in the database.
5. Define columns for `short` and `long`. Set the column type to `string` and mark the columns as required. This matches the non-optional `String` properties in the model. The field names must match the key of the property wrapper, **not** the name of the property itself.
6. Create the table in the database.
7. Implement `revert(on:)` as required by `Migration`. You call this function when you revert your migrations. This deletes the table referenced with `schema(_:)`.

All references to column names and table names are strings. This is deliberate as using properties causes issues if those property names change in the future. Chapter 35, "Production Concerns & Redis" describes one solution for improving this and making it type-safe.

Migrations only run *once*; once they have run in a database, they are never executed again. It's important to remember this as Fluent won't attempt to recreate a table if you change the migration.

Now that you have a migration for `Acronym` you can tell Fluent to create the table. Open **configure.swift** and, after `app.databases.use(_:as:)`, add the following:

```
// 1
app.migrations.add(CreateAcronym())

// 2
app.logger.logLevel = .debug

// 3
try app.autoMigrate().wait()
```

Here's what your new code does:

1. Add `CreateAcronym` to the list of migrations to run.
2. Set the log level for the application to debug. This provides more information and enables you to see your migrations.
3. Automatically run migrations and wait for the result. Fluent allows you to choose when to run your migrations. This is helpful when you need to schedule them, for example. You can use `wait()` here since you're not running on an `EventLoop`.

To test with PostgreSQL, you'll run the Postgres server in a Docker container. Open `Terminal` and enter the following command:

```
docker run --name postgres -e POSTGRES_DB=vapor_database \
  -e POSTGRES_USER=vapor_username \
  -e POSTGRES_PASSWORD=vapor_password \
  -p 5432:5432 -d postgres
```

Here's what this does:

- Run a new container named **postgres**.
- Specify the database name, username and password through environment variables.
- Allow applications to connect to the Postgres server on its default port: 5432.
- Run the server in the background as a daemon.
- Use the Docker image named **postgres** for this container. If the image is not present on your machine, Docker automatically downloads it.

To check that your database is running, enter the following in Terminal to list all active containers:

```
docker ps
```

Now you're ready to run the app! Set the active scheme to **TILApp** with **My Mac** as the destination. Build and run. Check the console and see that the migrations have run.

You should see something similar to the following:

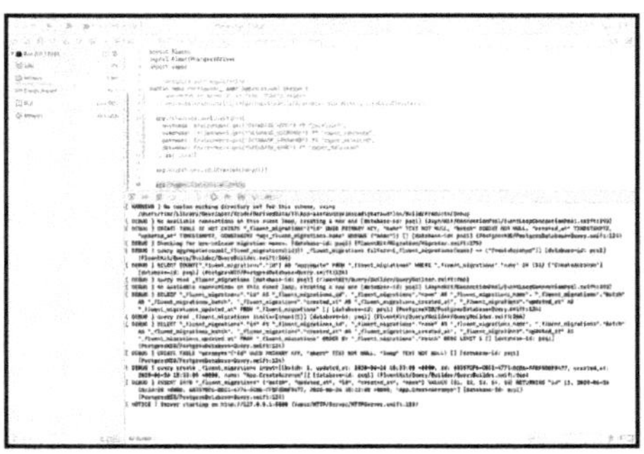

Saving models

When your app's user enters a new acronym, you need a way to save it.

In Vapor 4, `Codable` makes this trivial. Vapor provides `Content`, a wrapper around `Codable`, which allows you to convert models and other data between various formats.

This is used extensively in Vapor, and you'll see it throughout the book.

Open **Acronym.swift** and add the following to the end of the file to make `Acronym` conform to `Content`:

```
extension Acronym: Content {}
```

Since `Acronym` already conforms to `Codable` via `Model`, you don't have to add anything else. To create an acronym, the user's browser sends a POST request containing a JSON payload that looks similar to the following:

```
{
  "short": "OMG",
  "long": "Oh My God"
}
```

You'll need a route to handle this POST request and save the new acronym. Open **routes.swift** and add the following to the end of `routes(_:)`:

```
// 1
app.post("api", "acronyms") { req -> EventLoopFuture<Acronym> in
  // 2
  let acronym = try req.content.decode(Acronym.self)
  // 3
  return acronym.save(on: req.db).map {
    // 4
    acronym
  }
}
```

Here's what this does:

1. Register a new route at **/api/acronyms** that accepts a POST request and returns EventLoopFuture<Acronym>. It returns the acronym once it's saved.
2. Decode the request's JSON into an Acronym model using Codable.
3. Save the model using Fluent and the database from Request.
4. save(on:) returns EventLoopFuture<Void> so use map to return the acronym when the save completes.

Fluent and Vapor's integrated use of Codable makes this simple. Since Acronym conforms to Content, it's easily converted between JSON and Model.

This allows Vapor to return the model as JSON in the response without any effort on your part. Build and run the application to try it out.

A good tool to test this is **RESTed**, available as a free download from the Mac App Store. Other tools such as Paw and Postman are suitable as well.

In RESTed, configure the request as follows:

- **URL**: http://localhost:8080/api/acronyms
- **method**: POST
- **Parameter encoding**: JSON-encoded

Add two parameters with names and values:

- **short**: OMG
- **long**: Oh My God

Setting the parameter encoding to **JSON-encoded** ensures the data is sent as JSON.

It's important to note this also sets the Content-Type header to application/json, which tells Vapor the request contains JSON. If you're using a different client to send the request, you may need to set this manually.

Click **Send Request** and you'll see the acronym provided in the response.

The `id` field will have a value as it has now been saved in the database:

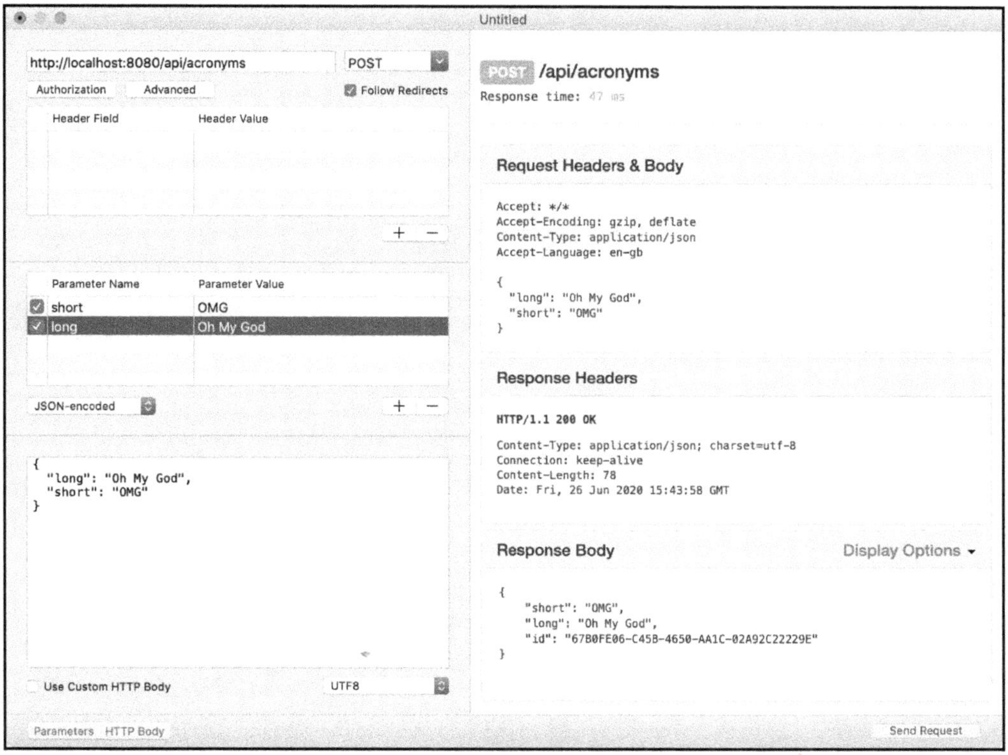

Where to go from here?

This chapter has introduced you to Fluent and how to create models in Vapor and save them in the database. The next chapters build on this application to create a full-featured TIL application.

Chapter 6: Configuring a Database

By Tim Condon

Databases allow you to persist data in your applications. In this chapter, you'll learn how to configure your Vapor application to integrate with the database of your choice.

> This chapter, and most of the book, uses **Docker** to host the database. Docker is a containerization technology that allows you to run independent images on your machine without the overhead of virtual machines. You can spin up different databases and not worry about installing dependencies or databases interfering with each other.

Why use a database?

Databases provide a reliable, performant means of storing and retrieving data. If your application stores information in memory, it's lost when you stop the application. It's good practice to decouple storage from your application as this allows you to scale your application across multiple instances, all backed by the same database. Indeed, most hosting solutions don't have persistent file storage.

Choosing a database

Vapor has official, Swift-native drivers for:

- **SQLite**
- **MySQL**
- **PostgreSQL**
- **MongoDB**

There are two types of databases: **relational**, or **SQL** databases, and **non-relational**, or **NoSQL** databases. Relational databases store their data in structured tables with defined columns. They are efficient at storing and querying data whose structure is known up front. You create and query tables with a **structured query language** (SQL) that allows you to retrieve data from multiple, related tables. For example, if you have a list of pets in one table and list of owners in another, you can retrieve a list of pets with their owners' names with a single query.

While relational databases are good for rigid structures, this can be an issue if you must change that structure. Recently, NoSQL databases have become popular as a way of storing large amounts of unstructured data. Social networks, for example, can store settings, images, locations, statuses and metrics all in a single document. This allows for much greater flexibility than traditional databases.

MySQL and PostgreSQL are examples of relational databases. MongoDB is an example of a non-relational database. Fluent supports both types of databases with different underlying drivers. Be warned though you can't make full use of the database you choose directly with Fluent. Fluent has to support both types and provide equal features to every database. However you can extend Fluent's functionality for a specific database, for example to add support for PostGIS. It's also easy to perform raw queries if needed.

SQLite

SQLite is a simple, file-based relational database system. It's designed to be embedded into an application and is useful for single-process applications such as iOS applications. It relies on file locks to maintain database integrity, so it's not suitable for write-intensive applications. This also means you can't use it across servers. It is, however, a good database for both testing and prototyping applications.

MySQL

MySQL is another open-source, relational database made popular by the LAMP web application stack (Linux, Apache, MySQL, PHP). It's become the most popular database due to its ease of use and support from most cloud providers and website builders.

PostgreSQL

PostgreSQL — frequently shortened to Postgres — is an open-source, relational database system focused on extensibility and standards and is designed for enterprise use. Postgres also has native support for geometric primitives, such as coordinates. Fluent supports these primitives as well as saving nested types, such as dictionaries, directly into Postgres.

MongoDB

MongoDB is a popular open-source, document-based, non-relational database designed to process large amounts of unstructured data and to be extremely scalable. It stores its data in JSON-like documents in human readable formats that do not require any particular structure.

Configuring Vapor

Configuring your Vapor application to use a database follows the same steps for all supported databases as shown below.

- Add the **Fluent Provider** as a dependency to the project.
- Configure the **database**.

Each database recipe in this chapter starts with **TILApp** as you left it in Chapter 5, "Fluent & Persisting Models". You'll also need to have Docker installed and running. Visit https://www.docker.com/get-docker and follow the instructions to install it. The toolbox allows you to choose which database to support, but you'll learn how to choose a different one manually.

SQLite

Unlike the other database types, SQLite doesn't require you to run a database server since SQLite uses a local file. Open **Package.swift** in your project directory. Replace the contents with the following:

```
// swift-tools-version:5.2

import PackageDescription

let package = Package(
  name: "TILApp",
  platforms: [
    .macOS(.v10_15)
  ],
  dependencies: [
    .package(
      url: "https://github.com/vapor/vapor.git",
      from: "4.0.0"),
    .package(
      url: "https://github.com/vapor/fluent.git",
      from: "4.0.0"),
    // 1
    .package(
      url: "https://github.com/vapor/fluent-sqlite-driver.git",
      from: "4.0.0")
  ],
  targets: [
    .target(
      name: "App",
      dependencies: [
        .product(name: "Fluent", package: "fluent"),
        // 2
        .product(
          name: "FluentSQLiteDriver",
          package: "fluent-sqlite-driver"),
        .product(name: "Vapor", package: "vapor")
      ],
      swiftSettings: [
        .unsafeFlags(
          ["-cross-module-optimization"],
          .when(configuration: .release))
      ]
    ),
    .target(name: "Run", dependencies: [.target(name: "App")]),
    .testTarget(name: "AppTests", dependencies: [
      .target(name: "App"),
      .product(name: "XCTVapor", package: "vapor"),
    ])
  ]
)
```

Here's what this does:

1. Specify `FluentSQLiteDriver` as a package dependency.
2. Specify that the App target depends on `FluentSQLiteDriver` to ensure it links correctly.

Like the other databases, database configuration happens in **Sources/App/configure.swift**. To switch to SQLite, replace the contents of the file with:

```
import Fluent
// 1
import FluentSQLiteDriver
import Vapor

// configures your application
public func configure(_ app: Application) throws {
  app.databases.use(.sqlite(.memory), as: .sqlite)

  app.migrations.add(CreateAcronym())

  app.logger.logLevel = .debug

  try app.autoMigrate().wait()

  // register routes
  try routes(app)
}
```

The changes are:

1. Import `FluentSQLiteDriver`.
2. Configure the application to use an in-memory SQLite database with the `.sqlite` identifier.

You can configure SQLite to use an in-memory database — this means the application creates a new instance of the database at every run. The database resides in memory, it's not persisted to disk and is lost when the application terminates. This is useful for testing and prototyping.

If you want persistent storage with SQLite, provide `SQLiteDatabase` with a path as shown below:

```
app.databases.use(.sqlite(.file("db.sqlite")), as: .sqlite)
```

This creates a database file at the specified path, if the file doesn't exist. If the file exists, Fluent uses it.

Make sure you have the deployment target set to **My Mac**, then build and run your application.

Look for the migration messages in the console.

MySQL

To test with MySQL, run the MySQL server in a Docker container. Enter the following command in Terminal:

```
docker run --name mysql \
  -e MYSQL_USER=vapor_username \
  -e MYSQL_PASSWORD=vapor_password \
  -e MYSQL_DATABASE=vapor_database \
  -e MYSQL_RANDOM_ROOT_PASSWORD=yes \
  -p 3306:3306 -d mysql
```

Here's what this does:

- Run a new container named **mysql**.
- Specify the database name, username and password through environment variables.
- Set `MYSQL_RANDOM_ROOT_PASSWORD` which sets the required root password to a random value.
- Allow applications to connect to the MySQL server on its default port: 3306.
- Run the server in the background as a daemon.
- Use the Docker image named **mysql** for this container. If the image is not present on your machine, Docker automatically downloads it.

To check that your database is running, enter the following in Terminal to list all active containers:

```
docker ps
```

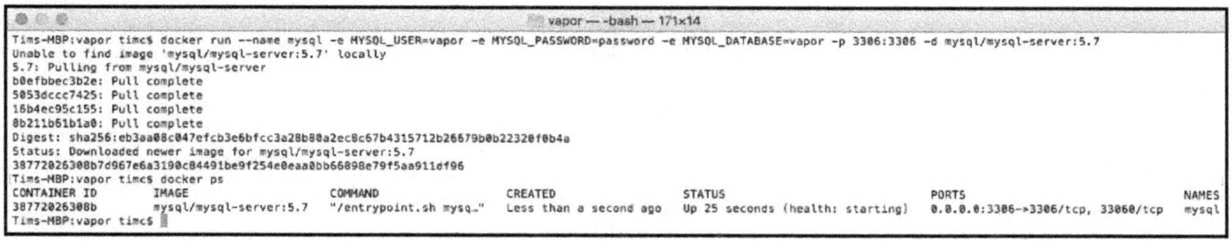

Now that MySQL is running, set up your Vapor application. Open **Package.swift**; replace its contents with the following:

```
// swift-tools-version:5.2
import PackageDescription

let package = Package(
  name: "TILApp",
  platforms: [
    .macOS(.v10_15)
  ],
  dependencies: [
    .package(
      url: "https://github.com/vapor/vapor.git",
      from: "4.0.0"),
    .package(
      url: "https://github.com/vapor/fluent.git",
      from: "4.0.0"),
    // 1
    .package(
```

```
        url: "https://github.com/vapor/fluent-mysql-driver.git",
        from: "4.0.0")
    ],
    targets: [
      .target(
        name: "App",
        dependencies: [
          .product(name: "Fluent", package: "fluent"),
          // 2
          .product(
            name: "FluentMySQLDriver",
            package: "fluent-mysql-driver"),
          .product(name: "Vapor", package: "vapor")
        ],
        swiftSettings: [
          .unsafeFlags(
            ["-cross-module-optimization"],
            .when(configuration: .release))
        ]
      ),
      .target(name: "Run", dependencies: [.target(name: "App")]),
      .testTarget(name: "AppTests", dependencies: [
        .target(name: "App"),
        .product(name: "XCTVapor", package: "vapor"),
      ])
    ]
)
```

Here's what this does:

1. Specify `FluentMySQLDriver` as a package dependency.
2. Specify that the `App` target depends on `FluentMySQLDriver` to ensure it links correctly.

Next, open **configure.swift**. To switch to MySQL, replace the contents with the following:

```
import Fluent
// 1
import FluentMySQLDriver
import Vapor

// configures your application
public func configure(_ app: Application) throws {
  // 2
  app.databases.use(.mysql(
    hostname: Environment.get("DATABASE_HOST") ?? "localhost",
    username: Environment.get("DATABASE_USERNAME")
      ?? "vapor_username",
    password: Environment.get("DATABASE_PASSWORD")
```

```
      ?? "vapor_password",
    database: Environment.get("DATABASE_NAME")
      ?? "vapor_database",
    tlsConfiguration: .forClient(certificateVerification: .none)
  ), as: .mysql)

  app.migrations.add(CreateAcronym())

  app.logger.logLevel = .debug

  try app.autoMigrate().wait()

  // register routes
  try routes(app)
}
```

The changes are:

1. Import `FluentMySQLDriver`.
2. Register the database with the application using the `.mysql` identifier. You provide the credentials for the database using environment variables. If the environment variables don't exist, the configuration uses the same hard-coded values you provided to docker.

> **Note:** MySQL uses a TLS connection by default. When running in Docker, MySQL generates a self-signed certificate. Your application doesn't know about this certificate. To allow your app to connect you need to disable certificate verification. You **must not** use this for a production application. You should provide the certificate to trust for a production application.

Make sure you have the deployment target set to **My Mac**, then build and run your application.

Look for the migration messages in the console.

MongoDB

To test with MongoDB, run the MongoDB server in a Docker container. Enter the following command in Terminal:

```
docker run --name mongo \
  -e MONGO_INITDB_DATABASE=vapor \
  -p 27017:27017 -d mongo
```

Here's what this does:

- Run a new container named **mongo**.
- Specify the database name through an environment variable.
- Allow applications to connect to the MongoDB server on its default port: 27017.
- Run the server in the background as a daemon.
- Use the Docker image named **mongo** for this container. If the image is not present on your machine, Docker automatically downloads it.

To check that your database is running, enter the following in Terminal to list all active containers:

```
docker ps
```

Now that MongoDB is running, set up your Vapor application. Open **Package.swift**; replace its contents with the following:

```
// swift-tools-version:5.2
import PackageDescription

let package = Package(
  name: "TILApp",
  platforms: [
    .macOS(.v10_15)
  ],
  dependencies: [
    .package(
      url: "https://github.com/vapor/vapor.git",
      from: "4.0.0"),
    .package(
      url: "https://github.com/vapor/fluent.git",
      from: "4.0.0"),
    // 1
    .package(
      url: "https://github.com/vapor/fluent-mongo-driver.git",
      from: "1.0.0")
  ],
  targets: [
    .target(
      name: "App",
      dependencies: [
        .product(name: "Fluent", package: "fluent"),
        // 2
        .product(
          name: "FluentMongoDriver",
          package: "fluent-mongo-driver"),
```

```
            .product(name: "Vapor", package: "vapor")
        ],
        swiftSettings: [
            .unsafeFlags(
                ["-cross-module-optimization"],
                .when(configuration: .release))
        ]
    ),
    .target(name: "Run", dependencies: [.target(name: "App")]),
    .testTarget(name: "AppTests", dependencies: [
        .target(name: "App"),
        .product(name: "XCTVapor", package: "vapor"),
    ])
  ]
)
```

Here's what this does:

1. Specify `FluentMongoDriver` as a package dependency.
2. Specify that the `App` target depends on `FluentMongoDriver` to ensure it links correctly.

Next, open **configure.swift**. To switch to MongoDB, replace the contents with the following:

```
import Fluent
// 1
import FluentMongoDriver
import Vapor

// configures your application
public func configure(_ app: Application) throws {
  // 2
  try app.databases.use(.mongo(
    connectionString: "mongodb://localhost:27017/vapor"),
    as: .mongo)

  app.migrations.add(CreateAcronym())

  app.logger.logLevel = .debug

  try app.autoMigrate().wait()

  // register routes
  try routes(app)
}
```

The changes are:

1. Import `FluentMongoDriver`.
2. Register the database with the application using the `.mongo` identifier. MongoDB uses a connection URL as shown here. The URL specifies the host — in this case `localhost` — the port and the path to the database. The path is the same as the database name provided to Docker. By default, MongoDB doesn't require authentication, but you would provide it here if needed.

Make sure you have the deployment target set to **My Mac**, then build and run your application.

Look for the migration messages in the console.

PostgreSQL

The Vapor app from Chapter 5, "Fluent & Persisting Models" you created already uses PostgreSQL. Remember, you created a PostgreSQL database in Docker with the following command in Terminal:

```
docker run --name postgres \
  -e POSTGRES_DB=vapor_database \
  -e POSTGRES_USER=vapor_username \
  -e POSTGRES_PASSWORD=vapor_password \
  -p 5432:5432 -d postgres
```

Here's what this does:

- Run a new container named **postgres**.
- Specify the database name, username and password through environment variables.
- Allow applications to connect to the Postgres server on its default port: 5432.
- Run the server in the background as a daemon.
- Use the Docker image named **postgres** for this container. If the image is not present on your machine, Docker automatically downloads it.

To check that your database is running, enter the following in Terminal to list all active containers:

```
docker ps
```

To understand how your Vapor application uses PostgreSQL. open **Package.swift**. It will look similar to the following:

```
// swift-tools-version:5.2
import PackageDescription

let package = Package(
  name: "TILApp",
  platforms: [
    .macOS(.v10_15)
  ],
  dependencies: [
    // 💧 A server-side Swift web framework.
    .package(
      url: "https://github.com/vapor/vapor.git",
      from: "4.0.0"),
```

```
    .package(
      url: "https://github.com/vapor/fluent.git",
      from: "4.0.0"),
    .package(
      url:
        "https://github.com/vapor/fluent-postgres-driver.git",
      from: "2.0.0")
  ],
  targets: [
    .target(
      name: "App",
      dependencies: [
        .product(name: "Fluent", package: "fluent"),
        .product(
          name: "FluentPostgresDriver",
          package: "fluent-postgres-driver"),
        .product(name: "Vapor", package: "vapor")
      ],
      swiftSettings: [
        .unsafeFlags(
          ["-cross-module-optimization"],
          .when(configuration: .release))
      ]
    ),
    .target(name: "Run", dependencies: [.target(name: "App")]),
    .testTarget(name: "AppTests", dependencies: [
      .target(name: "App"),
      .product(name: "XCTVapor", package: "vapor"),
    ])
  ]
)
```

You can see your app depends upon FluentPostgresDriver. Database configuration happens in **configure.swift**, like all the other database types. Your **configure.swift** should contain the following:

```
import Fluent
// 1
import FluentPostgresDriver
import Vapor

// configures your application
public func configure(_ app: Application) throws {
  // 2
  app.databases.use(.postgres(
    hostname: Environment.get("DATABASE_HOST")
      ?? "localhost",
    username: Environment.get("DATABASE_USERNAME")
      ?? "vapor_username",
    password: Environment.get("DATABASE_PASSWORD")
      ?? "vapor_password",
```

```
      database: Environment.get("DATABASE_NAME")
        ?? "vapor_database"
    ), as: .psql)

    // 3
    app.migrations.add(CreateAcronym())

    app.logger.logLevel = .debug

    // 4
    try app.autoMigrate().wait()

    // register routes
    try routes(app)
}
```

Here's what this does:

1. Import `FluentPostgresDriver`.
2. Configure the PostgreSQL database with the `.psql` identifier. This either uses credentials passed as environment variables or hard-coded credentials that match those passed to Docker.
3. Add `CreateAcronym` to the app's list of migrations.
4. Run the migrations automatically on application launch.

When you run your app for the first time, you'll see the migrations run:

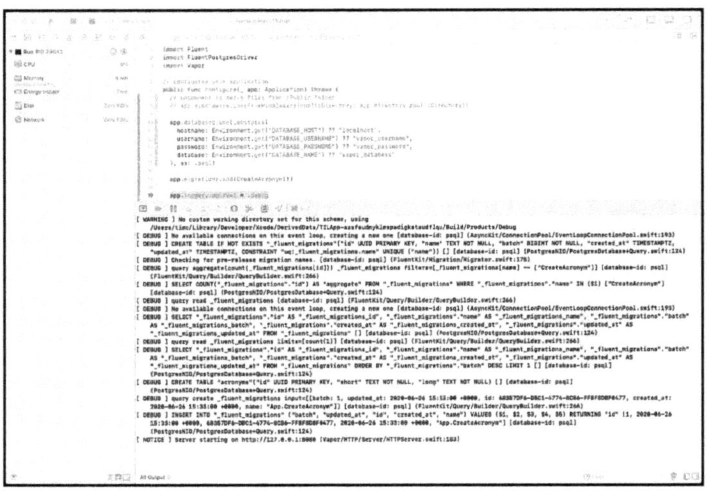

Where to go from here?

In this chapter, you've learned how to configure a database for your application. The next chapter introduces CRUD operations so you can create, retrieve, update and delete your acronyms.

Chapter 7: CRUD Database Operations

By Tim Condon

Chapter 5, "Fluent & Persisting Models", explained the concept of models and how to store them in a database using Fluent. This chapter concentrates on how to interact with models in the database. You'll learn about CRUD operations and how they relate to REST APIs. You'll also see how to leverage Fluent to perform complex queries on your models.

> **Note**: This chapter requires you to use PostgreSQL. Follow the steps in Chapter 5, "Fluent & Persisting Models", to set up PostgreSQL in Docker and configure your Vapor application.

CRUD and REST

CRUD operations — Create, Retrieve, Update, Delete — form the four basic functions of persistent storage. With these, you can perform most actions required for your application. You actually implemented the first function, create, in Chapter 5.

RESTful APIs provide a way for clients to call the CRUD functions in your application. Typically you have a resource URL for your models. For the TIL application, this is the acronym resource: **http://localhost:8080/api/acronyms**. You then define routes on this resource, paired with appropriate HTTP request methods, to perform the CRUD operations. For example:

- **GET http://localhost:8080/api/acronyms/**: get all the acronyms.
- **POST http://localhost:8080/api/acronyms**: create a new acronym.
- **GET http://localhost:8080/api/acronyms/1**: get the acronym with ID 1.
- **PUT http://localhost:8080/api/acronyms/1**: update the acronym with ID 1.
- **DELETE http://localhost:8080/api/acronyms/1**: delete the acronym with ID 1.

Create

In Chapter 5, "Fluent & Persisting Models", you implemented the create route for an Acronym. You can either continue with your project or open the TILApp in the starter folder for this chapter. To recap, you created a new route handler in **routes.swift**:

```
// 1
app.post("api", "acronyms") {
  req -> EventLoopFuture<Acronym> in
  // 2
  let acronym = try req.content.decode(Acronym.self)
  // 3
  return acronym.save(on: req.db).map { acronym }
}
```

Here's what this does:

1. Register a new route at **/api/acronyms/** that accepts a POST request and returns `EventLoopFuture<Acronym>`.
2. Decode the request's JSON into an `Acronym`. This is simple because `Acronym` conforms to `Content`.
3. Save the model using Fluent. When the save completes, you return the model inside the completion handler for `map(_:)`. This returns an `EventLoopFuture` — in this case, `EventLoopFuture<Acronym>`.

Build and run the application, then open RESTed. Configure the request as follows:

- **URL**: http://localhost:8080/api/acronyms/
- **method**: POST
- **Parameter encoding**: JSON-encoded

Add two parameters with names and values:

- **short**: OMG
- **long**: Oh My God

Send the request and you'll see the response containing the created acronym:

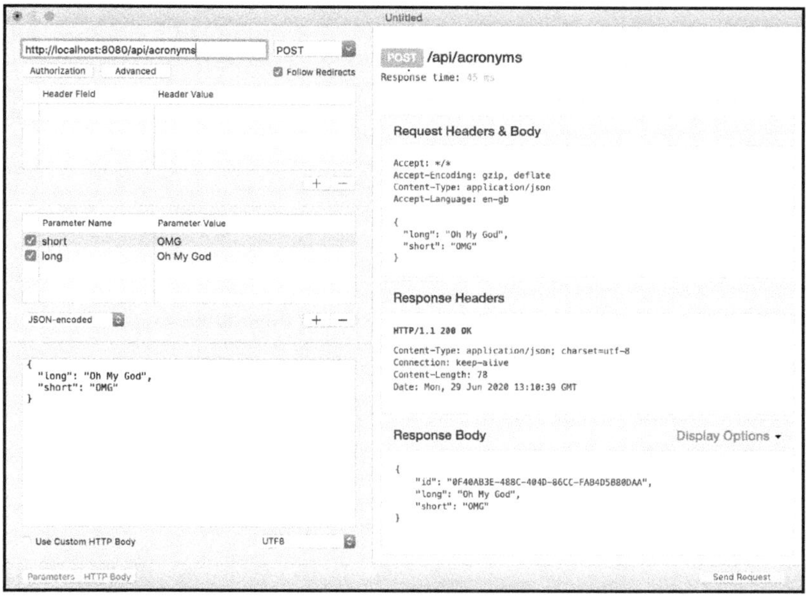

Retrieve

For TILApp, retrieve consists of two separate operations: retrieve all the acronyms and retrieve a single, specific acronym. Fluent makes both of these tasks easy.

Retrieve all acronyms

To retrieve all acronyms, create a route handler for GET requests to **/api/acronyms/**. Open **routes.swift** and add the following at the end of `routes(_:)`:

```
// 1
```

```
app.get("api", "acronyms") {
  req -> EventLoopFuture<[Acronym]> in
  // 2
  Acronym.query(on: req.db).all()
}
```

Here's what this does:

1. Register a new route handler that accepts a GET request which returns `EventLoopFuture<[Acronym]>`, a future array of `Acronyms`.
2. Perform a query to get all the acronyms.

Fluent adds functions to models to be able to perform queries on them. You must give the query a `Database`. This is almost always the database from the request and provides a connection for the query. `all()` returns all the models of that type in the database. This is equivalent to the SQL query `SELECT * FROM Acronyms;`.

Build and run your application, then create a new request in RESTed. Configure the request as follows:

- **URL**: http://localhost:8080/api/acronyms/
- **method**: GET

Send the request to see the acronyms already in the database:

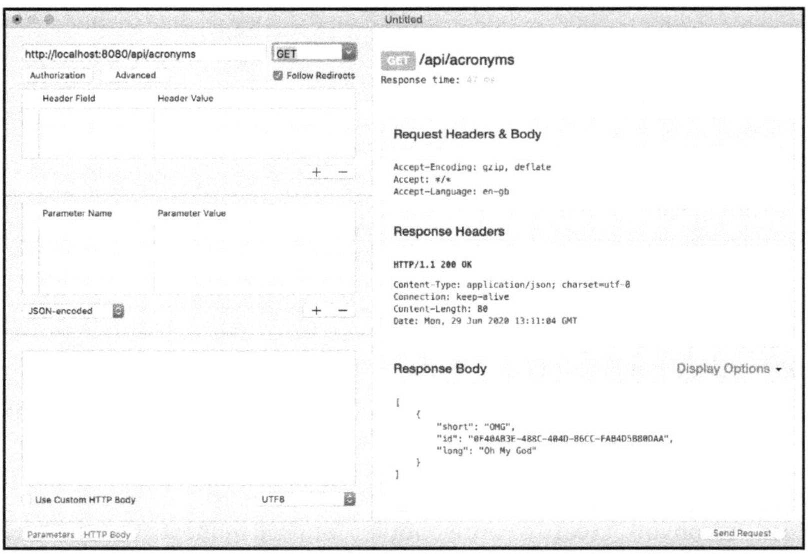

Retrieve a single acronym

Vapor's parameters integrate with Fluent's querying functions to make it easy to get acronyms by IDs. To get a single acronym, you need a new route handler. Open **routes.swift** and add the following at the end of `routes(_:)`:

```
// 1
app.get("api", "acronyms", ":acronymID") {
  req -> EventLoopFuture<Acronym> in
  // 2
  Acronym.find(req.parameters.get("acronymID"), on: req.db)
    // 3
    .unwrap(or: Abort(.notFound))
}
```

Here's what this does:

1. Register a route at **/api/acronyms/<ID>** to handle a GET request. The route takes the acronym's `id` property as the final path segment. This returns `EventLoopFuture<Acronym>`.
2. Get the parameter passed in with the name `acronymID`. Use `find(_:on:)` to query the database for an `Acronym` with that ID. Note that because `find(_:on:)` takes a UUID as the first parameter (because `Acronym`'s `id` type is `UUID`), `get(_:)` infers the return type as `UUID`. By default, it returns `String`. You can specify the type with `get(_:as:)`.
3. `find(_:on:)` returns `EventLoopFuture<Acronym?>` because an acronym with that ID might not exist in the database. Use `unwrap(or:)` to ensure that you return an acronym. If no acronym is found, `unwrap(or:)` returns a failed future with the error provided. In this case, it returns a **404 Not Found** error.

Build and run your application, then create a new request in RESTed. Configure the request as follows:

- **URL**: http://localhost:8080/api/acronyms/<ID> (replace the ID with the ID of the acronym you created earlier)
- **method**: GET

Send the request and you'll receive the first acronym as the response:

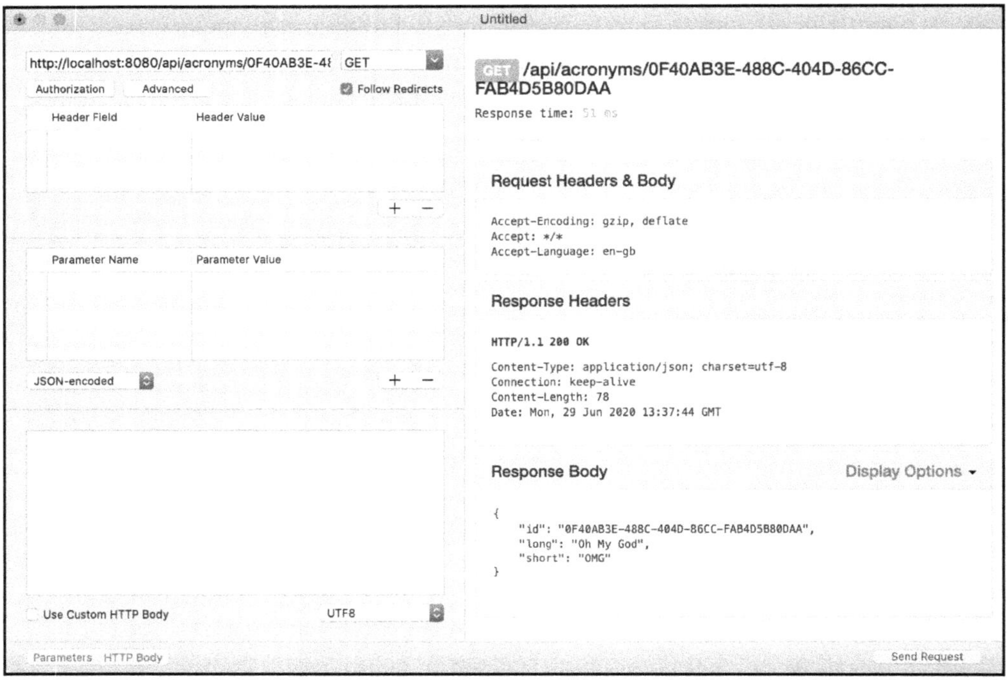

Update

In RESTful APIs, updates to single resources use a PUT request with the request data containing the new information.

Add the following at the end of `routes(_:)` to register a new route handler:

```
// 1
app.put("api", "acronyms", ":acronymID") {
  req -> EventLoopFuture<Acronym> in
  // 2
  let updatedAcronym = try req.content.decode(Acronym.self)
  return Acronym.find(
    req.parameters.get("acronymID"),
    on: req.db)
    .unwrap(or: Abort(.notFound)).flatMap { acronym in
      acronym.short = updatedAcronym.short
      acronym.long = updatedAcronym.long
      return acronym.save(on: req.db).map {
        acronym
      }
  }
}
```

Here's the play-by-play:

1. Register a route for a PUT request to **/api/acronyms/<ID>** that returns `EventLoopFuture<Acronym>`.
2. Decode the request body to `Acronym` to get the new details.
3. Get the acronym using the ID from the request URL. Use `unwrap(or:)` to return a **404 Not Found** if no acronym with the ID provided is found. This returns `EventLoopFuture<Acronym>` so use `flatMap(_:)` to wait for the future to complete.
4. Update the acronym's properties with the new values.
5. Save the acronym and wait for it to complete with `map(_:)`. Once the save has returned, return the updated acronym.

Build and run the application, then create a new acronym using RESTed. Configure the request as follows:

- **URL**: http://localhost:8080/api/acronyms/
- **method**: POST
- **Parameter encoding**: JSON-encoded

Add two parameters with names and values:

- **short**: WTF
- **long**: What The Flip

Send the request and you'll see the response containing the created acronym:

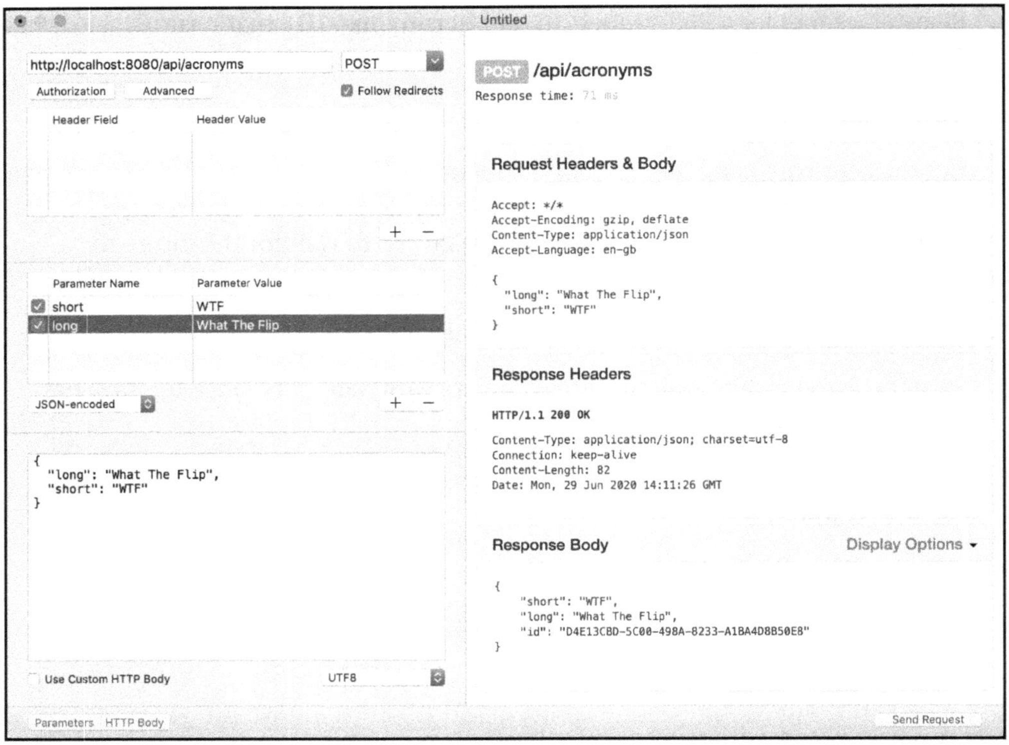

It turns out the meaning of WTF is not in fact "What The Flip", so it needs updating. Change the request in RESTed as follows:

- **URL**: http://localhost:8080/api/acronyms/<ID>

> **Note**: Use the ID from the returned create request.

- **method**: PUT
- **long**: What The Fudge

Send the request. You'll receive the updated acronym in the response:

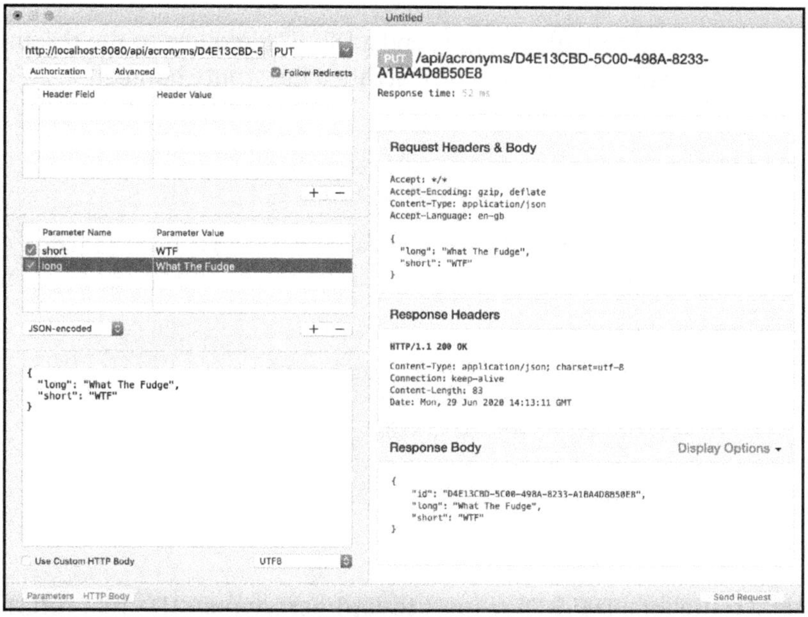

To ensure this has worked, send a request in RESTed to get all the acronyms. You'll see the updated acronym returned:

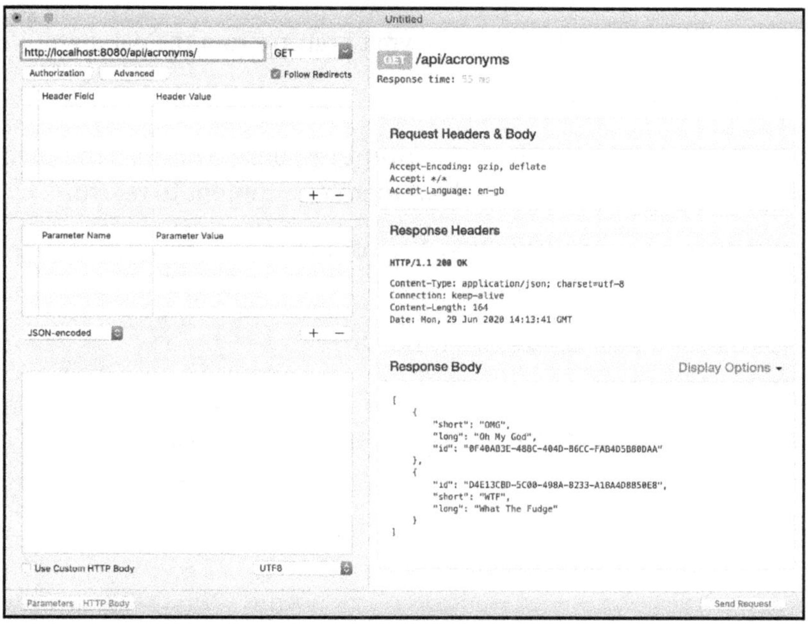

Delete

To delete a model in a RESTful API, you send a DELETE request to the resource. Add the following to the end of `routes(_:)` to create a new route handler:

```
// 1
app.delete("api", "acronyms", ":acronymID") {
  req -> EventLoopFuture<HTTPStatus> in
  // 2
  Acronym.find(req.parameters.get("acronymID"), on: req.db)
    .unwrap(or: Abort(.notFound))
    // 3
    .flatMap { acronym in
      // 4
      acronym.delete(on: req.db)
        // 5
        .transform(to: .noContent)
  }
}
```

Here's what this does:

1. Register a route for a DELETE request to **/api/acronyms/<ID>** that returns `EventLoopFuture<HTTPStatus>`.
2. Extract the acronym to delete from the request's parameters as before.
3. Use `flatMap(_:)` to wait for the acronym to return from the database.
4. Delete the acronym using `delete(on:)`.
5. Transform the result into a **204 No Content** response. This tells the client the request has successfully completed but there's no content to return.

Build and run the application. The "WTF" acronym is a little risqué so delete it. Configure a new request in RESTed as follows:

- **URL**: http://localhost:8080/api/acronyms/<ID>

> **Note**: Use ID of the WTF acronym from the previous request

- **method**: DELETE

Send the request; you'll receive a **204 No Content** response.

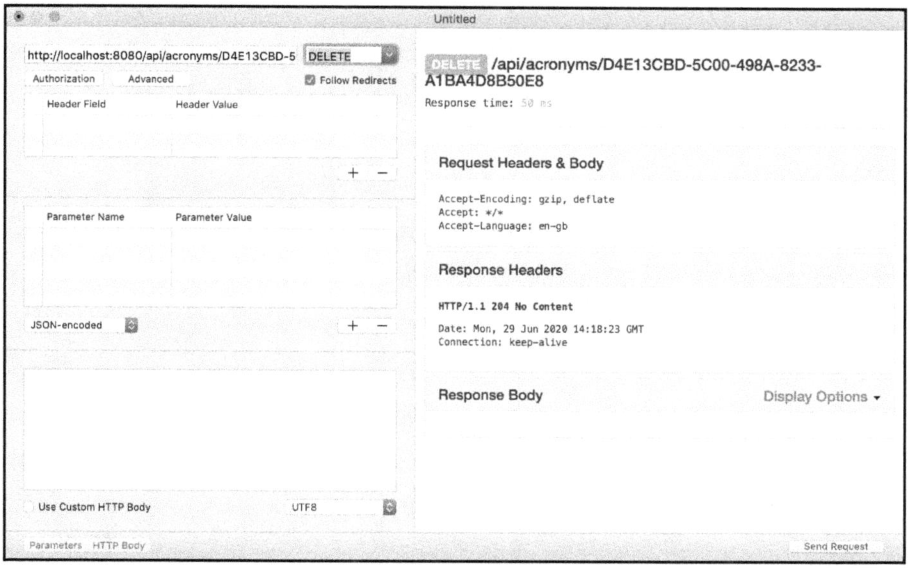

Send a request to get all the acronyms and you'll see the WTF acronym is no longer in the database.

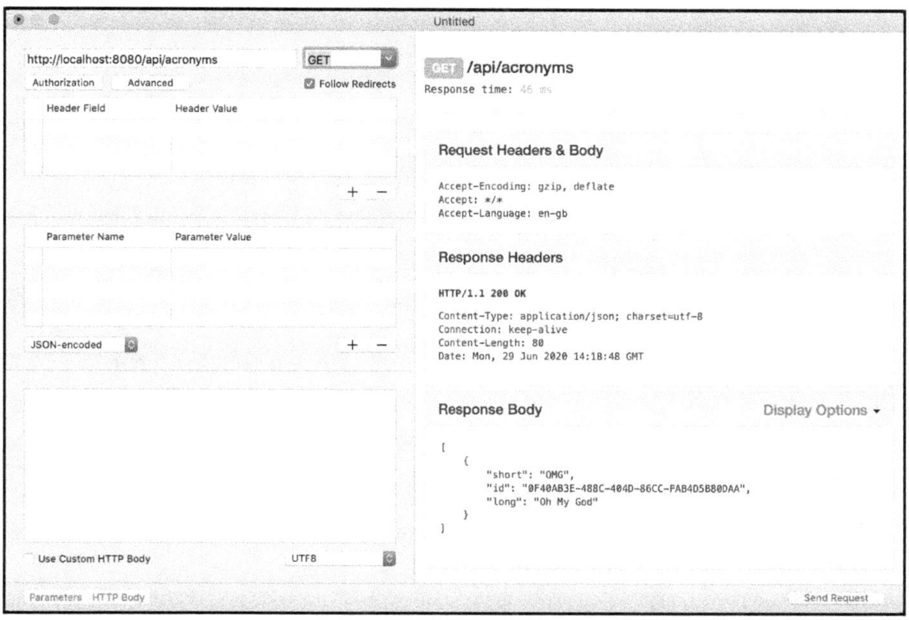

Fluent queries

You've seen how easy Fluent makes basic CRUD operations. It can perform more powerful queries just as easily.

Filter

Search functionality is a common feature in applications. If you want to search all the acronyms in the database, Fluent makes this easy. Ensure the following line of code is at the top of **routes.swift**:

```
import Fluent
```

Next, add a new route handler for searching at the end of `routes(_:)`:

```
// 1
app.get("api", "acronyms", "search") {
  req -> EventLoopFuture<[Acronym]> in
  // 2
  guard let searchTerm =
    req.query[String.self, at: "term"] else {
    throw Abort(.badRequest)
  }
  // 3
  return Acronym.query(on: req.db)
    .filter(\.$short == searchTerm)
    .all()
}
```

Here's what's going on to search the acronyms:

1. Register a new route handler that accepts a GET request for **/api/acronyms/search** and returns `EventLoopFuture<[Acronym]>`.

2. Retrieve the search term from the **URL query string**. If this fails, throw a `400 Bad Request` error.

> **Note**: Query strings in URLs allow clients to pass information to the server that doesn't fit sensibly in the path. For example, they are commonly used for defining the page number of a search result.

3. Use `filter(_:)` to find all acronyms whose `short` property matches the `searchTerm`. Because this uses key paths, the compiler can enforce type-safety on the properties and filter terms. This prevents run-time issues caused by specifying an invalid column name or invalid type to filter on. Fluent uses the property wrapper's projected value, instead of the value itself.

Fluent makes heavy use of property wrappers for fields when creating models. As described in the Swift documentation, "a property wrapper adds a layer of separation between code that manages how a property is stored and the code that defines a property". You can also provide a projected value to property wrappers. This allows you to expose additional functionality on the property wrapper. Fluent uses projected values to provide access to the key names and query functions for relationships.

In the above example, you provide the property wrapper's projected value to filter on instead of the value itself. The projected value provides Fluent with information from the property wrapper that it needs. For instance, Fluent needs the column name when performing the query for the filter. If you were to provide only the property, Fluent would have no way to access this data. You'll learn more about using property wrappers in the coming chapters.

If you require the actual value of a property, you use the property itself. For instance to read the short version of an acronym, you simply use `acronym.short`. In most instances, this is fine. However in some instances, this property may not have a value. You may want to reference a relation that you haven't yet loaded from the database. Or, you may have loaded the record but only retrieved selected fields. You'll learn about these different use cases in Chapter 9, "Parent-Child Relationships", Chapter 10, "Sibling Relationships" and Chapter 31, "Advanced Fluent".

Build and run your application, then create a new request in RESTed. Configure the request as follows:

- **URL**: http://localhost:8080/api/acronyms/search?term=OMG
- **method**: GET

Send the request and you'll see the OMG acronym returned with its meaning:

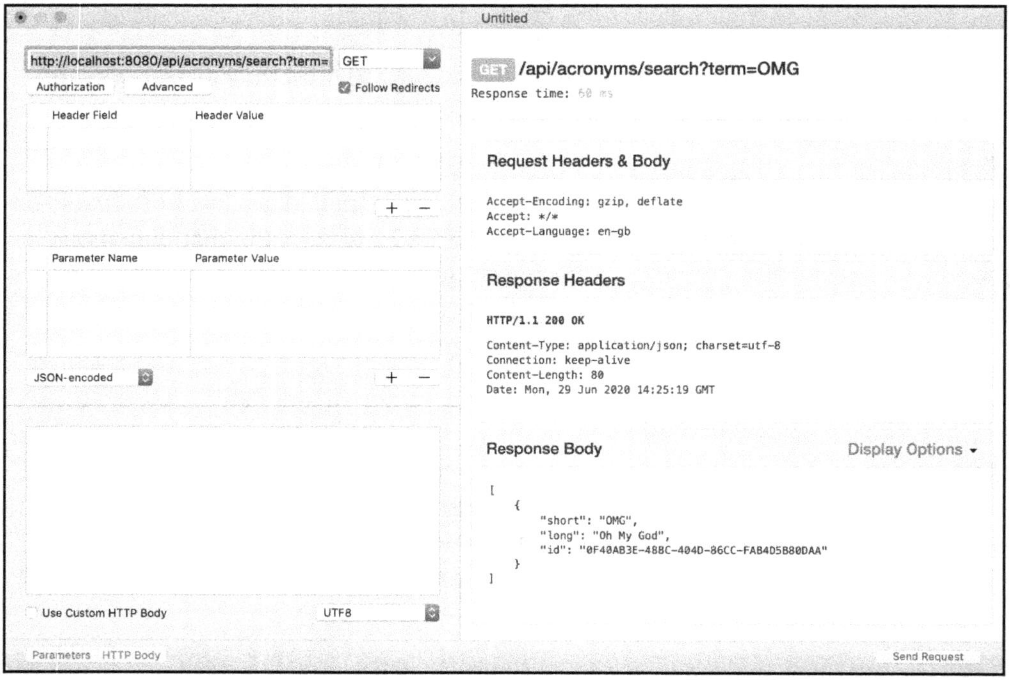

If you want to search multiple fields — for example both the short and long fields — you need to change your query. You can't chain `filter(_:)` functions as that would only match acronyms whose `short` and `long` properties were identical.

Instead, you must use a **filter group**. Replace:

```
return Acronym.query(on: req.db)
  .filter(\.$short == searchTerm)
  .all()
```

with the following:

```
// 1
return Acronym.query(on: req.db).group(.or) { or in
  // 2
  or.filter(\.$short == searchTerm)
  // 3
  or.filter(\.$long == searchTerm)
// 4
}.all()
```

Here's what this extra code does:

1. Create a filter group using the `.or` relation.
2. Add a filter to the group to filter for acronyms whose `short` property matches the search term.
3. Add a filter to the group to filter for acronyms whose `long` property matches the search term.
4. Return all the results.

This returns all acronyms that match the first filter *or* the second filter. Build and run the application and go back to RESTed. Resend the request from above and you'll still see the same result.

Change the URL to **http://localhost:8080/api/acronyms/search?term=Oh+My+God** and send the request. You'll get the OMG acronym back as a response:

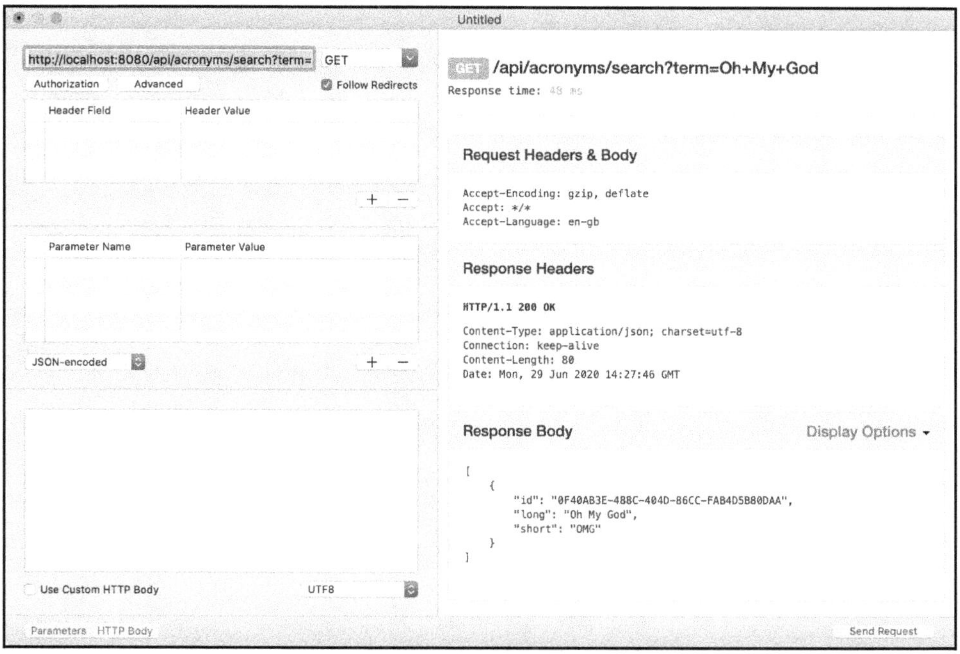

> **Note**: Spaces in URLs must be URL-encoded as either **%20** or + to be valid.

First result

Sometimes an application needs only the first result of a query. Creating a specific handler for this ensures the database only returns one result rather than loading all results into memory. Create a new route handler to return the first acronym at the end of `routes(_:)`:

```
// 1
app.get("api", "acronyms", "first") {
  req -> EventLoopFuture<Acronym> in
  // 2
  Acronym.query(on: req.db)
    .first()
    .unwrap(or: Abort(.notFound))
}
```

Here's what this function does:

1. Register a new HTTP GET route for **/api/acronyms/first** that returns `EventLoopFuture<Acronym>`.
2. Perform a query to get the first acronym. `first()` returns an optional as there may be no acronyms in the database. Use `unwrap(or:)` to ensure an acronym exists or throw a **404 Not Found** error.

You can also apply `.first()` to any query, such as the result of a filter.

Build and run the application, then open RESTed. Create new acronym with:

- **short**: IKR
- **long**: I Know Right

Now create a new RESTed request configured as:

- **URL**: http://localhost:8080/api/acronyms/first
- **method**: GET

Send the request and you'll see the first acronym you created returned:

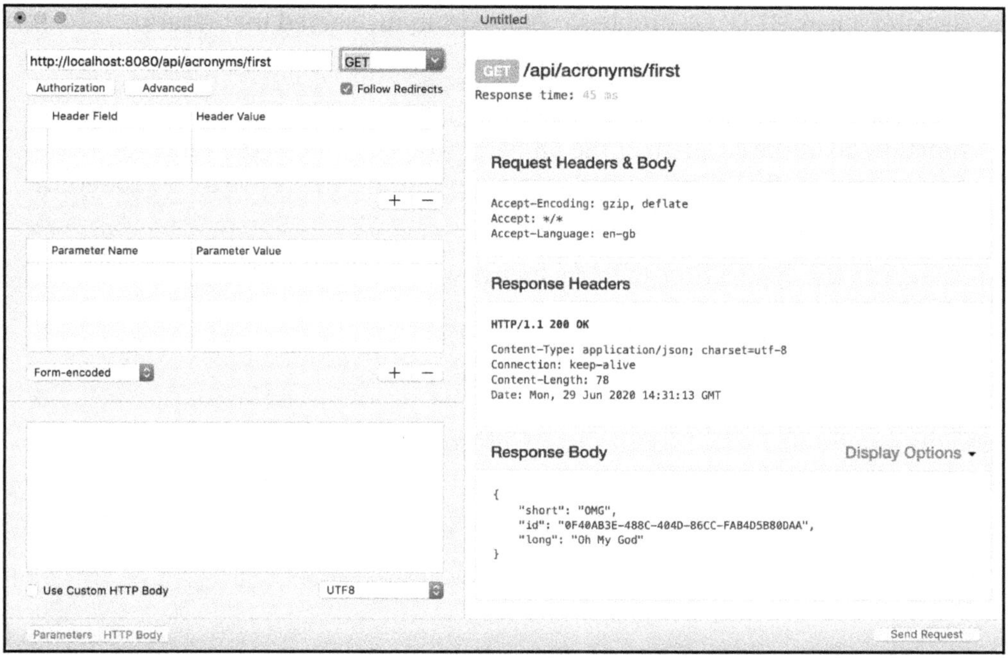

Sorting results

Apps commonly need to sort the results of queries before returning them. For this reason, Fluent provides a sort function.

Write a new route handler at the end of the `routes(_:)` function to return all the acronyms, sorted in ascending order by their `short` property:

```
// 1
app.get("api", "acronyms", "sorted") {
  req -> EventLoopFuture<[Acronym]> in
  // 2
  Acronym.query(on: req.db)
    .sort(\.$short, .ascending)
    .all()
}
```

Here's how this works:

1. Register a new HTTP GET route for **/api/acronyms/sorted** that returns `EventLoopFuture<[Acronym]>`.
2. Create a query for `Acronym` and use `sort(_:_:)` to perform the sort. This function takes the key path of the property wrapper's projected value for that field to sort on. It also takes the direction to sort in. Finally use `all()` to return all the results of the query.

Build and run the application, then create a new request in RESTed:

- **URL**: http://localhost:8080/api/acronyms/sorted
- **method**: GET

Send the request and you'll see the acronyms sorted alphabetically by their `short` property:

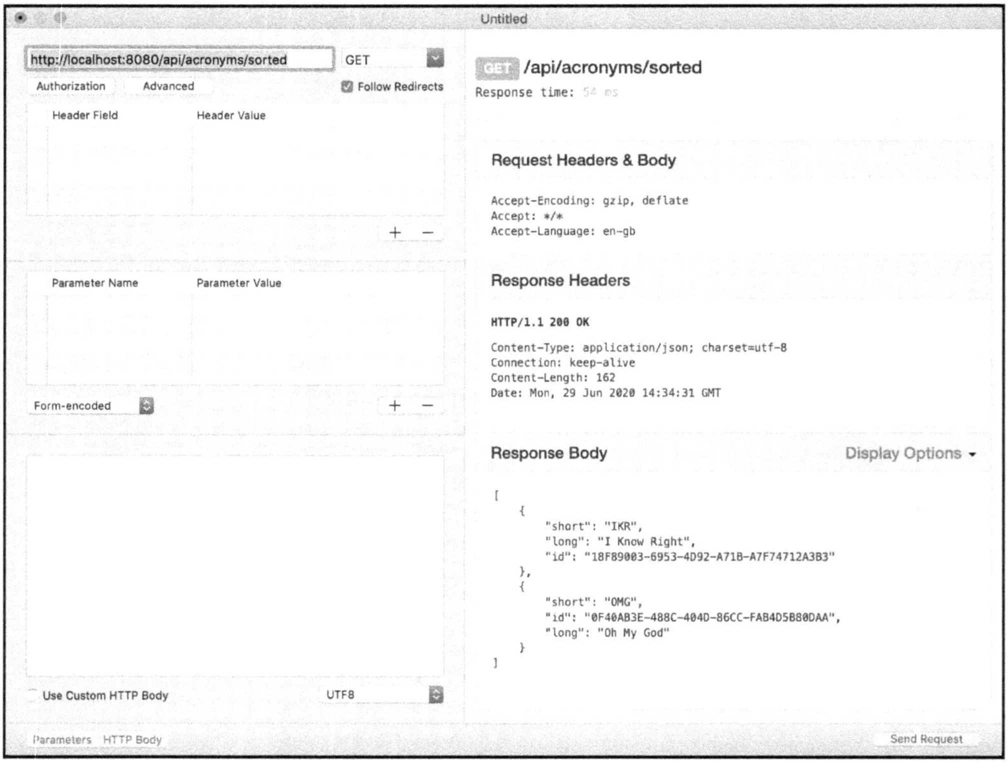

Where to go from here?

You now know how to use Fluent to perform the different CRUD operations and advanced queries. At this stage, **routes.swift** is getting cluttered with all the code from this chapter. The next chapter looks at how to better organize your code using controllers.

Chapter 8: Controllers

By Tim Condon

In previous chapters, you've written all the route handlers in **routes.swift**. This isn't sustainable for large projects as the file quickly becomes too big and cluttered. This chapter introduces the concept of controllers to help manage your routes and models, using both basic controllers and RESTful controllers.

> **Note**: This chapter requires that you have set up and configured PostgreSQL. Follow the steps in Chapter 6, "Configuring a Database", to set up PostgreSQL in Docker and configure the Vapor application.

Controllers

Controllers in Vapor serve a similar purpose to controllers in iOS. They handle interactions from a client, such as requests, process them and return the response. Controllers provide a way to better organize your code. It's good practice to have all interactions with a model in a dedicated controller. For example in the TIL application, an acronym controller can handle all CRUD operations on an acronym.

Controllers are also used to organize your application. For instance, you may use one controller to manage an older version of your API and another to manage the current version. This allows a clear separation of responsibilities in your code and keeps code maintainable.

Getting started with controllers

In Xcode, create a new Swift file to hold the acronyms controller. Create the file in **Sources/App/Controllers** and call it **AcronymsController.swift**.

Route collections

Inside a controller, you define different route handlers. To access these routes, you must register these handlers with the router. A simple way to do this is to call the functions inside your controller from **routes.swift**. For example:

```
app.get(
  "api",
  "acronyms",
  use: acronymsController.getAllHandler)
```

This example calls `getAlllHandler(_:)` on the `acronymsController`. This call is like the route handlers you wrote in Chapter 7. However, instead of passing a closure as the final parameter, you pass the function to use.

This works well for small applications. But if you've a large number of routes to register, **routes.swift** again becomes unmanageable. It's good practice for controllers to be responsible for registering the routes they control. Vapor provides the protocol `RouteCollection` to enable this.

Open **AcronymsController.swift** in Xcode and add the following to create an `AcronymsController` that conforms to `RouteCollection`:

```
import Vapor
import Fluent

struct AcronymsController: RouteCollection {
  func boot(routes: RoutesBuilder) throws {
  }
}
```

RouteCollection requires you to implement boot(router:) to register routes. Add a new route handler after boot(routes:):

```
func getAllHandler(_ req: Request)
    -> EventLoopFuture<[Acronym]> {
  Acronym.query(on: req.db).all()
}
```

The body of the handler is identical to the one you wrote earlier and the signature matches the signature of the closure you used before. Register the route in boot(router:):

```
routes.get("api", "acronyms", use: getAllHandler)
```

This makes a GET request to **/api/acronyms** call getAllHandler(_:). You wrote this same route earlier in **routes.swift**. Now, it's time to remove that one. Open **routes.swift** and delete the following handler:

```
app.get("api", "acronyms") {
  req -> EventLoopFuture<[Acronym]> in
  Acronym.query(on: req.db).all()
}
```

Next, add the following to the end of routes(_:):

```
// 1
let acronymsController = AcronymsController()
// 2
try app.register(collection: acronymsController)
```

Here's what this does:

1. Create a new AcronymsController.
2. Register the new type with the application to ensure the controller's routes get registered.

Build and run the application, then create a new request in RESTed. Configure the request as follows:

- **URL**: http://localhost:8080/api/acronyms/
- **method**: GET

Send the request and you'll get the existing acronyms in your database:

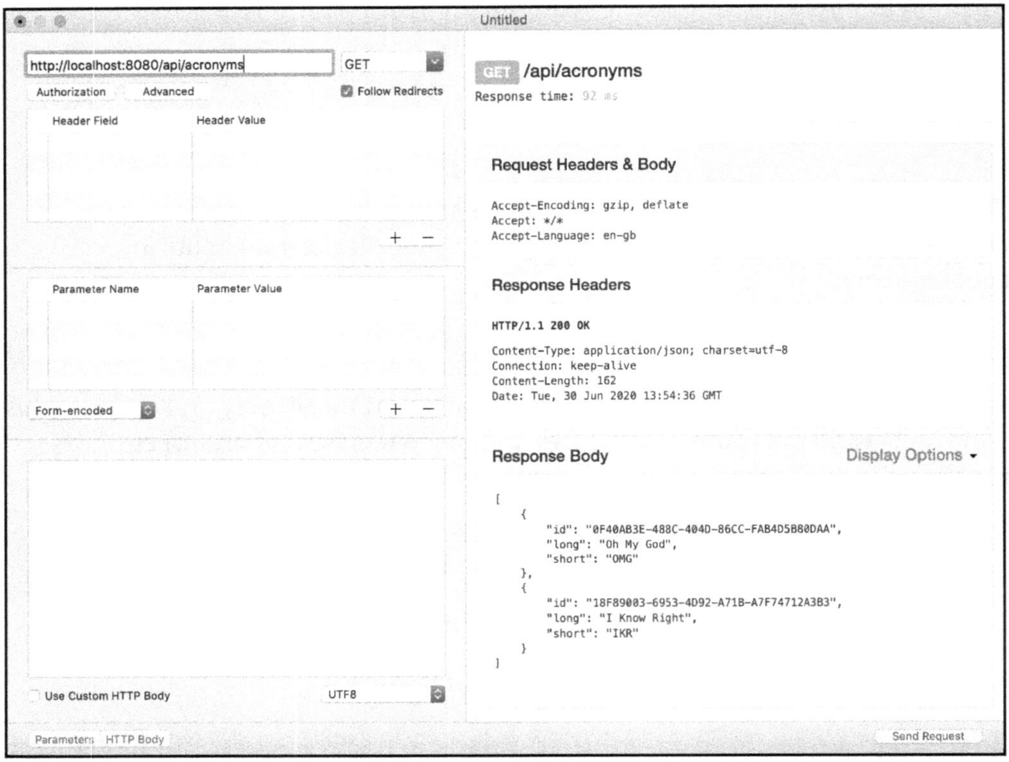

Route groups

All of the REST routes created for acronyms in the previous chapters use the same initial path, e.g.:

```
app.post("api", "acronyms") {
  req -> EventLoopFuture<Acronym> in
  let acronym = try req.content.decode(Acronym.self)
  return acronym.save(on: req.db).map { acronym }
}
```

If you need to change the **/api/acronyms/** path, you have to change the path in multiple locations. If you add a new route, you have to remember to add both parts of the path. Vapor provides **route groups** to simplify this. Open **AcronymsController.swift** and create a route group at the beginning of `boot(routes:)`:

```
let acronymsRoutes = routes.grouped("api", "acronyms")
```

This creates a new route group for the path **/api/acronyms**. Next, replace:

```
routes.get("api", "acronyms", use: getAllHandler)
```

with the following:

```
acronymsRoutes.get(use: getAllHandler)
```

This works as it did before but greatly simplifies the code, making it easier to maintain.

Next, open **routes.swift** and remove the remaining acronym route handlers:

- `router.post("api", "acronyms")`
- `router.get("api", "acronyms", Acronym.parameter)`
- `router.put("api", "acronyms", Acronym.parameter)`
- `router.delete("api", "acronyms", Acronym.parameter)`
- `router.get("api", "acronyms", "search")`
- `router.get("api", "acronyms", "first")`
- `router.get("api", "acronyms", "sorted")`

Next, remove any other routes from the template. You should only have the `AcronymsController` registration left in `routes(_:)`. Next, open **AcronymsController.swift** and recreate the handlers by adding each of the following after `boot(router:)`

```
func createHandler(_ req: Request) throws
    -> EventLoopFuture<Acronym> {
  let acronym = try req.content.decode(Acronym.self)
  return acronym.save(on: req.db).map { acronym }
}

func getHandler(_ req: Request)
    -> EventLoopFuture<Acronym> {
  Acronym.find(req.parameters.get("acronymID"), on: req.db)
    .unwrap(or: Abort(.notFound))
}

func updateHandler(_ req: Request) throws
    -> EventLoopFuture<Acronym> {
  let updatedAcronym = try req.content.decode(Acronym.self)
  return Acronym.find(
    req.parameters.get("acronymID"),
    on: req.db)
    .unwrap(or: Abort(.notFound)).flatMap { acronym in
```

```
        acronym.short = updatedAcronym.short
        acronym.long = updatedAcronym.long
        return acronym.save(on: req.db).map {
          acronym
        }
      }
  }

  func deleteHandler(_ req: Request)
      -> EventLoopFuture<HTTPStatus> {
    Acronym.find(req.parameters.get("acronymID"), on: req.db)
      .unwrap(or: Abort(.notFound))
      .flatMap { acronym in
        acronym.delete(on: req.db)
          .transform(to: .noContent)
      }
  }

  func searchHandler(_ req: Request) throws
      -> EventLoopFuture<[Acronym]> {
    guard let searchTerm = req
      .query[String.self, at: "term"] else {
        throw Abort(.badRequest)
    }
    return Acronym.query(on: req.db).group(.or) { or in
      or.filter(\.$short == searchTerm)
      or.filter(\.$long == searchTerm)
    }.all()
  }

  func getFirstHandler(_ req: Request)
      -> EventLoopFuture<Acronym> {
    return Acronym.query(on: req.db)
      .first()
      .unwrap(or: Abort(.notFound))
  }

  func sortedHandler(_ req: Request)
      -> EventLoopFuture<[Acronym]> {
    return Acronym.query(on: req.db)
      .sort(\.$short, .ascending).all()
  }
```

Each of these handlers is identical the ones you created in Chapter 7. If you need a reminder of what they do, that's the place to look!

Finally, register these route handlers using the route group. Add the following to the bottom of `boot(routes:)`:

```
// 1
acronymsRoutes.post(use: createHandler)
// 2
acronymsRoutes.get(":acronymID", use: getHandler)
// 3
acronymsRoutes.put(":acronymID", use: updateHandler)
// 4
acronymsRoutes.delete(":acronymID", use: deleteHandler)
// 5
acronymsRoutes.get("search", use: searchHandler)
// 6
acronymsRoutes.get("first", use: getFirstHandler)
// 7
acronymsRoutes.get("sorted", use: sortedHandler)
```

Here's what this does:

1. Register `createHandler(_:)` to process POST requests to **/api/acronyms**.
2. Register `getHandler(_:)` to process GET requests to **/api/acronyms/<ACRONYM ID>**.
3. Register `updateHandler(_:)` to process PUT requests to **/api/acronyms/<ACRONYM ID>**.
4. Register `deleteHandler(_:)` to process DELETE requests to **/api/acronyms/<ACRONYM ID>**.
5. Register `searchHandler(_:)` to process GET requests to **/api/acronyms/search**.
6. Register `getFirstHandler(_:)` to process GET requests to **/api/acronyms/first**.
7. Register `sortedHandler(_:)` to process GET requests to **/api/acronyms/sorted**.

Build and run the application, then create a new request in RESTed. Configure the request as follows:

- **URL**: http://localhost:8080/api/acronyms/first
- **method**: GET

Send the request and you'll see a previously created acronym using the new controller:

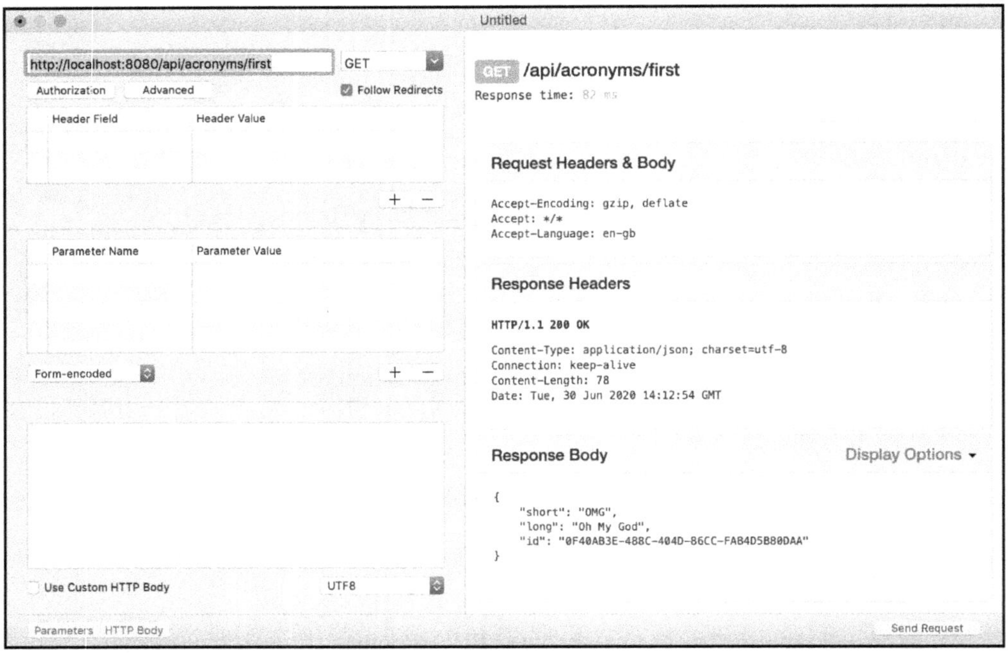

Where to go from here?

This chapter introduced controllers as a way of better organizing code. They help split out route handlers into separate areas on responsibility. This allows applications to grow in a maintainable way. The next chapters look at how to bring together different models with relationships in Fluent.

Chapter 9: Parent-Child Relationships

By Tim Condon

Chapter 5, "Fluent & Persisting Models", introduced the concept of models. In this chapter, you'll learn how to set up a parent-child relationship between two models. You'll also learn the purpose of these relationships, how to model them in Vapor and how to use them with routes.

> **Note**: This chapter requires that you have set up and configured PostgreSQL. Follow the steps in Chapter 6, "Configuring a Database", to set up PostgreSQL in Docker and configure the Vapor application.

Parent-child relationships

Parent-child relationships describe a relationship where one model has "ownership" of one or more models. They are also known as **one-to-one** and **one-to-many** relationships.

For instance, if you model the relationship between people and pets, one person can have one or more pets. A pet can only ever have one owner. In the TIL application, users will create acronyms. Users (the parent) can have many acronyms, and an acronym (the child) can only be created by one user.

Creating a user

In Xcode, create a new file for the `User` class called **User.swift** in **Sources/App/Models**. Next, create a migration file, **CreateUser.swift**, in **Sources/App/Migrations**. Finally, create a file called **UsersController.swift** in **Sources/App/Controllers** for the `UsersController`.

User model

In Xcode, open **User.swift** and create a basic model for the user:

```
import Fluent
import Vapor

final class User: Model, Content {
  static let schema = "users"

  @ID
  var id: UUID?

  @Field(key: "name")
  var name: String

  @Field(key: "username")
  var username: String

  init() {}

  init(id: UUID? = nil, name: String, username: String) {
    self.name = name
    self.username = username
  }
}
```

The model contains two `String` properties to hold the user's name and username. It also contains an optional `id` property that stores the ID of the model assigned by the database when it's saved. You annotate each property with the relevant property wrapper.

Next, open **CreateUser.swift** and insert the following:

```
import Fluent

// 1
struct CreateUser: Migration {
  // 2
  func prepare(on database: Database) -> EventLoopFuture<Void> {
```

```
    // 3
    database.schema("users")
      // 4
      .id()
      // 5
      .field("name", .string, .required)
      .field("username", .string, .required)
      // 6
      .create()
  }

  // 7
  func revert(on database: Database) -> EventLoopFuture<Void> {
    database.schema("users").delete()
  }
}
```

This is what your migration does:

1. Create a new type for the migration to create the users table in the database.
2. Implement `prepare(on:)` as required by `Migration`.
3. Set up the schema for `User` with the name of the table as `users`.
4. Create the ID column using the default properties.
5. Create the columns for the two other properties. These are both `String` and required. The name of the columns match the keys defined in the property wrapper for each property.
6. Create the table.
7. Implement `revert(on:)` as required by `Migration`. This deletes the table named `users`.

Finally, open **configure.swift** to add `CreateUser` to the migration list. Insert the following after `app.migrations.add(CreateAcronym())`:

```
app.migrations.add(CreateUser())
```

This adds the new model to the migrations so Fluent prepares the table in the database at the next application start.

User controller

Open **UsersController.swift** and create a new controller that can create users:

```
import Vapor

// 1
struct UsersController: RouteCollection {
  // 2
  func boot(routes: RoutesBuilder) throws {
    // 3
    let usersRoute = routes.grouped("api", "users")
    // 4
    usersRoute.post(use: createHandler)
  }

  // 5
  func createHandler(_ req: Request)
    throws -> EventLoopFuture<User> {
    // 6
    let user = try req.content.decode(User.self)
    // 7
    return user.save(on: req.db).map { user }
  }
}
```

This should look familiar by now; here's what it does:

1. Define a new type `UsersController` that conforms to `RouteCollection`.
2. Implement `boot(routes:)` as required by `RouteCollection`.
3. Create a new route group for the path **/api/users**.
4. Register `createHandler(_:)` to handle a POST request to **/api/users**.
5. Define the route handler function.
6. Decode the user from the request body.
7. Save the decoded user. `save(on:)` returns `EventLoopFuture<Void>` so use `map(_:)` to wait for the save to complete and return the saved user.

Finally, open **routes.swift** and add the following to the end of `routes(_:)`:

```
// 1
let usersController = UsersController()
// 2
try app.register(collection: usersController)
```

Here's what this does:

1. Create a `UsersController` instance.
2. Register the new controller instance with the router to hook up the routes.

Open **UsersController.swift** again and add the following to the end of `UsersController`. These functions return a list of all users and a single user, respectively:

```
// 1
func getAllHandler(_ req: Request)
  -> EventLoopFuture<[User]> {
  // 2
  User.query(on: req.db).all()
}

// 3
func getHandler(_ req: Request)
  -> EventLoopFuture<User> {
  // 4
  User.find(req.parameters.get("userID"), on: req.db)
      .unwrap(or: Abort(.notFound))
}
```

Here's what this does:

1. Define a new route handler, `getAllHandler(_:)`, that returns `EventLoopFuture<[User]>`.
2. Return all the users using a Fluent query.
3. Define a new route handler, `getHandler(_:)`, that returns `EventLoopFuture<User>`.
4. Return the user specified by the request's parameter named `userID`.

Register these two route handlers at the end of `boot(routes:)`:

```
// 1
usersRoute.get(use: getAllHandler)
// 2
usersRoute.get(":userID", use: getHandler)
```

Here's what this does:

1. Register `getAllHandler(_:)` to process GET requests to **/api/users/**.
2. Register `getHandler(_:)` to process GET requests to **/api/users/<USER ID>**.

This uses a dynamic path component that matches the parameter you search for in `getHandler(_:)`.

Build and run the application, then create a new request in RESTed. Configure the request as follows:

- **URL**: http://localhost:8080/api/users
- **method**: POST
- **Parameter encoding**: JSON-encoded

Add two parameters with names and values:

- **name**: your name
- **username**: a username of your choice

Send the request and you'll see the saved user in the response:

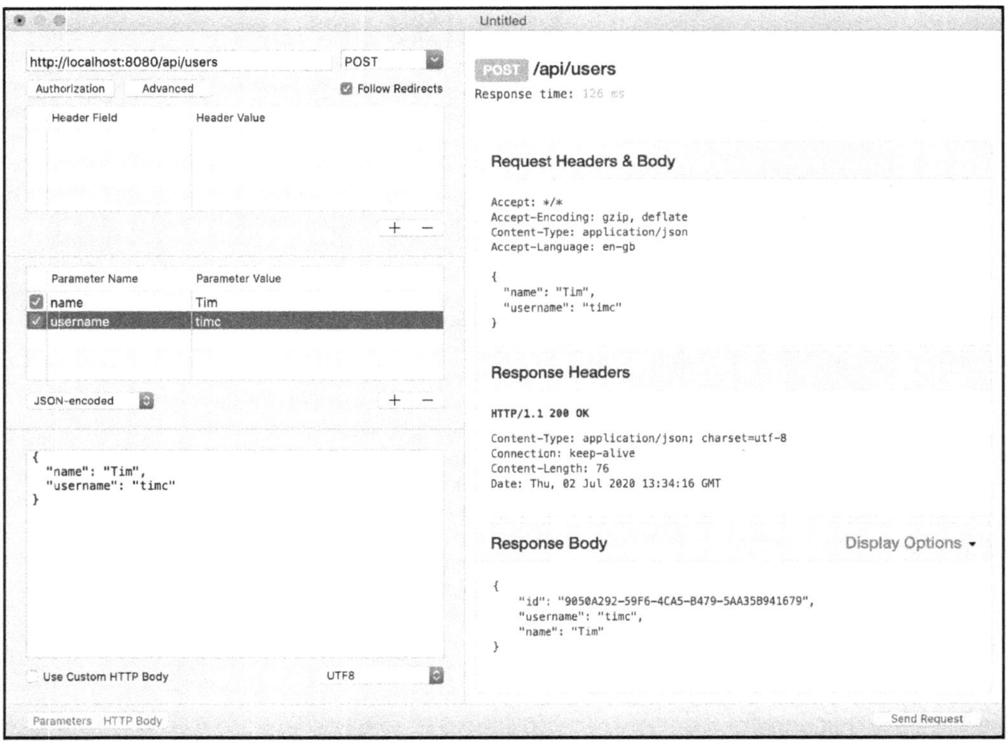

Setting up the relationship

Modeling a parent-child relationship in Vapor matches how a database models the relationship, but in a "Swifty" way. Because a user owns each acronym, you add a user property to the acronym. The database represents this as a reference to the user in the acronyms table. This allows Fluent to search the database efficiently.

To get all the acronyms for a user, you retrieve all acronyms that contain that user reference. To get the user of an acronym, you use the user from that acronym. Fluent uses property wrappers to make all this possible.

Open **Acronym.swift** and add a new property after `var long: String`:

```
@Parent(key: "userID")
var user: User
```

This adds a `User` property of to the model. It uses the `@Parent` property wrapper to create the link between the two models. Note this type is not optional, so an acronym must have a user. `@Parent` is another special Fluent property wrapper. It tells Fluent that this property represents the parent of a parent-child relationship. Fluent uses this to query the database. `@Parent` also allows you to create an `Acronym` using only the ID of a `User`, without needing a full `User` object. This helps avoid additional database queries.

Replace the initializer with the following to reflect this:

```
// 1
init(
  id: UUID? = nil,
  short: String,
  long: String,
  userID: User.IDValue
) {
  self.id = id
  self.short = short
  self.long = long
  // 2
  self.$user.id = userID
}
```

Here's what you changed:

1. Add a new parameter to the initializer for the user's ID of type `User.IDValue`. This is a typealias defined by `Model`, which resolves to UUID.
2. Set the ID of the projected value of the `user` property wrapper. As discussed above, this avoids you having to perform a lookup to get the full `User` model to create an `Acronym`.

Finally, open **CreateAcronym.swift**. Before `.create()` add the following line:

```
.field("userID", .uuid, .required)
```

This adds the new column for `user` using the key provided to the `@Parent` property wrapper. The column type, `uuid`, matches the ID column type from `CreateUser`.

Domain Transfer Objects (DTOs)

You can send a request with a JSON payload to match the new `Acronym` model. However, it looks like:

```
{
  "short": "OMG",
  "long": "Oh My God",
  "user": {
    "id": "2074AD1A-21DC-4238-B3ED-D076BBE5D135"
  }
}
```

Because `Acronym` has a `user` property, the JSON must match this. The property wrapper allows you to only send an `id` for `user`, but it's still complex to create. To solve this, you use a **Domain Transfer Object** or DTO. A DTO is a type that represents what a client should send or receive. Your route handler then accepts a DTO and converts it into something your code can use. At the bottom of **AcronymsController.swift**, add the following code:

```
struct CreateAcronymData: Content {
  let short: String
  let long: String
  let userID: UUID
}
```

This DTO represents the JSON we expect from the client:

```
{
  "short": "OMG",
  "long": "Oh My God",
  "userID": "2074AD1A-21DC-4238-B3ED-D076BBE5D135"
}
```

Next, replace the body of `createHandler(_:)` with the following:

```
// 1
let data = try req.content.decode(CreateAcronymData.self)
// 2
let acronym = Acronym(
  short: data.short,
  long: data.long,
  userID: data.userID)
return acronym.save(on: req.db).map { acronym }
```

Here's what the updated code changes:

1. Decode the request body to `CreateAcronymData` instead of `Acronym`.
2. Create an `Acronym` from the data received.

That's all you need to do to set up the relationship! Before you run the application, you need to reset the database. Fluent has already run the `CreateAcronym` migration but the table has a new column now. To add the new column to the table, you must delete the database so Fluent will run the migration again. Stop the application in Xcode and then in Terminal, enter:

```
# 1
docker stop postgres
# 2
docker rm postgres
# 3
docker run --name postgres -e POSTGRES_DB=vapor_database \
  -e POSTGRES_USER=vapor_username \
  -e POSTGRES_PASSWORD=vapor_password \
  -p 5432:5432 -d postgres
```

Here's what this does:

1. Stop the running Docker container **postgres**. This is the container currently running the database.
2. Remove the Docker container **postgres** to delete any existing data.
3. Start a new Docker container running PostgreSQL. For more information, see Chapter 6, "Configuring a Database".

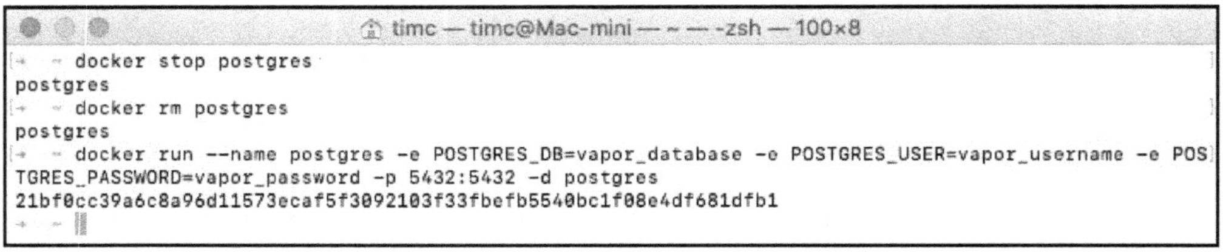

> **Note**: New migrations can also alter tables so you don't lose production data when changing your models. Chapter 27, "Database/API Versioning & Migration" covers this.

Build and run the application in Xcode and the migrations run. Open RESTed and create a user following the steps from earlier in the chapter. Make sure you copy the returned ID.

Create a new request in RESTed and configure it as follows:

- **URL**: http://localhost:8080/api/acronyms
- **method**: POST
- **Parameter encoding**: JSON-encoded

Add three parameters with names and values:

- **short**: OMG
- **long**: Oh My God
- **userID**: the ID you copied earlier

Click **Send Request**. Your application creates the acronym with the user specified:

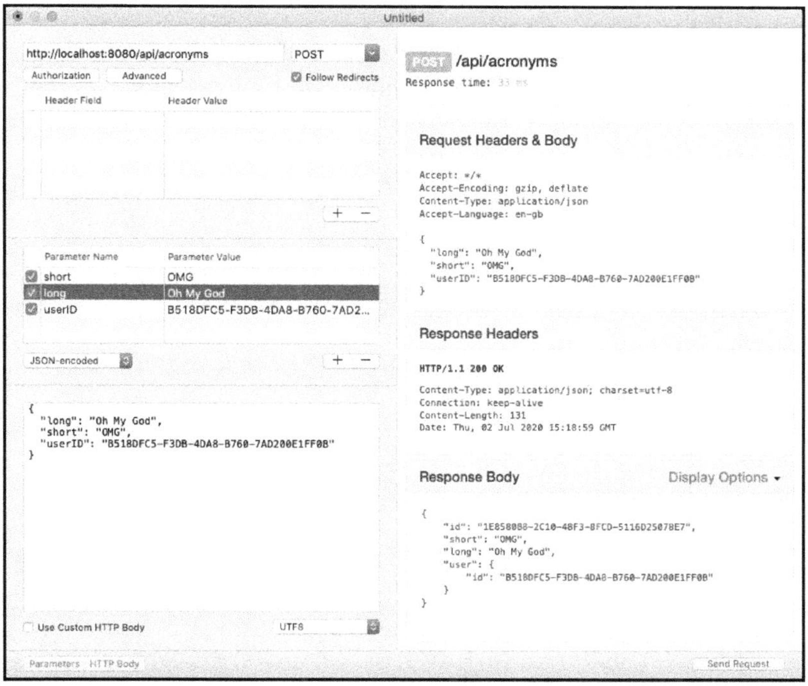

Finally, open **AcronymsController.swift** and replace `updateHandler(_:)` with the following to account for the new property on `Acronym`:

```
func updateHandler(_ req: Request) throws
    -> EventLoopFuture<Acronym> {
  let updateData =
    try req.content.decode(CreateAcronymData.self)
  return Acronym
    .find(req.parameters.get("acronymID"), on: req.db)
    .unwrap(or: Abort(.notFound))
    .flatMap { acronym in
      acronym.short = updateData.short
      acronym.long = updateData.long
      acronym.$user.id = updateData.userID
      return acronym.save(on: req.db).map {
        acronym
      }
    }
}
```

This updates the acronym's properties with the new values provided in the request, including the new user ID.

Querying the relationship

Users and acronyms are now linked with a parent-child relationship. However, this isn't very useful until you can query these relationships. Once again, Fluent makes that easy.

Getting the parent

Open **AcronymsController.swift** and add a new route handler after `sortedHandler(_:)`:

```
// 1
func getUserHandler(_ req: Request)
  -> EventLoopFuture<User> {
  // 2
  Acronym.find(req.parameters.get("acronymID"), on: req.db)
    .unwrap(or: Abort(.notFound))
    .flatMap { acronym in
      // 3
      acronym.$user.get(on: req.db)
    }
}
```

Here's what this route handler does:

1. Define a new route handler, `getUserHandler(_:)`, that returns `EventLoopFuture<User>`.
2. Fetch the acronym specified in the request's parameters and unwrap the returned future.
3. Use the property wrapper to get the acronym's owner from the database. This performs a query on the `User` table to find the user with the ID saved in the database. If you try to access the property with `acronym.user`, you'll get an error because you haven't retrieved the user from the database. Chapter 31, "Advanced Fluent", discusses eager loading and working with properties.

Register the route handler at the end of `boot(routes:)`:

```
acronymsRoutes.get(":acronymID", "user", use: getUserHandler)
```

This connects an HTTP GET request to **/api/acronyms/<ACRONYM ID>/user** to `getUserHandler(_:)`.

Build and run the application, then create a new request in RESTed. Configure the request as follows:

- **URL**: http://localhost:8080/api/acronyms/<ID of your acronym>/user
- **method**: GET

Send the request and you'll see the response returns the acronym's user:

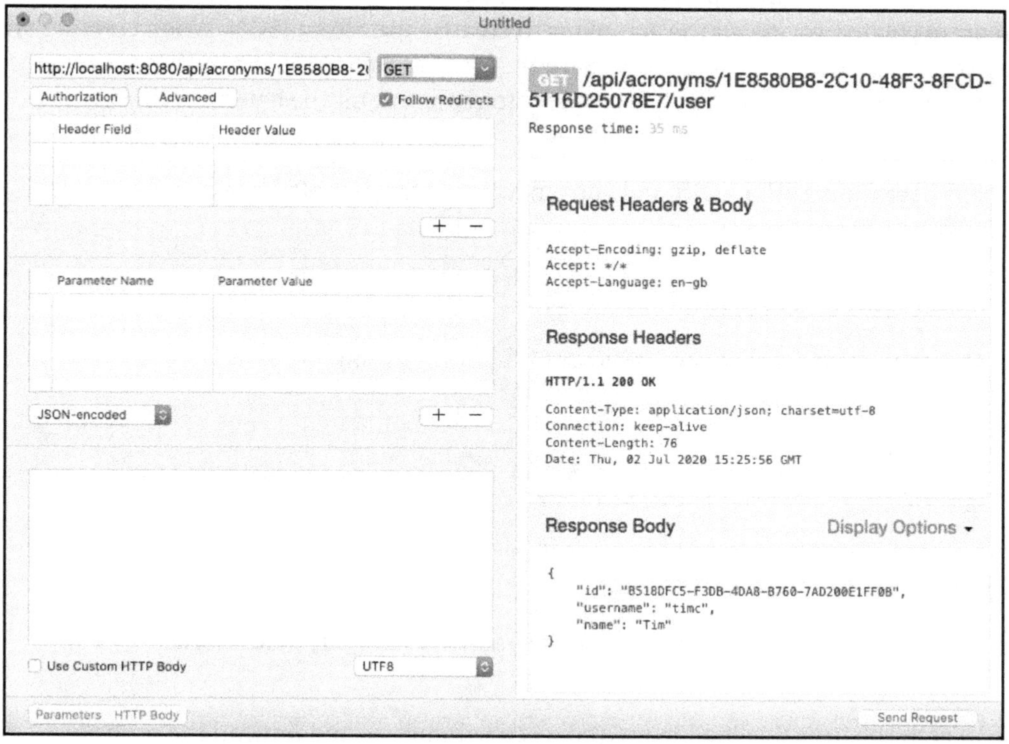

Getting the children

Getting the children of a model follows a similar pattern. Open **User.swift** and add a new property below `var username: String`:

```
@Children(for: \.$user)
var acronyms: [Acronym]
```

This defines a new property — the user's acronyms. You annotate the property with the `@Children` property wrapper. `@Children` tells Fluent that `acronyms` represents the children in a parent-child relationship. This is like `@ID` and `@Field`, which you saw in Chapter 5, "Fluent & Persisting Models".

Unlike `@Parent`, `@Children` doesn't represent any column in the database. Fluent uses it to know what to link for the relationship. You pass the property wrapper a keypath to the parent property wrapper on the child model. In this case, you use `\Acronym.$user`, or just `\.$user`. Fluent uses this to query the database when retrieving all the children.

Fluent's use of property wrappers also allows it to handle encoding and decoding of models. `User` contains a property for all the acronyms. Normally `Codable` would require you to provide all the acronyms to create a user from JSON. When creating an acronym, you would have to instantiate the array as well. `@Children` allows you to have the best of both worlds — a property to represent all the children without having to specify it to create the model.

Open **UsersController.swift** and add a new route handler after `getHandler(_:)`:

```
// 1
func getAcronymsHandler(_ req: Request)
  -> EventLoopFuture<[Acronym]> {
  // 2
  User.find(req.parameters.get("userID"), on: req.db)
    .unwrap(or: Abort(.notFound))
    .flatMap { user in
      // 3
      user.$acronyms.get(on: req.db)
    }
}
```

Here's what this route handler does:

1. Define a new route handler, `getAcronymsHandler(_:)`, that returns `EventLoopFuture<[Acronym]>`.
2. Fetch the user specified in the request's parameters and unwrap the returned future.
3. Use the new property wrapper created above to get the acronyms using a Fluent query to return all the acronyms. Remember, this uses the property wrapper's projected value, **not** the wrapped value.

Register the route handler at the end of `boot(routes:)`:

```
usersRoute.get(
  ":userID",
  "acronyms",
  use: getAcronymsHandler)
```

This connects an HTTP GET request to **/api/users/<USER ID>/acronyms** to `getAcronymsHandler(_:)`.

Build and run the application, then create a new request in RESTed. Configure the request as follows:

- **URL**: http://localhost:8080/api/users/<ID of your user>/acronyms
- **method**: GET

Send the request and you'll see the response returns the user's acronyms:

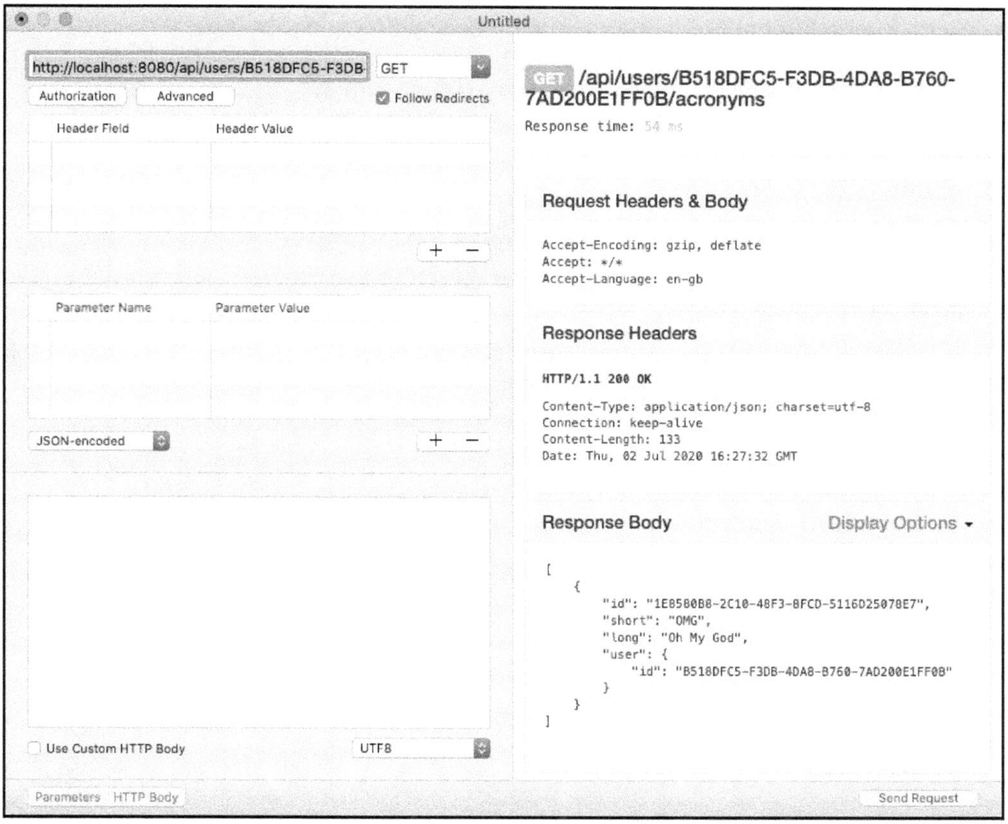

Foreign key constraints

Foreign key constraints describe a link between two tables. They are frequently used for validation. Currently, there's no link between the user table and the acronym table in the database. Fluent is the only thing that has knowledge of the link.

Using foreign key constraints has a number of benefits:

- It ensures you can't create acronyms with users that don't exist.
- You can't delete users until you've deleted all their acronyms.
- You can't delete the user table until you've deleted the acronym table.

Foreign key constraints are set up in the migration. Open **CreateAcronym.swift**, and replace `.field("userID", .uuid, .required)` with the following:

```
.field("userID", .uuid, .required, .references("users", "id"))
```

This is the same as before but also adds a reference from the `userID` column to the `id` column in the Users table.

Finally, because you're linking the acronym's `userID` property to the `User` table, you must create the `User` table first. In **configure.swift**, move the `User` migration to before the `Acronym` migration:

```
app.migrations.add(CreateUser())
app.migrations.add(CreateAcronym())
```

This ensures Fluent creates the tables in the correct order.

Stop the application in Xcode and follow the steps from earlier to **delete the database**.

Build and run the application, then create a new request in RESTed. Configure the request as follows:

- **URL**: http://localhost:8080/api/acronyms/
- **method**: POST
- **Parameter encoding**: JSON-encoded

Add three parameters with names and values:

- **short**: OMG
- **long**: Oh My God
- **userID**: E92B49F2-F239-41B4-B26D-85817F0363AB

This is a valid UUID string, but doesn't refer to any user since the database is empty. Send the request; you'll get an error saying there's a foreign key constraint violation:

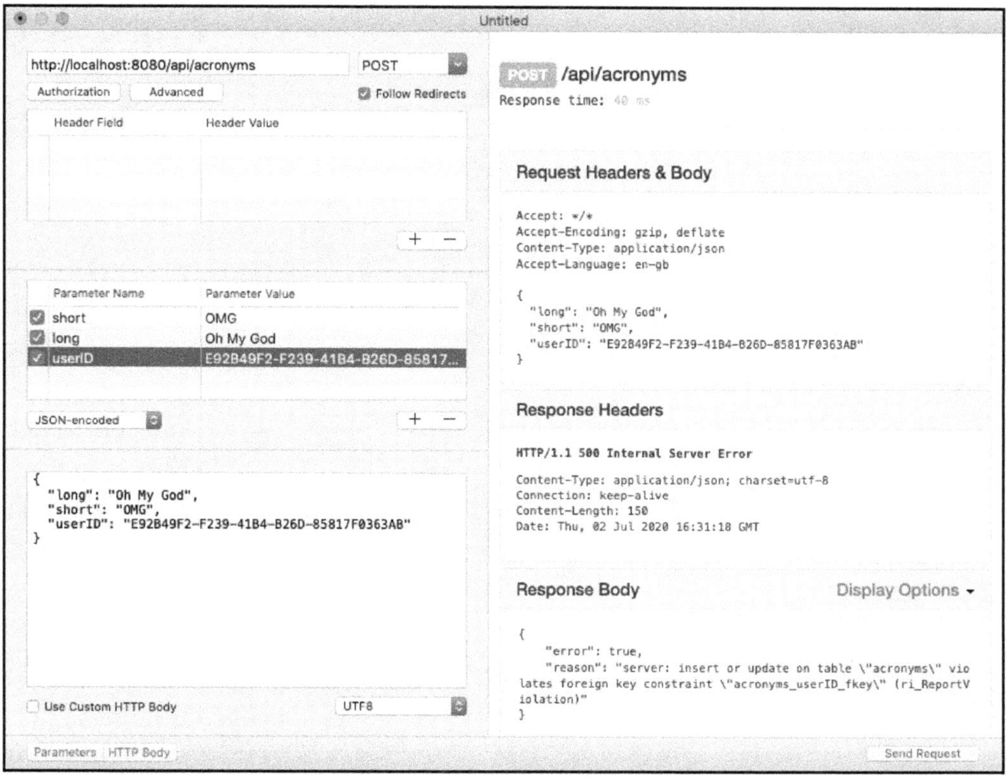

Create a user as you did earlier and copy the ID. Send the create acronym request again, this time using the valid ID. The application creates the acronym without any errors.

Where to go from here?

In this chapter, you learned how to implement parent-child relationships in Vapor using Fluent. This allows you to start creating complex relationships between models in the database. The next chapter covers the other type of relationship in databases: sibling relationships.

Chapter 10: Sibling Relationships

By Tim Condon

In Chapter 9, "Parent-Child Relationships", you learned how to use Fluent to build parent-child relationships between models. This chapter shows you how to implement the other type of relationship: sibling relationships. You'll learn how to model them in Vapor and how to use them in routes.

> **Note**: This chapter requires that you have set up and configured PostgreSQL. Follow the steps in Chapter 6, "Configuring a Database", to set up PostgreSQL in Docker and configure the Vapor application.

Sibling relationships

Sibling relationships describe a relationship that links two models to each other. They are also known as **many-to-many** relationships. Unlike parent-child relationships, there are no constraints between models in a sibling relationship.

For instance, if you model the relationship between pets and toys, a pet can have one or more toys and a toy can be used by one or more pets. In the TIL application, you'll be able to categorize acronyms. An acronym can be part of one or more categories and a category can contain one or more acronyms.

Creating a category

To implement categories, you'll need to create a model, a migration, a controller and a pivot. Begin by creating the model.

Category model

In Xcode, create a new file **Category.swift** in **Sources/App/Models**. Open the file and insert a basic model for a category:

```
import Fluent
import Vapor

final class Category: Model, Content {
  static let schema = "categories"

  @ID
  var id: UUID?

  @Field(key: "name")
  var name: String

  init() {}

  init(id: UUID? = nil, name: String) {
    self.id = id
    self.name = name
  }
}
```

The model contains a `String` property to hold the category's name. The model also contains an optional `id` property that stores the ID of the model when it's set. You annotate both the properties with their respective property wrappers.

Next, create a new file **CreateCategory.swift** in **Sources/App/Migrations**. Insert the following into the new file:

```
import Fluent

struct CreateCategory: Migration {
  func prepare(on database: Database) -> EventLoopFuture<Void> {
    database.schema("categories")
      .id()
      .field("name", .string, .required)
      .create()
  }

  func revert(on database: Database) -> EventLoopFuture<Void> {
```

```
      database.schema("categories").delete()
    }
  }
```

This should be clear to you now! It creates the table using the same value as `schema` defined in the model with the necessary properties. The migration deletes the table in `revert(on:)`.

Finally, open **configure.swift** and add `CreateCategory` to the migration list, after `app.migrations.add(CreateAcronym())`:

```
app.migrations.add(CreateCategory())
```

This adds the new migration to the application's migrations so that Fluent creates the table in the database at the next application start.

Category controller

Now it's time to create the controller. In **Sources/App/Controllers**, create a new file called **CategoriesController.swift**. Open the file and add code for a new controller to create and retrieve categories:

```
import Vapor

// 1
struct CategoriesController: RouteCollection {
  // 2
  func boot(routes: RoutesBuilder) throws {
    // 3
    let categoriesRoute = routes.grouped("api", "categories")
    // 4
    categoriesRoute.post(use: createHandler)
    categoriesRoute.get(use: getAllHandler)
    categoriesRoute.get(":categoryID", use: getHandler)
  }

  // 5
  func createHandler(_ req: Request)
    throws -> EventLoopFuture<Category> {
    // 6
    let category = try req.content.decode(Category.self)
    return category.save(on: req.db).map { category }
  }

  // 7
  func getAllHandler(_ req: Request)
    -> EventLoopFuture<[Category]> {
    // 8
```

```
    Category.query(on: req.db).all()
  }

  // 9
  func getHandler(_ req: Request)
    -> EventLoopFuture<Category> {
    // 10
    Category.find(req.parameters.get("categoryID"), on: req.db)
      .unwrap(or: Abort(.notFound))
  }
}
```

Here's what the controller does:

1. Define a new `CategoriesController` type that conforms to `RouteCollection`.
2. Implement `boot(routes:)` as required by `RouteCollection`. This is where you register route handlers.
3. Create a new route group for the path **/api/categories**.
4. Register the route handlers to their routes.
5. Define `createHandler(_:)` that creates a category.
6. Decode the category from the request and save it.
7. Define `getAllHandler(_:)` that returns all the categories.
8. Perform a Fluent query to retrieve all the categories from the database.
9. Define `getHandler(_:)` that returns a single category.
10. Get the ID from the request and use it to find the category.

Finally, open **routes.swift** and register the controller by adding the following to the end of `routes(_:)`:

```
let categoriesController = CategoriesController()
try app.register(collection: categoriesController)
```

As in previous chapters, this instantiates a controller and registers it with the app to enable its routes.

Build and run the application, then create a new request in RESTed. Configure the request as follows:

- **URL**: http://localhost:8080/api/categories
- **method**: POST
- **Parameter encoding**: JSON-encoded

Add a single parameter with name and value:

- **name**: Teenager

Send the request and you'll see the saved category in the response:

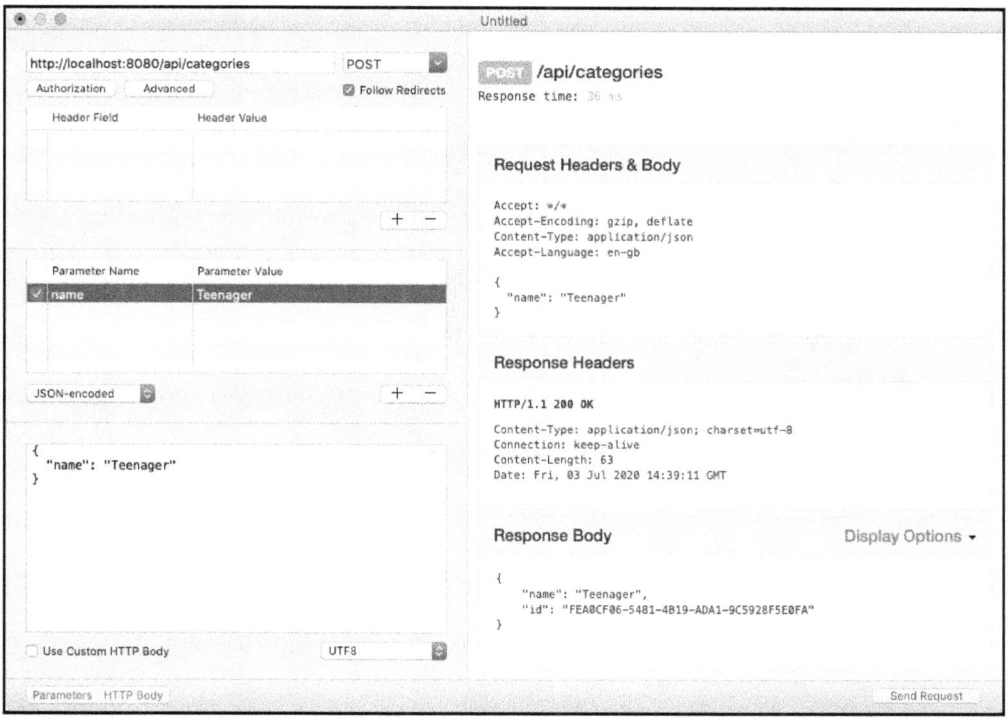

Creating a pivot

In Chapter 9, "Parent-Child Relationships", you added a reference to the user in the acronym to create the relationship between an acronym and a user. However, you can't model a sibling relationship like this as it would be too inefficient to query. If you had an array of acronyms inside a category, to search for all categories of an acronym you'd have to inspect every category. If you had an array of categories inside an acronym, to search for all acronyms in a category you'd have to inspect every acronym. You need a separate model to hold on to this relationship. In Fluent, this is a **pivot**.

A pivot is another model type in Fluent that contains the relationship. In Xcode, create this new model file called **AcronymCategoryPivot.swift** in **Sources/App/Models**. Open **AcronymCategoryPivot.swift** and add the following to create the pivot:

```
import Fluent
import Foundation

// 1
final class AcronymCategoryPivot: Model {
  static let schema = "acronym-category-pivot"

  // 2
  @ID
  var id: UUID?

  // 3
  @Parent(key: "acronymID")
  var acronym: Acronym

  @Parent(key: "categoryID")
  var category: Category

  // 4
  init() {}

  // 5
  init(
    id: UUID? = nil,
    acronym: Acronym,
    category: Category
  ) throws {
    self.id = id
    self.$acronym.id = try acronym.requireID()
    self.$category.id = try category.requireID()
  }
}
```

Here's what this model does:

1. Define a new object `AcronymCategoryPivot` that conforms to `Model`.
2. Define an `id` for the model. Note this is a `UUID` type so you must import the Foundation module.
3. Define two properties to link to the `Acronym` and `Category`. You annotate the properties with the `@Parent` property wrapper. A pivot record can point to only one `Acronym` and one `Category`, but each of those types can point to multiple pivots.
4. Implement the empty initializer, as required by `Model`.
5. Implement an initializer that takes the two models as arguments. This uses `requireID()` to ensure the models have an ID set.

Next create the migration for the pivot. Create a new file, **CreateAcronymCategoryPivot.swift**, in **Sources/App/Migrations**. Open the new file and insert the following:

```
import Fluent

// 1
struct CreateAcronymCategoryPivot: Migration {
  // 2
  func prepare(on database: Database) -> EventLoopFuture<Void> {
    // 3
    database.schema("acronym-category-pivot")
      // 4
      .id()
      // 5
      .field("acronymID", .uuid, .required,
        .references("acronyms", "id", onDelete: .cascade))
      .field("categoryID", .uuid, .required,
        .references("categories", "id", onDelete: .cascade))
      // 6
      .create()
  }

  // 7
  func revert(on database: Database) -> EventLoopFuture<Void> {
    database.schema("acronym-category-pivot").delete()
  }
}
```

Here's what the new migration does:

1. Define a new type, `CreateAcronymCategoryPivot` that conforms to `Migration`.
2. Implement `prepare(on:)` as required by `Migration`.
3. Select the table using the schema name defined for `AcronymCategoryPivot`.
4. Create the ID column.
5. Create the two columns for the two properties. These use the key provided to the property wrapper, set the type to UUID, and mark the column as required. They also set a reference to the respective model to create a foreign key constraint. As in Chapter 9, "Parent-Child Relationships," it's good practice to use foreign key constraints with sibling relationships. The current `AcronymCategoryPivot` does not check the IDs for the acronyms and categories. Without the constraint you can delete acronyms and categories that are still linked by the pivot and the relationship will remain, without flagging an error. The migration also sets a cascade schema reference action when you delete the model. This causes the database to remove the relationship automatically instead of throwing an error.
6. Call `create()` to create the table in the database.
7. Implement `revert(on:)` as required by `Migration`. This deletes the table in the database.

Finally, open **configure.swift** and add `CreateAcronymCategoryPivot` to the migration list, after `app.migrations.add(CreateCategory())`:

```
app.migrations.add(CreateAcronymCategoryPivot())
```

This adds the new pivot model to the application's migrations so that Fluent prepares the table in the database at the next application start.

To actually create a relationship between two models, you need to use the pivot. Fluent provides convenience functions for creating and removing relationships. First, open **Acronym.swift** and add a new property to the model below `var user: User`:

```
@Siblings(
  through: AcronymCategoryPivot.self,
  from: \.$acronym,
  to: \.$category)
var categories: [Category]
```

This adds a new property to allow you to query the sibling relationship. You annotate the new property with the `@Siblings` property wrapper. `@Siblings` take three parameters:

- the pivot's model type
- the key path from the pivot which references the root model. In this case you use the `acronym` property on `AcronymCategoryPivot`.
- the key path from the pivot which references the related model. In this case you use the `category` property on `AcronymCategoryPivot`.

Like `@Parent`, `@Siblings` allows you to specify related models as a property without needing them to initialize an instance. The property wrapper also tells Fluent how to map the siblings when performing queries in the database.

While `@Parent` uses the parent ID column in the database, `@Siblings` has to join between the two different models and the pivot in the database. Thankfully, Fluent abstracts this away for you and makes it easy!

Open **AcronymsController.swift** and add the following route handler below `getUserHandler(_:)` to set up the relationship between an acronym and a category:

```
// 1
func addCategoriesHandler(_ req: Request)
  -> EventLoopFuture<HTTPStatus> {
  // 2
  let acronymQuery =
    Acronym.find(req.parameters.get("acronymID"), on: req.db)
      .unwrap(or: Abort(.notFound))
  let categoryQuery =
    Category.find(req.parameters.get("categoryID"), on: req.db)
      .unwrap(or: Abort(.notFound))
  // 3
  return acronymQuery.and(categoryQuery)
    .flatMap { acronym, category in
      acronym
        .$categories
        // 4
        .attach(category, on: req.db)
        .transform(to: .created)
    }
}
```

Here's what the route handler does:

1. Define a new route handler, `addCategoriesHandler(_:)`, that returns `EventLoopFuture<HTTPStatus>`.
2. Define two properties to query the database and get the acronym and category from the IDs provided to the request. Each property is an `EventLoopFuture`.
3. Use `and(_:)` to wait for both futures to return.
4. Use `attach(_:on:)` to set up the relationship between `acronym` and `category`. This creates a pivot model and saves it in the database. Transform the result into a **201 Created** response. Like many of Fluent's operations, you call `attach(_:on:)` on the property wrappers projected value, rather than the property itself.

Register this route handler at the bottom of `boot(routes:)`:

```
acronymsRoutes.post(
  ":acronymID",
  "categories",
  ":categoryID",
  use: addCategoriesHandler)
```

This routes an HTTP POST request to **/api/acronyms/<ACRONYM_ID>/categories/<CATEGORY_ID>** to `addCategoriesHandler(_:)`.

Build and run the application and launch RESTed. If you do not have any acronyms in the database, create one now. Then, create a new request configured as follows:

- **URL**: http://localhost:8080/api/acronyms/<ACRONYM_ID>/categories/<CATEGORY_ID>
- **method**: POST

This creates a sibling relationship between the acronym and the category with the provided IDs. You created the category earlier in the chapter.

Click **Send Request** and you'll see a **201 Created** response:

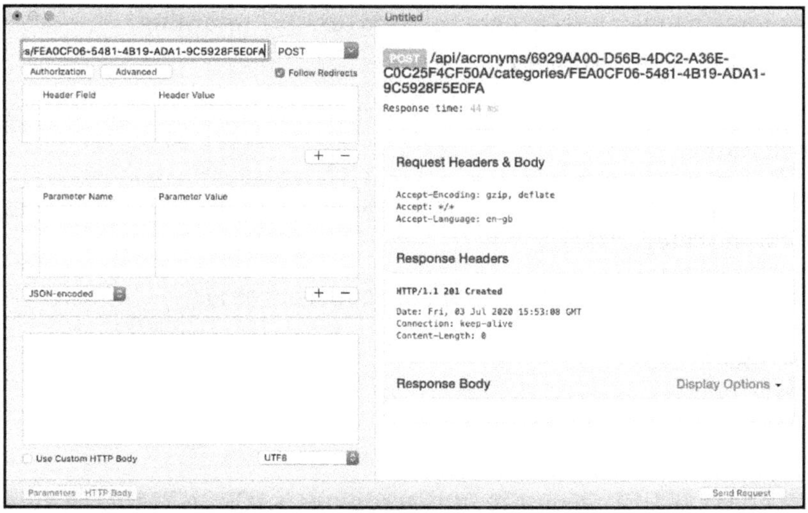

Querying the relationship

Acronyms and categories are now linked with a sibling relationship. But this isn't very useful if you can't view these relationships! Fluent provides functions that allow you to query these relationships. You've already used one above to create the relationship.

Acronym's categories

Open **AcronymsController.swift** and add a new route handler after `addCategoriesHandler(:_)`:

```
// 1
func getCategoriesHandler(_ req: Request)
  -> EventLoopFuture<[Category]> {
  // 2
  Acronym.find(req.parameters.get("acronymID"), on: req.db)
    .unwrap(or: Abort(.notFound))
    .flatMap { acronym in
      // 3
      acronym.$categories.query(on: req.db).all()
    }
}
```

Here's what this does:

1. Defines route handler `getCategoriesHandler(_:)` returning `EventLoopFuture<[Category]>`.
2. Get the acronym from the database using the provided ID and unwrap the returned future.
3. Use the new property wrapper to get the categories. Then use a Fluent query to return all the categories.

Register this route handler at the bottom of `boot(routes:)`:

```
acronymsRoutes.get(
  ":acronymID",
  "categories",
  use: getCategoriesHandler)
```

This routes an HTTP GET request to **/api/acronyms/<ACRONYM_ID>/categories** to `getCategoriesHandler(:_)`.

Build and run the application and launch RESTed. Create a request with the following properties:

- **URL**: http://localhost:8080/api/acronyms/<ACRONYM_ID>/categories
- **method**: GET

Send the request and you'll receive the array of categories that the acronym is in:

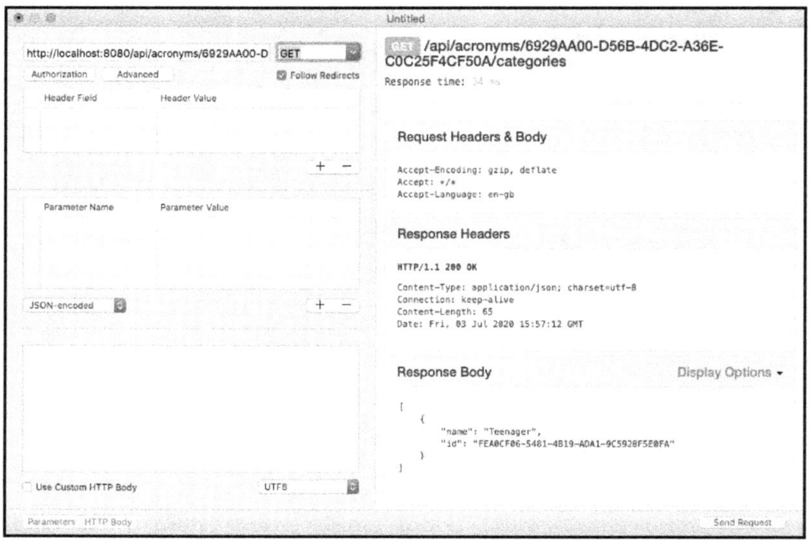

Category's acronyms

Open **Category.swift** and add a new property annotated with `@Siblings` below `var name: String`:

```
@Siblings(
  through: AcronymCategoryPivot.self,
  from: \.$category,
  to: \.$acronym)
var acronyms: [Acronym]
```

Like before, this adds a new property to allow you to query the sibling relationship. `@Siblings` provides all the required syntactic sugar to set up, query and work with the sibling relationship.

Open **CategoriesController.swift** and add a new route handler after `getHandler(_:)`:

```
// 1
func getAcronymsHandler(_ req: Request)
  -> EventLoopFuture<[Acronym]> {
  // 2
  Category.find(req.parameters.get("categoryID"), on: req.db)
    .unwrap(or: Abort(.notFound))
    .flatMap { category in
      // 3
      category.$acronyms.get(on: req.db)
    }
}
```

Here's what this does:

1. Define a new route handler, `getAcronymsHandler(_:)`, that returns `EventLoopFuture<[Acronym]>`.
2. Get the category from the database using the ID provided to the request. Ensure one is returned and unwrap the future.
3. Use the new property wrapper to get the acronyms. This uses `get(on:)` to perform the query for you. This is the same as `query(on: req.db).all()` from earlier.

Register this route handler at the bottom of `boot(routes:)`:

```
categoriesRoute.get(
  ":categoryID",
  "acronyms",
```

```
    use: getAcronymsHandler)
```

This routes an HTTP GET request to **/api/categories/<CATEGORY_ID>/acronyms** to `getAcronymsHandler(_:)`.

Build and run the application and launch RESTed. Create a request as follows:

- **URL**: http://localhost:8080/api/categories/<CATEGORY_ID>/acronyms
- **method**: GET

Send the request and you'll receive an array of the acronyms in that category:

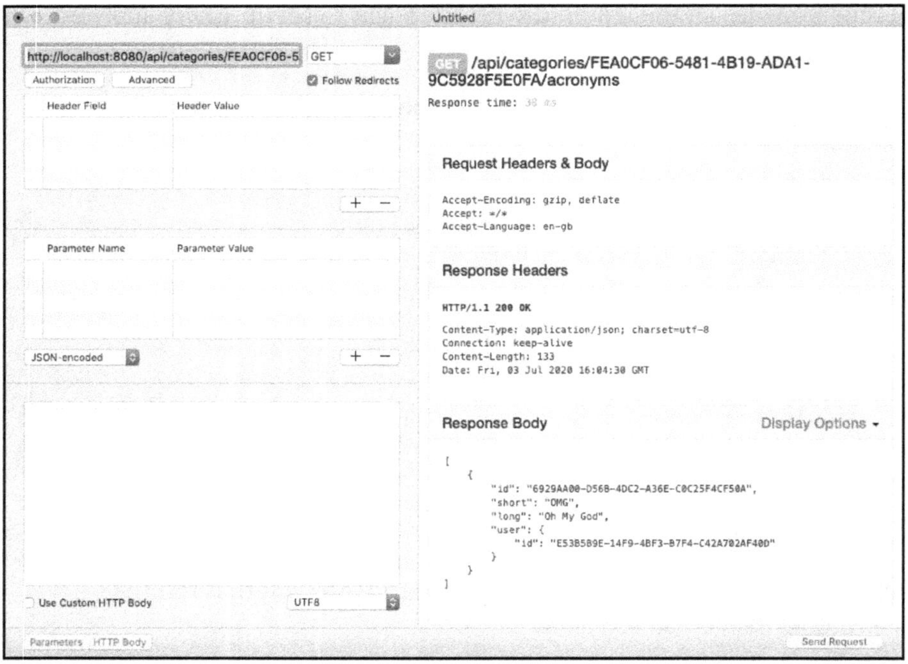

Removing the relationship

Removing a relationship between an acronym and a category is very similar to adding the relationship. Open **AcronymsController.swift** and add the following below `getCategoriesHandler(req:)`:

```
// 1
func removeCategoriesHandler(_ req: Request)
  -> EventLoopFuture<HTTPStatus> {
  // 2
```

```
    let acronymQuery =
      Acronym.find(req.parameters.get("acronymID"), on: req.db)
        .unwrap(or: Abort(.notFound))
    let categoryQuery =
      Category.find(req.parameters.get("categoryID"), on: req.db)
        .unwrap(or: Abort(.notFound))
    // 3
    return acronymQuery.and(categoryQuery)
      .flatMap { acronym, category in
        // 4
        acronym
          .$categories
          .detach(category, on: req.db)
          .transform(to: .noContent)
      }
  }
```

Here's what the new route handler does:

1. Define a new route handler, `removeCategoriesHandler(_:)`, that returns an `EventLoopFuture<HTTPStatus>`.
2. Perform two queries to get the acronym and category from the IDs provided.
3. Use `and(_:)` to wait for both futures to return.
4. Use `detach(_:on:)` to remove the relationship between `acronym` and `category`. This finds the pivot model in the database and deletes it. Transform the result into a **204 No Content** response.

Finally, register the route at the bottom of `boot(routes:)`:

```
acronymsRoutes.delete(
  ":acronymID",
  "categories",
  ":categoryID",
  use: removeCategoriesHandler)
```

This routes an HTTP DELETE request to **/api/acronyms/<ACRONYM_ID>/categories/<CATEGORY_ID>** to `removeCategoriesHandler(_:)`.

Build and run the application and launch RESTed. Create a request with the following properties:

- **URL**: http://localhost:8080/api/acronyms/<ACRONYM_ID>/categories/<CATEGORY_ID>
- **method**: DELETE

Send the request and you'll receive a **204 No Content** response:

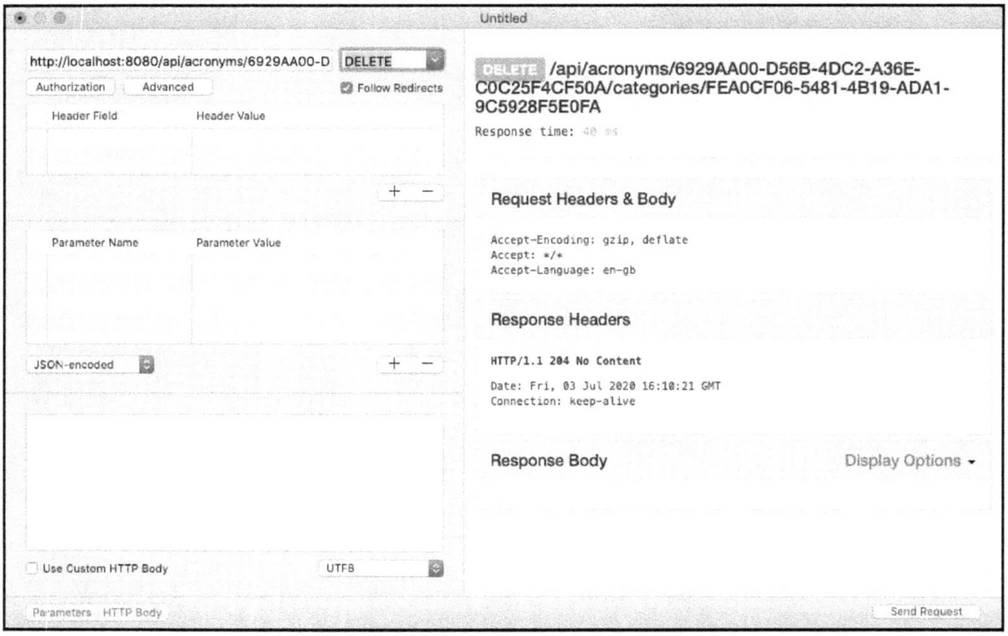

If you send the request to get the acronym's categories again, you'll receive an empty array.

Where to go from here?

In this chapter, you learned how to implement sibling relationships in Vapor using Fluent. Over the course of this section, you learned how to use Fluent to model all types of relationships and perform advanced queries. The TIL API is fully featured and ready for use by clients.

In the next chapter, you'll learn how to write tests for the application to ensure that your code is correct. Then, the next section of this book shows you how to create powerful clients to interact with the API — both on iOS and on the web.

Chapter 11: Testing

By Tim Condon

Testing is an important part of the software development process. Writing unit tests and automating them as much as possible allows you to develop and evolve your applications quickly.

In this chapter, you'll learn how to write tests for your Vapor applications. You'll learn why testing is important and how it works with Swift Package Manager. Next, you'll learn how to write tests for the TIL application from the previous chapters. Finally, you'll see why testing matters on Linux and how to test your code on Linux using Docker.

Why should you write tests?

Software testing is as old as software development itself. Modern server applications are deployed many times *a day*, so it's important that you're sure everything works as expected. Writing tests for your application gives you confidence the code is sound.

Testing also gives you confidence when you refactor your code. Over the last several chapters, you've evolved and changed the TIL application. Testing every part of the application manually is slow and laborious, and this application is small! To develop new features quickly, you want to ensure the existing features don't break. Having an expansive set of tests allows you to verify everything still works as you change your code.

Testing can also help you design your code. Test-driven development is a popular development process in which you write tests before writing code. This helps ensure you have full test coverage of your code. Test-driven development also helps you design your code and APIs.

Writing tests with SwiftPM

On iOS, Xcode links tests to a specific test target. Xcode configures a scheme to use that target and you run your tests from within Xcode. The Objective-C runtime scans your `XCTestCases` and picks out the methods whose names begin with `test`. On Linux, and with SwiftPM, there's no Objective-C runtime. There's also no Xcode project to remember schemes and which tests belong where.

In Xcode, open **Package.swift**. There's a test target defined in the `targets` array:

```
.testTarget(name: "AppTests", dependencies: [
  .target(name: "App"),
  .product(name: "XCTVapor", package: "vapor"),
])
```

This defines a `testTarget` type with a dependency on `App` and Vapor's `XCTVapor`. Tests must live in the **Tests/** directory. In this case, that's **Tests/AppTests**.

Xcode creates the **TILApp** scheme and adds `AppTests` as a test target to that scheme. You can run these tests as normal with **Command-U**, or **Product ▸ Test**:

Testing users

Writing your first test

Create a new file in **Tests/AppTests** called **UserTests.swift**. This file will contain all the user-related tests. Open the new file and insert the following:

```
@testable import App
import XCTVapor

final class UserTests: XCTestCase {
}
```

This creates the `XCTestCase` you'll use to test your users and imports the necessary modules to make everything work.

Next, add the following inside `UserTests` to test getting the users from the API:

```
func testUsersCanBeRetrievedFromAPI() throws {
  // 1
  let expectedName = "Alice"
  let expectedUsername = "alice"

  // 2
  let app = Application(.testing)
  // 3
  defer { app.shutdown() }
  // 4
  try configure(app)

  // 5
  let user = User(
    name: expectedName,
    username: expectedUsername)
  try user.save(on: app.db).wait()
  try User(name: "Luke", username: "lukes")
    .save(on: app.db)
    .wait()

  // 6
  try app.test(.GET, "/api/users", afterResponse: { response in
    // 7
    XCTAssertEqual(response.status, .ok)

    // 8
    let users = try response.content.decode([User].self)

    // 9
    XCTAssertEqual(users.count, 2)
```

```
      XCTAssertEqual(users[0].name, expectedName)
      XCTAssertEqual(users[0].username, expectedUsername)
      XCTAssertEqual(users[0].id, user.id)
    })
  }
```

There's a lot going on in this test; here's the breakdown:

1. Define some expected values for the test: a user's name and username.
2. Create an `Application`, similar to **main.swift**. This creates an entire `Application` object but doesn't start running the application. Note, you're using the `.testing` environment here.
3. Shutdown the application at the end of the test. This ensures that you close database connections correctly and clean up event loops.
4. Configure your application for testing. This helps ensure you configure your real application correctly as your test calls the same `configure(_:)`.
5. Create a couple of users and save them in the database, using the application's database object.
6. Use XCTVapor — Vapor's testing module — to send a **GET** request to **/api/users**. With XCTVapor you specify a path and HTTP method. XCTVapor also allows you to provide closures to run before you send the request and after you receive the response.
7. Ensure the response received contains the expected status code.
8. Decode the response body into an array of `Users`.
9. Ensure there are the correct number of users in the response and the first user matches the one created at the start of the test.

Next, you must update your app's configuration to support testing. Open **configure.swift** and before `app.databases.use` add the following:

```
let databaseName: String
let databasePort: Int
// 1
if (app.environment == .testing) {
  databaseName = "vapor-test"
  databasePort = 5433
} else {
  databaseName = "vapor_database"
  databasePort = 5432
}
```

This sets properties for the database name and port depending on the environment. You'll use different names and ports for testing and running the application. Next, replace the call to `app.databases.use` with the following:

```
app.databases.use(.postgres(
  hostname: Environment.get("DATABASE_HOST")
    ?? "localhost",
  port: databasePort,
  username: Environment.get("DATABASE_USERNAME")
    ?? "vapor_username",
  password: Environment.get("DATABASE_PASSWORD")
    ?? "vapor_password",
  database: Environment.get("DATABASE_NAME")
    ?? databaseName
), as: .psql)
```

This sets the database port and name from the properties set above if you don't provide environment variables. These changes allow you to run your tests on a database other than your production database. This ensures you start each test in a known state and don't destroy live data. Since you're using Docker to host your database, setting up another database on the same machine is simple. In Terminal, type the following:

```
docker run --name postgres-test \
  -e POSTGRES_DB=vapor-test \
  -e POSTGRES_USER=vapor_username \
  -e POSTGRES_PASSWORD=vapor_password \
  -p 5433:5432 -d postgres
```

This is similar to the command you used in Chapter 6, "Configuring a Database", but it changes the container name and database name. The Docker container is also mapped to host port 5433 to avoid conflicting with the existing database.

Run the tests and they should pass. However, if you run the tests again, they'll fail. The first test run added two users to the database and the second test run now has four users since the database wasn't reset.

Open **UserTests.swift** and add the following after `try configure(app)`:

```
try app.autoRevert().wait()
try app.autoMigrate().wait()
```

This adds commands to revert any migrations in the database and then run the migrations again. This provides you with a clean database for every test.

Build and run the tests again and this time they'll pass!

Test extensions

The first test contains a lot of code that all tests need. Extract the common parts to make the tests easier to read and to simplify future tests. In **Tests/AppTests** create a new file for one of these extensions, called **Application+Testable.swift**. Open the new file and add the following:

```
import XCTVapor
import App

extension Application {
  static func testable() throws -> Application {
    let app = Application(.testing)
    try configure(app)

    try app.autoRevert().wait()
    try app.autoMigrate().wait()

    return app
  }
}
```

This function allows you to create a testable `Application` object, configure it and set up the database. Next, create a new file in **Tests/AppTests** called **Models+Testable.swift**. Open the new file and create an extension to create a `User`:

```
@testable import App
import Fluent

extension User {
  static func create(
    name: String = "Luke",
    username: String = "lukes",
    on database: Database
  ) throws -> User {
    let user = User(name: name, username: username)
    try user.save(on: database).wait()
    return user
  }
}
```

This function saves a user, created with the supplied details, in the database. It has default values so you don't have to provide any if you don't care about them.

With all this created, you can now rewrite your user test. Open **UserTests.swift** and delete `testUsersCanBeRetrievedFromAPI()`.

Next, in `UserTests` create the common properties for all the tests:

```
let usersName = "Alice"
let usersUsername = "alicea"
let usersURI = "/api/users/"
var app: Application!
```

Next implement `setUpWithError()` to run the code that must execute before each test:

```
override func setUpWithError() throws {
  app = try Application.testable()
}
```

This creates an `Application` for the test, which also resets the database.

Next, implement `tearDownWithError()` to shut the application down:

```
override func tearDownWithError() throws {
  app.shutdown()
}
```

Finally, rewrite `testUsersCanBeRetrievedFromAPI()` to use all the new helper methods:

```
func testUsersCanBeRetrievedFromAPI() throws {
  let user = try User.create(
    name: usersName,
    username: usersUsername,
    on: app.db)
  _ = try User.create(on: app.db)

  try app.test(.GET, usersURI, afterResponse: { response in
    XCTAssertEqual(response.status, .ok)
    let users = try response.content.decode([User].self)

    XCTAssertEqual(users.count, 2)
    XCTAssertEqual(users[0].name, usersName)
    XCTAssertEqual(users[0].username, usersUsername)
    XCTAssertEqual(users[0].id, user.id)
  })
}
```

This test does exactly the same as before but is far more readable. It also makes the next tests much easier to write. Run the tests again to ensure they still work.

Testing the User API

Open **UserTests.swift** and using the test helper methods add the following to test saving a user via the API:

```
func testUserCanBeSavedWithAPI() throws {
  // 1
  let user = User(name: usersName, username: usersUsername)

  // 2
  try app.test(.POST, usersURI, beforeRequest: { req in
    // 3
    try req.content.encode(user)
  }, afterResponse: { response in
    // 4
    let receivedUser = try response.content.decode(User.self)
    // 5
    XCTAssertEqual(receivedUser.name, usersName)
    XCTAssertEqual(receivedUser.username, usersUsername)
    XCTAssertNotNil(receivedUser.id)

    // 6
    try app.test(.GET, usersURI,
      afterResponse: { secondResponse in
        // 7
        let users =
          try secondResponse.content.decode([User].self)
        XCTAssertEqual(users.count, 1)
        XCTAssertEqual(users[0].name, usersName)
        XCTAssertEqual(users[0].username, usersUsername)
        XCTAssertEqual(users[0].id, receivedUser.id)
      })
  })
}
```

Here's what the test does:

1. Create a `User` object with known values.
2. Use `test(_:_:beforeRequest:afterResponse:)` to send a POST request to the API
3. Encode the request with the created user before you send the request.
4. Decode the response body into a `User` object.
5. Assert the response from the API matches the expected values.
6. Make another request to get all the users from the API.
7. Ensure the response only contains the user you created in the first request.

Run the tests to ensure that the new test works!

Next, add the following test to retrieve a single user from the API:

```
func testGettingASingleUserFromTheAPI() throws {
  // 1
  let user = try User.create(
    name: usersName,
    username: usersUsername,
    on: app.db)

  // 2
  try app.test(.GET, "\(usersURI)\(user.id!)",
    afterResponse: { response in
      let receivedUser = try response.content.decode(User.self)
      // 3
      XCTAssertEqual(receivedUser.name, usersName)
      XCTAssertEqual(receivedUser.username, usersUsername)
      XCTAssertEqual(receivedUser.id, user.id)
    })
}
```

Here's what the test does:

1. Save a user in the database with known values.
2. Get the user at **/api/users/<USER ID>**.
3. Assert the values are the same as provided when creating the user.

The final part of the user's API to test retrieves a user's acronyms. Open **Models+Testable.swift** and, at the end of the file, create a new extension to create acronyms:

```
extension Acronym {
  static func create(
    short: String = "TIL",
    long: String = "Today I Learned",
    user: User? = nil,
    on database: Database
  ) throws -> Acronym {
    var acronymsUser = user

    if acronymsUser == nil {
      acronymsUser = try User.create(on: database)
    }

    let acronym = Acronym(
      short: short,
      long: long,
      userID: acronymsUser!.id!)
    try acronym.save(on: database).wait()
    return acronym
  }
}
```

This creates an acronym and saves it in the database with the provided values. If you don't provide any values, it uses defaults. If you don't provide a user for the acronym, it creates a user to use first.

Next, open **UserTests.swift** and create a method to test getting a user's acronyms:

```
func testGettingAUsersAcronymsFromTheAPI() throws {
  // 1
  let user = try User.create(on: app.db)
  // 2
  let acronymShort = "OMG"
  let acronymLong = "Oh My God"

  // 3
  let acronym1 = try Acronym.create(
    short: acronymShort,
    long: acronymLong,
    user: user,
    on: app.db)
  _ = try Acronym.create(
    short: "LOL",
    long: "Laugh Out Loud",
    user: user,
    on: app.db)
```

```
  // 4
  try app.test(.GET, "\(usersURI)\(user.id!)/acronyms",
    afterResponse: { response in
      let acronyms = try response.content.decode([Acronym].self)
      // 5
      XCTAssertEqual(acronyms.count, 2)
      XCTAssertEqual(acronyms[0].id, acronym1.id)
      XCTAssertEqual(acronyms[0].short, acronymShort)
      XCTAssertEqual(acronyms[0].long, acronymLong)
  })
}
```

Here's what the test does:

1. Create a user for the acronyms.
2. Define some expected values for an acronym.
3. Create two acronyms in the database using the created user. Use the expected values for the first acronym.
4. Get the user's acronyms from the API by sending a request to **/api/users/<USER ID>/acronyms**.
5. Assert the response returns the correct number of acronyms and the first one matches the expected values.

Run the tests to ensure the changes work!

Testing acronyms and categories

Open **Models+Testable.swift** and, at the bottom of the file, add a new extension to simplify creating categories:

```
extension App.Category {
  static func create(
    name: String = "Random",
    on database: Database
  ) throws -> App.Category {
    let category = Category(name: name)
    try category.save(on: database).wait()
    return category
  }
}
```

Like the other model helper functions, `create(name:on:)` takes the `name` as a parameter and creates a category in the database. The tests for the acronyms API and categories API are part of the starter project for this chapter. Open **CategoryTests.swift** and uncomment all the code. The tests follow the same pattern as the user tests.

Open **AcronymTests.swift** and uncomment all the code. These tests also follow a similar pattern to before but there are some extra tests for the extra routes in the acronyms API. These include updating an acronym, deleting an acronym and the different Fluent query routes.

Run all the tests to make sure they all work. You should have a sea of green tests with every route tested!

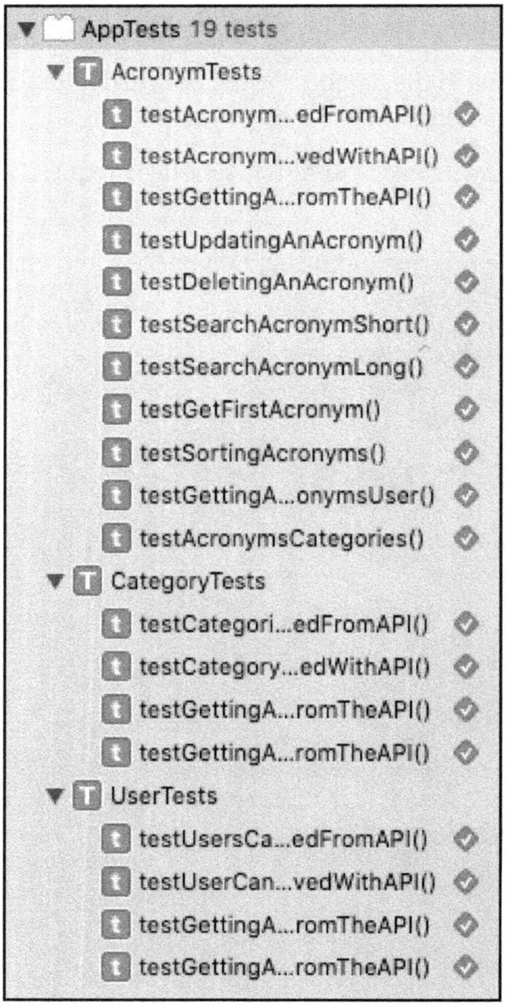

Testing on Linux

Earlier in the chapter you learned why testing your application is important. For server-side Swift, testing on Linux is especially important. When you deploy your application to Heroku, for instance, you're deploying to an operating system different from the one you used for development. It's vital that you test your application on the same environment that you deploy it on.

Why is this so? Foundation on Linux isn't the same as Foundation on macOS. Foundation on macOS still uses the Objective-C framework, which has been thoroughly tested over the years. Linux uses the pure-Swift Foundation framework, which isn't as battle-tested. The implementation status list, github.com/apple/swift-corelibs-foundation/blob/master/Docs/Status.md, shows that many features remain unimplemented on Linux. If you use these features, your application may crash. While the situation improves constantly, you must still ensure everything works as expected on Linux.

Running tests in Linux

Running tests on Linux requires you to do things differently from running them on macOS. As mentioned earlier, the Objective-C runtime determines the test methods your `XCTestCases` provide. On Linux there's no runtime to do this, so you must point Swift in the right direction. Swift 5.1 introduced test discovery, which parses your test classes to find tests to run.

When you call `swift test` on Linux, you must pass the `--enable-test-discovery` flag.

Early feedback is always valuable in software development and running tests on Linux is no exception. Using a Continuous Integration system to automatically test on Linux is vital, but what happens if you want to test on Linux on your Mac?

Well, you're already running Linux for the PostgreSQL database using Docker! So, you can also use Docker to run your tests in a Linux environment. In the project directory, create a new file called **testing.Dockerfile**.

Open the file in a text editor and add the following:

```
# 1
FROM swift:5.2

# 2
WORKDIR /package
```

```
# 3
COPY . ./
# 4
CMD ["swift", "test", "--enable-test-discovery"]
```

Here's what the **Dockerfile** does:

1. Use the Swift 5.2 image.
2. Set the working directory to **/package**.
3. Copy the contents of the current directory into **/package** in the container.
4. Set the default command to `swift test --enable-test-discovery`. This is the command Docker executes when you run the Dockerfile.

The tests need a PostgreSQL database in order to run. By default, Docker containers can't see each other. However, Docker has a tool, Docker Compose, designed to link together different containers for testing and running applications. Vapor already provides a compose file for running your applications, but you'll use a different one for testing. Create a new file called **docker-compose-testing.yml** in the project directory.

Open the file in an editor and add the following:

```
# 1
version: '3'
# 2
services:
  # 3
  til-app:
    # 4
    depends_on:
      - postgres
    # 5
    build:
      context: .
      dockerfile: testing.Dockerfile
    # 6
    environment:
      - DATABASE_HOST=postgres
      - DATABASE_PORT=5432
  # 7
  postgres:
    # 8
    image: "postgres"
    # 9
    environment:
      - POSTGRES_DB=vapor-test
```

```
      - POSTGRES_USER=vapor_username
      - POSTGRES_PASSWORD=vapor_password
```

Here's what this does:

1. Specify the Docker Compose version.
2. Define the services for this application.
3. Define a service for the TIL application.
4. Set a dependency on the Postgres container, so Docker Compose starts the Postgres container first.
5. Build **testing.Dockerfile** in the current directory — the Dockerfile you created earlier.
6. Inject the `DATABASE_HOST` environment variable. Docker Compose has an internal DNS resolver. This allows the `til-app` container to connect to the `postgres` container with the hostname `postgres`. Also set the port for the database.
7. Define a service for the Postgres container.
8. Use the standard Postgres image.
9. Set the same environment variables as used at the start of the chapter for the test database.

Finally open **configure.swift** in Xcode and allow the database port to be set as an environment variable for testing. Replace:

```
if (app.environment == .testing) {
  databaseName = "vapor-test"
  databasePort = 5433
} else {
```

with the following:

```
if (app.environment == .testing) {
  databaseName = "vapor-test"
  if let testPort = Environment.get("DATABASE_PORT") {
    databasePort = Int(testPort) ?? 5433
  } else {
    databasePort = 5433
  }
} else {
```

This uses the `DATABASE_PORT` environment variable if set, otherwise defaults the port to 5433. This allows you to use the port set in **docker-compose-testing.yml**. To test your application in Linux, open Terminal and type the following:

```
# 1
docker-compose -f docker-compose-testing.yml build
# 2
docker-compose -f docker-compose-testing.yml up \
  --abort-on-container-exit
```

Here's what this does:

1. Build the different docker containers using the compose file created earlier.
2. Spin up the different containers from the compose file created earlier and run the tests. `--abort-on-container-exit` tells Docker Compose to stop the `postgres` container when the `til-app` container stops. The `postgres` container used for this test is different from, and doesn't conflict with, the one you've been using during development.

When the tests finish running, you'll see the output in Terminal with all tests passing:

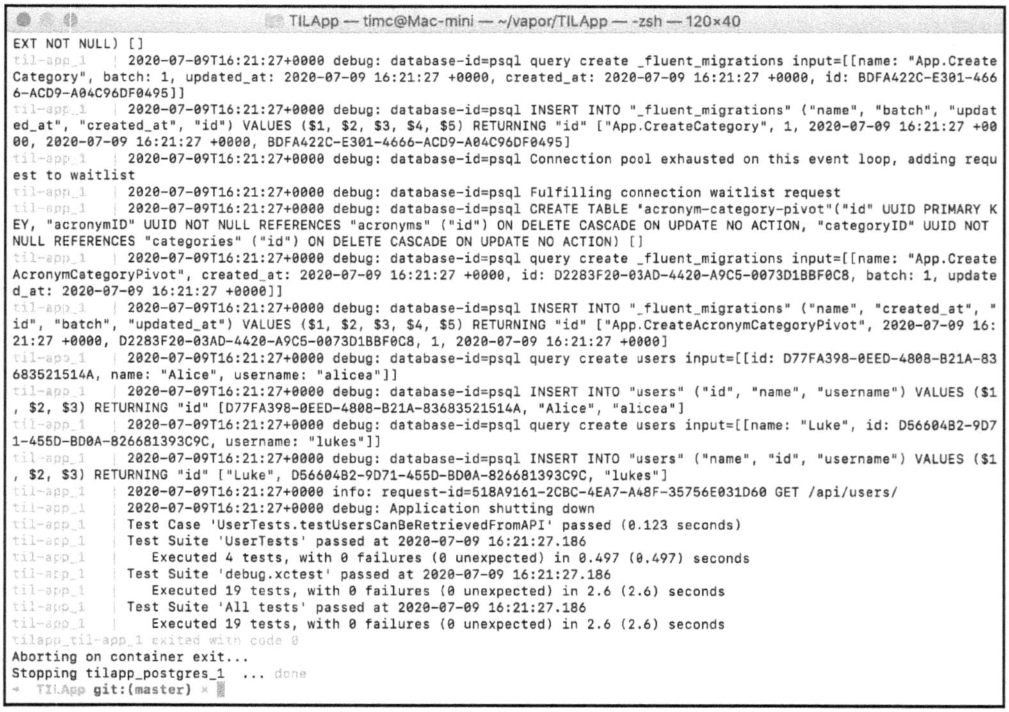

Where to go from here?

In this chapter, you learned how to test your Vapor applications to ensure they work correctly. Writing tests for your application also means you can run these tests on Linux. This gives you confidence your application will work when you deploy it. Having a good test suite allows you to evolve and adapt your applications quickly.

Vapor's architecture has a heavy reliance on protocols. This, combined with Vapor's use of Swift extensions and switchable services, makes testing simple and scalable. For large applications, you may even want to introduce a data abstraction layer so you aren't testing with a real database.

This means you don't have to connect to a database to test your main logic and will speed up the tests.

It's important you run your tests regularly. Using a continuous integration (CI) system such as Jenkins or GitHub Actions allows you to test every commit.

You must also keep your tests up to date. In future chapters where the behavior changes, such as when authentication is introduced, you'll change the tests to work with these new features.

Chapter 12: Creating a Simple iPhone App, Part 1

By Tim Condon

In the previous chapters, you created an API and interacted with it using RESTed. However, users expect something a bit nicer to use TIL! The next two chapters show you how to build a simple iOS app that interacts with the API. In this chapter, you'll learn how to create different models and get models from the database.

At the end of the two chapters, you'll have an iOS application that can do everything you've learned up to this point. It will look similar to the following:

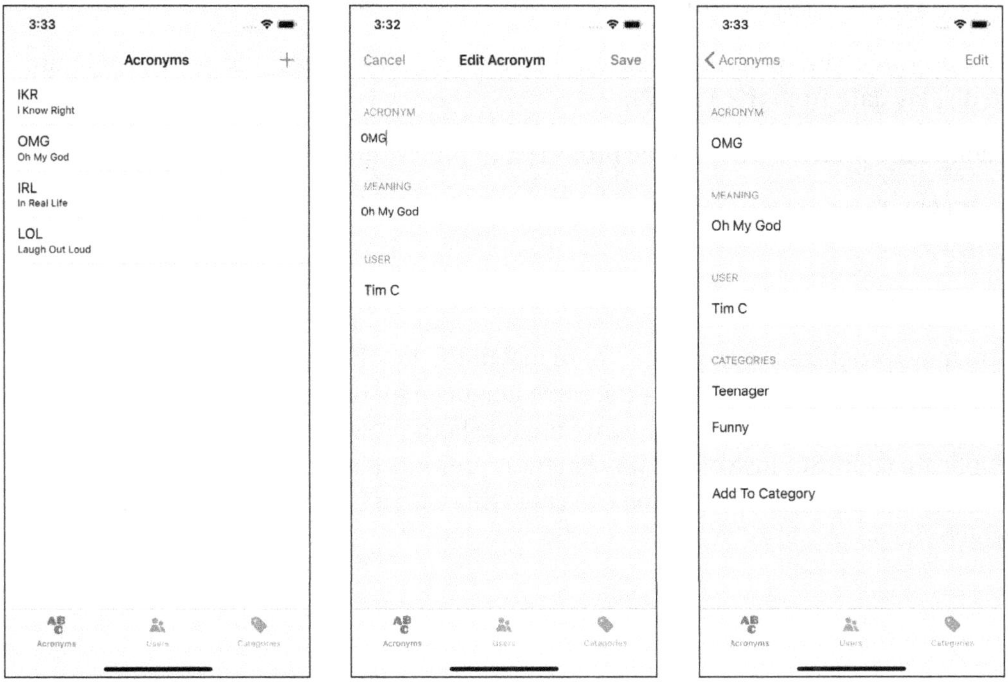

Getting started

To kick things off, download the materials for this chapter. In Terminal, go the directory where you downloaded the materials and type:

```
cd TILApp
swift run
```

This builds and runs the TIL application that the iOS app will talk to. You can use your existing TIL app if you like.

> **Note:** This requires that your Docker container for the database is running. See Chapter 6, "Configuring a Database", for instructions.

Next, open the **TILiOS** project. **TILiOS** contains a skeleton application that interacts with the TIL API. It's a tab bar application with three tabs:

- **Acronyms**: view all acronyms, view details about an acronym and add acronyms.
- **Users**: view all users and create users.
- **Categories**: view all categories and create categories.

The project contains several empty table view controllers ready for you to configure to display data from the TIL API.

Look at the **Models** group in the project; it provides three model classes:

- `Acronym`
- `User`
- `Category`

You may recognize the models — these match the models found API application! This shows how powerful using the same language for both client and server can be. It's even possible to create a separate module both projects use so you don't have to duplicate code. Because of the way Fluent represents parent-child relationships, the `Acronym` is slightly different. You can solve this with a DTO like `CreateAcronymData`, which the project also includes.

Viewing the acronyms

The first tab's table displays all the acronyms. Create a new **Swift** file in the **Utilities** group called **ResourceRequest.swift**. Open the file and create a type to manage making resource requests:

```
// 1
struct ResourceRequest<ResourceType>
  where ResourceType: Codable {
  // 2
  let baseURL = "http://localhost:8080/api/"
  let resourceURL: URL

  // 3
  init(resourcePath: String) {
    guard let resourceURL = URL(string: baseURL) else {
      fatalError("Failed to convert baseURL to a URL")
    }
    self.resourceURL =
      resourceURL.appendingPathComponent(resourcePath)
  }
}
```

Here's what this does:

1. Define a generic `ResourceRequest` type whose generic parameter must conform to `Codable`.
2. Set the base URL for the API. This uses `localhost` for now. Note that this requires you to disable ATS (App Transport Security) in the app's **Info.plist**. This is already set up for you in the sample project.
3. Initialize the URL for the particular resource.

Next, you need a way to fetch all instances of a particular resource type. Add the following method after `init(resourcePath:)`:

```
// 1
func getAll(
  completion: @escaping
    (Result<[ResourceType], ResourceRequestError>) -> Void
) {
  // 2
  let dataTask = URLSession.shared
    .dataTask(with: resourceURL) { data, _, _ in
      // 3
      guard let jsonData = data else {
        completion(.failure(.noData))
          return
```

```
      }
      do {
        // 4
        let resources = try JSONDecoder()
          .decode(
            [ResourceType].self,
            from: jsonData)
        // 5
        completion(.success(resources))
      } catch {
        // 6
        completion(.failure(.decodingError))
      }
    }
    // 7
    dataTask.resume()
  }
```

Here's what this does:

1. Define a function to get all values of the resource type from the API. This takes a completion closure as a parameter which uses Swift's `Result` type.
2. Create a data task with the resource URL.
3. Ensure the response returns some data. Otherwise, call the `completion(_:)` closure with the appropriate `.failure` case.
4. Decode the response data into an array of `ResourceTypes`.
5. Call the `completion(_:)` closure with the `.success` case and return the array of `ResourceTypes`.
6. Catch any errors and return the correct failure case.
7. Start the `dataTask`.

Open **AcronymsTableViewController.swift** and add the following under `// MARK: - Properties`:

```
// 1
var acronyms: [Acronym] = []
// 2
let acronymsRequest =
  ResourceRequest<Acronym>(resourcePath: "acronyms")
```

Here's what this does:

1. Declare an array of acronyms. These are the acronyms the table displays.
2. Create a `ResourceRequest` for acronyms.

Getting the acronyms

Whenever the view appears on screen, the table view controller calls `refresh(_:)`. Replace the implementation of `refresh(_:)` with the following:

```
// 1
acronymsRequest.getAll { [weak self] acronymResult in
  // 2
  DispatchQueue.main.async {
    sender?.endRefreshing()
  }

  switch acronymResult {
  // 3
  case .failure:
    ErrorPresenter.showError(
      message: "There was an error getting the acronyms",
      on: self)
  // 4
  case .success(let acronyms):
    DispatchQueue.main.async { [weak self] in
      guard let self = self else { return }
      self.acronyms = acronyms
      self.tableView.reloadData()
    }
  }
}
```

Here's what this does:

1. Call `getAll(completion:)` to get all the acronyms. This returns a result in the completion closure.
2. As the request is complete, call `endRefreshing()` on the refresh control.
3. If the fetch fails, use the `ErrorPresenter` utility to display an alert controller with an appropriate error message.
4. If the fetch succeeds, update the `acronyms` array from the result and reload the table.

Displaying acronyms

Still in **AcronymsTableViewController.swift**, update `tableView(_:numberOfRowsInSection:)` to return the correct number of acronyms by replacing `return 1` with the following:

```
return acronyms.count
```

Next, update `tableView(_:cellForRowAt:)` to display the acronyms in the table. Add the following before `return cell`:

```
let acronym = acronyms[indexPath.row]
cell.textLabel?.text = acronym.short
cell.detailTextLabel?.text = acronym.long
```

This sets the title and subtitle text to the acronym short and long properties for each cell.

Build and run and you'll see your table populated with acronyms from the database:

Viewing the users

Viewing all the users follows a similar pattern. Most of the view controller is already set up. Open **UsersTableViewController.swift** and under:

```
var users: [User] = []
```

add the following:

```
let usersRequest =
  ResourceRequest<User>(resourcePath: "users")
```

This creates a `ResourceRequest` to get the users from the API. Next, replace the implementation of `refresh(_:)` with the following:

```
// 1
usersRequest.getAll { [weak self] result in
  // 2
  DispatchQueue.main.async {
    sender?.endRefreshing()
  }
  switch result {
  // 3
  case .failure:
    ErrorPresenter.showError(
      message: "There was an error getting the users",
      on: self)
  // 4
  case .success(let users):
    DispatchQueue.main.async { [weak self] in
      guard let self = self else { return }
      self.users = users
      self.tableView.reloadData()
    }
  }
}
```

Here's what this does:

1. Call `getAll(completion:)` to get all the users. This returns a result in the completion closure.
2. As the request is complete, call `endRefreshing()` on the refresh control.
3. If the fetch fails, use the `ErrorPresenter` utility to display an alert view with an appropriate error message.
4. If the fetch succeeds, update the `users` array from the result and reload the table.

Build and run. Go to the **Users** tab and you'll see the table populated with users from your database:

Viewing the categories

Follow a similar pattern to view all the categories. Open **CategoriesTableViewController.swift** and under:

```
var categories: [Category] = []
```

add the following:

```
let categoriesRequest =
  ResourceRequest<Category>(resourcePath: "categories")
```

This sets up a `ResourceRequest` to get the categories from the API. Next, replace the implementation of `refresh(_:)` with the following:

```
// 1
categoriesRequest.getAll { [weak self] result in
  // 2
  DispatchQueue.main.async {
    sender?.endRefreshing()
  }
  switch result {
  // 3
```

```
    case .failure:
      let message = "There was an error getting the categories"
      ErrorPresenter.showError(message: message, on: self)
    // 4
    case .success(let categories):
      DispatchQueue.main.async { [weak self] in
        guard let self = self else { return }
        self.categories = categories
        self.tableView.reloadData()
      }
    }
  }
```

Here's what this does:

1. Call `getAll(completion:)` to get all the categories. This returns a result in the completion closure.
2. As the request is complete, call `endRefreshing()` on the refresh control.
3. If the fetch fails, use the `ErrorPresenter` utility to display an alert view with an appropriate error message.
4. If the fetch succeeds, update the `categories` array from the result and reload the table.

Build and run. Go to the **Categories** tab and you'll see the table populated with categories from the TIL application:

Creating users

In the TIL API, you must have a user to create acronyms, so set up that flow first. Open **ResourceRequest.swift** and add a new method at the bottom of `ResourceRequest` to save a model:

```
// 1
func save<CreateType>(
  _ saveData: CreateType,
  completion: @escaping
    (Result<ResourceType, ResourceRequestError>) -> Void
) where CreateType: Codable {
  do {
    // 2
    var urlRequest = URLRequest(url: resourceURL)
    // 3
    urlRequest.httpMethod = "POST"
    // 4
    urlRequest.addValue(
      "application/json",
      forHTTPHeaderField: "Content-Type")
    // 5
    urlRequest.httpBody =
      try JSONEncoder().encode(saveData)
    // 6
    let dataTask = URLSession.shared
      .dataTask(with: urlRequest) { data, response, _ in
        // 7
        guard
          let httpResponse = response as? HTTPURLResponse,
          httpResponse.statusCode == 200,
          let jsonData = data
          else {
            completion(.failure(.noData))
            return
        }

        do {
          // 8
          let resource = try JSONDecoder()
            .decode(ResourceType.self, from: jsonData)
          completion(.success(resource))
        } catch {
          // 9
          completion(.failure(.decodingError))
        }
      }
    // 10
    dataTask.resume()
  // 11
  } catch {
```

```
      completion(.failure(.encodingError))
    }
  }
```

Here's what the new method does:

1. Declare a method `save(_:completion:)` that takes a generic `Codable` type to save and a completion handler that takes the save result. This uses a generic type instead of `ResourceRequest` because the save `Acronym` API uses `CreateAcronymData` instead of `Acronym`.
2. Create a `URLRequest` for the save request.
3. Set the HTTP method for the request to **POST**.
4. Set the **Content-Type** header for the request to **application/json** so the API knows there's JSON data to decode.
5. Set the request body as the encoded save data.
6. Create a data task with the request.
7. Ensure there's an HTTP response. Check the response status is **200 OK**, the code returned by the API upon a successful save. Ensure there's data in the response body.
8. Decode the response body into the resource type. Call the completion handler with a success result.
9. Catch a decode error and call the completion handler with a failure result.
10. Start the data task.
11. Catch any encoding errors from `try JSONEncoder().encode(resourceToSave)` and call the completion handler with a failure result.

Next, open **CreateUserTableViewController.swift** and replace the implementation of `save(_:)` with the following:

```
// 1
guard
  let name = nameTextField.text,
  !name.isEmpty
  else {
    ErrorPresenter
      .showError(message: "You must specify a name", on: self)
    return
}
```

```
// 2
guard
  let username = usernameTextField.text,
  !username.isEmpty
  else {
    ErrorPresenter.showError(
      message: "You must specify a username",
      on: self)
    return
}

// 3
let user = User(name: name, username: username)
// 4
ResourceRequest<User>(resourcePath: "users")
  .save(user) { [weak self] result in
    switch result {
    // 5
    case .failure:
      let message = "There was a problem saving the user"
      ErrorPresenter.showError(message: message, on: self)
    // 6
    case .success:
      DispatchQueue.main.async { [weak self] in
        self?.navigationController?
          .popViewController(animated: true)
      }
    }
}
```

Here's what this does:

1. Ensure the name text field contains a non-empty string.
2. Ensure the username text field contains a non-empty string.
3. Create a new user from the provided data.
4. Create a `ResourceRequest` for `User` and call `save(_:completion:)`.
5. If the save fails, display an error message.
6. If the save succeeds, return to the previous view: the users table.

Build and run. Go to the **Users** tab and tap the + button to open the **Create User** screen. Fill in the two fields and tap **Save**.

If the save succeeds, the screen closes and the new user appears in the table:

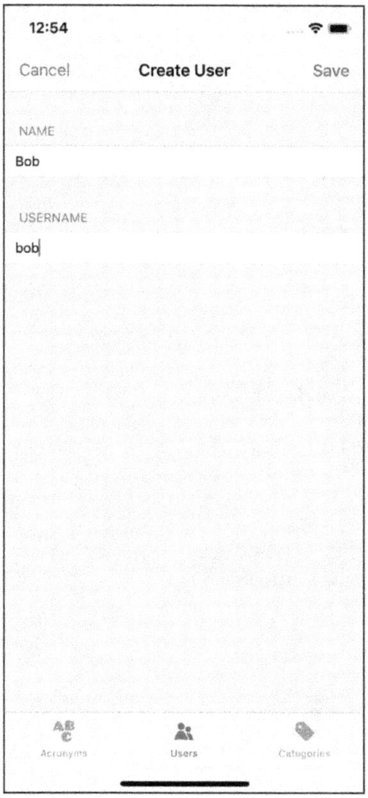

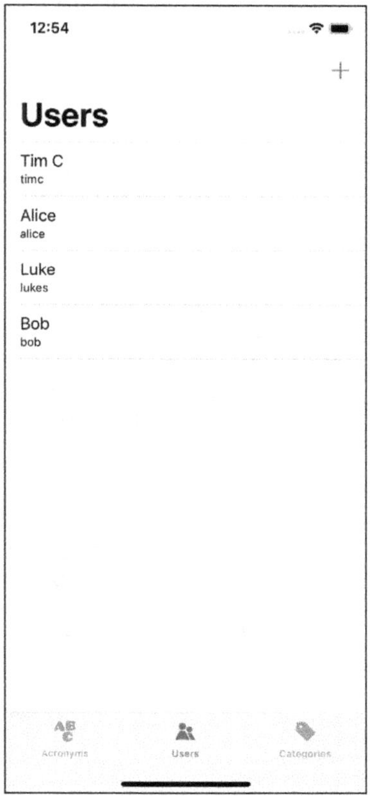

Creating acronyms

Now that you have the ability to create users, it's time to implement creating acronyms. After all, what good is an acronym dictionary app if you can't add to it.

Selecting users

When you create an acronym with the API, you must provide a user ID. Asking a user to remember and input a UUID isn't a good user experience! The iOS app should allow a user to select a user by name.

Open **CreateAcronymTableViewController.swift** and create a new method under `viewDidLoad()` to populate the User cell in the create acronym form with a default user:

```
func populateUsers() {
  // 1
  let usersRequest =
    ResourceRequest<User>(resourcePath: "users")

  usersRequest.getAll { [weak self] result in
    switch result {
    // 2
    case .failure:
      let message = "There was an error getting the users"
      ErrorPresenter
        .showError(message: message, on: self) { _ in
          self?.navigationController?
            .popViewController(animated: true)
        }
    // 3
    case .success(let users):
      DispatchQueue.main.async { [weak self] in
        self?.userLabel.text = users[0].name
      }
      self?.selectedUser = users[0]
    }
  }
}
```

Here's what this does:

1. Get all users from the API.
2. Show an error if the request fails. Return from the create acronym view when the user dismisses the alert controller. This uses the `dismissAction` on `showError(message:on:dismissAction:)`.
3. If the request succeeds, set the user field to the first user's name and update `selectedUser`.

At the end of `viewDidLoad()` add the following:

```
populateUsers()
```

Your app's user can tap the **USER** cell to select a different user for creating an acronym. This gesture opens the **Select A User** screen.

Open **SelectUserTableViewController.swift**. Under:

```
var users: [User] = []
```

add the following:

```
var selectedUser: User
```

This property holds the selected user. Next, in `init?(coder:selectedUser:)` assign the provided user to the new property before `super.init(coder: coder)`:

```
self.selectedUser = selectedUser
```

Next, add the following implementation to `loadData()` so the table displays the users when the view loads:

```
// 1
let usersRequest =
  ResourceRequest<User>(resourcePath: "users")

usersRequest.getAll { [weak self] result in
  switch result {
  // 2
  case .failure:
    let message = "There was an error getting the users"
    ErrorPresenter
      .showError(message: message, on: self) { _ in
        self?.navigationController?
          .popViewController(animated: true)
      }
    // 3
  case .success(let users):
    self?.users = users
    DispatchQueue.main.async { [weak self] in
      self?.tableView.reloadData()
    }
  }
}
```

Here's what this does:

1. Get all the users from the API.
2. If the request fails, show an error message. Return to the previous view once a user taps dismiss on the alert.
3. If the request succeeds, save the users and reload the table data.

In tableView(_:cellForRowAt:) before return cell add the following:

```
if user.name == selectedUser.name {
  cell.accessoryType = .checkmark
} else {
  cell.accessoryType = .none
}
```

This compares the current cell against the currently selected user. If they are the same, set a checkmark on that cell.

SelectUserTableViewController uses an unwind segue to navigate back to the CreateAcronymTableViewController when a user taps a cell.

Add the following implementation of prepare(for:) in SelectUserTableViewController to set the selected user for the segue:

```
// 1
if segue.identifier == "UnwindSelectUserSegue" {
  // 2
  guard
    let cell = sender as? UITableViewCell,
    let indexPath = tableView.indexPath(for: cell)
    else {
      return
  }
  // 3
  selectedUser = users[indexPath.row]
}
```

Here's what this does:

1. Verify this is the expected segue.
2. Get the index path of the cell that triggered the segue.
3. Update selectedUser to the user for the tapped cell.

The unwind segue calls updateSelectedUser(_:) in CreateAcronymTableViewController. Open **CreateAcronymTableViewController.swift** and add the following implementation to the updateSelectedUser(_:):

```
// 1
guard let controller = segue.source
  as? SelectUserTableViewController
  else {
    return
}
```

```
// 2
selectedUser = controller.selectedUser
userLabel.text = selectedUser?.name
```

Here's what this does:

1. Ensure the segue came from `SelectUserTableViewController`.
2. Update `selectedUser` with the new value and update the user label.

Finally, replace the implementation for `makeSelectUserViewController(_:)` with the following:

```
guard let user = selectedUser else {
  return nil
}
return SelectUserTableViewController(
  coder: coder,
  selectedUser: user)
```

This ensures we have a selected user and creates a `SelectUserTableViewController` with that user. When a user taps the user field, the app uses the `@IBSegueAction` to create the select user screen.

Build and run. In the Acronyms tab, tap + to bring up the **Create An Acronym** view. Tap the user row and the application opens the **Select A User** view, allowing you to select a user.

When you tap a user, that user is then set on the **Create An Acronym** page:

Saving acronyms

Now that you can successfully select a user, it's time to implement saving the new acronym to the database. Replace the implementation of `save(_:)` in **CreateAcronymTableViewController.swift** with the following:

```
// 1
guard
  let shortText = acronymShortTextField.text,
  !shortText.isEmpty
  else {
    ErrorPresenter.showError(
      message: "You must specify an acronym!",
      on: self)
    return
}
guard
  let longText = acronymLongTextField.text,
  !longText.isEmpty
  else {
    ErrorPresenter.showError(
      message: "You must specify a meaning!",
      on: self)
    return
}
guard let userID = selectedUser?.id else {
  let message = "You must have a user to create an acronym!"
  ErrorPresenter.showError(message: message, on: self)
  return
}

// 2
let acronym = Acronym(
  short: shortText,
  long: longText,
  userID: userID)
let acronymSaveData = acronym.toCreateData()
// 3
ResourceRequest<Acronym>(resourcePath: "acronyms")
  .save(acronymSaveData) { [weak self] result in
    switch result {
    // 4
    case .failure:
      let message = "There was a problem saving the acronym"
      ErrorPresenter.showError(message: message, on: self)
    // 5
    case .success:
      DispatchQueue.main.async { [weak self] in
        self?.navigationController?
          .popViewController(animated: true)
      }
```

```
        }
    }
```

Here are the steps to save the acronym:

1. Ensure the user has filled in the acronym and meaning. Check the selected user is not `nil` and the user has a valid ID.
2. Create a new `Acronym` from the supplied data. Convert the acronym to `CreateAcronymData` using the `toCreateData()` helper method.
3. Create a `ResourceRequest` for `Acronym` and call `save(_:)` using the create data.
4. If the save request fails, show an error message.
5. If the save request succeeds, return to the previous view: the acronyms table.

Build and run. On the **Acronyms** tab, tap +. Fill in the fields to create an acronym and tap **Save**.

The saved acronym appears in the table:

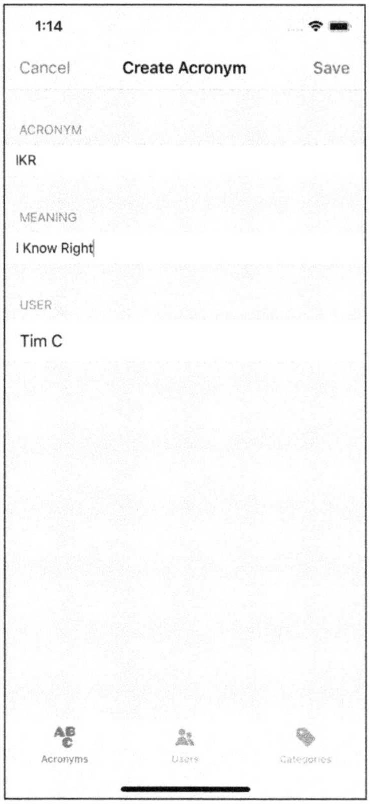

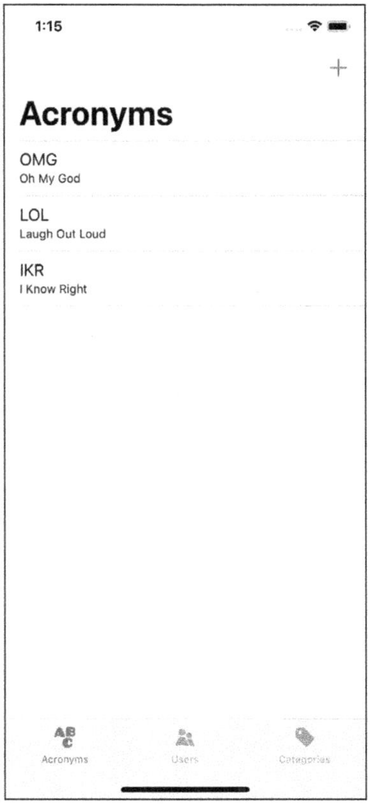

Where to go from here?

In this chapter, you learned how to interact with the API from an iOS application. You saw how to create different models and retrieve them from the API. You also learned how to manage the required relationships in a user-friendly way.

The next chapter builds upon this to view details about a single acronym. You'll also learn how to implement the rest of the CRUD operations. Finally, you'll see how to set up relationships between categories and acronyms.

Chapter 13: Creating a Simple iPhone App, Part 2

By Tim Condon

In the previous chapter, you created an iPhone application that can create users and acronyms. In this chapter, you'll expand the app to include viewing details about a single acronym. You'll also learn how to perform the final CRUD operations: edit and delete. Finally, you'll learn how to add acronyms to categories.

> **Note**: This chapter expects you have a TIL Vapor application running. It also expects you've completed the iOS app from the previous chapter. If not, grab the starter projects and pick up from there. See Chapter 12, "Creating a Simple iPhone App, Part 1", for details on how to run the Vapor application.

Getting started

In the previous chapter, you learned how to view all the acronyms in a table. Now, you want to show all the information about a single acronym when a user taps a table cell. The starter project contains the necessary plumbing; you simply need to implement the details.

Open **AcronymsTableViewController.swift**. Replace the implementation for `makeAcronymsDetailTableViewController(_:)` with the following:

```
// 1
guard let indexPath = tableView.indexPathForSelectedRow else {
  return nil
}
// 2
let acronym = acronyms[indexPath.row]
// 3
return AcronymDetailTableViewController(
  coder: coder,
  acronym: acronym)
```

You run this code when a user taps an acronym. The code does the following:

1. Ensure that there's a selected index path.
2. Get the acronym corresponding to the tapped row.
3. Create an `AcronymDetailTableViewController` using the selected acronym.

Create a new Swift file called **AcronymRequest.swift** in the **Utilities** group. Open the new file and create a new type to represent an acronym resource request:

```
struct AcronymRequest {
  let resource: URL

  init(acronymID: UUID) {
    let resourceString =
      "http://localhost:8080/api/acronyms/\(acronymID)"
    guard let resourceURL = URL(string: resourceString) else {
      fatalError("Unable to createURL")
    }
    self.resource = resourceURL
  }
}
```

This sets the `resource` property to the URL for that acronym. At the bottom of `AcronymRequest`, add a method to get the acronym's user:

```
func getUser(
  completion: @escaping (
    Result<User, ResourceRequestError>
  ) -> Void
) {
  // 1
  let url = resource.appendingPathComponent("user")

  // 2
```

```
    let dataTask = URLSession.shared
      .dataTask(with: url) { data, _, _ in
        // 3
        guard let jsonData = data else {
          completion(.failure(.noData))
          return
        }
        do {
        // 4
          let user = try JSONDecoder()
            .decode(User.self, from: jsonData)
          completion(.success(user))
        } catch {
          // 5
          completion(.failure(.decodingError))
        }
      }
    // 6
    dataTask.resume()
  }
```

Here's what this does:

1. Create the URL to get the acronym's user.
2. Create a data task using the shared `URLSession`.
3. Check the response contains a body, otherwise fail with the appropriate error.
4. Decode the response body into a `User` object and call the completion handler with the success result.
5. Catch any decoding errors and call the completion handler with the failure result.
6. Start the network task.

Next, below `getUser(completion:)`, add the following method to get the acronym's categories:

```
  func getCategories(
    completion: @escaping (
      Result<[Category], ResourceRequestError>
    ) -> Void
  ) {
    let url = resource.appendingPathComponent("categories")
    let dataTask = URLSession.shared
      .dataTask(with: url) { data, _, _ in
        guard let jsonData = data else {
          completion(.failure(.noData))
          return
        }
```

```
      do {
        let categories = try JSONDecoder()
          .decode([Category].self, from: jsonData)
        completion(.success(categories))
      } catch {
        completion(.failure(.decodingError))
      }
    }
  dataTask.resume()
}
```

This works exactly like the other request methods in the project, decoding the response body into `[Category]`.

Open **AcronymDetailTableViewController.swift** and add the following implementation to `getAcronymData()`:

```
// 1
guard let id = acronym.id else {
  return
}

// 2
let acronymDetailRequester = AcronymRequest(acronymID: id)
// 3
acronymDetailRequester.getUser { [weak self] result in
  switch result {
  case .success(let user):
    self?.user = user
  case .failure:
    let message =
      "There was an error getting the acronym's user"
    ErrorPresenter.showError(message: message, on: self)
  }
}

// 4
acronymDetailRequester.getCategories { [weak self] result in
  switch result {
  case .success(let categories):
    self?.categories = categories
  case .failure:
    let message =
      "There was an error getting the acronym's categories"
    ErrorPresenter.showError(message: message, on: self)
  }
}
```

Here's the play by play:

1. Ensure the acronym has a non-nil ID.
2. Create an `AcronymRequest` to gather information.
3. Get the acronym's user. If the request succeeds, update the `user` property. Otherwise, display an appropriate error message.
4. Get the acronym's categories. If the request succeeds, update the `categories` property. Otherwise, display an appropriate error message.

The project displays acronym data in a table view with four sections. These are:

- the acronym
- its meaning
- its user
- its categories

Build and run. Tap an acronym in the Acronyms table and the application will show the detail view with all the information:

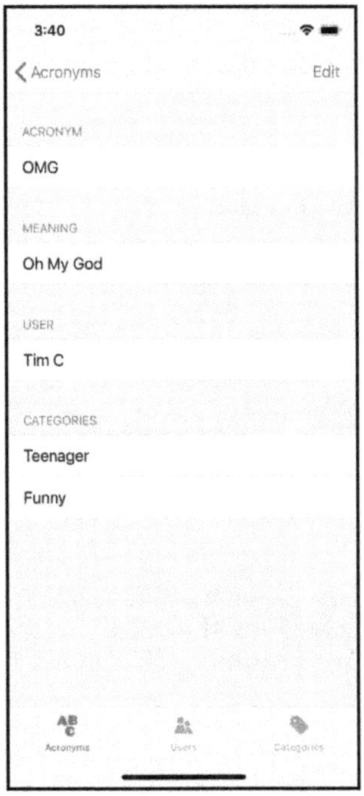

Editing acronyms

To edit an acronym, users tap the **Edit** button in the Acronym detail view. Open **CreateAcronymTableViewController.swift**. The `acronym` property exists to store the current acronym. If this property is set — by `prepare(for:sender:)` in **AcronymDetailTableViewController.swift** — then the user is editing the acronym. Otherwise, the user is creating a new acronym.

In `viewDidLoad()`, replace `populateUsers()` with:

```
if let acronym = acronym {
  acronymShortTextField.text = acronym.short
  acronymLongTextField.text = acronym.long
  userLabel.text = selectedUser?.name
  navigationItem.title = "Edit Acronym"
} else {
  populateUsers()
}
```

If the acronym is set, you're in edit mode, so populate the display fields with the correct values and update the view's title. If you're in create mode, call `populateUsers()` as before.

To update an acronym, you make a PUT request to the acronym's resource in the API. Open **AcronymRequest.swift** and add a method at the bottom of `AcronymRequest` to update an acronym:

```
func update(
  with updateData: CreateAcronymData,
  completion: @escaping (
    Result<Acronym, ResourceRequestError>
  ) -> Void
) {
  do {
    // 1
    var urlRequest = URLRequest(url: resource)
    urlRequest.httpMethod = "PUT"
    urlRequest.httpBody = try JSONEncoder().encode(updateData)
    urlRequest.addValue(
      "application/json",
      forHTTPHeaderField: "Content-Type")
    let dataTask = URLSession.shared
      .dataTask(with: urlRequest) { data, response, _ in
        // 2
        guard
          let httpResponse = response as? HTTPURLResponse,
          httpResponse.statusCode == 200,
          let jsonData = data
```

```
          else {
            completion(.failure(.noData))
            return
        }
        do {
        // 3
          let acronym = try JSONDecoder()
            .decode(Acronym.self, from: jsonData)
          completion(.success(acronym))
        } catch {
          completion(.failure(.decodingError))
        }
      }
    dataTask.resume()
  } catch {
    completion(.failure(.encodingError))
  }
}
```

This method works like other requests you've built. The differences are:

1. Create and configure a `URLRequest`. The method must be **PUT** and the body contains the encoded `CreateAcronymData`. Set the correct header so the Vapor application knows the request contains JSON.
2. Ensure the response is an HTTP response, the status code is 200 and the response has a body.
3. Decode the response body into an `Acronym` and call the completion handler with a success result.

Return to **CreateAcronymTableViewController.swift**. Inside `save(_:)` after:

```
let acronymSaveData = acronym.toCreateData()
```

Replace the rest of the function with the following:

```
if self.acronym != nil {
  // update code goes here
} else {
  ResourceRequest<Acronym>(resourcePath: "acronyms")
    .save(acronymSaveData) { [weak self] result in
      switch result {
      case .failure:
        let message = "There was a problem saving the acronym"
        ErrorPresenter.showError(message: message, on: self)
      case .success:
        DispatchQueue.main.async { [weak self] in
          self?.navigationController?
            .popViewController(animated: true)
```

```
        }
      }
    }
  }
```

This checks the class's `acronym` property to see if it has been set. If the property is `nil`, then the user is saving a new acronym so the function performs the same save request as before.

Inside the `if` block after `// update code goes here`, add the following code to update an acronym:

```
// 1
guard let existingID = self.acronym?.id else {
  let message = "There was an error updating the acronym"
  ErrorPresenter.showError(message: message, on: self)
  return
}
// 2
AcronymRequest(acronymID: existingID)
  .update(with: acronymSaveData) { result in
    switch result {
    // 3
    case .failure:
      let message = "There was a problem saving the acronym"
      ErrorPresenter.showError(message: message, on: self)
    case .success(let updatedAcronym):
      self.acronym = updatedAcronym
      DispatchQueue.main.async { [weak self] in
        // 4
        self?.performSegue(
          withIdentifier: "UpdateAcronymDetails",
          sender: nil)
      }
    }
  }
```

Here's what the update code does:

1. Ensure the acronym has a valid ID.
2. Create an `AcronymRequest` and call `update(with:completion:)`.
3. If the update fails, display an error message.
4. If the update succeeds, store the updated acronym and trigger an unwind segue to the `AcronymsDetailTableViewController`.

Next, open **AcronymsDetailTableViewController.swift** and add the following implementation to the end of `prepare(for:sender:)`:

```
if segue.identifier == "EditAcronymSegue" {
  // 1.
  guard
    let destination = segue.destination
      as? CreateAcronymTableViewController else {
    return
  }

  // 2.
  destination.selectedUser = user
  destination.acronym = acronym
}
```

Here's what this does:

1. Ensure the destination is a `CreateAcronymTableViewController`.

2. Set the `selectedUser` and `acronym` properties on the destination.

Next, add the following implementation to the unwind segue's target, `updateAcronymDetails(_:)`:

```
guard let controller = segue.source
  as? CreateAcronymTableViewController else {
  return
}

user = controller.selectedUser
if let acronym = controller.acronym {
  self.acronym = acronym
}
```

This captures the updated acronym, if set, and user, triggering an update to its own view.

Build and run. Tap an acronym to open the acronym detail view and tap **Edit**. Change the details and tap **Save**. The view will return to the acronyms details page with the updated values:

Deleting acronyms

The final CRUD operation to implement is D: delete. Open **AcronymRequest.swift** and add the following method after `update(with:completion:)`:

```
func delete() {
  // 1
  var urlRequest = URLRequest(url: resource)
  urlRequest.httpMethod = "DELETE"
  // 2
  let dataTask = URLSession.shared.dataTask(with: urlRequest)
  dataTask.resume()
}
```

Here's what `delete()` does:

1. Create a `URLRequest` and set the HTTP method to **DELETE**.
2. Create a data task for the request using the shared `URLSession` and send the request. This ignores the result of the request.

Open **AcronymsTableViewController.swift**. To enable deletion of a table row, add the following after `tableView(_:cellForRowAt:)`:

```
override func tableView(
  _ tableView: UITableView,
  commit editingStyle: UITableViewCell.EditingStyle,
  forRowAt indexPath: IndexPath
) {
  if let id = acronyms[indexPath.row].id {
    // 1
    let acronymDetailRequester = AcronymRequest(acronymID: id)
    acronymDetailRequester.delete()
  }

  // 2
  acronyms.remove(at: indexPath.row)
  // 3
  tableView.deleteRows(at: [indexPath], with: .automatic)
}
```

This enables "swipe-to-delete" functionality on the table view. Here's how it works:

1. If the acronym has a valid ID, create an `AcronymRequest` for the acronym and call `delete()` to delete the acronym in the API.
2. Remove the acronym from the local array of acronyms.
3. Remove the acronym's row from the table view.

Build and run. Swipe left on an acronym and the **Delete** button will appear. Tap **Delete** to remove the acronym.

If you pull-to-refresh the table view, the acronym doesn't reappear as the application has deleted it in the API:

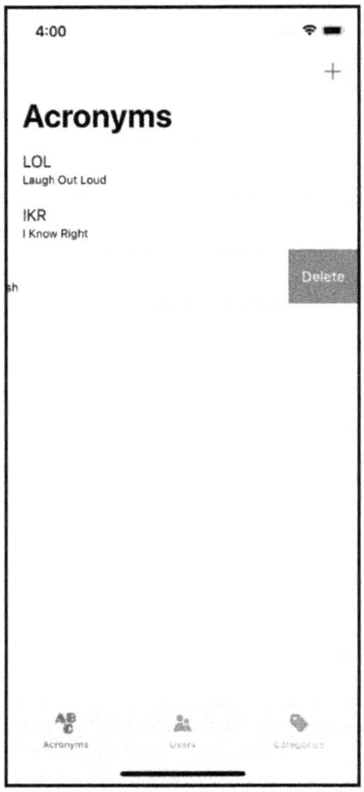

Creating categories

Setting up the create category table is like setting up the create users table. Open **CreateCategoryTableViewController.swift** and replace the implementation of `save(_:)` with:

```
// 1
guard
  let name = nameTextField.text,
  !name.isEmpty
  else {
    ErrorPresenter.showError(
      message: "You must specify a name", on: self)
    return
}

// 2
let category = Category(name: name)
// 3
ResourceRequest<Category>(resourcePath: "categories")
  .save(category) { [weak self] result in
```

```
    switch result {
    // 5
    case .failure:
      let message = "There was a problem saving the category"
      ErrorPresenter.showError(message: message, on: self)
    // 6
    case .success:
      DispatchQueue.main.async { [weak self] in
        self?.navigationController?
          .popViewController(animated: true)
      }
    }
  }
```

This is just like the save(_:) method for saving a user. Build and run. On the Categories tab, tap the + button to open the **Create Category** screen. Fill in a name and tap **Save**. If the save is successful, the screen will close and the new category will appear in the table:

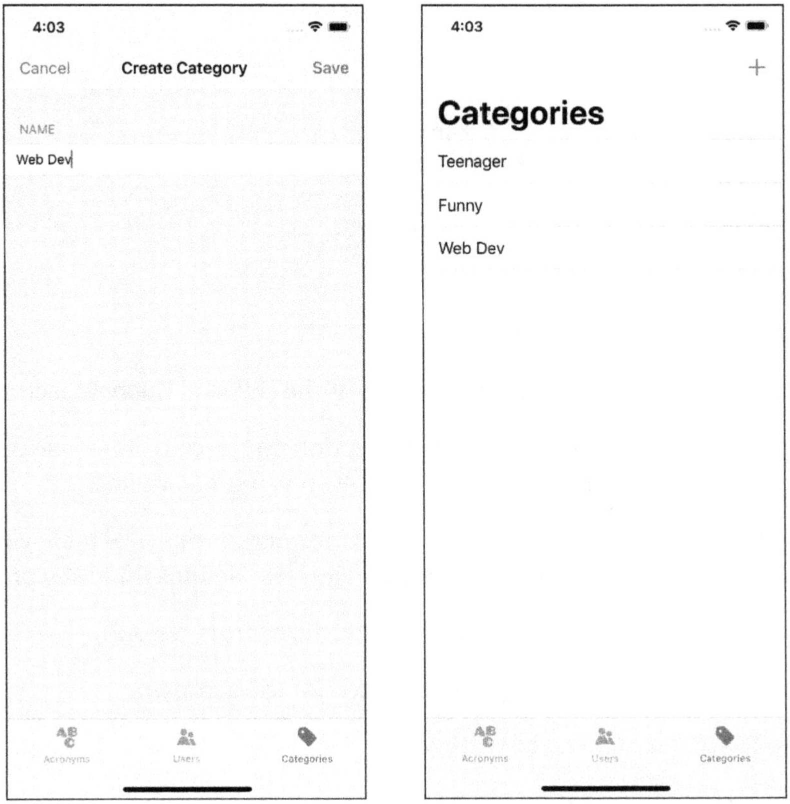

Adding acronyms to categories

The finish up, you must implement the ability to add acronyms to categories. Add a new table row section to the acronym detail view that contains a button to add the acronym to a category.

Open **AcronymsDetailTableViewController.swift**. Change the `return` statement in `numberOfSections(in:)` to:

```
return 5
```

In `tableView(_:cellForRowAt:)`, add a new case to the `switch` before `default`:

```
// 1
case 4:
  cell.textLabel?.text = "Add To Category"
```

Next, add the following just before `return cell`:

```
// 2
if indexPath.section == 4 {
  cell.selectionStyle = .default
  cell.isUserInteractionEnabled = true
} else {
  cell.selectionStyle = .none
  cell.isUserInteractionEnabled = false
}
```

These steps:

1. Set the table cell title to "Add To Category" if the cell is in the new section.
2. If the cell is in the new section, enable selection on the cell, otherwise disable selection. This allows a user to select the new row but no others.

The starter project already contains the view controller for this new table view: **AddToCategoryTableViewController.swift**. The class defines three key properties:

- `categories`: an array for all the categories retrieved from the API.
- `selectedCategories`: the categories selected for the acronym.
- `acronym`: the acronym to add to categories.

The class also contains an extension for the `UITableViewDataSource` methods. `tableView(_:cellForRowAt:)` sets the `accessoryType` on the cell if the category is in the `selectedCategories` array.

Open **AddToCategoryTableViewController.swift** and add the following implementation to `loadData()` to get all the categories from the API:

```
// 1
let categoriesRequest =
  ResourceRequest<Category>(resourcePath: "categories")
// 2
categoriesRequest.getAll { [weak self] result in
  switch result {
  // 3
  case .failure:
    let message =
      "There was an error getting the categories"
    ErrorPresenter.showError(message: message, on: self)
  // 4
  case .success(let categories):
    self?.categories = categories
    DispatchQueue.main.async { [weak self] in
      self?.tableView.reloadData()
    }
  }
}
```

Here's what this does:

1. Create a `ResourceRequest` for categories.
2. Get all the categories from the API.
3. If the fetch fails, show an error message.
4. If the fetch succeeds, populate the categories array and reload the table data.

Open **AcronymRequest.swift** and add the following method after `delete()`:

```
func add(
  category: Category,
  completion: @escaping (Result<Void, CategoryAddError>) -> Void
) {
  // 1
  guard let categoryID = category.id else {
    completion(.failure(.noID))
    return
  }
  // 2
  let url = resource
    .appendingPathComponent("categories")
    .appendingPathComponent("\(categoryID)")
  // 3
  var urlRequest = URLRequest(url: url)
  urlRequest.httpMethod = "POST"
```

```
    // 4
    let dataTask = URLSession.shared
      .dataTask(with: urlRequest) { _, response, _ in
        // 5
        guard
          let httpResponse = response as? HTTPURLResponse,
          httpResponse.statusCode == 201
          else {
            completion(.failure(.invalidResponse))
            return
        }
        // 6
        completion(.success(()))
      }
    dataTask.resume()
  }
```

Here's what this does:

1. Ensure the category has a valid ID, otherwise call the completion handler with the failure case and appropriate error. This uses `CategoryAddError` which is part of the starter project.
2. Build the `URL` for the request.
3. Create a `URLRequest` and set the HTTP method to **POST**.
4. Create a data task from the shared `URLSession`.
5. Ensure the response is an HTTP response and the response status is **201 Created**. Otherwise, call the completion handler with the right failure case.
6. Call the completion handler with the success case.

Open **AddToCategoryTableViewController.swift** and add the following `extension` at the end of the file:

```
// MARK: - UITableViewDelegate
extension AddToCategoryTableViewController {
  override func tableView(
    _ tableView: UITableView,
    didSelectRowAt indexPath: IndexPath
  ) {
    // 1
    let category = categories[indexPath.row]
    // 2
    guard let acronymID = acronym.id else {
      let message = """
        There was an error adding the acronym
        to the category - the acronym has no ID
```

```
      """
      ErrorPresenter.showError(message: message, on: self)
      return
    }
    // 3
    let acronymRequest = AcronymRequest(acronymID: acronymID)
    acronymRequest
      .add(category: category) { [weak self] result in
        switch result {
        // 4
        case .success:
          DispatchQueue.main.async { [weak self] in
            self?.navigationController?
              .popViewController(animated: true)
          }
        // 5
        case .failure:
          let message = """
            There was an error adding the acronym
            to the category
            """
          ErrorPresenter.showError(message: message, on: self)
        }
      }
  }
}
```

Here's what this function does:

1. Get the category the user has selected.
2. Ensure the acronym has a valid ID; otherwise, show an error message.
3. Create an `AcronymRequest` to add the acronym to the category.
4. If the request succeeds, return to the previous view.
5. If the request fails, show an error message.

Finally, open **AcronymDetailTableViewController.swift** to set up `AddToCategoryTableViewController`. Change the implementation of `makeAddToCategoryController(_:)` to the following:

```
AddToCategoryTableViewController(
  coder: coder,
  acronym: acronym,
  selectedCategories: categories)
```

This returns an `AddToCategoryTableViewController` created with the current acronym and its categories.

Build and run. Tap an acronym and, in the detail view, a new row labeled **Add To Category** now appears. Tap this cell and the categories list appears with already selected categories marked.

Select a new category and the view closes. The acronym detail view will now have the new category in its list:

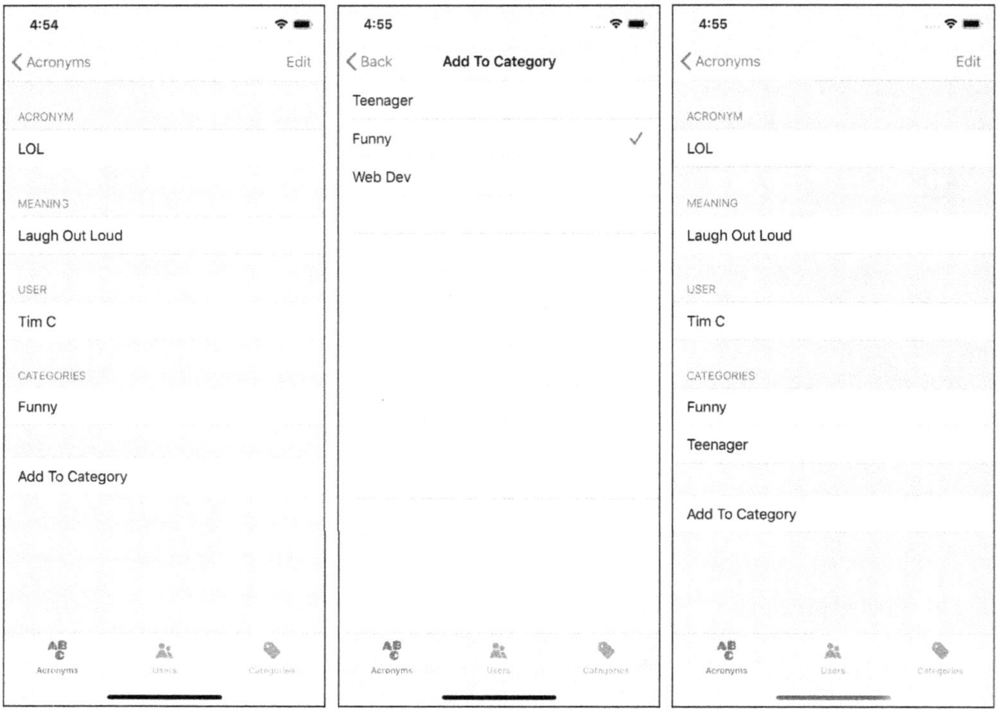

Where to go from here?

This chapter has shown you how to build an iOS application that interacts with the Vapor API. The application isn't fully-featured, however, and you could improve it. For example, you could add a category information view that displays all the acronyms for a particular category.

The next section of the book shows you how to build another type of client: a website.

Section II: Making a Simple Web App

This section teaches you how to build a front-end web site for your Vapor application. You'll learn to use Leaf, Vapor's templating engine, to generate dynamic web pages to display your app's data. You'll also learn how to accept data from a browser so that users can create and edit your models.This section will provide you the necessary building blocks to build a full website with Vapor.

Chapter 14: Templating with Leaf

By Tim Condon

In a previous section of the book, you learned how to create an API using Vapor and Fluent. You then learned how to create an iOS client to consume the API. In this section, you'll create another client — a website. You'll see how to use Leaf to create dynamic websites in Vapor applications.

Leaf

Leaf is Vapor's **templating language**. A templating language allows you to pass information to a page so it can generate the final HTML without knowing everything up front. For example, in the TIL application, you don't know every acronym that users will create when you deploy your application. Templating allows you handle this with ease.

Templating languages also allow you to reduce duplication in your webpages. Instead of multiple pages for acronyms, you create a single template and set the properties specific to displaying a particular acronym. If you decide to change the way you display an acronym, you only need change your code in one place and all acronym pages will show the new format.

Finally, templating languages allow you to embed templates into other templates. For example, if you have navigation on your website, you can create a single template that generates the code for your navigation. You embed the navigation template in all templates that need navigation rather than duplicating code.

Configuring Leaf

To use Leaf, you need to add it to your project as a dependency. Using the TIL application from Chapter 11, "Testing", or the starter project from this chapter, open **Package.swift**. Replace its contents with the following:

```
// swift-tools-version:5.2
import PackageDescription

let package = Package(
  name: "TILApp",
  platforms: [
    .macOS(.v10_15)
  ],
  dependencies: [
    // 💧 A server-side Swift web framework.
    .package(
      url: "https://github.com/vapor/vapor.git",
      from: "4.0.0"),
    .package(
      url: "https://github.com/vapor/fluent.git",
      from: "4.0.0"),
    .package(
      url:
        "https://github.com/vapor/fluent-postgres-driver.git",
      from: "2.0.0"),
    .package(
      url: "https://github.com/vapor/leaf.git",
      from: "4.0.0")
  ],
  targets: [
    .target(
      name: "App",
      dependencies: [
        .product(name: "Fluent", package: "fluent"),
        .product(
          name: "FluentPostgresDriver",
          package: "fluent-postgres-driver"),
        .product(name: "Vapor", package: "vapor"),
        .product(name: "Leaf", package: "leaf")
      ],
      swiftSettings: [
        .unsafeFlags(
          ["-cross-module-optimization"],
          .when(configuration: .release))
      ]
    ),
    .target(name: "Run", dependencies: [.target(name: "App")]),
    .testTarget(name: "AppTests", dependencies: [
      .target(name: "App"),
```

```
        .product(name: "XCTVapor", package: "vapor"),
      ])
    ]
  )
```

The changes made were:

- Make the `TILApp` package depend upon the Leaf package.
- Make the `App` target depend upon the `Leaf` target to ensure it links properly.

By default, Leaf expects templates to be in the **Resources/Views** directory. In Terminal, type the following to create these directories:

```
mkdir -p Resources/Views
```

Finally, you must create new routes for the website. Create a new controller to contain these routes. In Xcode, create a new Swift file named **WebsiteController.swift** in **Sources/App/Controllers**.

Rendering a page

Open **WebsiteController.swift** and replace its contents with the following, to create a new type to hold all the website routes and a route that returns an index template:

```
import Vapor
import Leaf

// 1
struct WebsiteController: RouteCollection {
  // 2
  func boot(routes: RoutesBuilder) throws {
    // 3
    routes.get(use: indexHandler)
  }

  // 4
  func indexHandler(_ req: Request)
    -> EventLoopFuture<View> {
      // 5
      return req.view.render("index")
  }
}
```

Here's what this does:

1. Declare a new `WebsiteController` type that conforms to `RouteCollection`.
2. Implement `boot(routes:)` as required by `RouteCollection`.
3. Register `indexHandler(_:)` to process GET requests to the router's root path, i.e., a request to /.
4. Implement `indexHandler(_:)` that returns `EventLoopFuture<View>`.
5. Render the **index** template and return the result. You'll learn about `req.view` in a moment.

Leaf generates a page from a template called **index.leaf** inside the **Resources/Views** directory.

Note that the file extension's not required by the `render(_:)` call. Create **Resources/Views/index.leaf** and replace its contents with the following:

```
<!DOCTYPE html>
<!-- 1 -->
<html lang="en">
<head>
  <meta charset="utf-8" />
  <!-- 2 -->
  <title>Hello World</title>
</head>
<body>
  <!-- 3 -->
  <h1>Hello World</h1>
</body>
</html>
```

Here's what this file does:

1. Declare a basic HTML 5 page with a `<head>` and `<body>`.
2. Set the page title to **Hello World** — this is the title displayed in a browser's tab.
3. Set the body to be a single `<h1>` title that says **Hello World**.

> **Note**: You can create your **.leaf** files using any text editor you choose, including Xcode. If you use Xcode, choose **Editor ▸ Syntax Coloring ▸ HTML** in order to get proper highlighting of elements and indentation support.

You must register your new `WebsiteController`. Open **routes.swift** and add the following to the end of `routes(_:)`:

```
let websiteController = WebsiteController()
try app.register(collection: websiteController)
```

Finally, also in **routes.swift**, remove the following code:

```
app.get { req in
  return "It works!"
}
```

`WebsiteController` now provides a route for / instead. Next, you must tell Vapor to use Leaf. Open **configure.swift** and add the following to the imports section below `import Vapor`:

```
import Leaf
```

Using the generic `req.view` to obtain a renderer allows you to switch to different templating engines easily. While this may not be useful when running your application, it's extremely useful for testing.

For example, it allows you to use a test renderer to produce plain text to verify against, rather than parsing HTML output in your test cases.

`req.view` asks Vapor to provide a type that conforms to `ViewRenderer`. Vapor provides `PlaintextRenderer` and LeafKit — the module Leaf is built upon — provides `LeafRenderer`. In **configure.swift**, add the following after `try app.autoMigrate().wait()`:

```
app.views.use(.leaf)
```

This tells Vapor to use Leaf when rendering views and `LeafRenderer` when asked for a `ViewRenderer` type.

Finally, you must tell Vapor where the app is running, because you might run the App from a standalone Xcode project or inside a workspace. To do this, set a custom working directory in Xcode. **Option-Click** the **Run** button in Xcode to open the scheme editor. On the **Options** tab, click to enable **Use custom working directory** and select the directory where the **Package.swift** file lives:

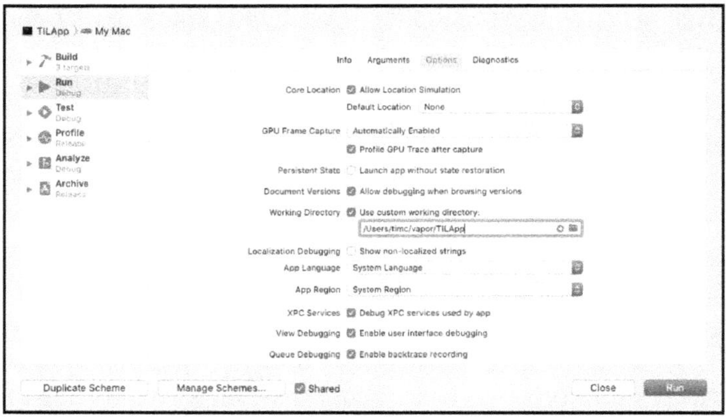

Build and run the application, remembering to choose the **Run** scheme, then open your browser. Enter the URL **http://localhost:8080** and you'll receive the page generated from the template:

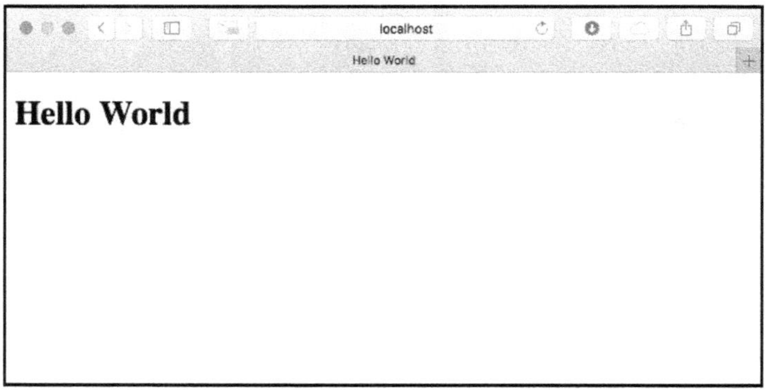

Injecting variables

The template is currently just a static page and not at all impressive! To make the page more dynamic, open **index.leaf** and change the <title> line to the following:

```
<title>#(title) | Acronyms</title>
```

This extracts a parameter called `title` using the `#()` Leaf function. Like a lot of Vapor, Leaf uses `Codable` to handle data.

At the bottom of **WebsiteController.swift**, add the following to create a new type to contain the title:

```
struct IndexContext: Encodable {
  let title: String
}
```

As data only flows to Leaf, you only need to conform to `Encodable`. `IndexContext` is the data for your view, similar to a view model in the MVVM design pattern. Next, change `indexHandler(_:)` to pass an `IndexContext` to the template. Replace the implementation with the following:

```
func indexHandler(_ req: Request)
  -> EventLoopFuture<View> {
    // 1
    let context = IndexContext(title: "Home page")
    // 2
    return req.view.render("index", context)
}
```

Here's what the new code does:

1. Create an `IndexContext` containing the desired title.
2. Pass the `context` to Leaf as the second parameter to `render(_:_:)`.

Build and run, then refresh the page in the browser. You'll see the updated title:

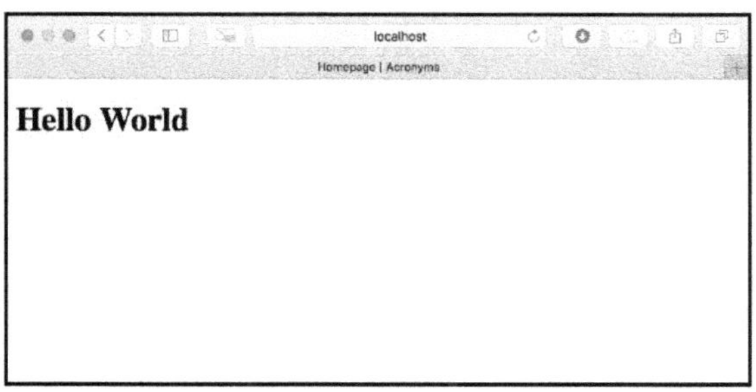

Using tags

The home page of the TIL website should display a list of all the acronyms. Still in **WebsiteController.swift**, add a new property to `IndexContext` underneath `title`:

```
let acronyms: [Acronym]?
```

This is an optional array of acronyms; it can be `nil` as there may be no acronyms in the database. Next, change `indexHandler(_:)` to get all the acronyms and insert them in the `IndexContext`.

Replace the implementation once more with the following:

```
func indexHandler(_ req: Request)
  -> EventLoopFuture<View> {
    // 1
    Acronym.query(on: req.db).all().flatMap { acronyms in
        // 2
        let acronymsData = acronyms.isEmpty ? nil : acronyms
        let context = IndexContext(
          title: "Home page",
          acronyms: acronymsData)
        return req.view.render("index", context)
    }
}
```

Here's what this does:

1. Use a Fluent query to get all the acronyms from the database.
2. Add the acronyms to `IndexContext` if there are any, otherwise set the property to `nil`. Leaf can check for `nil` in the template.

Finally open **index.leaf** and change the parts between the <body> tags to the following:

```
<!-- 1 -->
<h1>Acronyms</h1>

<!-- 2 -->
#if(acronyms):
  <!-- 3 -->
  <table>
    <thead>
      <tr>
        <th>Short</th>
        <th>Long</th>
      </tr>
```

```
      </thead>
      <tbody>
        <!-- 4 -->
        #for(acronym in acronyms):
          <tr>
            <!-- 5 -->
            <td>#(acronym.short)</td>
            <td>#(acronym.long)</td>
          </tr>
        #endfor
      </tbody>
    </table>
  <!-- 6 -->
  #else:
    <h2>There aren't any acronyms yet!</h2>
  #endif
```

Here's what the new code does:

1. Declare a new heading, "Acronyms".
2. Use Leaf's `#if()` tag to see if the `acronyms` variable is set. `#if()` can validate variables for nullability, work on booleans or even evaluate expressions.
3. If `acronyms` is set, create an HTML table. The table has a header row — `<thead>` — with two columns, **Short** and **Long**.
4. Use Leaf's `#for()` tag to loop through all the acronyms. This works in a similar way to Swift's `for` loop.
5. Create a row for each acronym. Use Leaf's `#()` function to extract the value. Since everything is `Encodable`, you can use dot notation to access properties on acronyms, just like Swift!
6. If there are no acronyms, print a suitable message.

Build and run, then refresh the page in the browser.

If you have no acronyms in the database, you'll see the correct message:

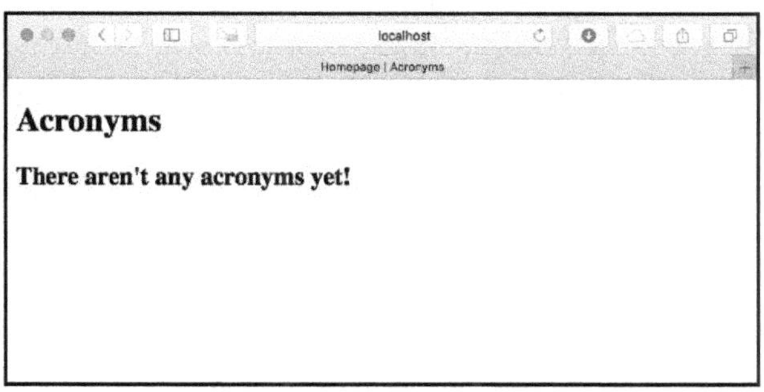

If there are acronyms in the database, you'll see them in the table:

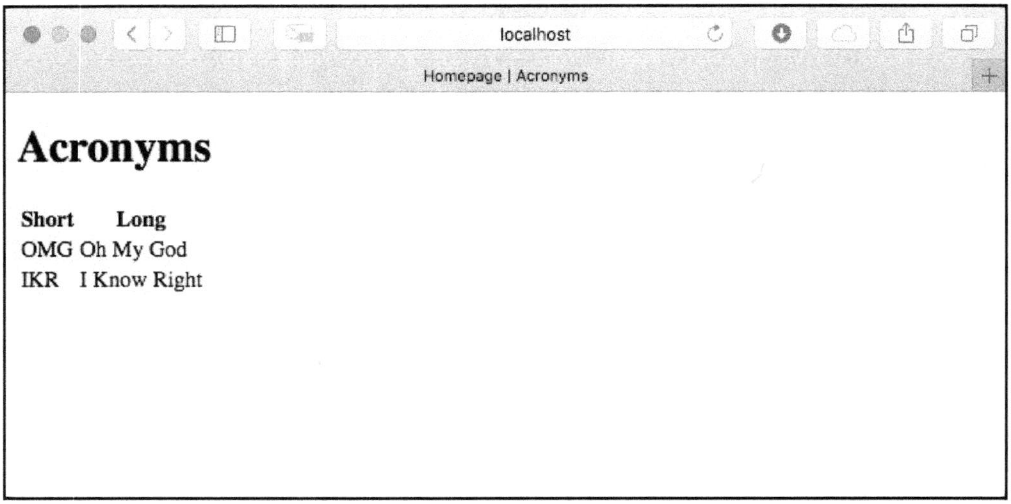

Acronym detail page

Now, you need a page to show the details for each acronym. At the end of **WebsiteController.swift**, create a new type to hold the context for this page:

```
struct AcronymContext: Encodable {
  let title: String
  let acronym: Acronym
  let user: User
}
```

This `AcronymContext` contains a title for the page, the acronym itself and the user who created the acronym. Create the following route handler for the acronym detail page under `indexHandler(_:)`:

```
// 1
func acronymHandler(_ req: Request)
  -> EventLoopFuture<View> {
    // 2
    Acronym.find(req.parameters.get("acronymID"), on: req.db)
      .unwrap(or: Abort(.notFound))
      .flatMap { acronym in
        // 3
        acronym.$user.get(on: req.db).flatMap { user in
          // 4
          let context = AcronymContext(
            title: acronym.short,
```

```
            acronym: acronym,
            user: user)
          return req.view.render("acronym", context)
        }
    }
}
```

Here's what this route handler does:

1. Declare a new route handler, `acronymHandler(_:)`, that returns `EventLoopFuture<View>`.
2. Extract the acronym from the request's parameters and unwrap the result. Return a **404 Not Found** if there is no acronym.
3. Get the user for acronym and unwrap the result.
4. Create an `AcronymContext` that contains the appropriate details and render the page using the **acronym.leaf** template.

Finally register the route at the bottom of `boot(routes:)`:

```
routes.get("acronyms", ":acronymID", use: acronymHandler)
```

This registers the `acronymHandler` route for **/acronyms/<ACRONYM ID>**, similar to the API. Create the **acronym.leaf** template inside the **Resources/Views** directory and open the new file and add the following:

```
<!DOCTYPE html>
<!-- 1 -->
<html lang="en">
<head>
  <meta charset="utf-8" />
  <!-- 2 -->
  <title>#(title) | Acronyms</title>
</head>
<body>
  <!-- 3 -->
  <h1>#(acronym.short)</h1>
  <!-- 4 -->
  <h2>#(acronym.long)</h2>

  <!-- 5 -->
  <p>Created by #(user.name)</p>
</body>
</html>
```

Here's what this template does:

1. Declare an HTML5 page like **index.leaf**.
2. Set the title to the value that's passed in.
3. Print the acronym's `short` property in an <h1> heading.
4. Print the acronym's `long` property in an <h2> heading.
5. Print the acronym's user in a <p> block

Finally, change **index.leaf** so you can navigate to the page. Replace the first column in the table for each acronym (`<td>#(acronym.short)</td>`) with:

```
<td><a href="/acronyms/#(acronym.id)">#(acronym.short)</a></td>
```

This wraps the acronym's `short` property in an HTML <a> tag, which is a link. The link sets the URL for each acronym to the route registered above. Build and run, then refresh the page in the browser:

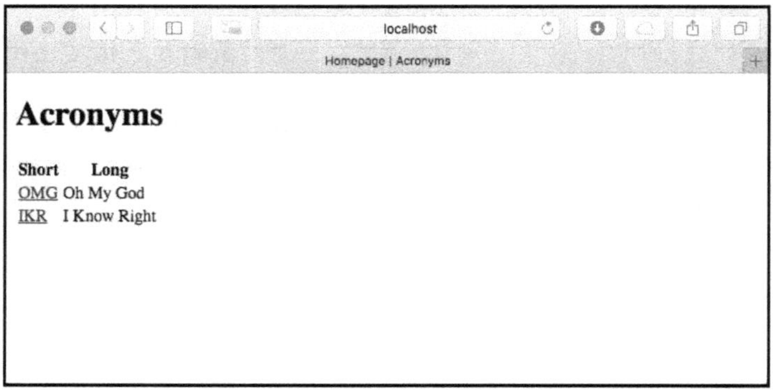

You'll see that each acronym's short form is now a link. Click the link and the browser navigates to the acronym's page:

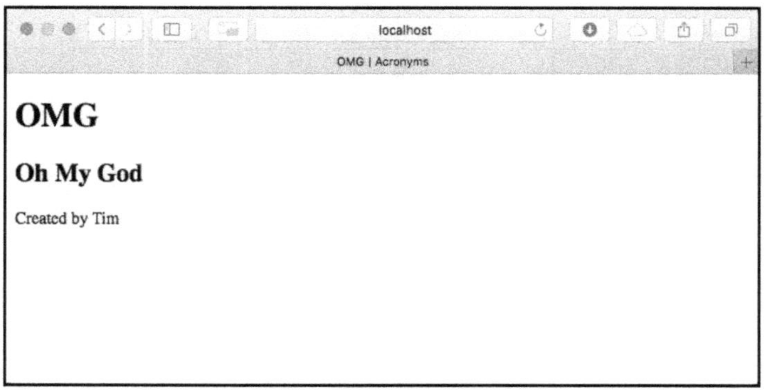

Where to go from here?

This chapter introduced Leaf and showed you how to start building a dynamic website. The next chapters in this section show you how to embed templates into other templates, beautify your application and create acronyms from the website.

Chapter 15: Beautifying Pages

By Tim Condon

In the previous chapter, you started building a powerful, dynamic website with Leaf. The web pages, however, only use simple HTML and aren't styled — they don't look great! In this chapter, you'll learn how to use the Bootstrap framework to add styling to your pages. You'll also learn how to embed templates so you only have to make changes in one place. Finally, you'll also see how to serve files with Vapor.

Embedding templates

Currently, if you change the index page template to add styling, you'll affect only that page. You'd have to duplicate the styling in the acronym detail page, and any other future pages.

Leaf allows you to embed templates into other templates. This enables you to create a "base" template that contains the code common to all pages and use it across your site.

In **Resources/Views** create a new file, **base.leaf**. Copy the contents of **index.leaf** into **base.leaf**. Remove everything between the `<body>` and `</body>` tags. The remaining code should look similar to the following:

```
<!DOCTYPE html>
<html lang="en">
<head>
  <meta charset="utf-8" />
  <title>#(title) | Acronyms</title>
</head>
<body>
```

```
</body>
</html>
```

This forms your base template and will be the same for all pages. Between the `<body>` and `</body>` tags add:

```
#import("content")
```

This uses Leaf's `#import()` tag to retrieve the `content` variable. To use the template, open **index.leaf** replace its contents with the following:

```
#extend("base"):

#endextend
```

This tells Leaf to extend the base template when rendering **index.leaf**. **base.leaf** requires one variable, `content`. Add the following, in between `#extend` and `#endextend` to define `content`:

```
#export("content"):
  <h1>Acronyms</h1>

  #if(acronyms):
    <table>
      <thead>
        <tr>
          <th>Short</th>
          <th>Long</th>
        </tr>
      </thead>
      <tbody>
        #for(acronym in acronyms):
          <tr>
            <td>
              <a href="/acronyms/#(acronym.id)">
                #(acronym.short)
              </a>
            </td>
            <td>#(acronym.long)</td>
          </tr>
        #endfor
      </tbody>
    </table>
  #else:
    <h2>There aren't any acronyms yet!</h2>
  #endif
#endexport
```

This takes the HTML specific to **index.leaf** and wraps it in an `#export` tag. When Leaf renders **base.leaf** as required by **index.leaf**, it takes `content` and inserts it into the base template.

Save the files, then build and run. Open your browser and enter the URL **http://localhost:8080/**. The page renders as before:

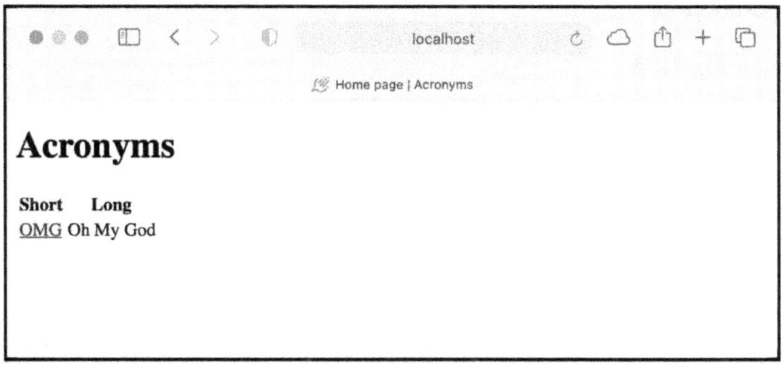

> **Note**: If you started fresh with the starter project from this chapter, you'll need to set a custom working directory in Xcode. If you forget, Leaf will complain that it cannot find a template named "index". See Chapter 14, "Templating with Leaf", for more information.

Next, open **acronym.leaf** and change it to use the base template by replacing its contents with the following:

```
#extend("base"):
  #export("content"):
    <h1>#(acronym.short)</h1>
    <h2>#(acronym.long)</h2>

    <p>Created by #(user.name)</p>
  #endexport
#endextend
```

Again, the changes made were:

- Remove all the HTML that now lives in the base template.
- Extend the base template to bring in the common code and render `content`.
- Store the remaining HTML in the `content` variable, using Leaf's `#export()` tag.

Save the file and, in your browser, navigate to an acronym page. The page renders as before with the new base template:

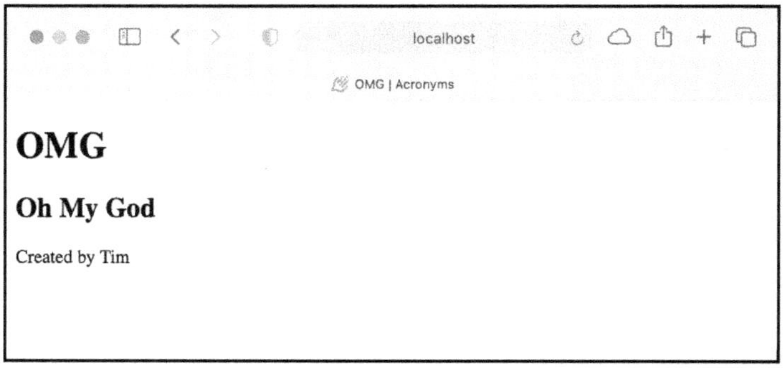

> **Note**: In debug mode, you can refresh pages to pick up Leaf changes. In release mode, Leaf caches the pages for performance, so you must restart your application to see changes.

Bootstrap

Bootstrap is an open-source, front-end framework for websites, originally built by Twitter. It provides easy-to-use components that you add to web pages. It's a mobile-first library and makes it simple to build a site that works on screens of all sizes.

To use Bootstrap go to getbootstrap.com and click **Get Started**. At the time of writing, Bootstrap is on version 4.5. Bootstrap provides a CSS file to provide the styling and Javascript files that provide functionality for Bootstrap components. You need to include these files in all pages. Since you've created a **base.leaf** template, this is easy to do!

On the **Get Started** page, find the **Starter template** section.

In the starter template's `<head>` section, copy the two `<meta>` tags — labeled "Required meta tags" — and the `<link>` tag for the CSS — labeled "Bootstrap CSS." Replace the current `<meta>` tag in **base.leaf** with the new tags.

At the bottom of the starter template, copy the two `<script>` tags from the Option 1. Put them in the **base.leaf** template, below `#import("content")` and before the `</body>` tag.

Save the file then, in your browser, visit **http://localhost:8080**. You'll notice the page looks a bit different. The page is now using Bootstrap's styling, but you need to add Bootstrap-specific components to make your page really shine.

Open **base.leaf** and replace `#import("content")` with the following:

```
<div class="container mt-3">
  #import("content")
</div>
```

This wraps the page's content in a **container**, which is a basic layout element in Bootstrap. The `<div>` also applies a margin at the top of the container.

If you save the file and refresh your web page, you'll see the page now has some space around the sides and top, and no longer looks cramped:

Navigation

The TIL website currently consists of two pages: a home page and an acronym detail page. As more and more pages are added, it can become difficult to find your way around the site. Currently, if you go to an acronym's detail page, there is no easy way to get back to the home page! Adding navigation to a website makes it more friendly for users.

HTML defines a `<nav>` element to denote the navigation section of a page. Bootstrap supplies classes and utilities to extend this for styling and mobile support. Open **base.leaf** and add the following above `<div class="container mt-3">`:

```
<!-- 1 -->
<nav class="navbar navbar-expand-md navbar-dark bg-dark">
  <!-- 2 -->
```

```
    <a class="navbar-brand" href="/">TIL</a>
    <!-- 3 -->
    <button class="navbar-toggler" type="button"
    data-toggle="collapse" data-target="\#navbarSupportedContent"
    aria-controls="navbarSupportedContent" aria-expanded="false"
    aria-label="Toggle navigation">
      <span class="navbar-toggler-icon"></span>
    </button>
    <!-- 4 -->
    <div class="collapse navbar-collapse"
    id="navbarSupportedContent">
      <!-- 5 -->
      <ul class="navbar-nav mr-auto">
        <!-- 6 -->
        <li class="nav-item
          #if(title == "Home page"): active #endif">
            <a href="/" class="nav-link">Home</a>
        </li>
      </ul>
    </div>
  </nav>
```

Here's what this new code does:

1. Define a <nav> element with some class names for styling. Bootstrap uses these classes to specify a Bootstrap navigation bar, allow the navigation bar to be full size in medium-sized screens and apply a dark theme to the bar.
2. Specify a root link to the home page.
3. Create a button that toggles the navigation bar for small screen sizes. This shows and hides the `navbarSupportedContent` section defined in the next element. Note that the link to the `navBarSupportContent` target uses an escaped # to avoid conflicting with Leaf's tag.
4. Create a collapsible section for small screens.
5. Define a list of navigation links to display. Bootstrap styles these `nav-item` list items for a navigation bar instead of a standard bulleted list.
6. Add a link for the home page. This uses Leaf's `#if` tag to check the page title. If the title is set to "Home page" then Leaf adds the `active` class to the item. This styles the link differently when on that page.

Save the file and refresh the page in the browser. The page is starting to look professional! For small screens you'll get a toggle button, which opens the navigation links:

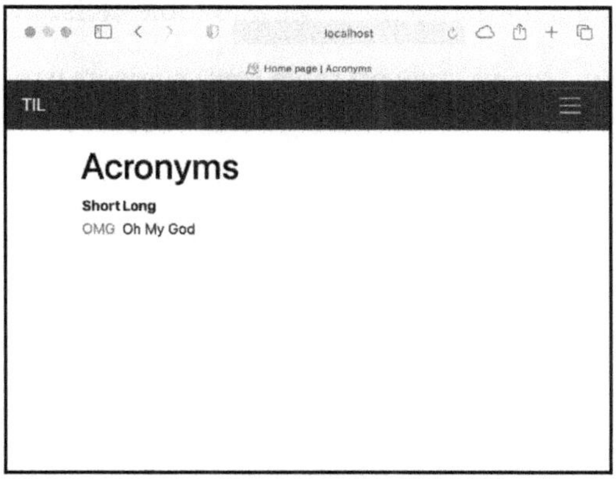

On larger screens, the navigation bar shows all the links:

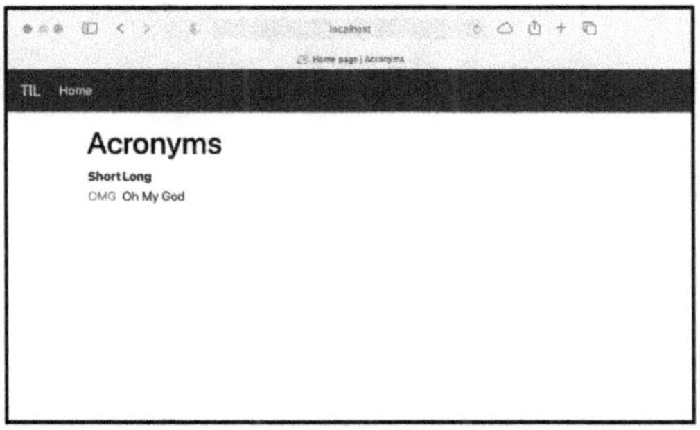

Now when you're on an acronym's detail page, you can use the navigation bar to return to the home screen!

Tables

Bootstrap provides classes to style tables with ease. Open **index.leaf** and replace the `<table>` tag with the following:

```
<table class="table table-bordered table-hover">
```

This adds the following Bootstrap classes to the table:

- `table`: apply standard Bootstrap table styling.
- `table-bordered`: add a border to the table and table cells.
- `table-hover`: enable a hover style on table rows so users can more easily see what row they are looking at.

Next, replace the `<thead>` tag with the following:

```
<thead class="thead-light">
```

This makes the table head stand out. Save the file and refresh the page. The home page now looks even more professional!

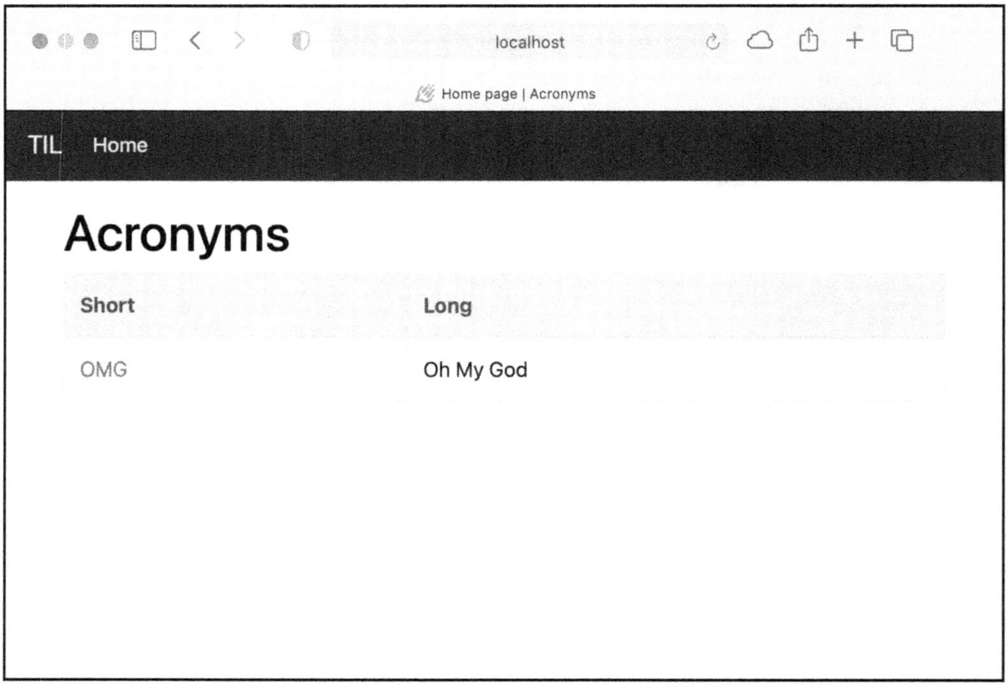

Serving files

Almost every website needs to be able to host static files, such as images or style sheets. Most of the time, you'll do this using a CDN (Content Delivery Network) or a server such as Nginx or Apache. However, Vapor provides a `FileMiddleware` module to serve files.

To enable this, open **configure.swift** in Xcode. At the start of `configure(_:)` add the following (uncomment it if the line already exists):

```
app.middleware.use(
  FileMiddleware(publicDirectory: app.directory.publicDirectory)
)
```

This adds `FileMiddleware` to the Application's middleware to serve files. It serves files in the **Public** directory in your project. For example, if you have a file in **Public/styles** called **stylesheet.css**, it is accessible from the path **/styles/stylesheet.css**.

The starter project for this chapter contains an **images** directory in the **Public** folder, with a logo inside for the website. If you've continued with your own project from the previous chapters, copy the **images** folder into your existing **Public** folder. Build and run, then open **index.leaf**.

Above `<h1>Acronyms</h1>` add the following:

```
<img src="/images/logo.png"
 class="mx-auto d-block" alt="TIL Logo" />
```

This adds an `<img>` tag — for an image — to the page. The page loads the image from **/images/logo.png**, which corresponds to **Public/images/logo.png** served by the `FileMiddleware`. The `mx-auto` and `d-block` classes tell Bootstrap to align the image centrally in the page. Finally the `alt` value provides an alternative title for the image. Screen readers uses this to help accessibility users.

Save the file and visit **http://localhost:8080** in the browser. The home page now displays the image, putting the final touches on the page:

Users

The website now has a page that displays all the acronyms and a page that displays an acronym's details. Next, you'll add pages to view all the users and a specific user's information.

Create a new file in **Resources/Views** called **user.leaf**. Implement the template like so:

```
<!-- 1 -->
#extend("base"):
  <!-- 2 -->
  #export("content"):
    <!-- 3 -->
    <h1>#(user.name)</h1>
    <!-- 4 -->
    <h2>#(user.username)</h2>

    <!-- 5 -->
    #if(count(acronyms) > 0):
      <table class="table table-bordered table-hover">
        <thead class="thead-light">
          <tr>
            <th>Short</th>
            <th>Long</th>
          </tr>
        </thead>
        <tbody>
          <!-- 6 -->
          #for(acronym in acronyms):
            <tr>
              <td>
                <a href="/acronyms/#(acronym.id)">
                  #(acronym.short)
                </a>
              </td>
              <td>#(acronym.long)</td>
            </tr>
          #endfor
        </tbody>
      </table>
    #else:
      <h2>There aren't any acronyms yet!</h2>
    #endif
  #endexport
#endextend
```

Here's what the new page does:

1. Extend the base template to bring in all the common HTML.
2. Set the `content` variable for the base template.
3. Display the user's name in an `<h1>` heading.
4. Display the user's username in an `<h2>` heading.
5. Use a combination of Leaf's `#if` tag and `count` tag to see if the user has any acronyms.
6. Display a table of acronyms from the injected `acronyms` property. This table is identical to the one in the **index.leaf** template.

In Xcode, open **WebsiteController.swift**. At the bottom of the file create a new context for the user page:

```
struct UserContext: Encodable {
  let title: String
  let user: User
  let acronyms: [Acronym]
}
```

This context has properties for:

- The title of the page, which is the user's name.
- The user object to which the page refers.
- The acronyms created by this user.

Next, add the following handler below `acronymHandler(_:)` for this page:

```
// 1
func userHandler(_ req: Request)
  -> EventLoopFuture<View> {
    // 2
    User.find(req.parameters.get("userID"), on: req.db)
        .unwrap(or: Abort(.notFound))
        .flatMap { user in
        // 3
        user.$acronyms.get(on: req.db).flatMap { acronyms in
          // 4
          let context = UserContext(
            title: user.name,
            user: user,
            acronyms: acronyms)
          return req.view.render("user", context)
```

```
            }
        }
    }
```

Here's what the route handler does:

1. Define the route handler for the user page that returns `EventLoopFuture<View>`.
2. Get the user from the request's parameters and unwrap the future.
3. Get the user's acronyms using the `@Children` property wrapper's project value and unwrap the future.
4. Create a `UserContext`, then render **user.leaf**, returning the result. In this case, you're not setting the acronyms array to `nil` if it's empty. This is not required as you're checking the count in template.

Finally, add the following to register this route at the end of `boot(routes:)`:

```
routes.get("users", ":userID", use: userHandler)
```

This registers the route for **/users/<USER ID>**, like the API. Build and run.

Next, open **acronym.leaf** to add a link to the new user page by replacing `<p>Created by #(user.name)</p>` with the following:

```
<p>Created by <a href="/users/#(user.id)/">#(user.name)</a></p>
```

Save the file, then open your browser. Go to **http://localhost:8080** and click one of the acronyms. The page now displays a link to the creating user's page. Click the link visit your newly created page:

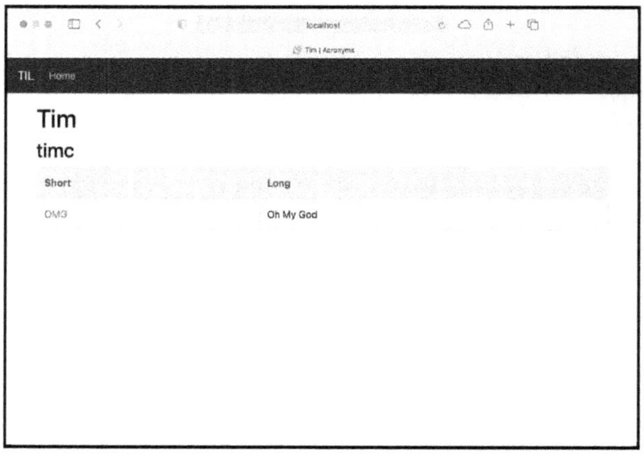

Listing all users

The final page for you to implement in this chapter displays a list of all users. Create a new file in **Resources/Views** called **allUsers.leaf**. Open the file and add the following:

```
#extend("base"):
  <!-- 1 -->
  #export("content"):
    <!-- 2 -->
    <h1>All Users</h1>

    <!-- 3 -->
    #if(count(users) > 0):
      <table class="table table-bordered table-hover">
        <thead class="thead-light">
          <tr>
            <th>Username</th>
            <th>Name</th>
          </tr>
        </thead>
        <tbody>
          #for(user in users):
            <tr>
              <td>
                <a href="/users/#(user.id)">
                  #(user.username)
                </a>
              </td>
              <td>#(user.name)</td>
            </tr>
          #endfor
        </tbody>
      </table>
    #else:
      <h2>There aren't any users yet!</h2>
    #endif
  #endexport
#endextend
```

Here's what the new page does:

1. Set the `content` variable for the base template.
2. Display an `<h1>` heading for "All Users".
3. See if the context provides any users. If so, create a table that contains two columns: username and name. This is like the acronyms table.

Save the file and open **WebsiteController.swift** in Xcode. At the bottom of the file, create a new context for the page:

```
struct AllUsersContext: Encodable {
  let title: String
  let users: [User]
}
```

This context contains a title and an array of users. Next, add the following below `userHandler(_:)` to create a route handler for the new page:

```
// 1
func allUsersHandler(_ req: Request)
  -> EventLoopFuture<View> {
    // 2
    User.query(on: req.db)
      .all()
      .flatMap { users in
        // 3
        let context = AllUsersContext(
          title: "All Users",
          users: users)
        return req.view.render("allUsers", context)
    }
}
```

Here's what the new route handler does:

1. Define a route handler for the "All Users" page that returns `EventLoopFuture<View>`.
2. Get the users from the database and unwrap the future.
3. Create an `AllUsersContext` and render the **allUsers.leaf** template, then return the result.

Next, register the route at the bottom of `boot(routes:)`:

```
routes.get("users", use: allUsersHandler)
```

This registers the route for **/users/**, like the API. Build and run, then open **base.leaf**. Add a link to the new page in the navigation bar above the `</ul>` tag:

```
<li class="nav-item #if(title == "All Users"): active #endif">
  <a href="/users" class="nav-link">All Users</a>
</li>
```

This adds a link to **/users** and sets the link to `active` if the page title is "All Users".

Save the file and open your browser.

Go to **http://localhost:8080** and you'll see a new link in the navigation bar. Click **All Users** and you'll see your new "All Users" page:

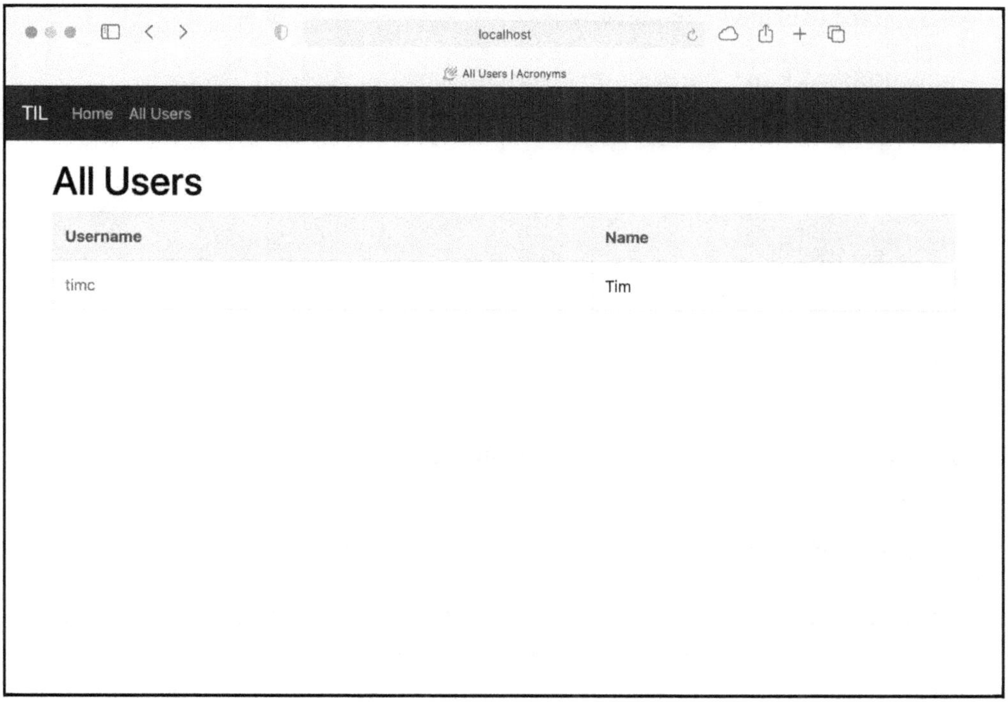

Sharing templates

The final thing to do in this chapter is to refactor your acronyms table. Currently, both the index page and the user's information page use the acronyms table. However, you've duplicated the code for the table. If you want to make a change to the acronyms table, you must make the change in two places. This is a problem templates should solve!

Create a new file in **Resources/Views** called **acronymsTable.leaf**. Open **user.leaf** and copy the table code into **acronymsTable.leaf**. The new file should contain the following:

```
#if(count(acronyms) > 0):
  <table class="table table-bordered table-hover">
    <thead class="thead-light">
      <tr>
```

```
          <th>Short</th>
          <th>Long</th>
        </tr>
      </thead>
      <tbody>
        #for(acronym in acronyms):
          <tr>
            <td>
              <a href="/acronyms/#(acronym.id)">
                #(acronym.short)
              </a>
            </td>
            <td>#(acronym.long)</td>
          </tr>
        #endfor
      </tbody>
    </table>
#else:
  <h2>There aren't any acronyms yet!</h2>
#endif
```

In **user.leaf**, remove the code that's now in **acronymsTable.leaf** and insert the following in it's place:

```
#extend("acronymsTable")
```

Like using **base.leaf**, this extends the contents of **acronymsTable.leaf** into your template. Save the file and in your browser, navigate to a user's page — it will show the user's acronyms, like before.

Open **index.leaf** and remove `#if(acronyms)` and all the code inside it. Again, insert the following in its place:

```
#extend("acronymsTable")
```

Save the file. Finally, open **WebsiteController.swift** and change `IndexContext` so `acronyms` is no longer optional:

```
let acronyms: [Acronym]
```

acronymsTable.leaf checks the count of the array to determine whether to show a table or not. This is easier to read and understand. In `indexHandler(_:)`, remove `acronymsData` and pass the array of acronyms directory to `IndexContext`:

```
let context = IndexContext(
  title: "Home page",
  acronyms: acronyms)
```

Build and run the application and navigate to **http://localhost:8080** in your browser. All the acronyms will still be there.

Where to go from here?

Now that you've completed the chapter, the website for the TIL application looks much better! Using the Bootstrap framework allows you to style the site easily. This makes a better impression on users visiting your application.

In the next chapters, you'll learn how to go from just displaying information on the page to implementing all the functionality to be able to create acronyms, categories and users.

Chapter 16: Making a Simple Web App, Part 1

By Tim Condon

In the previous chapters, you learned how to display data in a website and how to make the pages look nice with Bootstrap. In this chapter, you'll learn how to create different models and how to edit acronyms.

Categories

You've created pages for viewing acronyms and users. Now it's time to create similar pages for categories. Open **WebsiteController.swift**. At the bottom of the file, add a context for the "All Categories" page:

```
struct AllCategoriesContext: Encodable {
  // 1
  let title = "All Categories"
  // 2
  let categories: [Category]
}
```

Here's what this does:

1. Define the page's title for the template.
2. Define an array of categories to display in the page.

Next, add the following under `allUsersHandler(_:)` to create a new route handler for the “All Categories” page:

```
func allCategoriesHandler(_ req: Request)
  -> EventLoopFuture<View> {
  // 1
  Category.query(on: req.db).all().flatMap { categories in
    // 2
    let context = AllCategoriesContext(categories: categories)
    // 3
    return req.view.render("allCategories", context)
  }
}
```

Here’s what this route handler does:

1. Get all the categories from the database like before.
2. Create an `AllCategoriesContext`. Notice that the context includes the query result directly, since Leaf can handle futures.
3. Render the **allCategories.leaf** template with the provided context.

Create a new file in **Resources/Views** called **allCategories.leaf** for the “All Categories” page. Open the new file and add the following:

```
#extend("base"):
  <!-- 1 -->
  #export("content"):
    <h1>All Categories</h1>

    <!-- 2 -->
    #if(count(categories) > 0):
      <table class="table table-bordered table-hover">
        <thead class="thead-light">
          <tr>
            <th>Name</th>
          </tr>
        </thead>
        <tbody>
          <!-- 3 -->
          #for(category in categories):
            <tr>
              <td>
                <a href="/categories/#(category.id)">
                  #(category.name)
                </a>
              </td>
            </tr>
          #endfor
        </tbody>
```

```
      </table>
    #else:
      <h2>There aren't any categories yet!</h2>
    #endif
  #endexport
#endextend
```

This template is like the table for all acronyms, but the important points are:

1. Set the content variable for use by **base.leaf**.
2. Check if any categories exist.
3. Loop through each category and add a row to the table with the name, linking to a category page.

Now, you need a way to display all of the acronyms in a category. Open, **WebsiteController.swift** and add the following context at the bottom of the file for the new category page:

```
struct CategoryContext: Encodable {
  // 1
  let title: String
  // 2
  let category: Category
  // 3
  let acronyms: [Acronym]
}
```

Here's what the context contains:

1. A title for the page; you'll set this as the category name.
2. The category for the page.
3. The category's acronyms.

Next, add the following under allCategoriesHandler(_:) to create a route handler for the page:

```
func categoryHandler(_ req: Request)
  -> EventLoopFuture<View> {
  // 1
  Category.find(req.parameters.get("categoryID"), on: req.db)
    .unwrap(or: Abort(.notFound)).flatMap { category in
      // 2
      category.$acronyms.get(on: req.db).flatMap { acronyms in
        // 3
        let context = CategoryContext(
```

```
            title: category.name,
            category: category,
            acronyms: acronyms)
          // 4
          return req.view.render("category", context)
        }
    }
}
```

Here's what the route handler does:

1. Get the category from the request's parameters and unwrap the returned future.
2. Perform a query get all the acronyms for the category using Fluent's helpers.
3. Create a context for the page.
4. Return a rendered view using the **category.leaf** template.

Create the new template file, **category.leaf**, in **Resources/Views**. Open the new file and add the following:

```
#extend("base"):
  #export("content"):
    <h1>#(category.name)</h1>

    #extend("acronymsTable")
  #endexport
#endextend
```

This is almost the same as the user's page just with the category name for the title. Notice that you're using the **acronymsTable.leaf** template to display the table to acronyms. This avoids duplicating yet another table and, again, shows the power of templates. Open **base.leaf** and add the following after the link to the all users page:

```
<li class="nav-item
 #if(title == "All Categories"): active #endif">
  <a href="/categories" class="nav-link">All Categories</a>
</li>
```

This adds a new link to the navigation on the site for the all categories page. Finally, open **WebsiteController.swift** and, at the end of `boot(routes:)`, add the following to register the new routes:

```
// 1
routes.get("categories", use: allCategoriesHandler)
// 2
routes.get("categories", ":categoryID", use: categoryHandler)
```

Here's what this does:

1. Register a route at **/categories** that accepts GET requests and calls `allCategoriesHandler(_:)`.
2. Register a route at **/categories/<CATEGORY ID>** that accepts GET requests and calls `categoryHandler(_:)`.

Build and run, then go to **http://localhost:8080/** in your browser. Click the new **All Categories** link in the menu and you'll go to the new "All Categories" page:

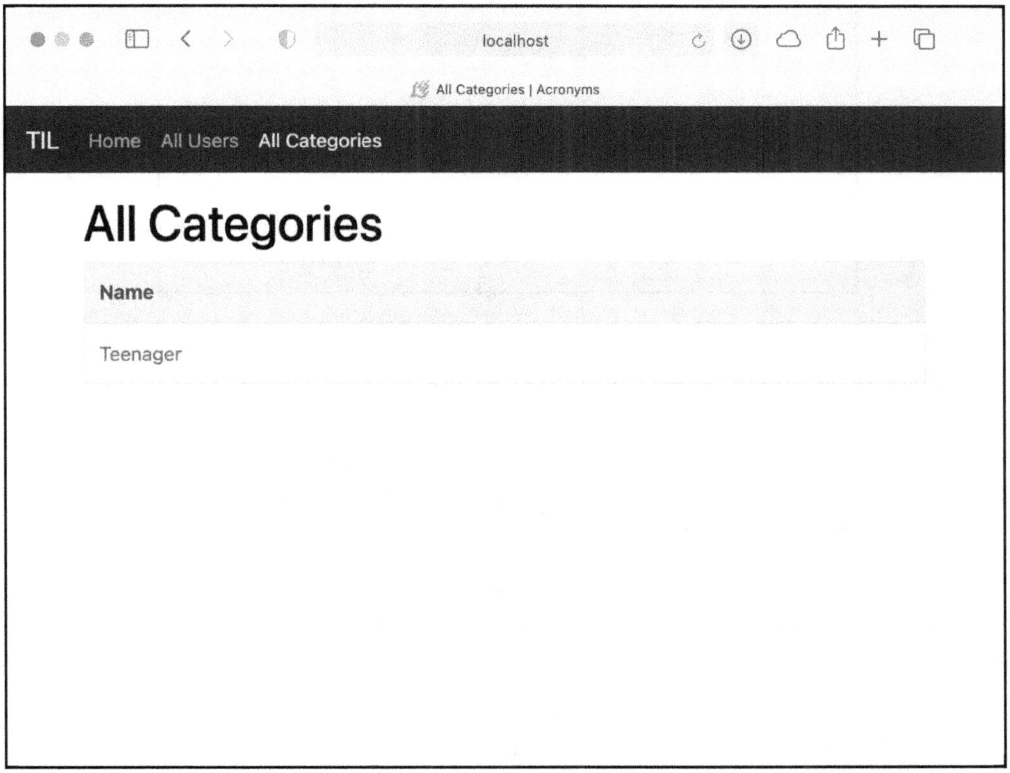

Click a category and you'll see the category information page with all the acronyms for that category:

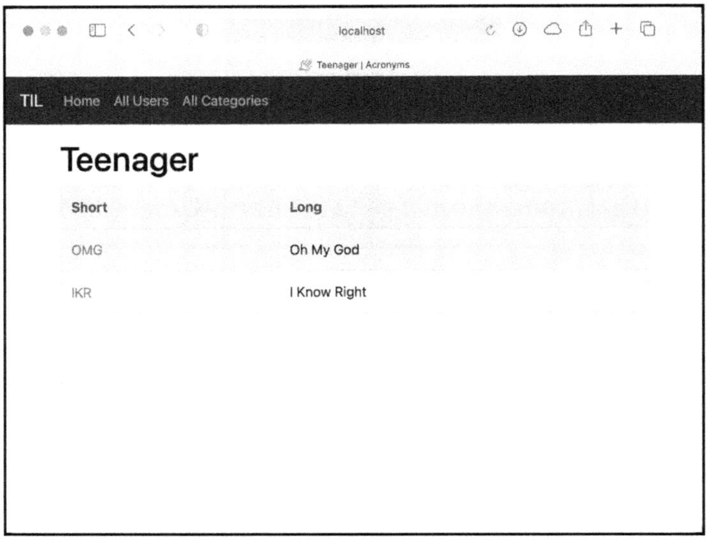

Create acronyms

To create acronyms in a web application, you must actually implement *two* routes. You handle a GET request to display the form to fill in. Then, you handle a POST request to accept the data the form sends.

The page to create an acronym needs a list of all the users to permit selecting which user owns the acronym. Create a context at the bottom of **WebsiteController.swift** to represent this:

```
struct CreateAcronymContext: Encodable {
  let title = "Create An Acronym"
  let users: [User]
}
```

Next, create a route handler to present the "Create An Acronym" page under `categoryHandler(_:)`:

```
func createAcronymHandler(_ req: Request)
  -> EventLoopFuture<View> {
  // 1
  User.query(on: req.db).all().flatMap { users in
    // 2
    let context = CreateAcronymContext(users: users)
```

```
    // 3
    return req.view.render("createAcronym", context)
  }
}
```

Here's what this does:

1. Get all the users from the database.
2. Create a context for the template.
3. Render the page using the **createAcronym.leaf** template.

Next, add the following below `createAcronymHandler(_:)` to create a route handler for the POST request:

```
// 1
func createAcronymPostHandler(_ req: Request) throws
  -> EventLoopFuture<Response> {
  // 2
  let data = try req.content.decode(CreateAcronymData.self)
  let acronym = Acronym(
    short: data.short,
    long: data.long,
    userID: data.userID)
  // 3
  return acronym.save(on: req.db).flatMapThrowing {
      // 4
      guard let id = acronym.id else {
        throw Abort(.internalServerError)
      }
      // 5
      return req.redirect(to: "/acronyms/\(id)")
  }
}
```

Here's what this does:

1. Declare a route handler that returns `EventLoopFuture<Response>`.
2. Decode the data from the request and use it to create an acronym. You do the same thing in `AcronymsController`.
3. Save the acronym and resolve the future. Note the use of `flatMapThrowing(_:)` here, since the closure doesn't return a future but can throw.
4. Ensure that the ID is set, otherwise throw a **500 Internal Server Error**.
5. Redirect to the page for the newly created acronym.

Next, to register these routes, add the following to the bottom of `boot(routes:)`:

```
// 1
routes.get("acronyms", "create", use: createAcronymHandler)
// 2
routes.post("acronyms", "create", use: createAcronymPostHandler)
```

Here's what the code does:

1. Register a route at **/acronyms/create** that accepts GET requests and calls `createAcronymHandler(_:)`.
2. Register a route at **/acronyms/create** that accepts POST requests and calls `createAcronymPostHandler(_:)`.

You now need a template to display the create acronym form. Create a new file in **Resources/Views** called **createAcronym.leaf**. Open the file and add the following:

```
<!-- 1 -->
#extend("base"):
  #export("content"):
    <h1>#(title)</h1>

    <!-- 2 -->
    <form method="post">
      <!-- 3 -->
      <div class="form-group">
        <label for="short">Acronym</label>
        <input type="text" name="short" class="form-control"
        id="short"/>
      </div>

      <!-- 4 -->
      <div class="form-group">
        <label for="long">Meaning</label>
        <input type="text" name="long" class="form-control"
        id="long"/>
      </div>

      <div class="form-group">
        <label for="userID">User</label>
        <!-- 5 -->
        <select name="userID" class="form-control" id="userID">
          <!-- 6 -->
          #for(user in users):
            <option value="#(user.id)">
              #(user.name)
            </option>
          #endfor
        </select>
      </div>
```

```
      <!-- 7 -->
      <button type="submit" class="btn btn-primary">
        Submit
      </button>
    </form>
  #endexport
#endextend
```

Here's what the template does:

1. Extend `base.leaf` and define the `content` variable required.
2. Create an HTML form. Set the method to POST. This means the browser sends the data to the same URL using a POST request when a user submits the form.
3. Create a group for the acronym's short value. Use HTML's `<input>` element to allow a user to insert text. The `name` property tells the browser what the key for this input should be when sending the data in the request.
4. Create a group for the acronym's long value using HTML's `<input>` element.
5. Create a group for the acronym's user. Use HTML's `<select>` element to display a drop-down menu of the different users.
6. Use Leaf's `#for()` loop to iterate through the provided users and add each as an option on the `<select>`.
7. Create a submit button the user can click to send the form to your web app.

Finally, add a link to the new page in **base.leaf** just before the `</ul>` tag:

```
<!-- 1 -->
<li class="nav-item
 #if(title == "Create An Acronym"): active #endif">
  <!-- 2 -->
  <a href="/acronyms/create" class="nav-link">
    Create An Acronym
  </a>
</li>
```

Here's what the code does:

1. Add a new navigation item to the nav bar. If you're on the "Create An Acronym" page, mark the item active.
2. Add a link to the create page.

Build and run, then open your browser. Navigate to **http://localhost:8080** and you'll see a new option, "Create An Acronym", in the navigation bar. Click the link to go to the new page. Fill in the form and click **Submit**.

The app redirects you to the new acronym's page:

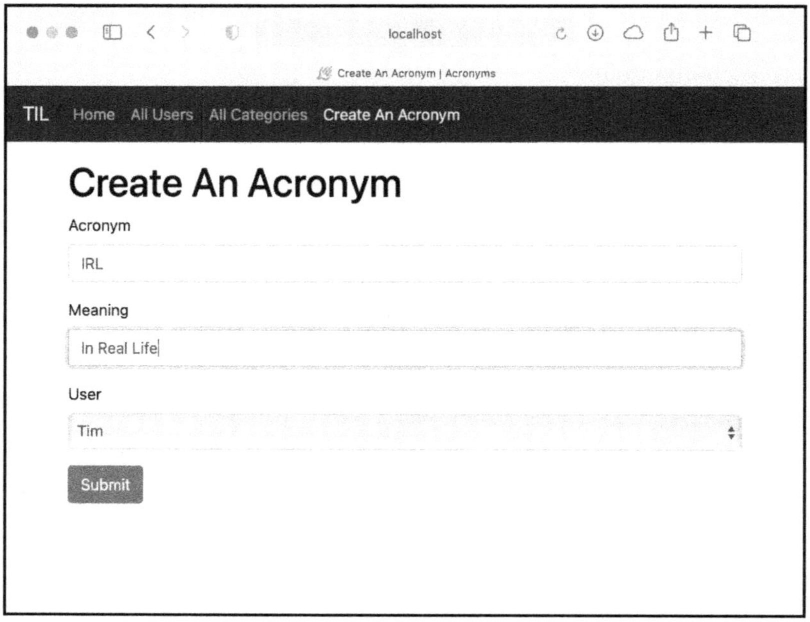

Editing acronyms

You now know how to create acronyms through the website. But what about editing an acronym? Thanks to Leaf, you can reuse many of the same components to allow users to edit acronyms. Open **WebsiteController.swift**.

At the end of the file, add the following context for editing an acronym:

```
struct EditAcronymContext: Encodable {
  // 1
  let title = "Edit Acronym"
  // 2
  let acronym: Acronym
  // 3
  let users: [User]
  // 4
  let editing = true
}
```

Here's what the context contains:

1. The title for the page: "Edit Acronym".
2. The acronym to edit.
3. An array of users to display in the form.
4. A flag to tell the template that the page is for editing an acronym.

Next, add the following route handler below `createAcronymPostHandler(_:)` to show the edit acronym form:

```
func editAcronymHandler(_ req: Request)
  -> EventLoopFuture<View> {
  // 1
  let acronymFuture = Acronym
    .find(req.parameters.get("acronymID"), on: req.db)
    .unwrap(or: Abort(.notFound))
  // 2
  let userQuery = User.query(on: req.db).all()
  // 3
  return acronymFuture.and(userQuery)
    .flatMap { acronym, users in
      // 4
      let context = EditAcronymContext(
        acronym: acronym,
        users: users)
      // 5
      return req.view.render("createAcronym", context)
  }
}
```

Here's what this route does:

1. Create a future to get the acronym to edit from the request's parameters.
2. Create a future to get all the users from the DB.
3. Use `.and(_:)` to chain the futures together and `flatMap(_:)` to wait for both futures to complete.
4. Create a context to edit the acronym, passing in all the users.
5. Render the page using the **createAcronym.leaf** template, the same template used for the create page.

Next, add the following route handler for the POST request from the edit acronym page below `editAcronymHandler(_:)`:

```
func editAcronymPostHandler(_ req: Request) throws
  -> EventLoopFuture<Response> {
  // 1
  let updateData =
    try req.content.decode(CreateAcronymData.self)
  // 2
  return Acronym
    .find(req.parameters.get("acronymID"), on: req.db)
    .unwrap(or: Abort(.notFound)).flatMap { acronym in
      // 3
      acronym.short = updateData.short
      acronym.long = updateData.long
      acronym.$user.id = updateData.userID
      // 4
      guard let id = acronym.id else {
        let error = Abort(.internalServerError)
        return req.eventLoop.future(error: error)
      }
      // 5
      let redirect = req.redirect(to: "/acronyms/\(id)")
      return acronym.save(on: req.db).transform(to: redirect)
  }
}
```

Here's what the route does:

1. Decode the request body to `CreateAcronymData`.
2. Get the acronym to edit from the request's parameters and resolve the future.
3. Update the acronym with the new data.
4. Ensure the ID is set, otherwise return a failed future with a **500 Internal Server Error**.
5. Save the updated acronym and transform the result to redirect to the updated acronym's page.

Next, add the following to register the two new routes at the bottom of `boot(routes:)`:

```
routes.get(
  "acronyms", ":acronymID", "edit",
   use: editAcronymHandler)
routes.post(
  "acronyms", ":acronymID", "edit",
  use: editAcronymPostHandler)
```

This registers a route at **/acronyms/<ACRONYM ID>/edit** to accept GET requests that calls `editAcronymHandler(_:)`. It also registers a route to handle POST requests to the same URL that calls `editAcronymPostHandler(_:)`.

Open **createAcronym.leaf** and change the template to accommodate editing an acronym. First, replace the input for the acronym short to accommodate editing:

```
<input type="text" name="short" class="form-control"
 id="short" #if(editing): value="#(acronym.short)" #endif/>
```

If the `editing` flag is set, this sets the `value` attribute of the `<input>` to the acronym's `short` property. This is how you pre-fill the form for editing. Do the same for the acronym's long input:

```
<input type="text" name="long" class="form-control"
 id="long" #if(editing): value="#(acronym.long)" #endif/>
```

Replace the users' `<select>` option for editing:

```
<option value="#(user.id)"
 #if(editing): #if(acronym.user.id == user.id):
   selected #endif #endif>
  #(user.name)
</option>
```

This sets the `<option>`'s `selected` property if the user's ID matches the acronym's `userID`. This makes that option in the drop-down menu appear as the selected one. Next, replace the button for submitting the form:

```
<button type="submit" class="btn btn-primary">
  #if(editing): Update #else: Submit #endif
</button>
```

This uses Leaf's `#if()/else` tags to set the text of the button to "Update" or "Submit" depending on the page's mode.

Finally, open **acronym.leaf** and add a button to edit that acronym at the bottom of `#export("content"):`:

```
<a class="btn btn-primary" href="/acronyms/#(acronym.id)/edit"
 role="button">Edit</a>
```

This creates an HTML link to **/acronyms/<ACRONYM ID>/edit** and uses Bootstrap to style the link as a button. Save the files and in Xcode, build and run the app. Open **http://localhost:8080/** in your browser.

Open an acronym page and there's now an **Edit** button at the bottom:

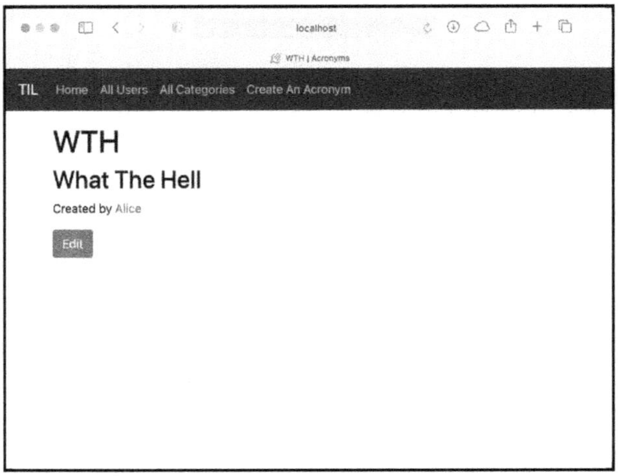

Click **Edit** to go to the edit acronym page with all the information pre-populated. The title and button are also different:

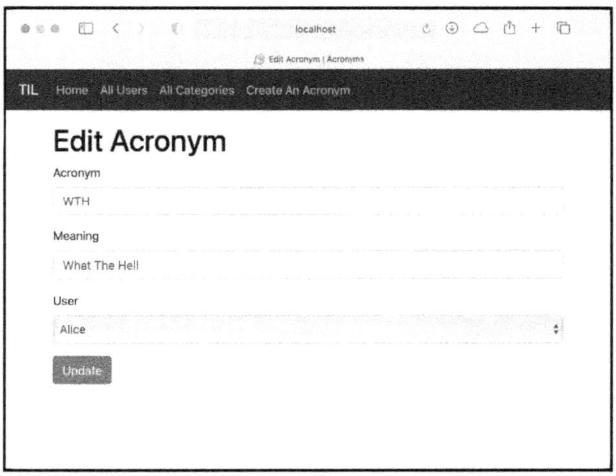

Change the acronym and click **Update**. The app redirects you to the acronym's page and you'll see the updated information.

Deleting acronyms

Unlike creating and editing acronyms, deleting an acronym only requires a single route. However, with web browsers there's no simple way to send a DELETE request.

Browsers can only send GET requests to request a page and POST requests to send data with forms.

> **Note**: It's possible to send a DELETE request with JavaScript, but that's outside the scope of this chapter.

To work around this, you'll send a POST request to a delete route.

Open, **WebsiteController.swift** and add the following route handler below `editAcronymPostHandler(_:)` to delete an acronym:

```
func deleteAcronymHandler(_ req: Request)
  -> EventLoopFuture<Response> {
  Acronym
    .find(req.parameters.get("acronymID"), on: req.db)
    .unwrap(or: Abort(.notFound)).flatMap { acronym in
      acronym.delete(on: req.db)
        .transform(to: req.redirect(to: "/"))
  }
}
```

This route extracts the acronym from the request's parameter, unwraps the future and calls `delete(on:)` on the acronym. The route then transforms the result to redirect the page to the home screen. Register the route at the bottom of `boot(routes:)`:

```
routes.post(
  "acronyms", ":acronymID", "delete",
  use: deleteAcronymHandler)
```

This registers a route at **/acronyms/<ACRONYM ID>/delete** to accept POST requests and call `deleteAcronymHandler(_:)`. Build and run. Open **acronym.leaf** and replace the edit button with the following:

```
<!-- 1 -->
<form method="post" action="/acronyms/#(acronym.id)/delete">
  <!-- 2 -->
  <a class="btn btn-primary" href="/acronyms/#(acronym.id)/edit"
   role="button">Edit</a> 
  <!-- 3 -->
  <input class="btn btn-danger" type="submit" value="Delete" />
</form>
```

Here's what the new code does:

1. Declare a form that sends a POST request. Set the `action` property to / **acronyms/<ACRONYM ID>/delete**. It's good practice to use a POST request for actions that modify the database, such as create or delete. This enables you to protect them with CSRF (Cross Site Request Forgery) tokens in the future, for example.
2. Incorporate the edit button that already exists on the page. This allows Bootstrap to align them. Use Bootstrap's button styling so the buttons look the same.
3. Create a submit button for the delete form.

Save the file, then open **http://localhost:8080/** in the browser. Open an acronym page and you'll see the delete button:

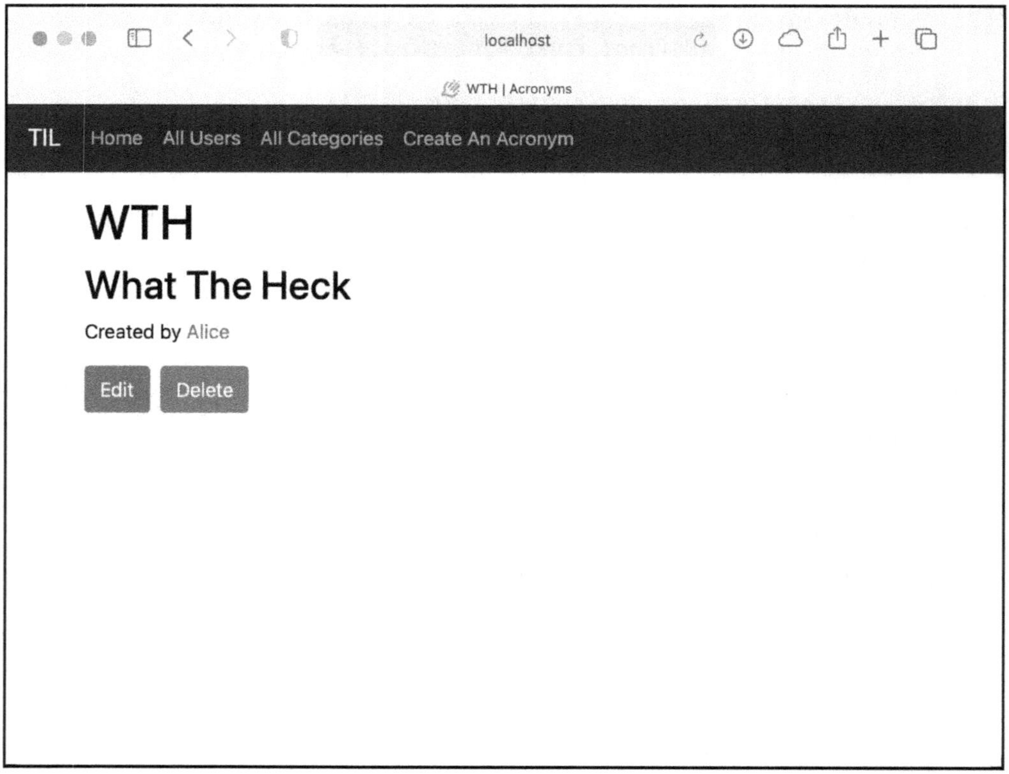

Click **Delete** to delete the acronym. The app redirects you to the homepage and the deleted acronym is no longer shown.

Where to go from here?

In this chapter, you learned how to display your categories and how to create, edit and delete acronyms. You still need to complete your support for categories, allowing your users to put acronyms into categories and remove them. You'll learn how to do that in the next chapter!

Chapter 17: Making a Simple Web App, Part 2

By Tim Condon

In the last chapter, you learned how to view categories and how to create, edit and delete acronyms. In this chapter, you'll learn how to allow users to add categories to acronyms in a user-friendly way.

Creating acronyms with categories

The final implementation task for the web app is to allow users to manage categories on acronyms. When using the API with a REST client such as the iOS app, you send multiple requests, one per category. However, this isn't feasible with a web browser.

The web app must accept all the information in one request and translate the request into the appropriate Fluent operations. Additionally, having to create categories before a user can select them doesn't create a good user experience.

Open **Category.swift** and add the following extension at the bottom:

```
extension Category {
  static func addCategory(
    _ name: String,
    to acronym: Acronym,
    on req: Request
  ) -> EventLoopFuture<Void> {
    // 1
    return Category.query(on: req.db)
      .filter(\.$name == name)
      .first()
      .flatMap { foundCategory in
        if let existingCategory = foundCategory {
          // 2
```

```
          return acronym.$categories
            .attach(existingCategory, on: req.db)
        } else {
          // 3
          let category = Category(name: name)
          // 4
          return category.save(on: req.db).flatMap {
            // 5
            acronym.$categories
              .attach(category, on: req.db)
          }
        }
      }
    }
  }
```

Here's what this new extension does:

1. Perform a query to search for a category with the provided name.
2. If the category exists, set up the relationship.
3. If the category doesn't exist, create a new `Category` object with the provided name.
4. Save the new category and unwrap the returned future.
5. Set up the relationship using the saved acronym.

Open **WebsiteController.swift** and add a new `Content` type at the bottom of the file to handle the accepting categories:

```
struct CreateAcronymFormData: Content {
  let userID: UUID
  let short: String
  let long: String
  let categories: [String]?
}
```

This is similar to the existing `CreateAcronymData` in **AcronymsController.swift**. `CreateAcronymFormData` adds an optional array of `Strings` to represent the categories. This allows users to submit existing *and* new categories instead of only existing ones.

Next, replace `createAcronymPostHandler(_:)` with the following:

```
func createAcronymPostHandler(_ req: Request) throws
  -> EventLoopFuture<Response> {
  // 1
```

```
    let data = try req.content.decode(CreateAcronymFormData.self)
    let acronym = Acronym(
      short: data.short,
      long: data.long,
      userID: data.userID)
    // 2
    return acronym.save(on: req.db).flatMap {
      guard let id = acronym.id else {
        // 3
        return req.eventLoop
          .future(error: Abort(.internalServerError))
      }
      // 4
      var categorySaves: [EventLoopFuture<Void>] = []
      // 5
      for category in data.categories ?? [] {
        categorySaves.append(
          Category.addCategory(
            category,
            to: acronym,
            on: req))
      }
      // 6
      let redirect = req.redirect(to: "/acronyms/\(id)")
      return categorySaves.flatten(on: req.eventLoop)
        .transform(to: redirect)
    }
  }
```

Here's what you changed:

1. Change `Content` type to decode `CreateAcronymFormData`.
2. Use `flatMap(_:)` instead of `map(:_)` as you now return an `EventLoopFuture` in the closure.
3. If the acronym save fails, return a failed `EventLoopFuture` instead of throwing the error as you can't throw inside `flatMap(_:)`.
4. Define an array of futures to store the save operations.
5. Loop through all the categories provided in the request and add the results of `Category.addCategory(_:to:on:)` to the array of futures.
6. Flatten the array to complete all the Fluent operations and transform the result to a `Response`. Redirect the page to the new acronym's page.

Next, you need to allow a user to specify categories when they create an acronym. Open **createAcronym.leaf** and, just above the `<button>` section, add the following:

```
<!-- 1 -->
<div class="form-group">
  <!-- 2 -->
  <label for="categories">Categories</label>
  <!-- 3 -->
  <select name="categories[]" class="form-control"
   id="categories" placeholder="Categories" multiple="multiple">
  </select>
</div>
```

Here's what this does:

1. Define a new `<div>` for categories that's styled with the `form-group` class.
2. Specify a label for the input.
3. Define a `<select>` input to allow a user to specify categories. The `multiple` attribute lets a user specify multiple options. The name `categories[]` allows the form to send the categories as a URL-encoded array.

Currently the form displays no categories. Using a `<select>` input only allows users to select pre-defined categories. To make this a nice user-experience, you'll use the Select2 JavaScript library (https://select2.org).

Open **base.leaf** and under `<link rel=stylesheet...` for the Bootstrap stylesheet add the following:

```
#if(title == "Create An Acronym" || title == "Edit Acronym"):
  <link rel="stylesheet" href="https://cdnjs.cloudflare.com/
ajax/libs/select2/4.0.13/css/select2.min.css" integrity="sha384-
KZO2FRYNmIHerhfYMjCIUaJeGBRXP7CN24SiNSG+wdDzgwvxWbl16wMVtWiJTcMt
" crossorigin="anonymous">
#endif
```

This adds the stylesheet for Select2 to the create and edit acronym pages. Note the complex Leaf statement. At the bottom of **base.leaf**, remove the first `<script>` tag for jQuery and replace it with the following:

```
<!-- 1 -->
<script src="https://code.jquery.com/jquery-3.5.1.min.js"
integrity="sha384-ZvpUoO/
+PpLXR1lu4jmpXWu80pZlYUAfxl5NsBMWOEPSjUn/6Z/hRTt8+pR6L4N2"
crossorigin="anonymous"></script>
<!-- 2 -->
#if(title == "Create An Acronym" || title == "Edit Acronym"):
```

```
  <script src="https://cdnjs.cloudflare.com/ajax/libs/
select2/4.0.13/js/select2.min.js" integrity="sha384-JnbsSLBmv2/
R0fUmF2XYIcAEMPHEA051Gitn9IjL4l89uFTIgtLF1+jqIqqd9FSk"
crossorigin="anonymous"></script>
  <!-- 3 -->
  <script src="/scripts/createAcronym.js"></script>
#endif
```

Here's what this does:

1. Include the full jQuery library. Bootstrap only requires the **slim** version, but Select2 requires functionality not included in the slim version, so must include the full library.
2. If the page is the create or edit acronym page, include the JavaScript for Select2.
3. Also include the local **createAcronym.js**.

Create a directory in **Public** called **scripts** for your local JavaScript file. In the new directory, create **createAcronym.js**. Open the new file and insert the following:

```
// 1
$.ajax({
  url: "/api/categories/",
  type: "GET",
  contentType: "application/json; charset=utf-8"
}).then(function (response) {
  var dataToReturn = [];
  // 2
  for (var i=0; i < response.length; i++) {
    var tagToTransform = response[i];
    var newTag = {
                   id: tagToTransform["name"],
                   text: tagToTransform["name"]
                 };
    dataToReturn.push(newTag);
  }
  // 3
  $("#categories").select2({
    // 4
    placeholder: "Select Categories for the Acronym",
    // 5
    tags: true,
    // 6
    tokenSeparators: [','],
    // 7
    data: dataToReturn
  });
});
```

Here's what the script does:

1. On page load, send a GET request to **/api/categories**. This gets all the categories in the TIL app.
2. Loop through each returned category and turn it into a JSON object and add it to `dataToReturn`. The JSON object looks like:

```
{
  "id": <id of the category>,
  "text": <name of the category>
}
```

3. Get the HTML element with the ID `categories` and call `select2()` on it. This enables Select2 on the `<select>` in the form.
4. Set the placeholder text on the Select2 input.
5. Enable tags in Select2. This allows users to dynamically create new categories that don't exist in the input.
6. Set the separator for Select2. When a user types , Select2 creates a new category from the entered text. This allows users to create categories with spaces.
7. Set the data — the options a user can choose from — to the existing categories.

Save the files, then build and run the app in Xcode. Navigate to the **Create An Acronym** page. The categories list allows you to input existing categories or create new ones. The list also allows you to add and remove the "tags" in a user-friendly way:

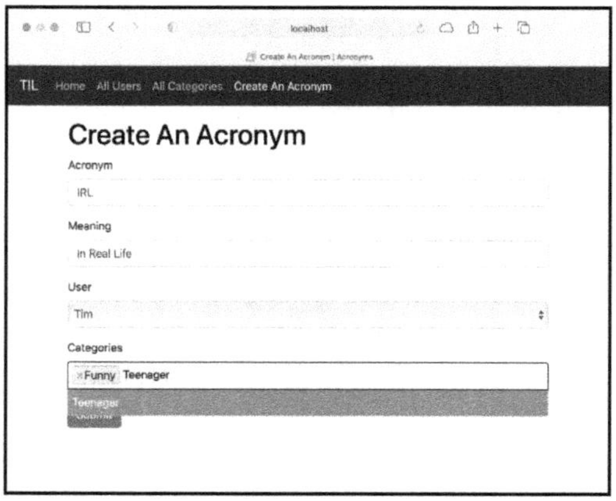

Displaying Categories

Now, open **acronym.leaf**. Under the "Created By" paragraph add the following:

```
<!-- 1 -->
#if(count(categories) > 0):
  <!-- 2 -->
  <h3>Categories</h3>
  <ul>
    <!-- 3 -->
    #for(category in categories):
      <li>
        <a href="/categories/#(category.id)">
          #(category.name)
        </a>
      </li>
    #endfor
  </ul>
#endif
```

Here's what this does:

1. Check if the template context has any categories.
2. If so, create a heading and a `<ul>` list.
3. Loop through the provided categories and add a link to each one.

Save the file and open **WebsiteController.swift**. Add a new property at the bottom of `AcronymContext` for the categories:

```
let categories: [Category]
```

In `acronymHandler(_:)`, replace:

```
acronym.$user.get(on: req.db).flatMap { user in
  let context = AcronymContext(
    title: acronym.short,
    acronym: acronym,
    user: user)
  return req.view.render("acronym", context)
}
```

With the following:

```
let userFuture = acronym.$user.get(on: req.db)
let categoriesFuture =
  acronym.$categories.query(on: req.db).all()
return userFuture.and(categoriesFuture)
```

```
    .flatMap { user, categories in
      let context = AcronymContext(
        title: acronym.short,
        acronym: acronym,
        user: user,
        categories: categories)
      return req.view.render("acronym", context)
  }
```

This gets the acronym's categories as well as its user. Build and run, then open the create acronym page in the browser. Create an acronym with categories in the browser and head to the acronym's page. You'll see the acronym's categories on the page:

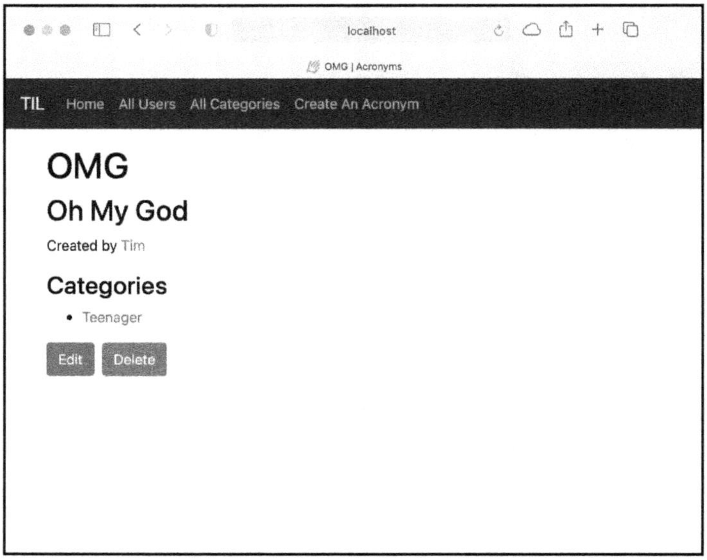

Editing acronyms

To allow adding and editing categories when editing an acronym, open **createAcronym.leaf**. In the categories `<div>`, between the `<select>` and `</select>` tags, add the following:

```
#if(editing):
  <!-- 1 -->
  #for(category in categories):
    <!-- 2 -->
    <option value="#(category.name)" selected="selected">
      #(category.name)
```

```
      </option>
    #endfor
  #endif
```

Here's what this does:

1. If the `editing` flag is set, loop through the array of provided categories.
2. Add each category as an `<option>` with the `selected` attribute set. This allows the category tags to be pre-populated when editing a form.

Save the file. Open **WebsiteController.swift** and add a new property at the bottom of `EditAcronymContext`:

```
let categories: [Category]
```

In `editAcronymHandler(_:)` replace:

```
let context = EditAcronymContext(acronym: acronym, users: users)
return req.view.render("createAcronym", context)
```

with the following:

```
acronym.$categories.get(on: req.db).flatMap { categories in
  let context = EditAcronymContext(
    acronym: acronym,
    users: users,
    categories: categories)
  return req.view.render("createAcronym", context)
}
```

This gets the acronyms categories and passes them to your new `EditAcronymContext`. Finally, replace `editAcronymPostHandler(_:)` with the following:

```
func editAcronymPostHandler(_ req: Request) throws
  -> EventLoopFuture<Response> {
  // 1
  let updateData =
    try req.content.decode(CreateAcronymFormData.self)
  return Acronym
    .find(req.parameters.get("acronymID"), on: req.db)
    .unwrap(or: Abort(.notFound)).flatMap { acronym in
      acronym.short = updateData.short
      acronym.long = updateData.long
      acronym.$user.id = updateData.userID
      guard let id = acronym.id else {
        return req.eventLoop
```

```
            .future(error: Abort(.internalServerError))
        }
        // 2
        return acronym.save(on: req.db).flatMap {
          // 3
          acronym.$categories.get(on: req.db)
        }.flatMap { existingCategories in
          // 4
          let existingStringArray = existingCategories.map {
            $0.name
          }

          // 5
          let existingSet = Set<String>(existingStringArray)
          let newSet = Set<String>(updateData.categories ?? [])

          // 6
          let categoriesToAdd = newSet.subtracting(existingSet)
          let categoriesToRemove = existingSet
            .subtracting(newSet)

          // 7
          var categoryResults: [EventLoopFuture<Void>] = []
          // 8
          for newCategory in categoriesToAdd {
            categoryResults.append(
              Category.addCategory(
                newCategory,
                to: acronym,
                on: req))
          }

          // 9
          for categoryNameToRemove in categoriesToRemove {
            // 10
            let categoryToRemove = existingCategories.first {
              $0.name == categoryNameToRemove
            }
            // 11
            if let category = categoryToRemove {
              categoryResults.append(
                acronym.$categories.detach(category, on: req.db))
            }
          }

          let redirect = req.redirect(to: "/acronyms/\(id)")
          // 12
          return categoryResults.flatten(on: req.eventLoop)
            .transform(to: redirect)
        }
    }
}
```

The important points in this new version are:

1. Change the content type the request decodes to `CreateAcronymFormData`.
2. Use `flatMap(_:)` on `save(on:)` but return all the acronym's categories. Note the chaining of futures instead of nesting them. This helps improve the readability of your code.
3. Get all categories from the database.
4. Create an array of category names from the categories in the database.
5. Create a `Set` for the categories in the database and another for the categories supplied with the request.
6. Calculate the categories to add to the acronym and the categories to remove.
7. Create an array of category operation results.
8. Loop through all the categories to add and call `Category.addCategory(_:to:on:)` to set up the relationship. Add each result to the results array.
9. Loop through all the category names to remove from the acronym.
10. Get the `Category` object from the name of the category to remove.
11. If the `Category` object exists, use `detach(_:on:)` to remove the relationship and delete the pivot.
12. Flatten all the future category results. Transform the result to redirect to the updated acronym's page.

Build and run, then open an acronym page in the browser.

Click **Edit** and you'll see the form populated with the existing categories:

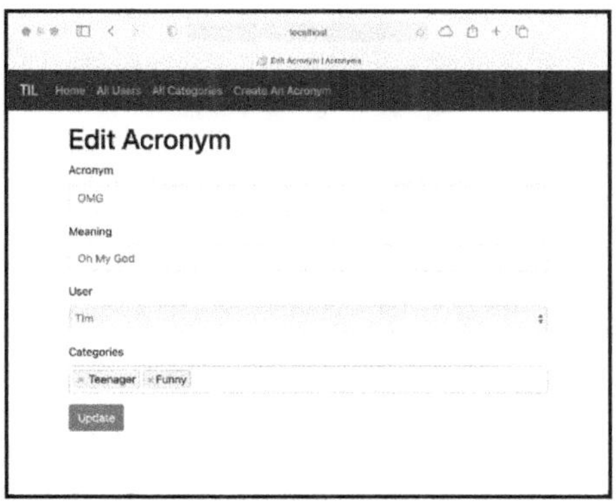

Add a new category and click **Update**. The page redirects to the acronym's page, with the updated acronym shown. Now try removing a category from an acronym.

Where to go from here?

In this section, you learned how to create a full-featured web app that performs the same functions as the iOS app. You learned how to use Leaf to display different types of data and work with futures. You also learned how to accept data from web forms and provide a good user-experience for handling data.

The TIL app contains both the API and the web app. This works well for small applications, but for very large applications you may consider splitting them up into their own apps. The web app then talks to the API like any other client would, such as the iOS app. This allows you to scale the different parts separately. Large applications may even be developed by different teams. Splitting them up lets the application grow and change, without reliance on the other team.

In the next section of the book, you'll learn how to apply authentication to your application. Currently anyone can create any acronyms in both the iOS app and the web app. This isn't desirable, especially for large systems. The next chapters show you how to protect both the API and web app with authentication.

Section III: Validation, Users & Authentication

This section shows you how to protect your Vapor application with authentication. You'll learn how to add password protection to both the API and the website, which lets you require users to log in. You'll learn about different types of authentication: HTTP Basic authentication and token-based authentication for the API, and cookie- and session-based authentication for the web site.

Finally, you'll learn how to integrate with Google, Github and Apple's OAuth providers. This allows you to delegate authentication and allow users to utilize their Google, Github or Apple account credentials to access your site.

These chapters will allow you to secure your important routes and keep only allowed routes as unauthenticated. You'll also learn how to delegate the authentication duties to third party vendors while still keeping your application secure.

Chapter 18: API Authentication, Part 1

By Tim Condon

The TILApp you've built so far has a ton of great features, but it also has one small problem: Anyone can create new users, categories or acronyms. There's no authentication on the API or the website to ensure only known users can change what's in the database. In this chapter, you'll learn how to protect your API with authentication. You'll learn how to implement both HTTP basic authentication and token authentication in your API. You'll also learn best-practices for storing passwords and authenticating users.

> **Note**: You must have PostgreSQL set up and configured in your project. If you still need to do this, follow the steps in Chapter 6, "Configuring a Database".

Passwords

Authentication is the process of verifying who someone is. This is different from **authorization**, which is verifying that a user has permission to perform a particular action. You commonly authenticate users with a username and password combination and TILApp will be no different.

Open the Vapor application in Xcode and open **User.swift**. Add the following property to User below var username: String:

```
@Field(key: "password")
var password: String
```

This property stores the user's password using the column name **password**. Next, to account for the new property, replace the initializer init(id:name:username) with the following:

```
init(
  id: UUID? = nil,
  name: String,
  username: String,
  password: String
) {
  self.name = name
  self.username = username
  self.password = password
}
```

Password storage

Thanks to Codable, you don't have to make any additional changes to create users with passwords. The existing UserController now automatically expects to find the password property in the incoming JSON. However, without any changes, you'll be saving the user's password in plain text.

You should ***never*** store passwords in plain text. You should ***always*** store passwords in a secure fashion. Bcrypt is an industry standard for hashing passwords and Vapor has it built in.

Bcrypt is a one-way hashing algorithm. This means that you can turn a password into a hash, but can't convert a hash back into a password. Since Bcrypt is designed to be slow, if someone steals a password hash, it takes a long time to brute-force the password. Bcrypt hashes a **salt** with the password. A salt is a unique, random value to help defend against common attacks. Bcrypt also provides a mechanism to verify a password using the password and a hash.

Open **UsersController.swift**, find createHandler(_:user:) and add the following after let user = try req.content.decode(User.self):

```
user.password = try Bcrypt.hash(user.password)
```

This hashes the user's password before saving it in the database.

Making usernames unique

In the coming sections of this chapter, you'll be using the username and password to uniquely identify users. At the moment, there's nothing to prevent multiple users from having the same username.

Open **CreateUser.swift**. Before `.create()` add:

```
.field("password", .string, .required)
.unique(on: "username")
```

This updates the migration to add a field for the password and a unique index to `username` of `User`. After the application runs the updated migration, any attempts to create duplicate usernames result in an error.

Fixing the tests

You changed the initializer for `User` so you need to update the tests so Xcode can compile your app. Open **UserTests.swift** and in `testUserCanBeSavedWithAPI()` replace `let user = User...` with the following:

```
let user = User(
  name: usersName,
  username: usersUsername,
  password: "password")
```

Next, open **Models+Testable.swift** and update `create(name:username:on:)` in the extension for `User`. Again, add a value for the `password` parameter:

```
let user = User(
  name: name,
  username: username,
  password: "password")
```

Returning users from the API

Since the model has changed, you need to reset the database. Fluent has already run the `User` migration, but the table has a new column now. To add the new column to the table, you must delete the database so Fluent will run the migration again. In Terminal, enter:

```
# 1
docker stop postgres
# 2
```

```
docker rm postgres
# 3
docker run --name postgres -e POSTGRES_DB=vapor_database \
  -e POSTGRES_USER=vapor_username \
  -e POSTGRES_PASSWORD=vapor_password \
  -p 5432:5432 -d postgres
```

Here's what this does:

1. Stop the running Docker container **postgres**. This is the container currently running the database.
2. Remove the Docker container **postgres** to delete any existing data.
3. Start a new Docker container running PostgreSQL. For more information, see Chapter 6, "Configuring a Database".

Now, build and run and Fluent will create a clean database with your new additions.

Launch RESTed, create a new request and configure it as follows:

- **URL**: http://localhost:8080/api/users/
- **method**: POST
- **Parameter encoding**: JSON-encoded

Add three parameters with names and values:

- **name**: your name
- **username**: a username of your choice
- **password**: a password of your choice

Click **Send Request**. Your application creates the requested user, but the response returns the password hash:

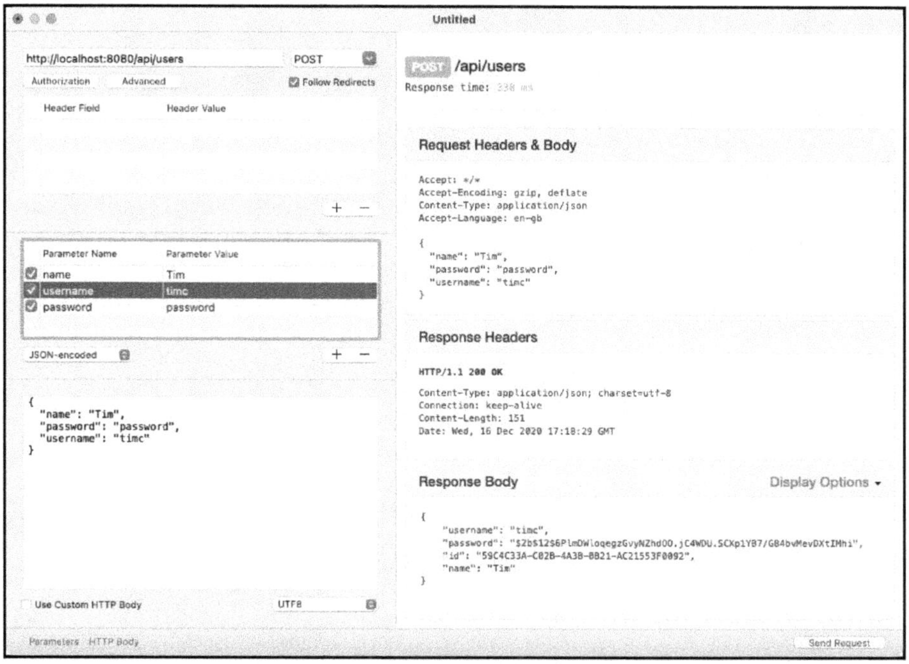

This isn't good! You should protect password hashes and never return them in responses. In fact, any user returned by the API includes the password hash, including listing all the users! This happens because you're returning `User` in all your routes. You should instead return a "public view" of `User`.

In Xcode, open **User.swift** and add the following below the `User` initializer:

```
final class Public: Content {
  var id: UUID?
  var name: String
  var username: String

  init(id: UUID?, name: String, username: String) {
    self.id = id
    self.name = name
    self.username = username
  }
}
```

This creates an inner class to represent a public view of `User` to return in responses. Next, add the following at the bottom of **User.swift**:

```
extension User {
  // 1
  func convertToPublic() -> User.Public {
    // 2
    return User.Public(id: id, name: name, username: username)
  }
}
```

Here's what the new method does:

1. Define a method on `User` that returns `User.Public`.
2. Create a public version of the current object.

Finally, add the following below the new extension:

```
// 1
extension EventLoopFuture where Value: User {
  // 2
  func convertToPublic() -> EventLoopFuture<User.Public> {
    // 3
    return self.map { user in
      // 4
      return user.convertToPublic()
    }
  }
}

// 5
extension Collection where Element: User {
  // 6
  func convertToPublic() -> [User.Public] {
    // 7
    return self.map { $0.convertToPublic() }
  }
}

// 8
extension EventLoopFuture where Value == Array<User> {
  // 9
  func convertToPublic() -> EventLoopFuture<[User.Public]> {
    // 10
    return self.map { $0.convertToPublic() }
  }
}
```

Here's what this does:

1. Define an extension for `EventLoopFuture<User>`.
2. Define a new method that returns a `EventLoopFuture<User.Public>`.
3. Unwrap the user contained in `self`.
4. Convert the `User` object to `User.Public`.
5. Define an extension for `[User]`.
6. Define a new method that returns `[User.Public]`.
7. Convert all the `User` objects in the array to `User.Public`.
8. Define an extension for `EventLoopFuture<[User]>`.
9. Define a new method that returns `EventLoopFuture<[User.Public]>`.
10. Unwrap the array contained in the future and use the previous extension to convert all the `Users` to `User.Public`.

These extensions allow you to call `convertToPublic()` on `EventLoopFuture<User>`, `[User]` and `EventLoopFuture<[User]>`. This helps tidy up your code and reduce nesting. These new methods allow you to change your route handlers to return public users.

First, open **UsersController.swift** and change the return type of `createHandler(_:user:)`:

```
func createHandler(_ req: Request)
  -> EventLoopFuture<User.Public> {
```

Next, change the result of `map` to return a public user instead:

```
return user.save(on: req.db).map { user.convertToPublic() }
```

This uses the new method to convert a `User` to `User.Public`. Build and run, then create a new user in RESTed. You'll notice the user's password hash is no longer returned:

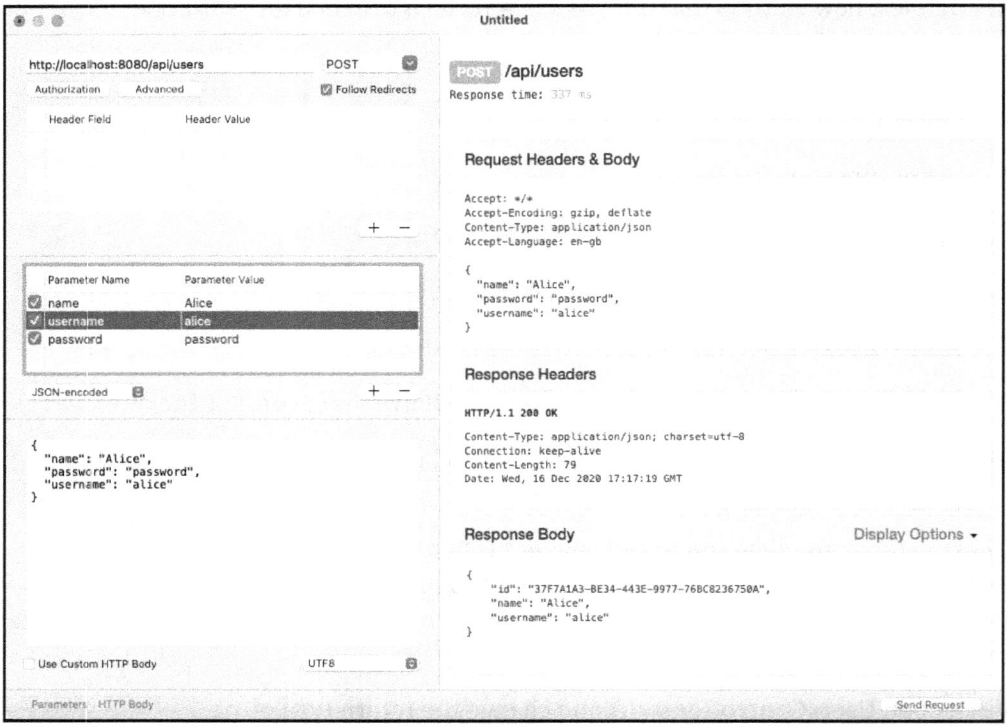

Now, you must update the rest of the routes that return `User`.

First, in **UsersController.swift** change the signature of `getAllHandler(_:)` to the following:

```
func getAllHandler(_ req: Request)
  -> EventLoopFuture<[User.Public]> {
```

Next, change the body of `getAllHandler(_:)` to the following:

```
User.query(on: req.db).all().convertToPublic()
```

This uses the extension for `EventLoopFuture<[User]>` to convert the users returned from the database to `User.Public`. Next, change the signature of `getHandler(_:)` to return a public user:

```
func getHandler(_ req: Request)
  -> EventLoopFuture<User.Public> {
```

Next, change the body to return a public user:

```
User.find(req.parameters.get("userID"), on: req.db)
  .unwrap(or: Abort(.notFound))
  .convertToPublic()
```

Finally, open **AcronymsController.swift** and replace `getUserHandler(_:)` so it returns a public user:

```
// 1
func getUserHandler(_ req: Request)
  -> EventLoopFuture<User.Public> {
  Acronym.find(req.parameters.get("acronymID"), on: req.db)
  .unwrap(or: Abort(.notFound))
  .flatMap { acronym in
    // 2
    acronym.$user.get(on: req.db).convertToPublic()
  }
}
```

Here's what changed:

1. Change the return type of the method to `Future<User.Public>`.
2. Call `convertToPublic()` on the acronym's user to return a public user.

Now, no calls to your API to retrieve a user will return a password hash.

Basic authentication

HTTP basic authentication is a standardized method of sending credentials via HTTP and is defined by RFC 7617 (https://tools.ietf.org/html/rfc7617). You typically include the credentials in an HTTP request's **Authorization** header.

To generate the token for this header, you combine the username and password, then Base64-encode the result.

For example, for the username **timc** and password **password** the combined credential string is:

```
timc:password
```

You then Base64-encode this which gives you:

```
dGltYzpwYXNzd29yZA==
```

The full header becomes:

```
Authorization: Basic dGltYzpwYXNzd29yZA==
```

Authentication is built into Vapor and contains helpers to use HTTP Basic authentication. Open **User.swift** and, at the bottom of the file, add the following:

```
// 1
extension User: ModelAuthenticatable {
  // 2
  static let usernameKey = \User.$username
  // 3
  static let passwordHashKey = \User.$password

  // 4
  func verify(password: String) throws -> Bool {
    try Bcrypt.verify(password, created: self.password)
  }
}
```

Here's what this does:

1. Conform `User` to `ModelAuthenticatable`. This is a protocol that allows Fluent `Model`s to use HTTP Basic Authentication.
2. Tell Vapor which key path of `User` is the username.
3. Tell Vapor which key path of `User` is the password hash.
4. Implement `verify(password:)` as required by `ModelAuthenticatable`. Since you hash the `User`'s password using Bcrypt, verify the hash with Bcrypt here.

Open **AcronymsController.swift** and add the following at the bottom of `boot(routes:)`:

```
// 1
let basicAuthMiddleware = User.authenticator()
// 2
let guardAuthMiddleware = User.guardMiddleware()
// 3
let protected = acronymsRoutes.grouped(
  basicAuthMiddleware,
  guardAuthMiddleware)
// 4
protected.post(use: createHandler)
```

Here's what this does:

1. Create an instance of `ModelAuthenticator` middleware, which uses HTTP Basic Authentication. Since `User` conforms to `ModelAuthenticatable`, this is available as a static method on the model.
2. Create an instance of `GuardAuthenticationMiddleware` which ensures that requests contain authenticated users.
3. Create a middleware group which uses `basicAuthMiddleware` and `guardAuthMiddleware`.
4. Connect the "create acronym" path to `createHandler(_:acronym:)` through this middleware group.

> **Middleware** allows you to intercept requests and responses in your application. In this example, `basicAuthMiddleware` intercepts the request and authenticates the user supplied. You can chain middleware together. In the above example, `basicAuthMiddleware` authenticates the user. Then `guardAuthMiddleware` ensures the request contains an authenticated user. If there's no authenticated user, `guardAuthMiddleware` throws an error. You can learn more about middleware in Chapter 29, "Middleware".

This ensures only requests authenticated using HTTP basic authentication can create acronyms.

Next, delete the following to remove the unauthenticated route:

```
acronymsRoutes.post(use: createHandler)
```

Build and run, then launch RESTed. Create a new request and configure it as follows:

- **URL**: http://localhost:8080/api/acronyms
- **method**: POST
- **Parameter encoding**: JSON-encoded

Add three parameters with names and values:

- **short**: OMG
- **long**: Oh My God
- **userID**: The ID of the user created earlier

Click **Send Request** and you'll receive a **401 Unauthorized** error response. You should see the following:

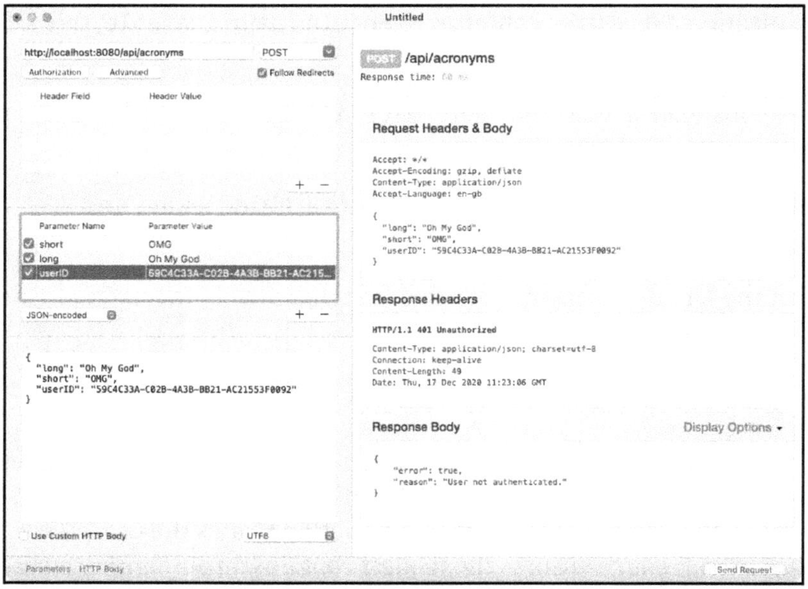

In RESTed, click **Authorization** and enter the username and password for the user created earlier. Check **Present Before Authentication Challenge** and click **OK**:

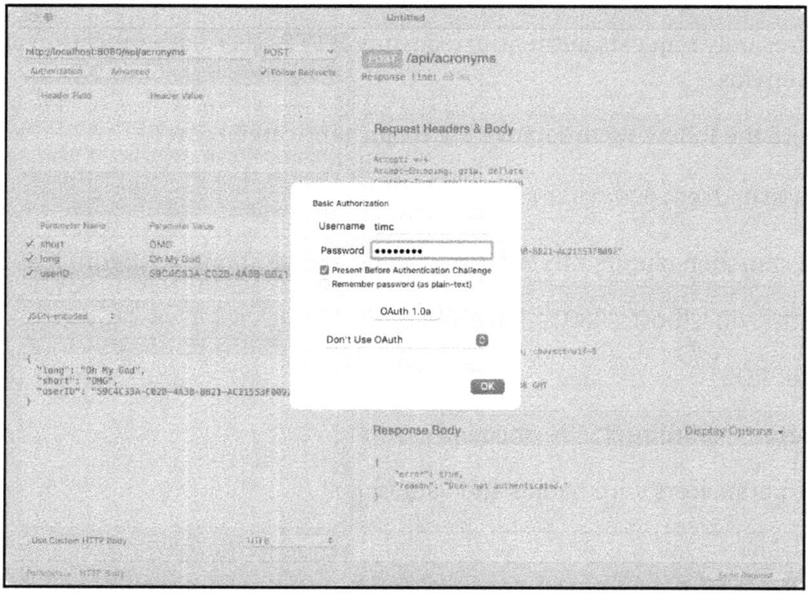

This sets the basic **Authorization** header as described above. Click **Send Request** again. This time the request succeeds:

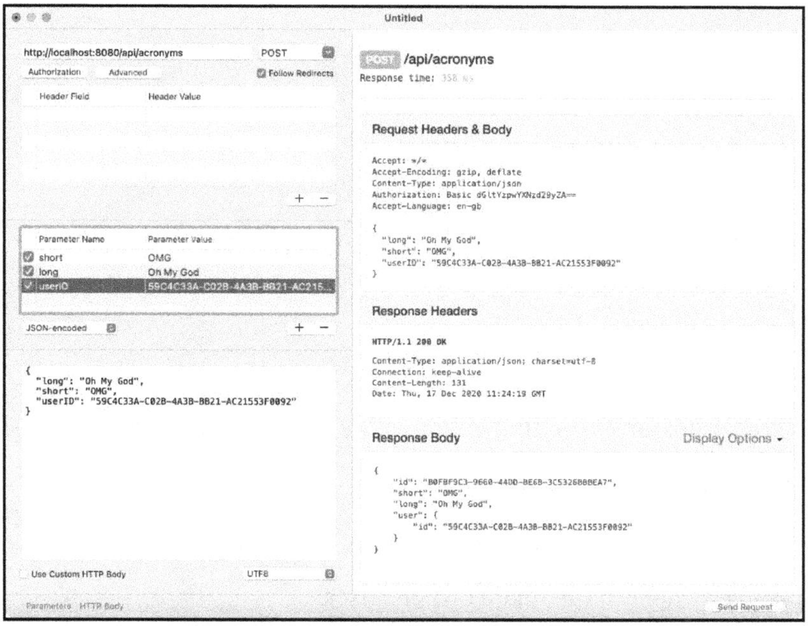

Token authentication

Getting a token

At this stage, only authenticated users can create acronyms. However, all other "destructive" routes are still unprotected. Asking a user to enter credentials with each request is impractical. You also don't want to store a user's password anywhere in your application since you'd have to store it in plain text. Instead, you'll allow users to log in to your API. When they log in, you exchange their credentials for a token the client can save.

Create a new file, **Token.swift** in **Sources/App/Models**. Open the new file and add the following:

```
import Vapor
import Fluent

final class Token: Model, Content {
  static let schema = "tokens"
```

```
  @ID
  var id: UUID?

  @Field(key: "value")
  var value: String

  @Parent(key: "userID")
  var user: User

  init() {}

  init(id: UUID? = nil, value: String, userID: User.IDValue) {
    self.id = id
    self.value = value
    self.$user.id = userID
  }
}
```

This defines a model for `Token` that contains the following properties:

- `id`: the ID of the model.
- `value`: the token string provided to clients.
- `user`: a `@Parent` field to the token owner's user.

Create a migration file, **CreateToken.swift** in **Sources/App/Migrations**, for the new model and insert the migration below:

```
import Fluent

struct CreateToken: Migration {
  func prepare(on database: Database) -> EventLoopFuture<Void> {
    database.schema("tokens")
      .id()
      .field("value", .string, .required)
      .field(
        "userID",
        .uuid,
        .required,
        .references("users", "id", onDelete: .cascade))
      .create()
  }

  func revert(on database: Database) -> EventLoopFuture<Void> {
    database.schema("tokens").delete()
  }
}
```

Like other migrations before, this creates the table for `Token`. It also creates a reference to `User` for the `userID` field. The reference is marked with a cascade deletion so that any tokens are automatically deleted when you delete a user. In **configure.swift**, add the following after `app.migrations.add(CreateAcronymCategoryPivot()):`

```
app.migrations.add(CreateToken())
```

This adds `CreateToken` to the list of migrations so Vapor creates the table when the application next starts. When a user logs in, the application must create a token for that user.

Open **Token.swift** and add the following at the bottom of the file:

```
extension Token {
  // 1
  static func generate(for user: User) throws -> Token {
    // 2
    let random = [UInt8].random(count: 16).base64
    // 3
    return try Token(value: random, userID: user.requireID())
  }
}
```

Here's what this extension does:

1. Define a static method to generate a token for a user.
2. Generate 16 random bytes to act as the token and Base64 encode it.
3. Create a `Token` using the Base64-encoded representation of the random bytes and the user's ID.

Open **UsersController.swift** and add the following under `getAcronymsHandler(_:):`

```
// 1
func loginHandler(_ req: Request) throws
  -> EventLoopFuture<Token> {
  // 2
  let user = try req.auth.require(User.self)
  // 3
  let token = try Token.generate(for: user)
  // 4
  return token.save(on: req.db).map { token }
}
```

Here's what this does:

1. Define a route handler for logging a user in.
2. Get the authenticated user from the request. You'll protect this route with the HTTP basic authentication middleware. This saves the user's identity in the request's authentication cache, allowing you to retrieve the user object later. `req.auth.require(_:)` throws an authentication error if there's no authenticated user.
3. Create a token for the user.
4. Save and return the token.

At the bottom of `boot(routes:)` add the following:

```
// 1
let basicAuthMiddleware = User.authenticator()
let basicAuthGroup = usersRoute.grouped(basicAuthMiddleware)
// 2
basicAuthGroup.post("login", use: loginHandler)
```

Here's what this does:

1. Create a protected route group using HTTP basic authentication, as you did for creating an acronym. This doesn't use `GuardAuthenticationMiddleware` since `req.auth.require(_:)` throws the correct error if a user isn't authenticated.
2. Connect **/api/users/login** to `loginHandler(_:)` through the protected group.

Build and run, then head back to RESTed.

Ensure you've configured the HTTP basic authentication and set the URL to **http://localhost:8080/api/users/login**.

Click **Send Request** and you'll receive a token back:

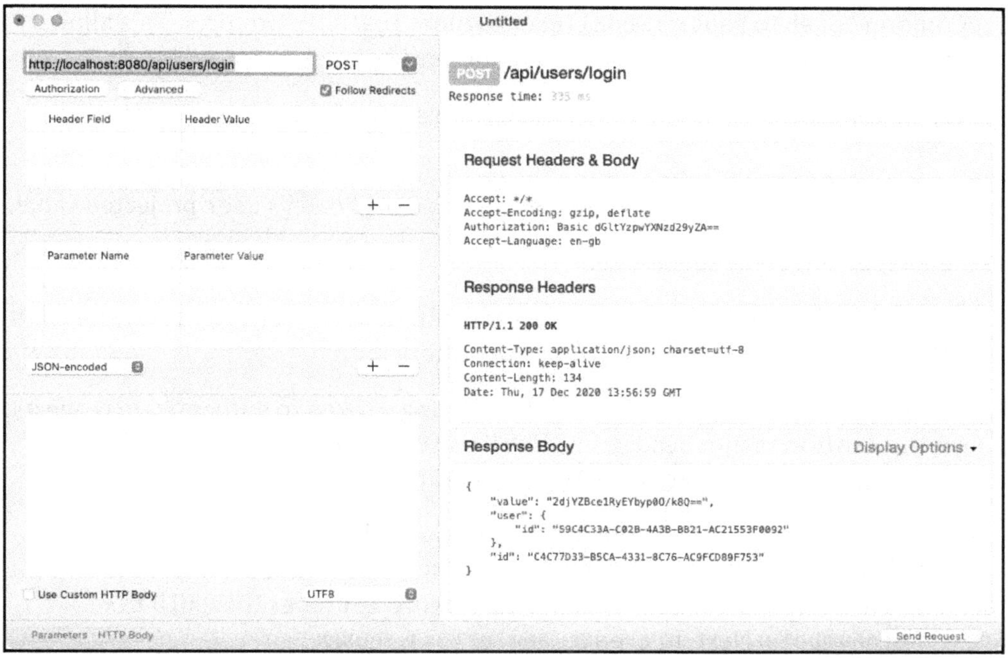

Using a token

Open **Token.swift** and add the following at the end of the file:

```
// 1
extension Token: ModelTokenAuthenticatable {
  // 2
  static let valueKey = \Token.$value
  // 3
  static let userKey = \Token.$user
  // 4
  typealias User = App.User
  // 5
  var isValid: Bool {
    true
  }
}
```

Here's what this does:

1. Conform `Token` to `Vapor`'s `ModelTokenAuthenticatable` protocol. This allows you to use the token with HTTP Bearer authentication.
2. Tell Vapor the key path to the value key, in this case, `Token`'s `value` projected value.
3. Tell Vapor the key path to the user key, in this case, `Token`'s `user` projected value.
4. Tell Vapor what type the user is.
5. Determine if the token is valid. Return `true` for now, but you might add an expiry date or a revoked property to check in the future.

Bearer authentication is a mechanism for sending a token to authenticate requests. It uses the **Authorization** header, like HTTP basic authentication, but the header looks like **Authorization: Bearer <TOKEN STRING>**.

Currently when users create acronyms, they must send their ID in the request. However, because you're requiring authentication, you now know which user sent each request. In **AcronymsController.swift**, remove `let userID: UUID` from `CreateAcronymData`. Next, in `createHandler(_:)`, replace:

```
let acronym = Acronym(
  short: data.short,
  long: data.long,
  userID: data.userID)
```

with the following:

```
// 1
let user = try req.auth.require(User.self)
// 2
let acronym = try Acronym(
  short: data.short,
  long: data.long,
  userID: user.requireID())
```

The changes made were:

1. Get the authenticated user from the request.
2. Create a new `Acronym` using the data from the request and the authenticated user.

Next, replace `updateHandler(_:)` with the following:

```
func updateHandler(_ req: Request) throws
  -> EventLoopFuture<Acronym> {
  let updateData =
    try req.content.decode(CreateAcronymData.self)
  // 1
  let user = try req.auth.require(User.self)
  // 2
  let userID = try user.requireID()
  return Acronym
    .find(req.parameters.get("acronymID"), on: req.db)
    .unwrap(or: Abort(.notFound))
    .flatMap { acronym in
      acronym.short = updateData.short
      acronym.long = updateData.long
      // 3
      acronym.$user.id = userID
      return acronym.save(on: req.db).map {
        acronym
      }
  }
}
```

The changes made were:

1. Get the authenticated user from the request.
2. Get the user ID from the user. It's useful to do this here as you can't throw inside `flatMap(_:)`.
3. Set the acronym's user's ID to the user ID from the step above.

Finally, update the tests so the project compiles. Open **AcronymTests.swift**. In `testAcronymCanBeSavedWithAPI()` replace `let createAcronymData = ...` with the following:

```
let createAcronymData =
  CreateAcronymData(short: acronymShort, long: acronymLong)
```

This removes the `userID` parameter as it's no longer required. While you're there, remove the line `let user = try User.create...` since it's no longer needed. Finally, in `testUpdatingAnAcronym()` replace `let updatedAcronymData = ...` with the following to remove the extra `userID` parameter:

```
let updatedAcronymData =
  CreateAcronymData(short: acronymShort, long: newLong)
```

Return to **AcronymsController.swift**. In `boot(routes:)`, remove the code you used earlier to protect the "create an acronym" route and replace it with the following:

```
// 1
let tokenAuthMiddleware = Token.authenticator()
let guardAuthMiddleware = User.guardMiddleware()
// 2
let tokenAuthGroup = acronymsRoutes.grouped(
  tokenAuthMiddleware,
  guardAuthMiddleware)
// 3
tokenAuthGroup.post(use: createHandler)
```

Here's what the new code does:

1. Create a `ModelTokenAuthenticator` middleware for `Token`. This extracts the bearer token out of the request and converts it into a logged in user.
2. Create a route group using `tokenAuthMiddleware` and `guardAuthMiddleware` to protect the route for creating an acronym with token authentication.
3. Connect the "create acronym" path to `createHandler(_:data:)` through this middleware group using the new `AcronymCreateData`.

Build and run, then head back to RESTed. Copy the token value string returned from the user login. Configure a request like so:

- **URL**: http://localhost:8080/api/acronyms/
- **method**: POST
- **Parameter encoding**: JSON-encoded

Add two parameters with names and values:

- **short**: IKR
- **long**: I Know Right

Create a new header field for **Authorization** with the value **Bearer <TOKEN STRING>**, using the token string you copied earlier. Remove the HTTP basic authentication credentials you used for logging in.

To do this, click **Authorization**, remove the username and password, and uncheck **Present Before Authentication Challenge**.

Click **Send Request** and you'll see the created acronym returned:

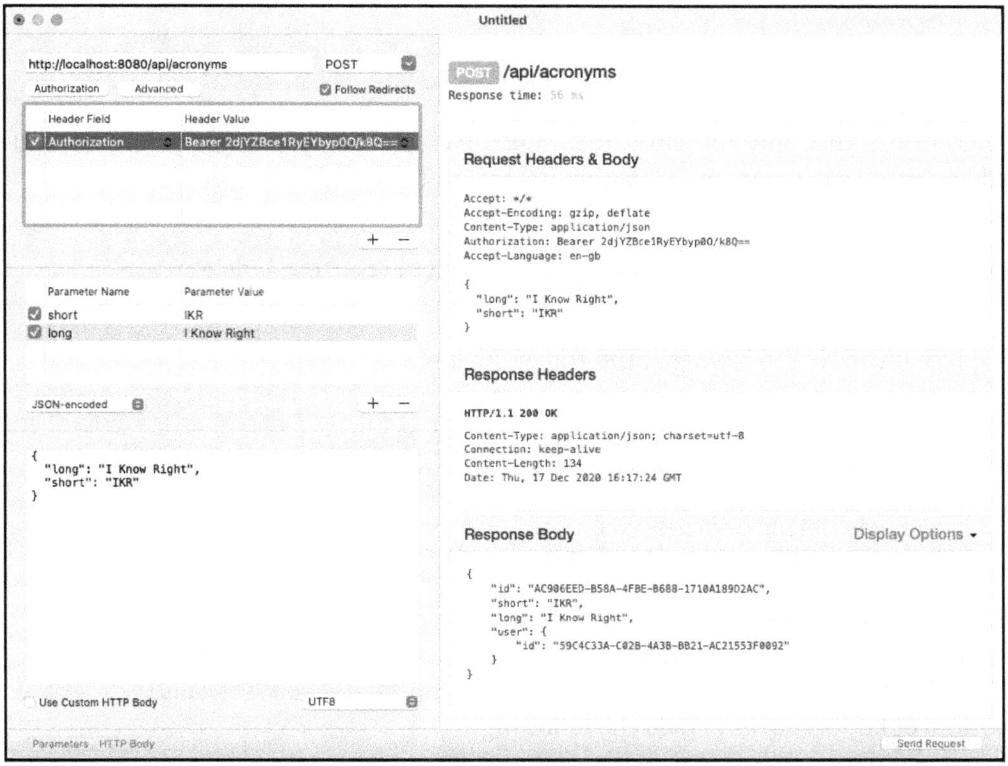

Open **AcronymsController.swift**, find `boot(routes:)`, and delete the following lines:

```
acronymsRoutes.put(":acronymID", use: updateHandler)
acronymsRoutes.delete(":acronymID", use: deleteHandler)
acronymsRoutes.post(":acronymID", "categories", ":categoryID",
                    use: addCategoriesHandler)
acronymsRoutes.delete(":acronymID", "categories", ":categoryID",
                      use: removeCategoriesHandler)
```

This is all of the original routes that are not `get()` routes. At the bottom of `boot(routes:)`, add their replacements:

```
tokenAuthGroup.delete(":acronymID", use: deleteHandler)
tokenAuthGroup.put(":acronymID", use: updateHandler)
tokenAuthGroup.post(
  ":acronymID",
  "categories",
  ":categoryID",
  use: addCategoriesHandler)
```

```
tokenAuthGroup.delete(
  ":acronymID",
  "categories",
  ":categoryID",
  use: removeCategoriesHandler)
```

This ensures that only authenticated users can create, edit and delete acronyms, and add categories to acronyms. Unauthenticated users can still view details about acronyms.

Now, open **CategoriesController.swift** and, in `boot(routes:)`, delete `categoriesRoute.post(use: createHandler)`.

Replace it with the following at the end of the method:

```
let tokenAuthMiddleware = Token.authenticator()
let guardAuthMiddleware = User.guardMiddleware()
let tokenAuthGroup = categoriesRoute.grouped(
  tokenAuthMiddleware,
  guardAuthMiddleware)
tokenAuthGroup.post(use: createHandler)
```

This uses the token middleware to protect category creation, just like creating an acronym, ensuring only authenticated users can create categories. Finally, open **UsersController.swift** and delete `usersRoute.post(use: createHandler)`. At the bottom of `boot(routes:)`, add the following:

```
let tokenAuthMiddleware = Token.authenticator()
let guardAuthMiddleware = User.guardMiddleware()
let tokenAuthGroup = usersRoute.grouped(
  tokenAuthMiddleware,
  guardAuthMiddleware)
tokenAuthGroup.post(use: createHandler)
```

Again, using `tokenAuthMiddleware` and `guardAuthMiddleware` ensures only authenticated users can create other users. This prevents anyone from creating a user to send requests to the routes you've just protected!

Now all API routes that can perform "destructive" actions — that is create, edit or delete resources — are protected. For those actions, the application only accept requests from authenticated users.

Database seeding

At this point the API is secure, but now there's another problem. When you deploy your application, or next revert the database, you won't have any users in the database.

But, you can't create a new user since that route requires authentication! One way to solve this is to seed the database and create a user when the application first boots up. In Vapor, you do this with a migration.

In **Sources/App/Migrations** create a new file, **CreateAdminUser.swift**. Open the new file and add the following:

```
import Fluent
import Vapor

// 1
struct CreateAdminUser: Migration {
  // 2
  func prepare(on database: Database) -> EventLoopFuture<Void> {
    // 3
    let passwordHash: String
    do {
      passwordHash = try Bcrypt.hash("password")
    } catch {
      return database.eventLoop.future(error: error)
    }
    // 4
    let user = User(
      name: "Admin",
      username: "admin",
      password: passwordHash)
    // 5
    return user.save(on: database)
  }

  // 6
  func revert(on database: Database) -> EventLoopFuture<Void> {
    // 7
    User.query(on: database)
      .filter(\.$username == "admin")
      .delete()
  }
}
```

Here's what this does:

1. Define a new type that conforms to `Migration`.
2. Implement the required `prepare(on:)`.
3. Create a password hash from the password. Catch any errors thrown and return a failed future.
4. Create a new user with the name **Admin**, username **admin** and the hashed password.
5. Save the user and return.
6. Implement the required `revert(on:)`.
7. Query `User` and delete any rows where the username matches **admin.** As usernames must be unique, this only deletes the one admin row.

> **Note**: Obviously, in a production system, you shouldn't use **password** as the password for your admin user! You also don't want to hard code the password in case it ends up in source control. You can either read an environment variable or generate a random password and print it out.

Open **configure.swift** and add the following after `app.migrations.add(CreateToken())`:

```
app.migrations.add(CreateAdminUser())
```

This adds `CreateAdminUser` to the list of migrations so the app executes the migration at the next app launch.

Build and run. Head to RESTed and try out all of your newly protected routes. You can even log in with the new admin user.

Where to go from here?

In this chapter, you learned about HTTP Basic and Bearer authentication. You saw how authentication middleware can simplify your code and do much of the heavy lifting for you. You saw how to modify your existing model to work with Vapor's authentication capabilities. You glued it all together to add authentication to your API.

But, there's much more to be done. Turn the page and get busy updating your test suite and your iOS app to work with the new authentication capabilities.

Chapter 19: API Authentication, Part 2

By Tim Condon

Now that you've implemented API authentication, neither your tests nor the iOS application work any longer. In this chapter, you'll learn the techniques needed to account for the new authentication requirements.

> **Note**: You must have PostgreSQL set up and configured in your project. If you still need to do this, follow the steps in Chapter 6, "Configuring a Database".

Updating the tests

In the previous chapter, you updated the tests to ensure they compile. However, many of the tests won't pass as you've protected all the routes in your API.

First, open **Models+Testable.swift** and, at the top of the file, add:

```
import Vapor
```

This allows the compiler to see the Bcrypt function used for password hashing. Next, replace `create(name:username:on:)` in the `User` extension with the following:

```
// 1
static func create(
  name: String = "Luke",
  username: String? = nil,
  on database: Database
) throws -> User {
  let createUsername: String
  // 2
  if let suppliedUsername = username {
    createUsername = suppliedUsername
  // 3
  } else {
    createUsername = UUID().uuidString
  }

  // 4
  let password = try Bcrypt.hash("password")
  let user = User(
    name: name,
    username: createUsername,
    password: password)
  try user.save(on: database).wait()
  return user
}
```

Here's what you changed:

1. Make the `username` parameter an optional string that defaults to `nil`.

2. If a username is supplied, use it.

3. If a username isn't supplied, create a new, random one using `UUID`. This ensures the username is unique as required by the migration.

4. Hash the password and create a user.

In Terminal, run the following:

```
# 1
docker rm  -f postgres-test
# 2
docker run --name postgres-test -e POSTGRES_DB=vapor-test \
  -e POSTGRES_USER=vapor_username \
```

```
  -e POSTGRES_PASSWORD=vapor_password \
  -p 5433:5432 -d postgres
```

Here's what this does:

1. Stop and remove the test PostgreSQL container, if it exists, so you start with a fresh database.

2. Run the test container again as described in Chapter 11, "Testing".

If you run the tests now, they crash since calls to any authenticated routes fail. You need to provide authentication for these requests.

Stop the tests, open **Application+Testable.swift** and replace:

```
import XCTVapor
import App
```

with the following:

```
@testable import App
@testable import XCTVapor
```

This enables you to use `Token`, `User` and `XCTApplicationTester`. Next, at the bottom of the file, insert:

```
// 1
extension XCTApplicationTester {
  // 2
  public func login(
    user: User
  ) throws -> Token {
    // 3
    var request = XCTHTTPRequest(
      method: .POST,
      url: .init(path: "/api/users/login"),
      headers: [:],
      body: ByteBufferAllocator().buffer(capacity: 0)
    )
    // 4
    request.headers.basicAuthorization =
      .init(username: user.username, password: "password")
    // 5
    let response = try performTest(request: request)
    // 6
    return try response.content.decode(Token.self)
  }
}
```

Here's what the new function does:

1. Add an extension to `XCTApplicationTester`, Vapor's test wrapper around `Application`.
2. Define a log in method that takes `User` and returns `Token`.
3. Create a test **POST** request to **/api/users/login** — the log in URL — with empty values where needed.
4. Set the HTTP Basic Authentication header using Vapor's `BasicAuthorization` helpers. **Note**: The password here must be plaintext text, not the hashed password from `User`.
5. Send the request to get the response.
6. Decode the response to `Token` and return the result.

Next, at the bottom of the `XCTApplicationTester` extension, add a new method to use the log in method you just created:

```
// 1
@discardableResult
public func test(
  _ method: HTTPMethod,
  _ path: String,
  headers: HTTPHeaders = [:],
  body: ByteBuffer? = nil,
  loggedInRequest: Bool = false,
  loggedInUser: User? = nil,
  file: StaticString = #file,
  line: UInt = #line,
  beforeRequest: (inout XCTHTTPRequest) throws -> () = { _ in },
  afterResponse: (XCTHTTPResponse) throws -> () = { _ in }
) throws -> XCTApplicationTester {
  // 2
  var request = XCTHTTPRequest(
    method: method,
    url: .init(path: path),
    headers: headers,
    body: body ?? ByteBufferAllocator().buffer(capacity: 0)
  )

  // 3
  if (loggedInRequest || loggedInUser != nil) {
    let userToLogin: User
    // 4
    if let user = loggedInUser {
      userToLogin = user
    } else {
```

```
        userToLogin = User(
          name: "Admin",
          username: "admin",
          password: "password")
      }

      // 5
      let token = try login(user: userToLogin)
      // 6
      request.headers.bearerAuthorization =
        .init(token: token.value)
    }

    // 7
    try beforeRequest(&request)

    // 8
    do {
      let response = try performTest(request: request)
      try afterResponse(response)
    } catch {
      XCTFail("\(error)", file: (file), line: line)
      throw error
    }
    return self
  }
```

Here's the details for the new method:

1. Add a new method that duplicates the existing `app.test(_:_:beforeRequest:afterResponse:)` you use in tests. This new method adds `loggedInRequest` and `loggedInUser` as parameters. You use these to tell your tests to send an Authorization header or use a specified user, as required.

2. Create a request to use in the test.

3. Determine if this request requires authentication.

4. Work out the user to use. **Note**: This requires you to know the user's password. As all the users in your tests have the password "password", this isn't an issue. If no user is specified, use "admin".

5. Get a token using `login(user:)`, which you created earlier.

6. Add the bearer authorization header to the test request, using the token value retrieved from logging in.
7. Apply `beforeRequest(_:)` to the request.
8. Get the response and apply `afterResponse(_:)`. Catch any errors and fail the test. This is the same as the standard `app.test(_:_:beforeRequest:afterResponse:)` method.

Open **AcronymTests.swift** and, in `testAcronymCanBeSavedWithAPI()`, add the following at the beginning:

```
let user = try User.create(on: app.db)
```

This creates a user to use in the test.

Next, change the call to `app.test(_:_:beforeRequest:afterResponse:)` to use the user you just created:

```
// 1
try app.test(
  .POST,
  acronymsURI,
  loggedInUser: user,
  beforeRequest: { request in
    try request.content.encode(createAcronymData)
  },
  afterResponse: { response in
    let receivedAcronym =
      try response.content.decode(Acronym.self)
    XCTAssertEqual(receivedAcronym.short, acronymShort)
    XCTAssertEqual(receivedAcronym.long, acronymLong)
    XCTAssertNotNil(receivedAcronym.id)
    // 2
    XCTAssertEqual(receivedAcronym.$user.id, user.id)

    try app.test(.GET, acronymsURI,
      afterResponse: { allAcronymsResponse in
        let acronyms =
          try allAcronymsResponse.content.decode([Acronym].self)
        XCTAssertEqual(acronyms.count, 1)
        XCTAssertEqual(acronyms[0].short, acronymShort)
        XCTAssertEqual(acronyms[0].long, acronymLong)
        XCTAssertEqual(acronyms[0].id, receivedAcronym.id)
        // 3
        XCTAssertEqual(acronyms[0].$user.id, user.id)
    })
})
```

The changes made were:

1. Pass in the created user for `loggedInUser` to authenticated the create acronym request using your new helper function.
2. Add a check to ensure the created acronym's user ID matches the ID of the user used to authenticate the create acronym request.
3. Add a check to ensure the returned acronym's user ID matches the ID of the user used to authenticate the create acronym request.

In `testUpdatingAnAcronym()`, pass the user into the send request helper:

```
try app.test(.PUT,
  "\(acronymsURI)\(acronym.id!)",
  loggedInUser: newUser,
  beforeRequest: { request in
    try request.content.encode(updatedAcronymData)
  })
```

In `testDeletingAnAcronym()`, set `loggedInRequest` when sending the **DELETE** request:

```
try app.test(
  .DELETE,
  "\(acronymsURI)\(acronym.id!)",
  loggedInRequest: true)
```

Next, in `testGettingAnAcronymsUser()`, change the decoded user type to `User.Public`:

```
let acronymsUser = try response.content.decode(User.Public.self)
```

Since the app no longer returns users' passwords in requests, you must change the decode type to `User.Public`.

Next, in `testAcronymsCategories()` replace the two **POST** requests with the following:

```
try app.test(
  .POST,
  "\(acronymsURI)\(acronym.id!)/categories/\(category.id!)",
  loggedInRequest: true)
try app.test(
  .POST,
  "\(acronymsURI)\(acronym.id!)/categories/\(category2.id!)",
  loggedInRequest: true)
```

Finally, replace the **DELETE** with the following:

```
try app.test(
  .DELETE,
  "\(acronymsURI)\(acronym.id!)/categories/\(category.id!)",
  loggedInRequest: true)
```

These requests now use an authenticated user.

Open **CategoryTests.swift** and change `testCategoryCanBeSavedWithAPI()` to use an authenticated request:

```
try app.test(.POST, categoriesURI, loggedInRequest: true,
  beforeRequest: { request in
    try request.content.encode(category)
}, afterResponse: { response in
  let receivedCategory =
    try response.content.decode(Category.self)
  XCTAssertEqual(receivedCategory.name, categoryName)
  XCTAssertNotNil(receivedCategory.id)

  try app.test(.GET, categoriesURI,
    afterResponse: { response in
      let categories =
        try response.content.decode([App.Category].self)
      XCTAssertEqual(categories.count, 1)
      XCTAssertEqual(categories[0].name, categoryName)
      XCTAssertEqual(categories[0].id, receivedCategory.id)
    })
})
```

Next, in `testGettingACategoriesAcronymsFromTheAPI()`, replace the two POST requests with the following to use an authenticated user:

```
try app.test(
  .POST,
  "/api/acronyms/\(acronym.id!)/categories/\(category.id!)",
  loggedInRequest: true)
try app.test(
  .POST,
  "/api/acronyms/\(acronym2.id!)/categories/\(category.id!)",
  loggedInRequest: true)
```

Now, open **UserTests.swift**. First, change the request in `testUsersCanBeRetrievedFromAPI()` from:

```
let users = try response.content.decode([User].self)
```

to the following:

```
let users = try response.content.decode([User.Public].self)
```

This changes the decode type to `User.Public`. Update the assertions to account for the admin user:

```
XCTAssertEqual(users.count, 3)
XCTAssertEqual(users[1].name, usersName)
XCTAssertEqual(users[1].username, usersUsername)
XCTAssertEqual(users[1].id, user.id)
```

Next, in `testUserCanBeSavedWithAPI()`, replace the body with:

```
let user = User(
  name: usersName,
  username: usersUsername,
  password: "password")

// 1
try app.test(.POST, usersURI, loggedInRequest: true,
  beforeRequest: { req in
    try req.content.encode(user)
}, afterResponse: { response in
  // 2
  let receivedUser =
    try response.content.decode(User.Public.self)
  XCTAssertEqual(receivedUser.name, usersName)
  XCTAssertEqual(receivedUser.username, usersUsername)
  XCTAssertNotNil(receivedUser.id)

  try app.test(.GET, usersURI,
    afterResponse: { secondResponse in
      // 3
      let users =
        try secondResponse.content.decode([User.Public].self)
      // 4
      XCTAssertEqual(users.count, 2)
      XCTAssertEqual(users[1].name, usersName)
      XCTAssertEqual(users[1].username, usersUsername)
      XCTAssertEqual(users[1].id, receivedUser.id)
    })
})
```

The changes made were:

1. Set `loggedInRequest` so the create user request works.
2. Decode the response to `User.Public`.
3. Decode the second response to an array of `User.Public`.
4. Update the assertions to take account of the admin user.

Finally, update the request in `testGettingASingleUserFromTheAPI()`:

```
let receivedUser = try response.content.decode(User.Public.self)
```

This changes the decode type to `User.Public` as the response no longer contains the user's password. Build and run the tests; they should all pass.

Updating the iOS application

With the API now requiring authentication, the iOS Application can no longer create acronyms. Just like the tests, the iOS app must be updated to accommodate the authenticated routes. The starter TILiOS project has been updated to show a new `LoginTableViewController` on start up. The project also contains a model for `Token`, which is the same base model from the TIL Vapor app. Finally, the "create user" view now accepts a password.

Ensure your TIL Vapor application is running before sending requests.

Logging in

Open **AppDelegate.swift**. In `application(_:didFinishLaunchingWithOptions:)`, the application checks the new `Auth` object for a token. If there's no token, it launches the login screen; otherwise, it displays the acronyms table as normal.

Open **Auth.swift**. The token check called from `AppDelegate` looks for a token in the Keychain using the **TIL-API-KEY** key. When you set a token in `Auth`, it saves that token in the keychain. **Auth+Keychain.swift** simplifies interacting with the keychain for you.

At the bottom of `Auth`, create a new method to log a user in:

```
func login(
  username: String,
```

```
    password: String,
    completion: @escaping (AuthResult) -> Void
  ) {
    // 2
    let path = "http://localhost:8080/api/users/login"
    guard let url = URL(string: path) else {
      fatalError("Failed to convert URL")
    }
    // 3
    guard
      let loginString = "\(username):\(password)"
        .data(using: .utf8)?
        .base64EncodedString()
    else {
      fatalError("Failed to encode credentials")
    }

    // 4
    var loginRequest = URLRequest(url: url)
    // 5
    loginRequest.addValue(
      "Basic \(loginString)",
      forHTTPHeaderField: "Authorization")
    loginRequest.httpMethod = "POST"

    // 6
    let dataTask = URLSession.shared
      .dataTask(with: loginRequest) { data, response, _ in
        // 7
        guard
          let httpResponse = response as? HTTPURLResponse,
          httpResponse.statusCode == 200,
          let jsonData = data
        else {
          completion(.failure)
          return
        }

        do {
          // 8
          let token = try JSONDecoder()
            .decode(Token.self, from: jsonData)
          // 9
          self.token = token.value
          completion(.success)
        } catch {
          // 10
          completion(.failure)
        }
      }
    // 11
    dataTask.resume()
  }
```

Here's what the new method does:

1. Declare a method to log a user in. It takes the user's username, password and a completion handler as parameters.
2. Construct the URL for the login request.
3. Create the Base64-encoded representation of the user's credentials for the header.
4. Create a `URLRequest` for the request to log a user in.
5. Add the necessary header for HTTP Basic authentication and set the HTTP method to **POST**.
6. Create a new `URLSessionDataTask` to send the request.
7. Ensure the response is valid, has a status code of 200 and contains a body.
8. Decode the response body into a `Token`.
9. Save the received token as the `Auth` token.
10. Catch any errors and call the completion handler with the `failure` case.
11. Start the data task to send the request.

Open **LoginTableViewController.swift**. When a user taps **Login**, the application calls `loginTapped(_:)`. At the end of `loginTapped(_:)`, add the following:

```
// 1
Auth().login(username: username, password: password) { result in
  switch result {
  case .success:
    DispatchQueue.main.async {
      let appDelegate =
        UIApplication.shared.delegate as? AppDelegate
      // 2
      appDelegate?.window?.rootViewController =
        UIStoryboard(name: "Main", bundle: Bundle.main)
        .instantiateInitialViewController()
    }
  case .failure:
    let message =
      "Could not login. Check your credentials and try again"
    // 3
    ErrorPresenter.showError(message: message, on: self)
  }
}
```

Here's what this does:

1. Create an instance of `Auth` and call `login(username:password:completion:)`.
2. If the login succeeds, load **Main.storyboard** to display the acronyms table.
3. If the login fails, show an alert using `ErrorPresenter`.

Build and run. When the application launches, it displays the login screen. Enter the admin credentials and tap **Login**:

The app logs you in and takes you to the main acronyms table.

Open **Auth.swift** and add the following implementation to `logout()`:

```
// 1
token = nil
DispatchQueue.main.async {
  guard let applicationDelegate =
    UIApplication.shared.delegate as? AppDelegate else {
      return
  }
  // 2
  let rootController =
    UIStoryboard(name: "Login", bundle: Bundle.main)
      .instantiateViewController(
        withIdentifier: "LoginNavigation")
```

```
    applicationDelegate.window?.rootViewController =
      rootController
  }
```

Here's what this does:

1. Delete any existing token.
2. Load **Login.storyboard** and switch to the login screen.

Build and run. Since you've already logged in, the app takes you to the main acronyms view. Switch to the **Users** tab and tap **Logout**. The app returns to the login screen.

Creating models

The starter project simplifies `CreateAcronymTableViewController` as you no longer have to provide a user when creating an acronym. Open **ResourceRequest.swift**. In `save(_:completion:)` before `var urlRequest = URLRequest(url: resourceURL)` add the following:

```
// 1
guard let token = Auth().token else {
  // 2
  Auth().logout()
  return
}
```

Here's what this does:

1. Get the token from the `Auth` service.
2. If the token doesn't exist, call `logout()` since the user needs to log in again to get a new token.

Next, under `urlRequest.addValue("application/json", forHTTPHeaderField: "Content-Type")` add:

```
urlRequest.addValue(
  "Bearer \(token)",
  forHTTPHeaderField: "Authorization")
```

This adds the token to the request using the **Authorization** header.

Finally, replace the `guard` clause inside the completionHandler of `dataTask(with:completionHandler:)` with the following:

```
guard let httpResponse = response as? HTTPURLResponse else {
  completion(.failure(.noData))
  return
}
guard
  httpResponse.statusCode == 200,
  let jsonData = data
else {
  if httpResponse.statusCode == 401 {
    Auth().logout()
  }
  completion(.failure(.noData))
  return
}
```

This checks the status code of the failure. If the response returns a **401 Unauthorized**, this means the token is invalid. Log the user out to trigger a new login sequence.

Build and run and log in again. Click + and you'll see the new create acronym page, without a user option:

Fill in the form and tap **Save** to create the acronym. You'll also be able to create users and categories. Note that the "create user" flow now includes a new model `CreateUser`. The app sends this model to the API as it contains the password property.

Acronym requests

You still need to add authentication to acronym requests. Open **AcronymRequest.swift** and in `update(with:completion:)`, before `var urlRequest = URLRequest(url: resource)` add the following:

```
guard let token = Auth().token else {
  Auth().logout()
  return
}
```

Like `ResourceRequest`, this gets the token from `Auth` and calls `logout()` if there's an error. After `urlRequest.addValue("application/json", forHTTPHeaderField: "Content-Type")` add:

```
urlRequest.addValue(
  "Bearer \(token)",
  forHTTPHeaderField: "Authorization")
```

This adds the token to the **Authorization** header. Next, replace the `guard` clause in `dataTask(with:completionHandler:)` with following:

```
guard let httpResponse = response as? HTTPURLResponse else {
  completion(.failure(.noData))
  return
}
guard
  httpResponse.statusCode == 200,
  let jsonData = data
else {
  if httpResponse.statusCode == 401 {
    Auth().logout()
  }
  completion(.failure(.noData))
  return
}
```

This calls `logout()` if the token was invalid. Next change `delete()` to add authentication to the request. At the start of the method add:

```
guard let token = Auth().token else {
```

```
    Auth().logout()
    return
  }
```

Next, after `urlRequest.httpMethod = "DELETE"` add the following:

```
  urlRequest.addValue(
    "Bearer \(token)",
    forHTTPHeaderField: "Authorization")
```

Finally, in `add(category:completion:)` before `let url = ...`, get the token:

```
  guard let token = Auth().token else {
    Auth().logout()
    return
  }
```

Next, after `urlRequest.httpMethod = "POST"` add the token to the request:

```
  urlRequest.addValue(
    "Bearer \(token)",
    forHTTPHeaderField: "Authorization")
```

Finally, replace the `guard` clause in `dataTask(with:completionHandler:)` to log the user out if the response returned a **401 Unauthorized**:

```
  guard let httpResponse = response as? HTTPURLResponse else {
    completion(.failure(.invalidResponse))
    return
  }
  guard httpResponse.statusCode == 201 else {
    if httpResponse.statusCode == 401 {
      Auth().logout()
    }
    completion(.failure(.invalidResponse))
    return
  }
```

Build and run. You can now delete and edit acronyms and add categories to them.

Where to go from here?

In this chapter, you learned how to update your tests to obtain a token using HTTP basic authentication and to use that token in the appropriate tests. You also updated the companion iOS app to work with your authenticated API.

At the moment, only authenticated users can create acronyms in the API. However, the website is still open and anyone can do anything! In the next chapter, you'll learn how to apply authentication to the web front-end. You'll learn the differences between authenticating an API and a website and how to use cookies and sessions.

Chapter 20: Web Authentication, Cookies & Sessions

By Tim Condon

In the previous chapters, you learned how to implement authentication in the TIL app's API. In this chapter, you'll see how to implement authentication for the TIL website. You'll learn how authentication works on the web and how Vapor's Authentication module provides all the necessary support. You'll then see how to protect different routes on the website. Finally, you'll learn how to use cookies and sessions to your advantage.

Web authentication

How it works

Earlier, you learned how to use HTTP basic authentication and bearer authentication to protect the API. As you'll recall, this works by sending tokens and credentials in the request headers. However, this isn't possible in web browsers. There's no way to add headers to requests your browser makes with normal HTML.

To work around this, browsers and web sites use **cookies**. A cookie is a small bit of data your application sends to the browser to store on the user's computer. Then, when the user makes a request to your application, the browser attaches the cookies for your site.

You combine this with **sessions** to authenticate users. Sessions allow you to persist state across requests. In Vapor, when you have sessions enabled, the application provides a cookie to the user with a unique ID. This ID identifies the user's session. When the user logs in, Vapor saves the user in the session. When you need to ensure a user has logged in or to get the current authenticated user, you query the session.

Implementing sessions

Vapor manages sessions using a middleware, `SessionsMiddleware`. Open the project in Xcode and open **configure.swift**. In the middleware configuration section, add the following below `app.middleware.use(FileMiddleware(publicDirectory: app.directory.publicDirectory))`:

```
app.middleware.use(app.sessions.middleware)
```

This registers the sessions middleware as a global middleware for your application. It also enables sessions for all requests. Next, open **User.swift** and add the following at the bottom of the file:

```
// 1
extension User: ModelSessionAuthenticatable {}
// 2
extension User: ModelCredentialsAuthenticatable {}
```

Here's what this does:

1. Conform `User` to `ModelSessionAuthenticatable`. This allows the application to save and retrieve your user as part of a session.

2. Conform `User` to `ModelCredentialsAuthenticatable`. This allows Vapor to authenticate users with a username and password when they log in. Since you've already implemented the necessary properties and function for `ModelCredentialsAuthenticatable` in `ModelAuthenticatable`, there's nothing to do here.

Log in

To log a user in, you need two routes — one for showing the login page and one for accepting the POST request from that page. Open **WebsiteController.swift** and add the following at the bottom of the file to create a context for the login page:

```
struct LoginContext: Encodable {
  let title = "Log In"
  let loginError: Bool

  init(loginError: Bool = false) {
    self.loginError = loginError
  }
}
```

This provides the title of the page and a flag to indicate a login error. Next, at the bottom of `WebsiteController`, add a route handler for the page:

```
// 1
func loginHandler(_ req: Request)
  -> EventLoopFuture<View> {
    let context: LoginContext
    // 2
    if let error = req.query[Bool.self, at: "error"], error {
      context = LoginContext(loginError: true)
    } else {
      context = LoginContext()
    }
    // 3
    return req.view.render("login", context)
}
```

Here's what this does:

1. Define a route handler for the login page that returns a future `View`.
2. If the request contains the **error** parameter and it's true, create a context with `loginError` set to `true`.
3. Render the **login.leaf** template, passing in the context.

Create the new template, **login.leaf**, in **Resources/Views** and open the file. Replace the contents of the file with the following:

```
<!-- 1 -->
#extend("base"):
  #export("content"):
    <!-- 2 -->
    <h1>#(title)</h1>

    <!-- 3 -->
    #if(loginError):
      <div class="alert alert-danger" role="alert">
        User authentication error. Either your username or
        password was invalid.
      </div>
    #endif

    <!-- 4 -->
    <form method="post">
      <!-- 5 -->
      <div class="form-group">
        <label for="username">Username</label>
        <input type="text" name="username" class="form-control"
         id="username"/>
      </div>

      <!-- 6 -->
      <div class="form-group">
        <label for="password">Password</label>
        <input type="password" name="password"
         class="form-control" id="password"/>
      </div>

      <!-- 7 -->
      <button type="submit" class="btn btn-primary">
        Log In
      </button>
    </form>
  #endexport
#endextend
```

Here's what's going on in the template:

1. Extend **base.leaf** and export `content` as required.
2. Set the title for the page using the provided `title` from the context.
3. If the context value for `loginError` is `true`, display a suitable message.
4. Define a `<form>` that sends a POST request to same URL when submitted.

5. Add an input for the user's username. The name of the input matches the name required by `ModelCredentialsAuthenticatable`.

6. Add an input for the user's password. Note the `type="password"` — this tells the browser to render the input as a password field. This uses the name for password required by `ModelCredentialsAuthenticatable`.

7. Add a submit button for the form.

Next, open **WebsiteController.swift** and, below `loginHandler(_:)`, add the following route handler for this request:

```
// 1
func loginPostHandler(
  _ req: Request
) -> EventLoopFuture<Response> {
  // 2
  if req.auth.has(User.self) {
    // 3
    return req.eventLoop.future(req.redirect(to: "/"))
  } else {
    // 4
    let context = LoginContext(loginError: true)
    return req
      .view
      .render("login", context)
      .encodeResponse(for: req)
  }
}
```

Here's what this does:

1. Define a route handler that returns `EventLoopFuture<Response>`.

2. Verify that the request has an authenticated `User`. You use middleware to perform the authentication.

3. Redirect to the home page after the login succeeds.

4. If the login failed, redirect back to the login page to show an error.

Finally, at the bottom of `boot(routes:)`, register the two routes:

```
// 1
routes.get("login", use: loginHandler)
// 2
let credentialsAuthRoutes =
  routes.grouped(User.credentialsAuthenticator())
// 3
credentialsAuthRoutes.post("login", use: loginPostHandler)
```

Here's what this does:

1. Route GET requests for **/login** to `loginHandler(_:)`.
2. Create a route group using `ModelCredentialsAuthenticator`. This middleware checks the request for the submitted form. It then verifies the credentials and authenticates the request if successful.
3. Route POST requests for **/login** to `loginPostHandler(_:userData:)` via `credentialsAuthRoutes`.

Build and run the application. In your browser, visit **http://localhost:8080/login**. Click **Log In** without entering data to see the error handling.

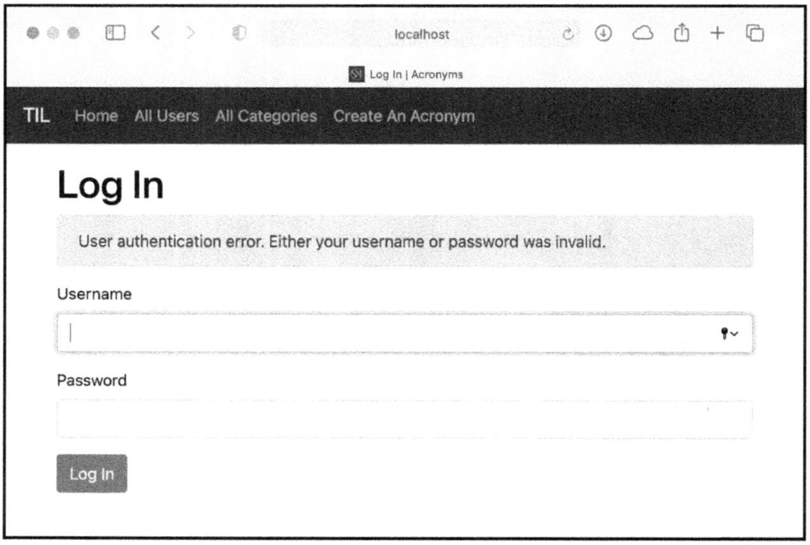

Next, enter your credentials and click **Log In** again. After the app validates your credentials, it redirects you to the main acronyms list.

Protecting routes

In the API, you used `GuardAuthenticationMiddleware` to assert that the request contained an authenticated user. This middleware throws an authentication error if there's no user, resulting in a **401 Unauthorized** response to the client.

On the web, this isn't the best user experience. Instead, you use `RedirectMiddleware` to redirect users to the login page when they try to access a protected route without logging in first. Before you can use this redirect, you must first translate the session cookie, sent by the browser, into an authenticated user.

In `WebsiteController`, replace the entire contents of `boot(routes:)`, including the new routes you just added with the following:

```
let authSessionsRoutes =
  routes.grouped(User.sessionAuthenticator())
```

This creates a route group that runs `DatabaseSessionAuthenticator` before the route handlers. This middleware reads the cookie from the request and looks up the session ID in the application's session list. If the session contains a user, `DatabaseSessionAuthenticator` adds it to the request's authentication cache, making the user available later in the process.

Next, register all the public routes, including the new login routes, in this route group:

```
authSessionsRoutes.get("login", use: loginHandler)
let credentialsAuthRoutes =
  authSessionsRoutes.grouped(User.credentialsAuthenticator())
credentialsAuthRoutes.post("login", use: loginPostHandler)
authSessionsRoutes.get(use: indexHandler)
authSessionsRoutes.get(
  "acronyms",
  ":acronymID",
  use: acronymHandler)
authSessionsRoutes.get("users", ":userID", use: userHandler)
authSessionsRoutes.get("users", use: allUsersHandler)
authSessionsRoutes.get("categories", use: allCategoriesHandler)
authSessionsRoutes.get(
  "categories",
  ":categoryID",
  use: categoryHandler)
```

This makes the `User` available to these pages, even though it's not required. This is useful for displaying user-specific content, such as a profile link, on any page you desire. Underneath these routes, add the following:

```
let protectedRoutes = authSessionsRoutes
  .grouped(User.redirectMiddleware(path: "/login"))
```

This creates a new route group, extending from `authSessionsRoutes`, that includes `RedirectMiddleware` for `User`. The application runs a request through `RedirectMiddleware` before it reaches the route handler, but *after* `DatabaseSessionAuthenticator`. This allows `RedirectMiddleware` to check for an authenticated user. `RedirectMiddleware` requires you to specify the path for redirecting unauthenticated users.

Finally, register the routes that require protection — creating, editing and deleting acronyms — to this route group:

```
protectedRoutes.get(
  "acronyms",
  "create",
  use: createAcronymHandler)
protectedRoutes.post(
  "acronyms",
  "create",
  use: createAcronymPostHandler)
protectedRoutes.get(
  "acronyms",
  ":acronymID",
  "edit",
  use: editAcronymHandler)
protectedRoutes.post(
  "acronyms",
  ":acronymID",
  "edit",
  use: editAcronymPostHandler)
protectedRoutes.post(
  "acronyms",
  ":acronymID",
  "delete",
  use: deleteAcronymHandler)
```

Remember this includes both the GET requests and the POST requests. Build and run, then visit **http://localhost:8080** in your browser.

Click **Create An Acronym** in the navigation bar and, this time, the app redirects you to the login page:

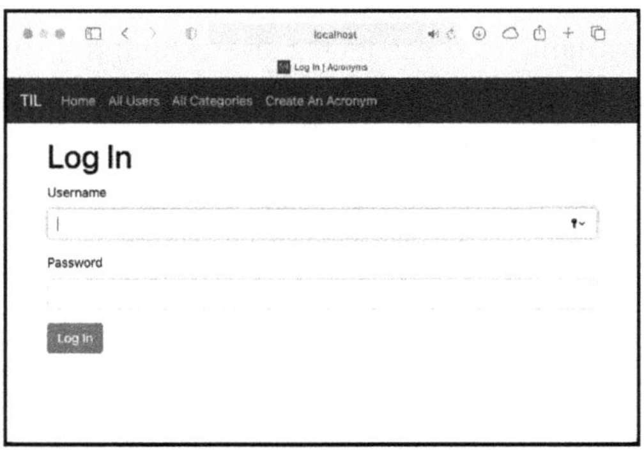

Enter the credentials for the seeded admin user and click **Log In**. The application redirects you to the main acronym list. If you click **Create An Acronym** again, the application lets you access the page.

Updating the site

Just like the API, now that users must login, the application knows which user is creating or editing an acronym. Still in **WebsiteController.swift**, find `CreateAcronymFormData` and remove the user ID:

```
let userID: UUID
```

This is no longer required since you can get it from the authenticated user. Next, find `createAcronymPostHandler(_:data:)` and replace:

```
let acronym = Acronym(
  short: data.short,
  long: data.long,
  userID: data.userID)
```

With the following:

```
let user = try req.auth.require(User.self)
let acronym = try Acronym(
  short: data.short,
  long: data.long,
  userID: user.requireID())
```

This gets the user from the request using `require(_:)`, as in the API. Next, in `editAcronymPostHandler(_:)`, add the following at the top of the method:

```
let user = try req.auth.require(User.self)
let userID = try user.requireID()
```

Again, this gets the authenticated user from the request and then gets the associated ID. It's useful to do it here as you can throw errors in the main body of `editAcronymPostHandler(_:)`. Finally, replace `acronym.$user.id = updateData.userID` with the following:

```
acronym.$user.id = userID
```

This uses the authenticated user's ID for the updated acronym. Now, both creating and editing acronyms use the authenticated user. As a result, you no longer need to show the users in the form. Open **createAcronym.leaf** and remove the following code:

```
<div class="form-group">
  <label for="userID">User</label>
  <select name="userID" class="form-control" id="userID">
```

```
      #for(user in users):
        <option value="#(user.id)"
          #if(editing):
            #if(acronym.user.id == user.id): selected #endif
          #endif>
          #(user.name)
        </option>
      #endfor
    </select>
  </div>
```

As you use the same template for creating and editing acronyms, you only need to remove this from one place! Next, open **WebsiteController.swift** and remove the following from `CreateAcronymContext`:

```
let users: [User]
```

This is no longer required as the template doesn't use `users` any longer. In `createAcronymHandler(_:)`, address the change by replacing the body of the method with:

```
let context = CreateAcronymContext()
return req.view.render("createAcronym", context)
```

Next, remove the following from `EditAcronymContext`:

```
let users: [User]
```

Next, replace `editAcronymHandler(_:)`, with the following:

```
func editAcronymHandler(_ req: Request)
  -> EventLoopFuture<View> {
  return Acronym
    .find(req.parameters.get("acronymID"), on: req.db)
    .unwrap(or: Abort(.notFound))
    .flatMap { acronym in
      acronym.$categories.get(on: req.db)
        .flatMap { categories in
          let context = EditAcronymContext(
            acronym: acronym,
            categories: categories)
          return req.view.render("createAcronym", context)
      }
  }
}
```

This removes the query to get all the users and the resulting extra future. Build and run, then visit **http://localhost:8080/** in your browser. Click **Create An Acronym** and log in again.

> **Note**: You need to log in again after restarting because the application keeps sessions in memory. For production applications, you can use Redis or a database to persist this information and share it across server instances.

Head back to **Create An Acronym** and the form no longer includes the list of users:

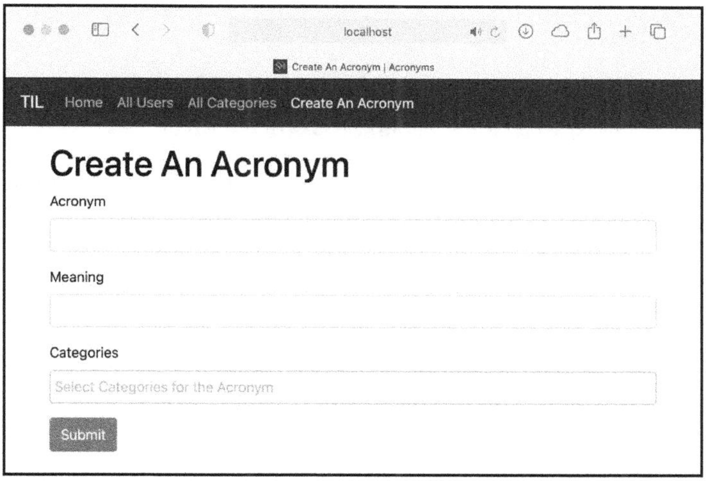

Create an acronym. When the application redirects you to the acronym's page, you'll see Vapor has used the authenticated user as the acronym's user:

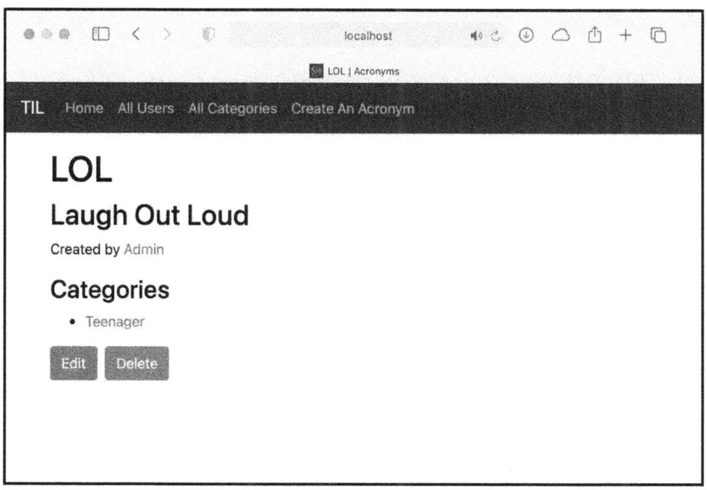

Log out

When you allow users to log in to your site, you should also allow them to log out. Still in **WebsiteController.swift**, add the following after `loginPostHandler(_:)`:

```
// 1
func logoutHandler(_ req: Request) -> Response {
  // 2
  req.auth.logout(User.self)
  // 3
  return req.redirect(to: "/")
}
```

Here's what this does:

1. Define a route handler that simply returns `Response`. There's no asynchronous work in this method, so it doesn't need to return a future.
2. Call `logout(_:)` on the request. This deletes the user from the session so it can't be used to authenticate future requests.
3. Return a redirect to the index page.

Register the route inside `boot(routes:)` after `credentialsAuthRoutes.post("login", use: loginPostHandler)`:

```
authSessionsRoutes.post("logout", use: logoutHandler)
```

This connects POST requests for **/logout** to `logoutHandler()`. You should always use POST requests for anything that changes application state. Modern browsers prefetch GET requests which could result in your users being unexpectedly logged out if you don't use POST!

Open **base.leaf** and after `</ul>` in the navigation bar add the following:

```
<!-- 1 -->
#if(userLoggedIn):
  <!-- 2 -->
  <form class="form-inline" action="/logout" method="POST">
    <!-- 3 -->
    <input class="nav-link btn btn-secondary mr-sm-2"
     type="submit" value="Log out">
  </form>
#endif
```

Here's what this does:

1. Check to see if `userLoggedIn` is set so you only display the logout option when a user's logged in.
2. Create a new form that sends a POST request to **/logout**.
3. Add a submit button to the form with the value **Log out** and style it like a button and align it to the right.

Save the file. Next, open **WebsiteController.swift** and, at the bottom of `IndexContext`, add the following:

```
let userLoggedIn: Bool
```

This is the flag you set to tell the template the request contains a logged in user. Finally, in `indexHandler(_:)`, replace `let context = IndexContext(title: "Home page", acronyms: acronyms)` with the following:

```
// 1
let userLoggedIn = req.auth.has(User.self)
// 2
let context = IndexContext(
  title: "Home page",
  acronyms: acronyms,
  userLoggedIn: userLoggedIn)
```

Here's what this does:

1. Check if the request contains an authenticated user.
2. Pass the result to the new flag in `IndexContext`.

Build and run, then head to your browser. Click **Create An Acronym** and log in. When the application redirects you to the home page, you'll see a new **Log out** option in the top right:

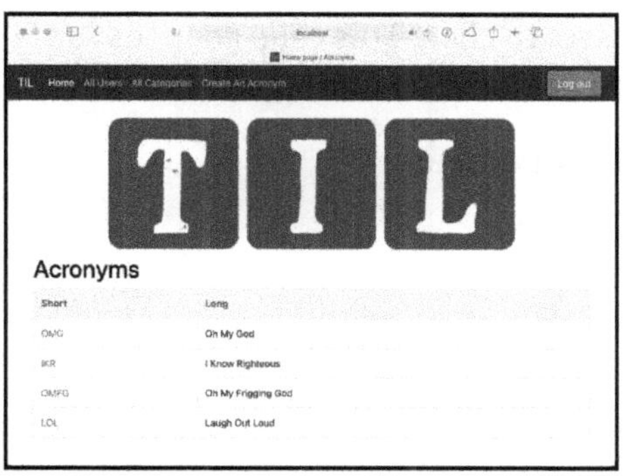

If you click this, then click **Create An Acronym** again, you'll need to sign in as the application has logged you out.

Cookies

Cookies are widely used on the web. Everyone's seen the cookie consent messages that pop up on a site when you first visit. You've already used cookies to implement authentication, but sometimes you want to set and read cookies manually.

A common way to handle the cookie consent message is to add a cookie when a user has accepted the notice (the irony!).

Open **base.leaf** and, above the script tag for jQuery, add the following:

```
<!-- 1 -->
#if(showCookieMessage):
  <!-- 2 -->
  <footer id="cookie-footer">
    <div id="cookieMessage" class="container">
      <span class="muted">
        <!-- 3 -->
        This site uses cookies! To accept this, click
        <a href="#" onclick="cookiesConfirmed()">OK</a>
      </span>
    </div>
  </footer>
  <!-- 4 -->
  <script src="/scripts/cookies.js"></script>
#endif
```

Here's what the code does:

1. Check whether a `showCookieMessage` flag is set for the template.
2. If so, add a `<footer>` for the cookie message, styled using Bootstrap.
3. Add an **OK** link for users to click. This calls `cookiesConfirmed()`, a JavaScript function that dismisses the cookie message.
4. Add the JavaScript file for cookies.

Next, in **base.leaf** above `<title>#(title) | Acronyms</title>`, add the following:

```
<link rel="stylesheet" href="/styles/style.css">
```

This includes a new stylesheet for the website. You'll use this to add custom styling to your site. Save the file.

To create this stylesheet, enter the following in Terminal:

```
mkdir Public/styles
touch Public/styles/style.css
```

Next, open **style.css** and add the following:

```
#cookie-footer {
  position: absolute;
  bottom: 0;
  width: 100%;
  height: 60px;
  line-height: 60px;
  background-color: #f5f5f5;
}
```

This styling pins the cookie message to the bottom of the page. Save the stylesheet. Next, enter the following into Terminal to create a new file in **Public/scripts** called **cookies.js** :

```
touch Public/scripts/cookies.js
```

Next, open **cookies.js** and add the following:

```
// 1
function cookiesConfirmed() {
  // 2
  $('#cookie-footer').hide();
  // 3
  var d = new Date();
  d.setTime(d.getTime() + (365*24*60*60*1000));
  var expires = "expires="+ d.toUTCString();
  // 4
  document.cookie = "cookies-accepted=true;" + expires;
}
```

Here's what the JavaScript does:

1. Define a function, `cookiesConfirmed()`, that the browser calls when the user clicks the OK link in the cookie message.
2. Hide the cookie message.
3. Create a date that's one year in the future. Then, create the **expires** string required for the cookie. By default, cookies are valid for the browser session — when the user closes the browser window or tab, the browser deletes the cookie. Adding the date ensures the browser persists the cookie for a year.
4. Add a cookie called `cookies-accepted` to the page using JavaScript. You'll check to see if this cookie exists when working out whether to show the cookie consent message.

Save the file. Open **WebsiteController.swift** in Xcode and add the following to the bottom of `IndexContext`:

```
let showCookieMessage: Bool
```

This flag indicates to the template whether it should display the cookie consent message. In `indexHandler(_:)`, replace `let context = IndexContext...` with the following:

```
// 1
let showCookieMessage =
  req.cookies["cookies-accepted"] == nil
// 2
let context = IndexContext(
  title: "Home page",
  acronyms: acronyms,
  userLoggedIn: userLoggedIn,
  showCookieMessage: showCookieMessage)
```

Here's what this does:

1. See if a cookie called `cookies-accepted` exists. If it doesn't, set the `showCookieMessage` flag to `true`. You can read cookies from the request and set them on a response.
2. Pass the flag to `IndexContext` so the template knows whether to show the message.

Build and run, then go to **http://localhost:8080** in your browser. The site shows the cookie consent message on the page:

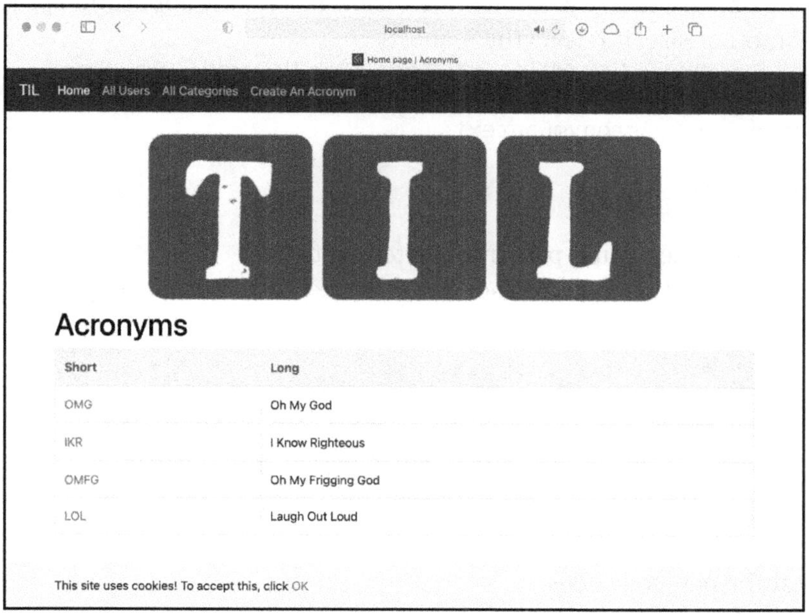

Click **OK** in the cookie consent message and your JavaScript code hides it. Refresh the page and the site won't show the message again.

Sessions

In addition to using cookies for web authentication, you've also made use of sessions. Sessions are useful in a number of scenarios, including authentication.

Another such scenario is Cross-Site Request Forgery (CSRF) prevention. CSRF is where an attacker tricks a user into sending an unexpected or unintended POST request, such as a request to a bank to transfer money. If the user is logged in, the site processes the request without any issue.

The same is possible with creating acronyms in the TIL website. If someone tricked an already-authenticated user into sending a POST request to **/acronyms/create**, the application would create the acronym!

A common approach to solving this problem involves including a CSRF token in the form. When the application receives the POST request, it verifies that the CSRF token matches the one issued to the form. If the tokens match, the application processes the request; otherwise, it rejects the request.

To add CSRF token support, open **WebsiteController.swift** and add the following to the bottom of `CreateAcronymContext`:

```
let csrfToken: String
```

This is the CSRF token you'll pass into the template. In `createAcronymHandler(_:)`, replace `let context = CreateAcronymContext()` with the following:

```
// 1
let token = [UInt8].random(count: 16).base64
// 2
let context = CreateAcronymContext(csrfToken: token)
// 3
req.session.data["CSRF_TOKEN"] = token
```

Here's what the new code does:

1. Create a token using 16 bytes of randomly generated data, Base64 encoded.
2. Initialize a `CreateAcronymContext` with the created token.
3. Save the token into the request's session data under the **CSRF_TOKEN** key.

Vapor persists the token in the session across different requests. When the user makes a new request and provides the cookie that identifies the session, all the session data is available. Open **createAcronym.leaf** and, underneath `<form method="post">`, add the following:

```
#if(csrfToken):
  <input type="hidden" name="csrfToken" value="#(csrfToken)">
#endif
```

This checks to see if the context contains a token. If so, the template adds a new input element to the form with the token as the value. Since this element is hidden, the browser doesn't display the token to the user.

Save the file. Back in **WebsiteController.swift**, add the following to the bottom of `CreateAcronymFormData`:

```
let csrfToken: String?
```

This is the CSRF token that the form sends using the hidden input. The token is optional as it's not required by the edit acronym page for now. Finally, in `createAcronymPostHandler(_:data:)` after `let user = try req.auth.require(User.self)`, add the following:

```
// 1
let expectedToken = req.session.data["CSRF_TOKEN"]
// 2
req.session.data["CSRF_TOKEN"] = nil
// 3
guard
  let csrfToken = data.csrfToken,
  expectedToken == csrfToken
else {
  throw Abort(.badRequest)
}
```

Here's what this does:

1. Get the expected token from the request's session data. This is the token you saved in `createAcronymHandler(_:)`.
2. Clear the CSRF token now that you've used it. You generate a new token with each form.
3. Ensure the provided token is not nil and matches the expected token; otherwise, throw a **400 Bad Request** error.

Build and run, then visit **http://localhost:8080** in your browser. Go to the **Create An Acronym** page once you've logged in and create a new acronym. The application creates the acronym as the form provided the correct CSRF token. If you send a request without the token, either by removing it from your page or using RESTed, you'll get a **400 Bad Request** response.

Where to go from here?

In this chapter, you learned how to add authentication to the application's web site. You also learned how to make use of both sessions and cookies. You might want to look at adding CSRF tokens to the other POST routes, such as deleting and editing acronyms. In the next chapter, you'll learn how to use Vapor's validation library to automatically validate objects, request data and inputs.

Chapter 21: Validation

By Tim Condon

In the previous chapters, you built a fully-functional API and website. Users can send requests and fill in forms to create acronyms, categories and other users. In this chapter, you'll learn how to use Vapor's Validation library to verify some of the information users send the application. You'll create a registration page on the website for users to sign up. You'll then validate the data from this form and display an error message if the data isn't correct.

The registration page

Create a new file in **Resources/Views** called **register.leaf**. This is the template for the registration page. Open **register.leaf** and replace its contents with the following:

```
#extend("base"):
  #export("content"):
    <h1>#(title)</h1>

    <form method="post">
        <div class="form-group">
        <label for="name">Name</label>
        <input type="text" name="name" class="form-control"
        id="name"/>
        </div>

        <div class="form-group">
        <label for="username">Username</label>
        <input type="text" name="username" class="form-control"
        id="username"/>
        </div>
```

```
      <div class="form-group">
      <label for="password">Password</label>
      <input type="password" name="password"
      class="form-control" id="password"/>
      </div>

      <div class="form-group">
      <label for="confirmPassword">Confirm Password</label>
      <input type="password" name="confirmPassword"
      class="form-control" id="confirmPassword"/>
      </div>

      <button type="submit" class="btn btn-primary">
      Register
      </button>
    </form>
  #endexport
#endextend
```

This is very similar to the templates for creating an acronym and logging in. The template contains four input fields for:

- name
- username
- password
- password confirmation

Save the file. Next, in Xcode, open **WebsiteController.swift** and, at the bottom of the file, add the following context for the registration page:

```
struct RegisterContext: Encodable {
  let title = "Register"
}
```

Next, below `logoutHandler(_:)`, add the following route handler for the registration page:

```
func registerHandler(_ req: Request) -> EventLoopFuture<View> {
  let context = RegisterContext()
  return req.view.render("register", context)
}
```

Like the other routes handlers, this creates a context then calls `render(_:_:)` to render **register.leaf**.

Next, create the `Content` for the POST request for registration, add the following to the end of **WebsiteController.swift**:

```
struct RegisterData: Content {
  let name: String
  let username: String
  let password: String
  let confirmPassword: String
}
```

This `Content` type matches the expected data received from the registration POST request. The variables match the names of the inputs in **register.leaf**. Next, create a route handler for this POST request, add the following after `registerHandler(_:)`:

```
// 1
func registerPostHandler(
  _ req: Request
) throws -> EventLoopFuture<Response> {
  // 2
  let data = try req.content.decode(RegisterData.self)
  // 3
  let password = try Bcrypt.hash(data.password)
  // 4
  let user = User(
    name: data.name,
    username: data.username,
    password: password)
  // 5
  return user.save(on: req.db).map {
    // 6
    req.auth.login(user)
    // 7
    return req.redirect(to: "/")
  }
}
```

Here's what's going on in the route handler:

1. Define a route handler that accepts a request and returns `EventLoopFuture<Response>`.
2. Decode the request body to `RegisterData`.
3. Hash the password submitted to the form.
4. Create a new `User`, using the data from the form and the hashed password.
5. Save the new user and unwrap the returned future.

6. Authenticate the session for the new user. This automatically logs users in when they register, thereby providing a nice user experience when signing up with the site.

7. Return a redirect back to the home page.

Next, in `boot(routes:)` add the following below `authSessionsRoutes.post("logout", use: logoutHandler)`:

```
// 1
authSessionsRoutes.get("register", use: registerHandler)
// 2
authSessionsRoutes.post("register", use: registerPostHandler)
```

Here's what this does:

1. Connect a GET request for **/register** to `registerHandler(_:)`.

2. Connect a POST request for **/register** to `registerPostHandler(_:data:)`.

Finally, open **base.leaf**. Before the closing `</ul>` in the navigation bar, add the following:

```
<!-- 1 -->
#if(!userLoggedIn):
  <!-- 2 -->
  <li class="nav-item #if(title == "Register"): active #endif">
    <!-- 3 -->
    <a href="/register" class="nav-link">Register</a>
  </li>
#endif
```

Here's what the new Leaf code does:

1. Check to see if there's a logged in user. You only want to display the register link if there's no user logged in.

2. Add a new navigation link to the navigation bar. Set the `active` class if the current page is the **Register** page.

3. Add a link to the new **/register** route.

Save the template then build and run the project in Xcode. Visit **http://localhost:8080** in your browser. You'll see the new navigation link:

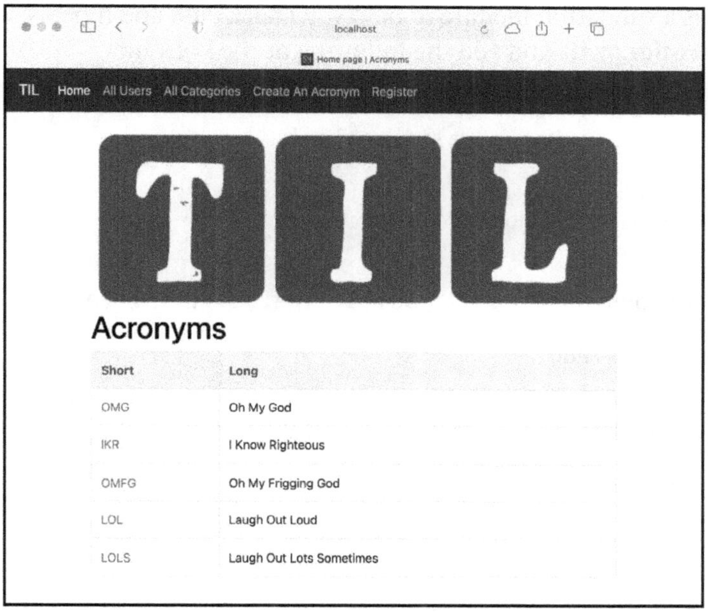

Click **Register** and you'll see the new register page:

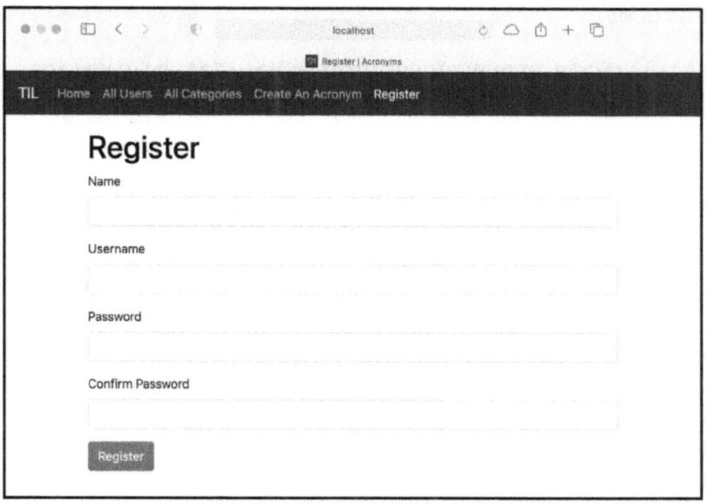

If you fill out the form and click **Register**, the app takes you to the home page. Notice the **Log out** button in the top right; this confirms that registration automatically logged you in.

Basic validation

Vapor provides a validation module to help you check data and models. Open **WebsiteController.swift** and add the following at the bottom:

```
// 1
extension RegisterData: Validatable {
  // 2
  public static func validations(
    _ validations: inout Validations
  ) {
    // 3
    validations.add("name", as: String.self, is: .ascii)
    // 4
    validations.add(
      "username",
      as: String.self,
      is: .alphanumeric && .count(3...))
    // 5
    validations.add(
      "password",
      as: String.self,
      is: .count(8...))
  }
}
```

Here's what this does:

1. Extend `RegisterData` to make it conform to `Validatable`. `Validatable` allows you to validate types with Vapor.
2. Implement `validations(_:)` as required by `Validatable`.
3. Add a validator to ensure `RegisterData`'s name contains only ASCII characters and is a `String`. **Note**: Be careful when adding restrictions on names like this. Some countries, such as China, don't have names with ASCII characters.
4. Add a validator to ensure the username contains only alphanumeric characters and is at least 3 characters long. `.count(_:)` takes a Swift `Range`, allowing you to create both open-ended and closed ranges, as necessary.
5. Add a validator to ensure the password is at least eight characters long. Currently, it's not possible to add a validation to two different properties. You must provide your own check that `password` and `confirmPassword` match.

As you can see, Vapor allows you to create powerful validations on models or incoming data. In `registerPostHandler(_:)`, add the following at the top of the method:

```
do {
  try RegisterData.validate(content: req)
} catch {
  return req.eventLoop.future(req.redirect(to: "/register"))
}
```

This calls `validate(content:)` on `RegisterData`, checking each each validator you added previously. `validate(content:)` can throw a number of `ValidationsErrors` depending on the checks you added. In an API, you can let this error propagate back to the user but, on a website, that doesn't make for a good user experience. In this case, you redirect the user back to the "register" page.

Build and run, then visit the "register" page in your browser. If you enter information that doesn't match the validators, the app sends you back to try again.

Custom validation

Vapor allows you to write expressive and complex validations, but sometimes you need more than the built-in options offer. For example, you may want to validate a US Zip code. To demonstrate this, at the bottom of **WebsiteController.swift**, add the following:

```
// 1
extension ValidatorResults {
  // 2
  struct ZipCode {
    let isValidZipCode: Bool
  }
}

// 3
extension ValidatorResults.ZipCode: ValidatorResult {
  // 4
  var isFailure: Bool {
    !isValidZipCode
  }

  // 5
  var successDescription: String? {
    "is a valid zip code"
  }
```

```
  // 6
  var failureDescription: String? {
    "is not a valid zip code"
  }
}
```

Here's what the new code does:

1. Create an extension for `ValidatorResults` to add your own results.
2. Create a `ZipCode` result that contains the result check.
3. Create an extension for the new `ZipCode` type that conforms to `ValidatorResult`.
4. Implement `isFailure` as required by `ValidatorResult`. Define what counts as a failure.
5. Implement `successDescription` as required by `ValidatorResult`.
6. Implement `failureDescription` as required by `ValidatorResult`. Vapor uses this when throwing an error when `isFailure` is true.

Next, at the bottom of the file add a new `Validator` for a zip code:

```
// 1
extension Validator where T == String {
  // 2
  private static var zipCodeRegex: String {
    "^\\d{5}(?:[-\\s]\\d{4})?$"
  }

  // 3
  public static var zipCode: Validator<T> {
    // 4
    Validator { input -> ValidatorResult in
      // 5
      guard
        let range = input.range(
          of: zipCodeRegex,
          options: [.regularExpression]),
        range.lowerBound == input.startIndex
          && range.upperBound == input.endIndex
      else {
        // 6
        return ValidatorResults.ZipCode(isValidZipCode: false)
      }
      // 7
      return ValidatorResults.ZipCode(isValidZipCode: true)
    }
```

```
    }
  }
```

Here's what the new validator does:

1. Create an extension for `Validator` that works on `String`s.
2. Define the regular expression to use to check for a valid US zip code.
3. Define a new validator type for a zip code.
4. Construct a new `Validator`. This takes a closure which has the data to validate as the parameter and returns `ValidatorResult`.
5. Check the zip code matches the regular expression.
6. If the zip code does not match, return `ValidatorResult` with `isValidZipCode` set to `false`.
7. Otherwise, return a successful `ValidatorResult`.

Finally, in the extension conforming `RegisterData` to `Validatable`, add the following to the end of `validations(_:)`:

```
validations.add(
  "zipCode",
  as: String.self,
  is: .zipCode,
  required: false)
```

This add a validation to a property called `zipCode` sent in the request body. The property must be a `String` and match the `zipCode` validation you added above. However, setting `required` to `false` marks the property as optional. Vapor will validate it if it exists, but won't throw an error if `zipCode` is not sent. This is useful as you don't have a zip code property on your registration form yet!

Displaying an error

Currently, when a user fills out the form incorrectly, the application redirects back to the form with no indication of what went wrong. Open **register.leaf** and add the following under `<h1>#(title)</h1>`:

```
#if(message):
  <div class="alert alert-danger" role="alert">
    Please fix the following errors:<br />
```

```
      #(message)
    </div>
  #endif
```

If the page context includes `message`, this displays it in a new `<div>`. You style the new message appropriately by setting the `alert` and `alert-danger` classes. Open **WebsiteController.swift** and add the following to the end of `RegisterContext`:

```
let message: String?

init(message: String? = nil) {
  self.message = message
}
```

This is the message to display on the registration page. Remember that Leaf handles `nil` gracefully, allowing you to use the default value in the normal case.

In `registerHandler(_:)`, replace:

```
let context = RegisterContext()
```

With the following:

```
let context: RegisterContext
if let message = req.query[String.self, at: "message"] {
  context = RegisterContext(message: message)
} else {
  context = RegisterContext()
}
```

This checks the request's query. If **message** exists — i.e., the URL is **/register?message=some-string** — the route handler includes it in the context Leaf uses to render the page.

Finally, in `registerPostHandler(_:data:)`, replace the `catch` block with:

```
catch let error as ValidationsError {
  let message =
    error.description
    .addingPercentEncoding(
      withAllowedCharacters: .urlQueryAllowed
    ) ?? "Unknown error"
  let redirect =
    req.redirect(to: "/register?message=\(message)")
  return req.eventLoop.future(redirect)
}
```

When validation fails, the route handler extracts the `description` from the `ValidationsError`. Vapor combines all the errors into one description. The code then escapes the description properly for inclusion in a URL or provides a default message if the description is `nil`. It then adds the message to the redirect URL. Finally, it redirects the user back to the registration page. Build and run, then visit **http://localhost:8080/register** in your browser.

Submit the empty form and you'll see the new message:

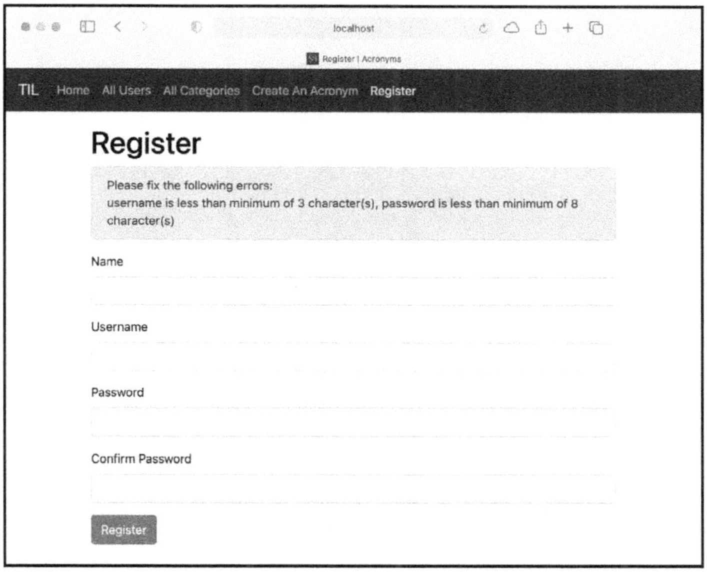

Where to go from here?

In this chapter, you learned how to use Vapor's validation library to check a request's data. You can apply validation to models and other types as well.

In the next chapter, you'll learn how to integrate the TIL application with an OAuth provider. This lets you delegate login and registration to online services such Google or GitHub, allowing users to sign in with an existing account.

Chapter 22: Google Authentication

By Tim Condon

In the previous chapters, you learned how to add authentication to the TIL web site. However, sometimes users don't want to create extra accounts for an application and would prefer to use their existing accounts.

In this chapter, you'll learn how to use OAuth 2.0 to delegate authentication to Google, so users can log in with their Google accounts instead.

OAuth 2.0

OAuth 2.0 (https://tools.ietf.org/html/rfc6749) is an authorization framework that allows third-party applications to access resources on behalf of a user. Whenever you log in to a website with your Google account, you're using OAuth.

When you click **Login with Google**, Google is the site that authenticates you. You then authorize the application to have access to your Google data, such as your email. Once you've allowed the application access, Google gives the application a token. The app uses this token to authenticate requests to Google APIs. You'll implement this technique in this chapter.

> **Note**: You must have a Google account to complete this chapter. If you don't have one, visit https://accounts.google.com/SignUp to create one.

Imperial

Writing all the necessary scaffolding to interact with Google's OAuth system and get a token is a time-consuming job!

There's a community package called Imperial, https://github.com/vapor-community/Imperial, that does the heavy lifting for you. It has integrations for Google, Facebook and GitHub and several more.

Adding to your project

Open **Package.swift** in Xcode to add the new dependency. Replace:

```
.package(
  url: "https://github.com/vapor/leaf.git",
  from: "4.0.0")
```

with the following:

```
.package(
  url: "https://github.com/vapor/leaf.git",
  from: "4.0.0"),
.package(
  url: "https://github.com/vapor-community/Imperial.git",
  from: "1.0.0")
```

Next, add the dependency to your `App` target's dependency array. Replace:

```
.product(name: "Leaf", package: "leaf")
```

with the following:

```
.product(name: "Leaf", package: "leaf"),
.product(name: "ImperialGoogle", package: "Imperial")
```

Next, create a file for a new controller to manage Imperial's routes. In **Sources/App/Controllers** create a file called **ImperialController.swift**. Open the new file and create a new empty controller:

```
import ImperialGoogle
import Vapor
import Fluent

struct ImperialController: RouteCollection {
  func boot(routes: RoutesBuilder) throws {
  }
```

```
}
```

This creates a new type, `ImperialController`, that conforms to `RouteCollection`, implementing the required `boot(routes:)`.

Finally, open **routes.swift** and add the controller to your application at the bottom of `routes(_:)`:

```
let imperialController = ImperialController()
try app.register(collection: imperialController)
```

Setting up your application with Google

To be able to use Google OAuth in your application, you must first register the application with Google. In your browser, go to https://console.developers.google.com/apis/credentials.

If this is the first time you've used Google's credentials, the site prompts you to create a project:

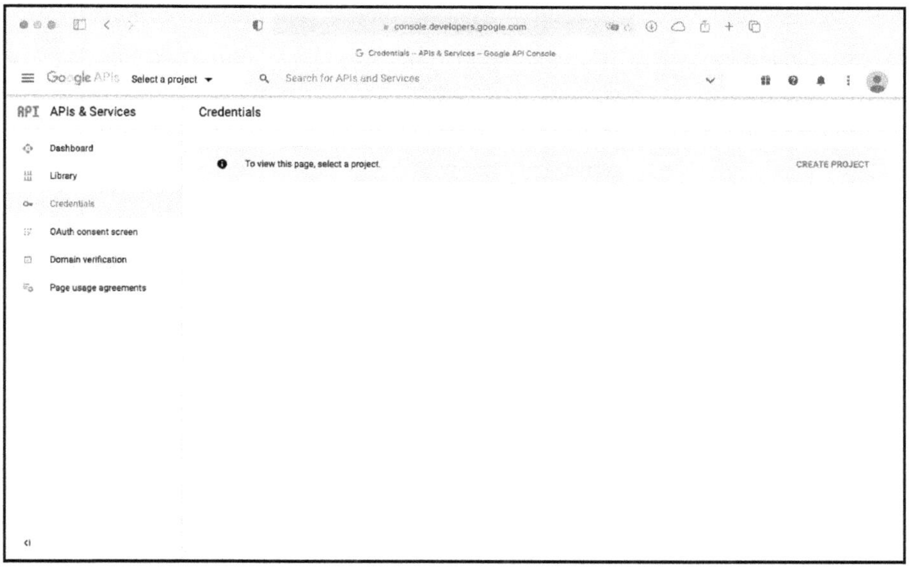

Click **Create Project** to create a project for the TIL application. Fill in the form with an appropriate name, e.g. **Vapor TIL**:

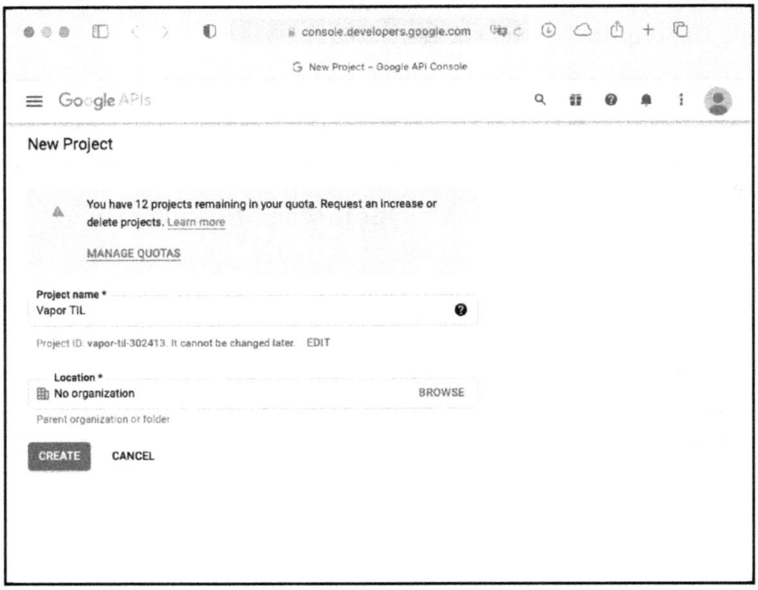

After it creates the project, the site takes you back to the Google credentials page for the newly created project. This time, click **Create Credentials** to create credentials for the TIL app and choose **OAuth client ID**:

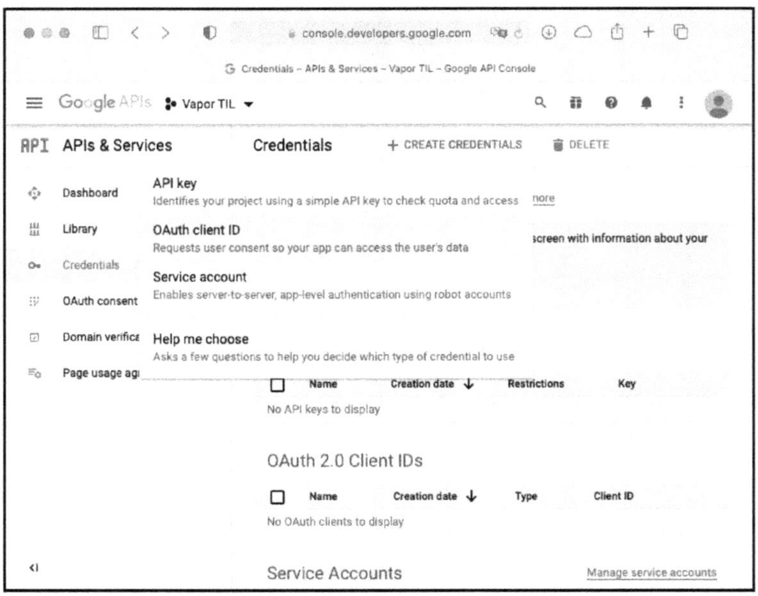

Next, click **Configure consent screen** to set up the page Google presents to users, so they can allow your application access to their details.

Choose **External** for the user type and click **Create**.

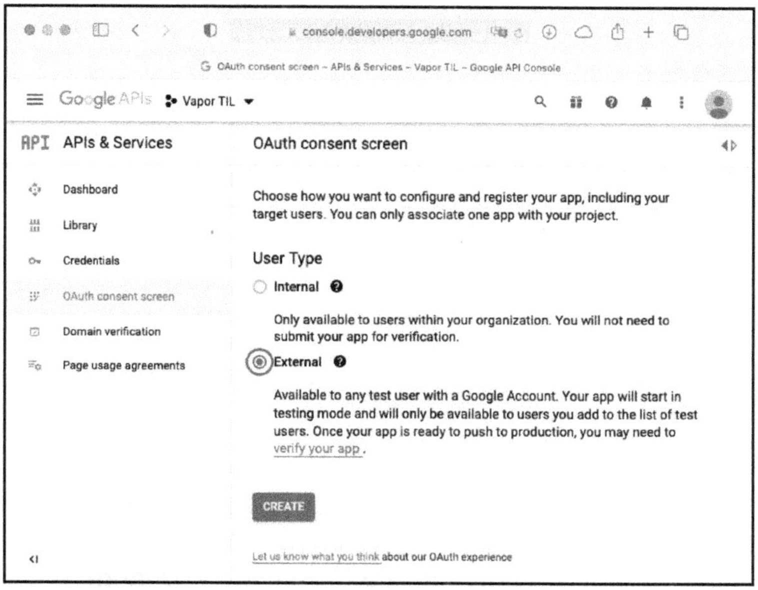

Add an app name and select the user support email.

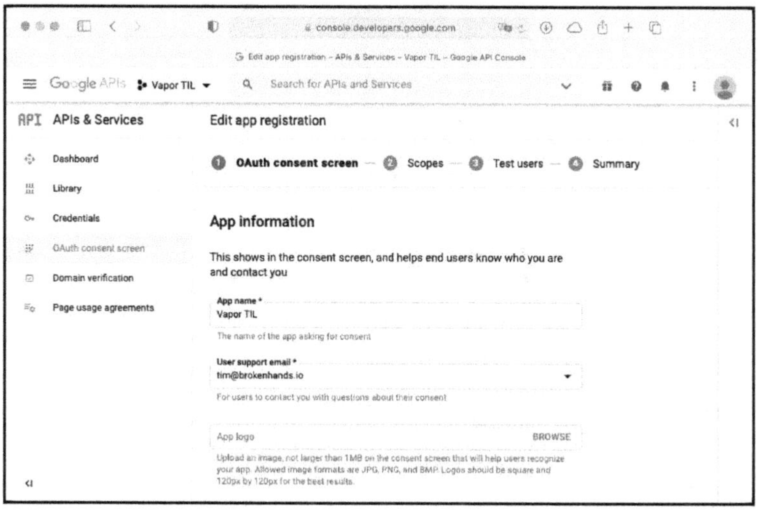

At the bottom of the page, add your developer contact information. Click **Save and Continue**.

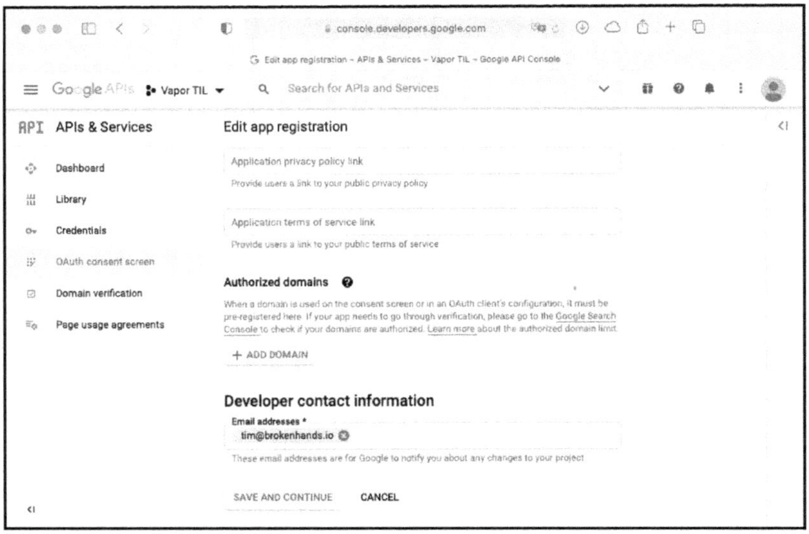

On the next screen, you configure the scopes for your application. These are the permissions you want to request from users, such as their email address. Click **Add or remove scopes** and select both **/auth/userinfo.email** and **/auth/userinfo.profile**. This gives you access to the user's email and profile which you need to create an account in the TIL app.

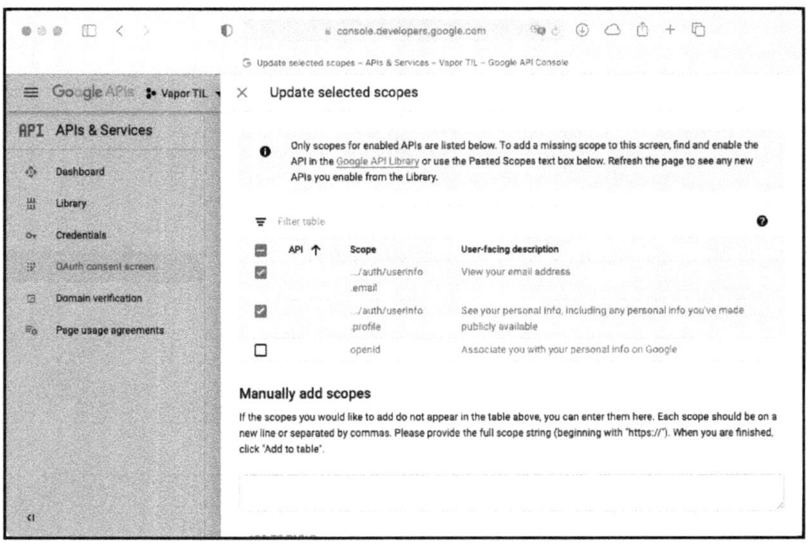

Once you've selected the scopes, click **Update** and then **Save and continue**. Next, you need to select the users you'll use for testing. Click **Add Users** and add any users you want to be able to log in. If you publish your app, you can verify your domain and app to remove this limitation. Click **Save and continue**.

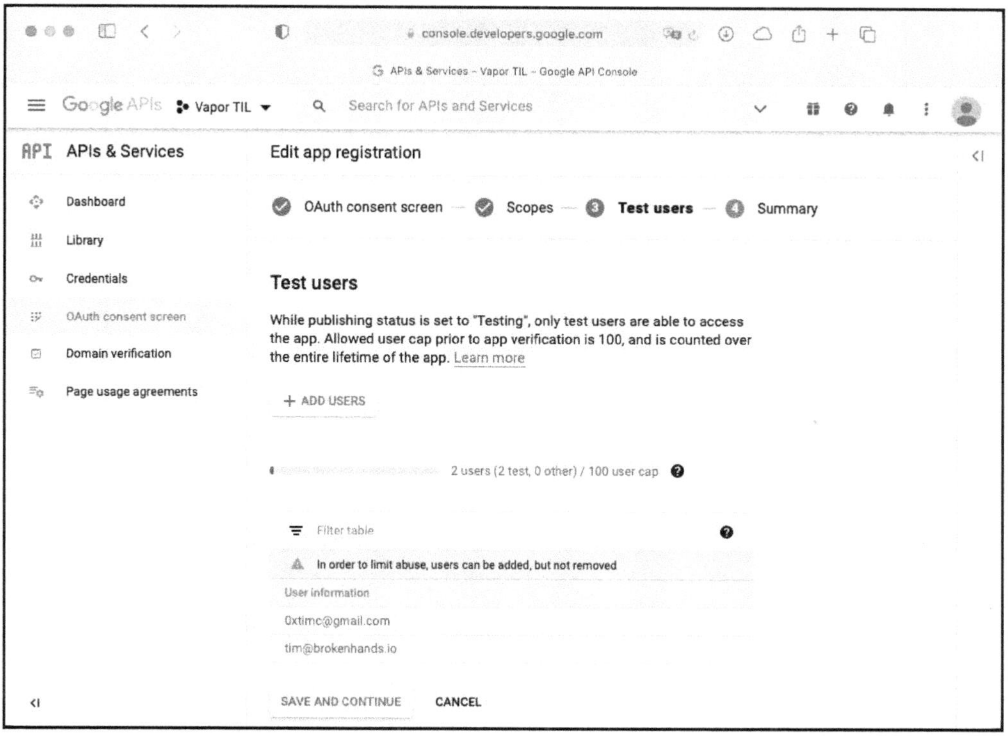

You've completed the OAuth consent screen so click **Back to dashboard**. Click the **Credentials** page again and click **Create Credentials** once more and choose OAuth client ID. When creating a client ID, choose **Web application**. Add a redirect URI for your application for testing — **http://localhost:8080/oauth/google**. This is the URL that Google redirects back to once users have allowed your application access to their data.

If you want to deploy your application to the internet, such as with AWS or Heroku, add another redirect for the URL for that site — e.g., **https://rw-til-vapor.herokuapp.com/oauth/google**:

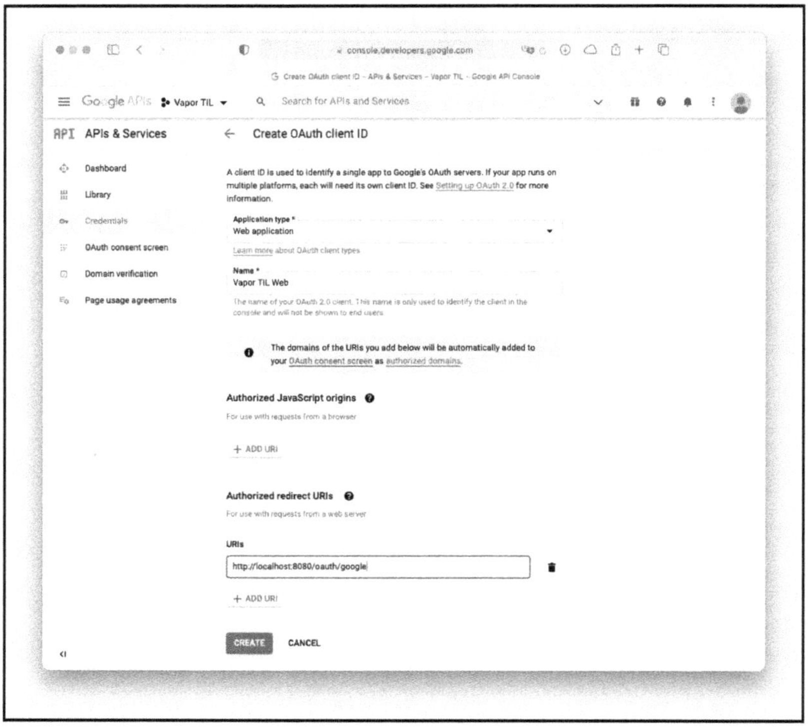

Click **Create** and the site gives you your client ID and client secret:

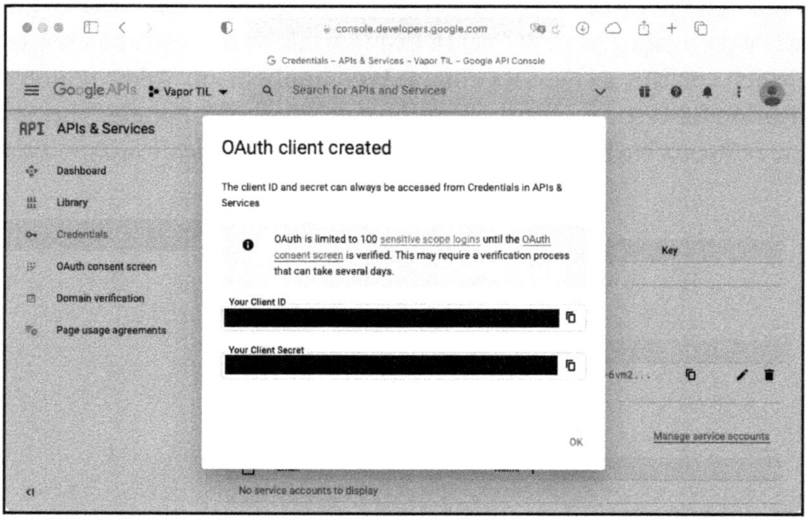

> **Note**: You *must* keep these safe and secure. Your secret allows you access to Google's APIs, and you should not share or check the secret into source control. You should treat it like a password.

Setting up the integration

Now that you've registered your application with Google, you can start integrating Imperial. Open **ImperialController.swift** and add the following under `boot(routes:)`:

```
func processGoogleLogin(request: Request, token: String)
  throws -> EventLoopFuture<ResponseEncodable> {
    request.eventLoop.future(request.redirect(to: "/"))
  }
```

This defines a method to handle the Google login. The handler simply redirects the user to the home page — the same way that the regular login works. Imperial uses this method as the final callback once it has handled the Google redirect. Notice the use of `eventLoop.future(_:)` to create a future from `request.redirect(to:)`. This is because the method that Imperial uses requires an `EventLoopFuture`.

Next, set up the Imperial routes by adding the following in `boot(routes:)`:

```
guard let googleCallbackURL =
  Environment.get("GOOGLE_CALLBACK_URL") else {
    fatalError("Google callback URL not set")
}
try routes.oAuth(
  from: Google.self,
  authenticate: "login-google",
  callback: googleCallbackURL,
  scope: ["profile", "email"],
  completion: processGoogleLogin)
```

Here's what this does:

- Get the callback URL for Google from an environment variable — this is the URL you set up in the Google console.
- Register Imperial's Google OAuth router with your app's router.
- Tell Imperial to use the Google handlers.
- Set up the `/login-google` route as the route that triggers the OAuth flow. This is the route the application uses to allow users to log in via Google.

- Provide the callback URL to Imperial.
- Request the **profile** and **email** scopes from Google — this matches the scopes you set when creating your application earlier.
- Set the completion handler to `processGoogleLogin(request:token:)` - the method you created above.

In order for Imperial to work, you need to provide it the client ID and client secret that Google gave you. You provide these to Imperial using environment variables. There are a number of ways to do this but Vapor has built in support for **.env** files. This allows you to define environment variables in a file that Vapor reads. This works from both the command line and Xcode. **Note**: **.env** files rely on you setting the custom working directory when running in Xcode. See Chapter 14, "Templating with Leaf" if you need more information about how to do this. Create a new file in your project directory called **.env** and open it in your favorite text editor. Insert the following:

```
GOOGLE_CALLBACK_URL=http://localhost:8080/oauth/google
GOOGLE_CLIENT_ID=<THE_CLIENT_ID_FROM_GOOGLE>
GOOGLE_CLIENT_SECRET=<THE_CLIENT_SECRET_FROM_GOOGLE>
```

Insert your client ID and client secret provided by Google.

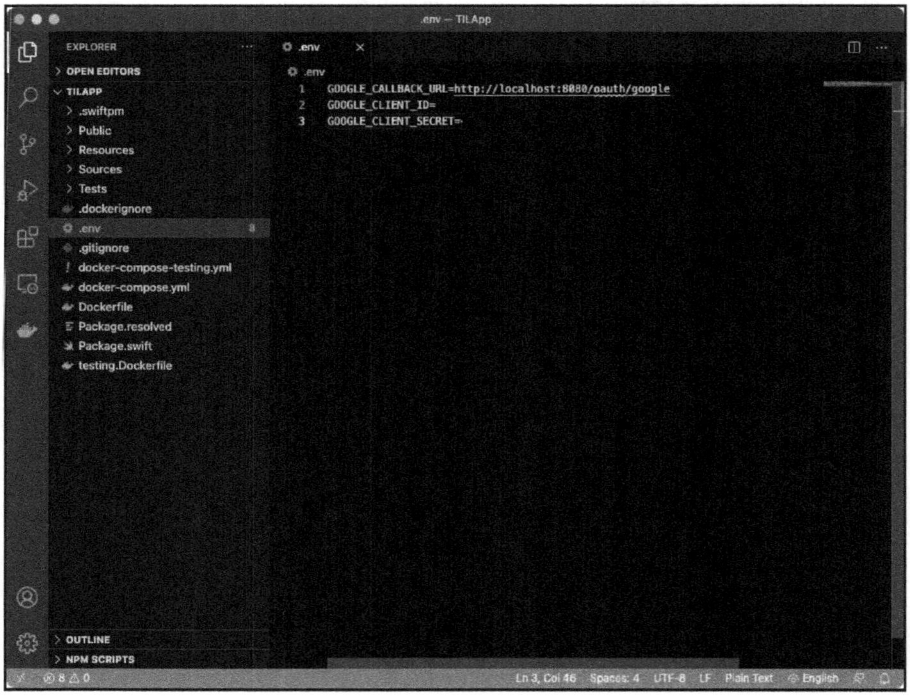

> **Note:** It's good practice to add **.env** files to **.gitignore** so you don't check secrets into source control.

Integrating with web authentication

It's important to provide a seamless experience for users and match the experience for the regular login. To do this, you need to create a new user when a user logs in with Google for the first time. To create a user, you can use Google's API to get the necessary details using the OAuth token.

Sending requests to third-party APIs

At the bottom of **ImperialController.swift**, add a new type to decode the data from Google's API:

```
struct GoogleUserInfo: Content {
  let email: String
  let name: String
}
```

The request to Google's API returns many fields. However, you only care about the email, which becomes the username, and the name.

Next, under `GoogleUserInfo`, add the following:

```
extension Google {
  // 1
  static func getUser(on request: Request)
    throws -> EventLoopFuture<GoogleUserInfo> {
      // 2
      var headers = HTTPHeaders()
      headers.bearerAuthorization =
        try BearerAuthorization(token: request.accessToken())

      // 3
      let googleAPIURL: URI =
        "https://www.googleapis.com/oauth2/v1/userinfo?alt=json"
      // 4
      return request
        .client
        .get(googleAPIURL, headers: headers)
        .flatMapThrowing { response in
        // 5
        guard response.status == .ok else {
```

```
        // 6
        if response.status == .unauthorized {
          throw Abort.redirect(to: "/login-google")
        } else {
          throw Abort(.internalServerError)
        }
      }
      // 7
      return try response.content
        .decode(GoogleUserInfo.self)
    }
  }
}
```

Here's what this does:

1. Add a new method to Imperial's `Google` service that gets a user's details from the Google API.
2. Set the headers for the request by adding the OAuth token to the authorization header.
3. Set the URL for the request — this is Google's API to get the user's information. This uses Vapor's `URI` type, which `Client` requires.
4. Use `request.client` to send the request to Google. `get()` sends an HTTP GET request to the URL provided. Unwrap the returned future response.
5. Ensure the response status is **200 OK**.
6. Otherwise, return to the login page if the response was **401 Unauthorized** or return an error.
7. Decode the data from the response to `GoogleUserInfo` and return the result.

Next, replace the contents of `processGoogleLogin(request:token:)` with the following:

```
// 1
try Google
  .getUser(on: request)
  .flatMap { userInfo in
    // 2
    User
      .query(on: request.db)
      .filter(\.$username == userInfo.email)
      .first()
      .flatMap { foundUser in
        guard let existingUser = foundUser else {
```

```
          // 3
          let user = User(
            name: userInfo.name,
            username: userInfo.email,
            password: UUID().uuidString)
          // 4
          return user
            .save(on: request.db)
            .map {
              // 5
              request.session.authenticate(user)
              return request.redirect(to: "/")
            }
        }
        // 6
        request.session.authenticate(existingUser)
        return request.eventLoop
          .future(request.redirect(to: "/"))
      }
  }
```

Here's what the new code does:

1. Get the user information from Google.
2. See if the user exists in the database by looking up the email as the username.
3. If the user doesn't exist, create a new `User` using the name and email from the user information from Google. Set the password to a UUID string, since you don't need it. This ensures that no one can login to this account via a normal password login.
4. Save the user and unwrap the returned future.
5. Call `session.authenticate(_:)` to save the created user in the session so the website allows access. Redirect back to the home page.
6. If the user already exists, authenticate the user in the session and redirect to the home page.

> **Note:** In a real world application, you may want to consider using a flag to separate out users registered on your site vs. logging in with OAuth.

The final thing to do is to add a button on the website to allow users to make use of the new functionality! Open **login.leaf** and, under `</form>`, add the following:

```
<a href="/login-google">
  <img class="mt-3" src="/images/sign-in-with-google.png"
   alt="Sign In With Google">
</a>
```

The sample project for this chapter contains a new, Google-provided image, **sign-in-with-google.png**, to display a **Sign in with Google** button. This adds the image as a link to **/login-google** — the route provided to Imperial to start the login.

Save the Leaf template and build and run the application in Xcode. Remember to set the custom working directory before running. Visit **http://localhost:8080** in your browser.

Click **Create An Acronym** and the application takes you to the login page. You'll see the new **Sign in with Google** button:

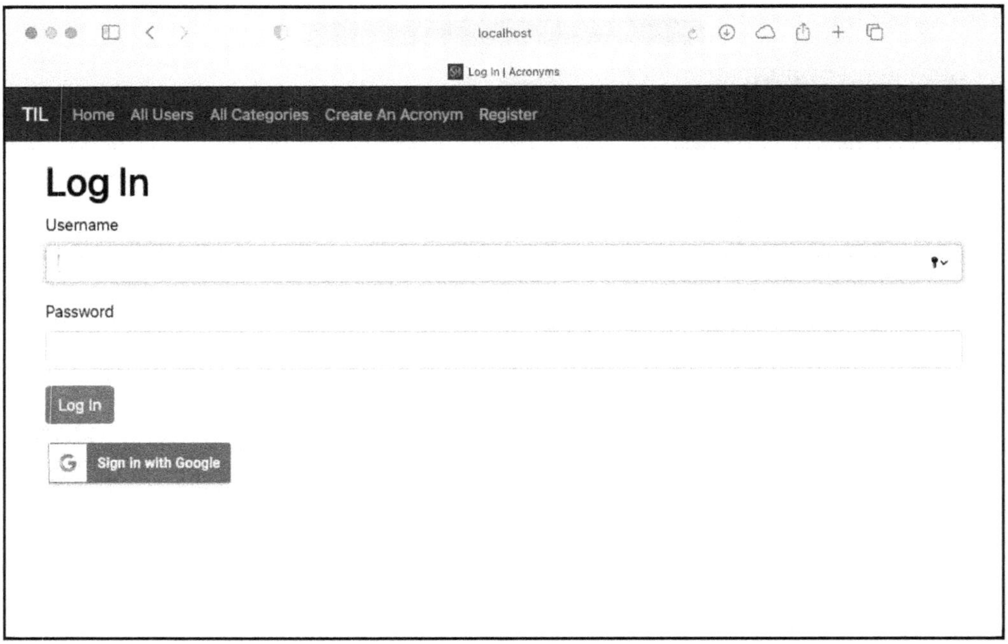

Click the new button and the application takes you to a Google page to allow the TIL application access to your information:

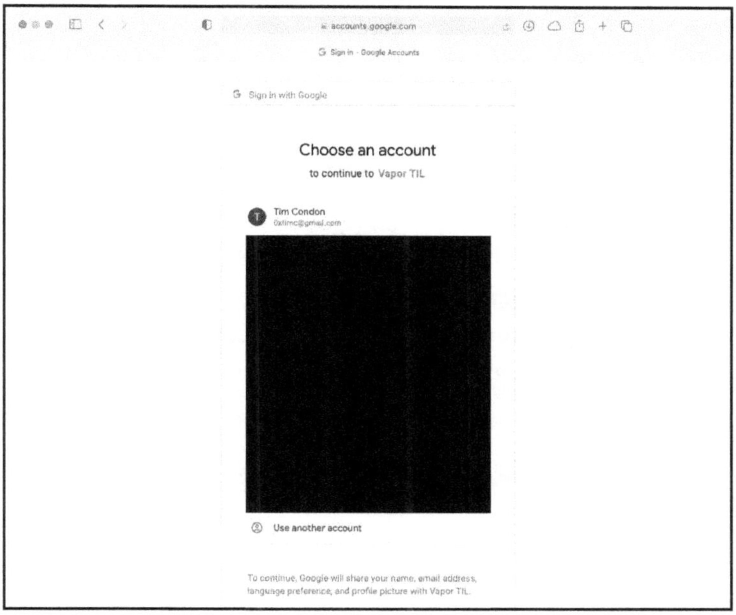

Select the account you want to use and the application redirects you back to the home page. Go to the **All Users** screen and you'll see your new user account. If you create an acronym, the application also uses that new user.

Integrating with iOS

You've integrated Imperial with the TIL website to allow users to sign in with Google. However, you also have another client — the iOS app. You can reuse most of the existing code to allow users to sign in to the iOS app with Google as well! In **ImperialController.swift** add a new route handler below `processGoogleLogin(_:)`:

```
func iOSGoogleLogin(_ req: Request) -> Response {
  // 1
  req.session.data["oauth_login"] = "iOS"
  // 2
  return req.redirect(to: "/login-google")
}
```

Here's what the new route does:

1. Add an entry to the request's session, noting that this OAuth login attempt came from iOS.
2. Redirect to the URL you created earlier to start the OAuth flow for logging in to the website using Google.

Register the new route at the bottom of `boot(routes:)`:

```
routes.get("iOS", "login-google", use: iOSGoogleLogin)
```

This routes a **GET** request to **/iOS/login-google** to `iOSGoogleLogin(_:)`. Then, below `iOSGoogleLogin(_:)`, add a new method to create the redirect for logging in:

```
// 1
func generateRedirect(on req: Request, for user: User)
  -> EventLoopFuture<ResponseEncodable> {
    let redirectURL: EventLoopFuture<String>
    // 2
    if req.session.data["oauth_login"] == "iOS" {
      do {
        // 3
        let token = try Token.generate(for: user)
        // 4
        redirectURL = token.save(on: req.db).map {
          "tilapp://auth?token=\(token.value)"
        }
      // 5
      } catch {
        return req.eventLoop.future(error: error)
      }
    } else {
      // 6
      redirectURL = req.eventLoop.future("/")
    }
    // 7
    req.session.data["oauth_login"] = nil
    // 8
    return redirectURL.map { url in
      req.redirect(to: url)
    }
}
```

Here's what the new code does:

1. Define a new method that takes both `Request` and `User` to generate a redirect. This new method returns `EventLoopFuture<ResponseEncodable>`.
2. Check the request's session data for the `oauth_login` flag to see if it matches the flag set in `iOSGoogleLogin(_:)`.
3. If the request is from iOS, generate a token for the user.
4. Save the token, resolve the returned future and return a redirect. This uses the **tilapp** scheme and returns the token as a query parameter. You'll use this in the iOS app.
5. Catch any errors thrown by generating the token and return a failed future.
6. If the request is not from iOS, create a future string for the original redirect URL.
7. Reset the `oauth_login` flag for the next session.
8. Resolve the future and return a redirect using the returned string.

Next, in `processGoogleLogin(request:token:)`, replace:

```
return user.save(on: request.db).map {
  request.session.authenticate(user)
  return request.redirect(to: "/")
}
```

with the following:

```
return user.save(on: request.db).flatMap {
  request.session.authenticate(user)
  return generateRedirect(on: request, for: user)
}
```

This returns a generated redirect for the new user instead of the hard-coded /. It also replaces `map` with `flatMap` as the closure now returns a future.

Finally, replace:

```
return request.eventLoop
  .future(request.redirect(to: "/"))
```

with the following:

```
return generateRedirect(on: request, for: existingUser)
```

This returns a redirect generated for the existing user. Build and run the app, then open the TILiOS starter project. The iOS project is similar to the final project from Chapter 19, "API Authentication, Part 2". The login screen now contains a new button for signing in with Google.

Open **LoginTableViewController.swift**. The **Sign in with Google** button triggers `signInWithGoogleButtonTapped(_:)` when tapped. This doesn't do anything at the moment. At the top of the file, below `import UIKit` add:

```
import AuthenticationServices
```

This imports the Authentication Services framework which you'll use for signing in. Then, in `signInWithGoogleButtonTapped(_:)`, add the following:

```
// 1
guard let googleAuthURL = URL(
  string: "http://localhost:8080/iOS/login-google")
else {
  return
}
// 2
let scheme = "tilapp"
// 3
let session = ASWebAuthenticationSession(
  url: googleAuthURL,
  callbackURLScheme: scheme) { callbackURL, error in
}
```

Here's what this does:

1. Create a `URL` that matches the route you created in TILApp for signing in with Google earlier.
2. Define the scheme to use. This matches the scheme of the redirect the TILApp you set earlier.
3. Create an instance of `ASWebAuthenticationSession`. This allows the user to authenticate with the TIL app using existing credentials from Safari.

Next, at the bottom of the file, add the following extension:

```
extension LoginTableViewController:
ASWebAuthenticationPresentationContextProviding {
  func presentationAnchor(
    for session: ASWebAuthenticationSession
  ) -> ASPresentationAnchor {
    guard let window = view.window else {
      fatalError("No window found in view")
```

```
    }
    return window
  }
}
```

This conforms the view controller to `ASWebAuthenticationPresentationContextProviding` and implements `presentationAnchor(for:)` as required by the protocol. Then, in the callback for `ASWebAuthenticationSession(url:callbackURLScheme:)` add the following:

```
// 1
guard
  error == nil,
  let callbackURL = callbackURL
else {
  return
}

// 2
let queryItems =
  URLComponents(string: callbackURL.absoluteString)?.queryItems
// 3
let token = queryItems?.first { $0.name == "token" }?.value
// 4
Auth().token = token
// 5
DispatchQueue.main.async {
  let appDelegate =
    UIApplication.shared.delegate as? AppDelegate
  appDelegate?.window?.rootViewController =
    UIStoryboard(name: "Main", bundle: Bundle.main)
      .instantiateInitialViewController()
}
```

Here's what's going on:

1. Ensure there's no error and a callback URL is set.
2. Get the query items from the callback URL.
3. Extract the token from the URL. This is the token provided in the redirect you set up earlier.
4. Set the token on the `Auth` instance.
5. Replace the root view controller to complete the log in process.

Finally, below `ASWebAuthenticationSession(url:callbackURLScheme:)` add the following:

```
session.presentationContextProvider = self
session.start()
```

This sets the session's `presentationContextProvider` to the current view controller. This allows iOS to know where to launch the browser from. It then starts the session to start the log in flow.

Build and run the app and log out if necessary in the **Users** tab. You'll see the new **Sign in with Google** button:

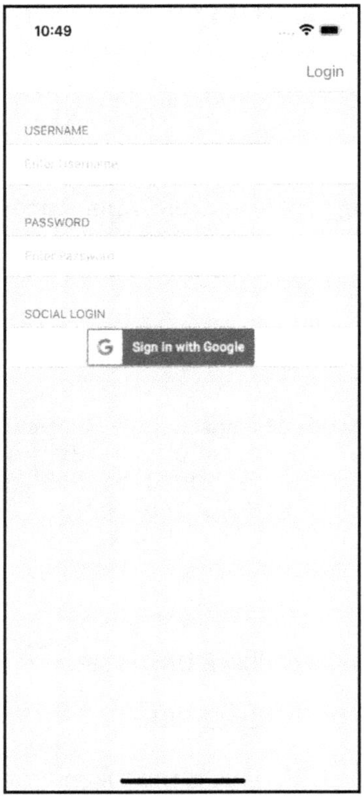

Tap the button and you'll get a prompt to allow the app to access the TIL website to log in:

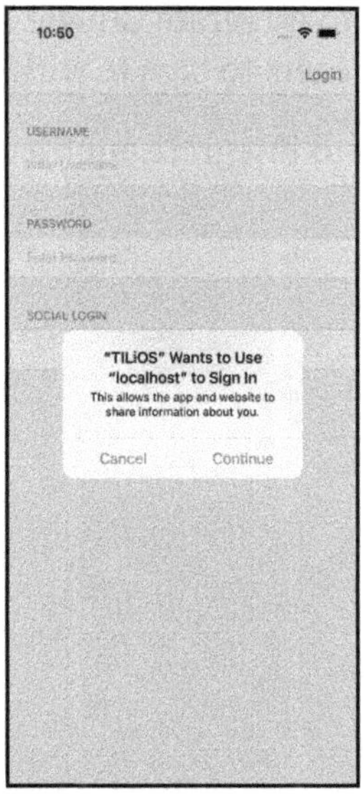

Click **Continue** and the app redirects you to Google to sign in or select an account to use. Complete the log in process and select an account and the app logs you in.

Where to go from here?

In this chapter, you learned how to integrate Google login into your website using Imperial and OAuth. This allows users to sign in with their existing Google accounts!

The next chapter shows you how to integrate another popular OAuth provider: GitHub.

Chapter 23: GitHub Authentication

By Tim Condon

In the previous chapter, you learned how to authenticate users using Google. In this chapter, you'll see how to build upon this and allow users to log in with their GitHub accounts.

Setting up your application with GitHub

To be able to use GitHub OAuth in your application, you must first register the application with GitHub. In your browser, go to https://github.com/settings/developers. Click **Register a new application**:

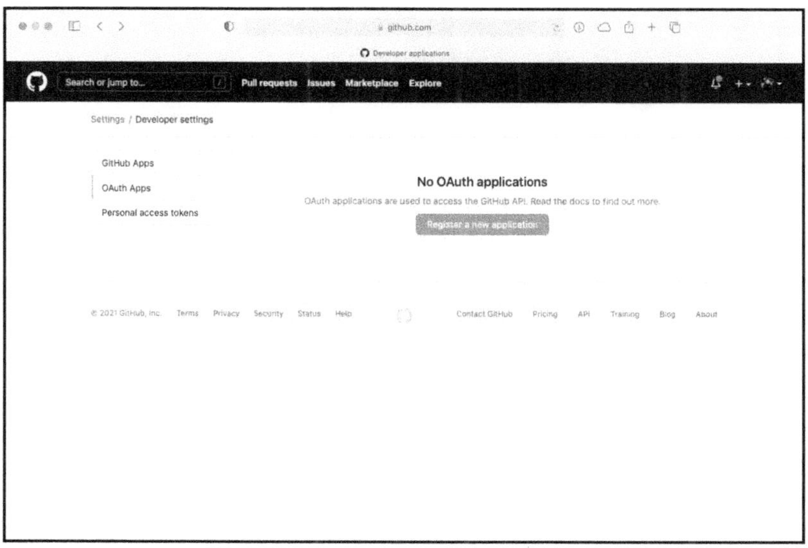

> **Note**: You must have a GitHub account to complete this chapter. If you don't have one, visit https://github.com/join to create one. This chapter also assumes you added Imperial as a dependency to your project in the previous chapter.

Fill in the form with an appropriate name, e.g. **Vapor TIL**. Set the **Homepage URL** to **http://localhost:8080** for this application and provide a sensible description. Set the **Authorization callback URL** to **http://localhost:8080/oauth/github**. This is the URL that GitHub redirects back to once users have allowed your application access to their data:

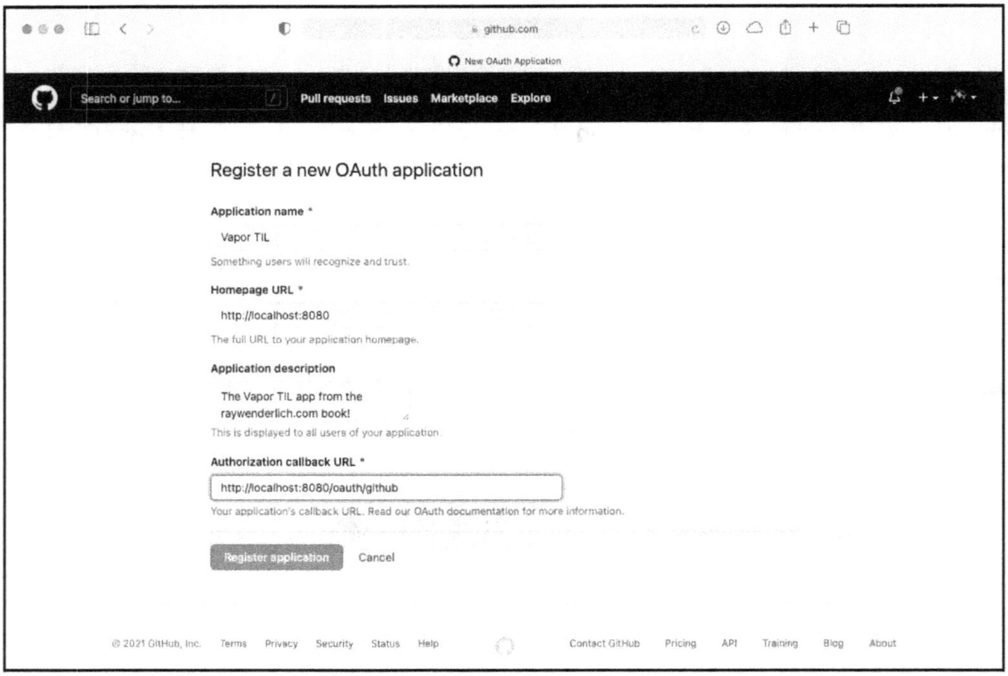

Click **Register application**. After it creates the application, the site takes you back to the application's information page. That page provides the client ID. Click **Generate a new client secret** to get a client secret:

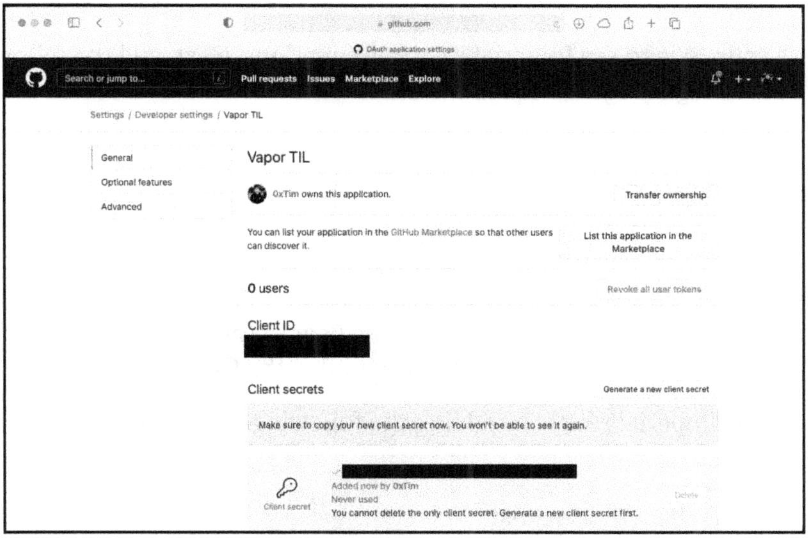

> **Note**: You *must* keep these safe and secure. Your secret allows you access to GitHub's APIs and you should not share or check the secret into source control. You should treat it like a password.

Integrating with Imperial

Now that you've registered your application with GitHub, you can start integrating Imperial. First, open **Package.swift** in Xcode and replace:

```
.product(name: "ImperialGoogle", package: "Imperial")
```

with the following:

```
.product(name: "ImperialGoogle", package: "Imperial"),
.product(name: "ImperialGitHub", package: "Imperial")
```

This adds Imperial's GitHub library as a dependency. Next, open **ImperialController.swift** and add the following below `import Fluent`:

```
import ImperialGitHub
```

This allows your code to see Imperial's GitHub functions. Next, add the following under `processGoogleLogin(request:token:)`:

```
func processGitHubLogin(request: Request, token: String)
  throws -> EventLoopFuture<ResponseEncodable> {
    return request.eventLoop.future(request.redirect(to: "/"))
  }
```

This defines a method to handle the GitHub login, similar to the initial handler for Google logins. The handler simply redirects the user to the home page. Imperial uses this method as the final callback once it has handled the GitHub redirect.

Next, set up the Imperial routes by adding the following at the bottom of `boot(routes:)`:

```
guard let githubCallbackURL =
  Environment.get("GITHUB_CALLBACK_URL") else {
    fatalError("GitHub callback URL not set")
}
try routes.oAuth(
  from: GitHub.self,
  authenticate: "login-github",
  callback: githubCallbackURL,
  completion: processGitHubLogin)
```

Here's what this does:

- Get the callback URL from an environment variable — this is the URL you set up when registering the application with GitHub.
- Register Imperial's GitHub OAuth router with your app's routes.
- Tell Imperial to use the GitHub handler.
- Set up the **/login-github** request as the route that triggers the OAuth flow. This is the route the application uses to allow users to log in via GitHub.
- Provide the callback URL to Imperial.
- Set the completion handler to `processGitHubLogin(request:token:)` — the method you created above.

As before, you need to provide Imperial the client ID and client secret that GitHub gave you using environment variables. You must also provide the redirect URL. Open **.env** in a text editor and add the following at the bottom of the file:

```
GITHUB_CALLBACK_URL=http://localhost:8080/oauth/github
GITHUB_CLIENT_ID=<YOUR_GITHUB_CLIENT_ID>
GITHUB_CLIENT_SECRET=<YOUR_GITHUB_CLIENT_SECRET>
```

Add the client ID and secret generate by GitHub earlier.

> **Note**: Be sure you still have environment variables set for **GOOGLE_CALLBACK_URL**, **GOOGLE_CLIENT_ID** and **GOOGLE_CLIENT_SECRET** or your app won't start.

Integrating with web authentication

As in the previous chapter, it's important to match the experience for a regular login. Again, you'll create a new user when a user logs in with GitHub for the first time. You can use GitHub's API with the user's OAuth token.

At the bottom of **ImperialController.swift**, add a new type to decode the data from GitHub's API:

```
struct GitHubUserInfo: Content {
  let name: String
  let login: String
}
```

The request to GitHub's API returns many fields. However, you only care about the login, which becomes the username, and the name.

Next, under `GitHubUserInfo`, add the following:

```
extension GitHub {
  // 1
  static func getUser(on request: Request)
    throws -> EventLoopFuture<GitHubUserInfo> {
      // 2
      var headers = HTTPHeaders()
      try headers.add(
        name: .authorization,
        value: "token \(request.accessToken())")
      headers.add(name: .userAgent, value: "vapor")
```

```
      // 3
      let githubUserAPIURL: URI = "https://api.github.com/user"
      // 4
      return request
        .client
        .get(githubUserAPIURL, headers: headers)
        .flatMapThrowing { response in
          // 5
          guard response.status == .ok else {
            // 6
            if response.status == .unauthorized {
              throw Abort.redirect(to: "/login-github")
            } else {
              throw Abort(.internalServerError)
            }
          }
          // 7
          return try response.content
            .decode(GitHubUserInfo.self)
      }
    }
}
```

Here's what this does:

1. Add a new method to Imperial's `GitHub` service which gets a user's details from the GitHub API.
2. Set the headers for the request by adding the OAuth token to the authorization header. Note that GitHub doesn't use a standard bearer authorization header, so you must define the header manually. Also set the **user-agent** header as GitHub's API requires this.
3. Set the URL for the request — this is GitHub's API to get the user's information. This uses Vapor's `URI` which the `Client` requires.
4. Use `request.client` to send an HTTP request. `get()` sends an HTTP GET request to the URL provided. Unwrap the returned future response.
5. Ensure the response status is **200 OK**.
6. Otherwise, return to the login page if the response was **401 Unauthorized** or return an error.
7. Decode the data from the response to `GitHub` and return the result.

Next, replace the body of `processGitHubLogin(request:token:)` with the following:

```
// 1
return try GitHub
  .getUser(on: request)
  .flatMap { userInfo in
    // 2
    return User
      .query(on: request.db)
      .filter(\.$username == userInfo.login)
      .first()
      .flatMap { foundUser in
        guard let existingUser = foundUser else {
          // 3
          let user = User(
            name: userInfo.name,
            username: userInfo.login,
            password: UUID().uuidString)
          // 4
          return user
            .save(on: request.db)
            .flatMap {
              // 5
              request.session.authenticate(user)
              return generateRedirect(on: request, for: user)
          }
        }
        // 6
        request.session.authenticate(existingUser)
        return generateRedirect(on: request, for: existingUser)
    }
}
```

Here's what the new code does:

1. Get the user information from GitHub.
2. See if the user exists in the database by looking up the login property as the username.
3. If the user doesn't exist, create a new `User` using the name and username from the user information from GitHub. Set the password to a UUID, since you don't need it.
4. Save the user and unwrap the returned future.

5. Call `session.authenticate(_:)` on `Request` to save the created user in the session so the website allows access. Use `generateRedirect(on:for:)` from the previous chapter to redirect back to the home page.

6. If the user already exists, authenticate the user in the session and redirect to the home page. Again, use `generateRedirect(on:for:)` to create the redirect.

The final thing to do is to add a button on the website to allow users to make use of the new functionality! Open **login.leaf** and, under </form>, add the following:

```
<a href="/login-github">
  <img class="mt-3" src="/images/sign-in-with-github.png"
   alt="Sign In With GitHub">
</a>
```

The sample project for this chapter contains a new image, **sign-in-with-github.png**, to display a **Sign in with GitHub** button. This adds the image as a link to **/login-github** — the route provided to Imperial to start the login. Build and run the application and then visit **http://localhost:8080** in your browser. Click **Create An Acronym** and the application takes you to the login page. You'll see the new **Sign in with GitHub** button next to the **Sign in with Google** button:

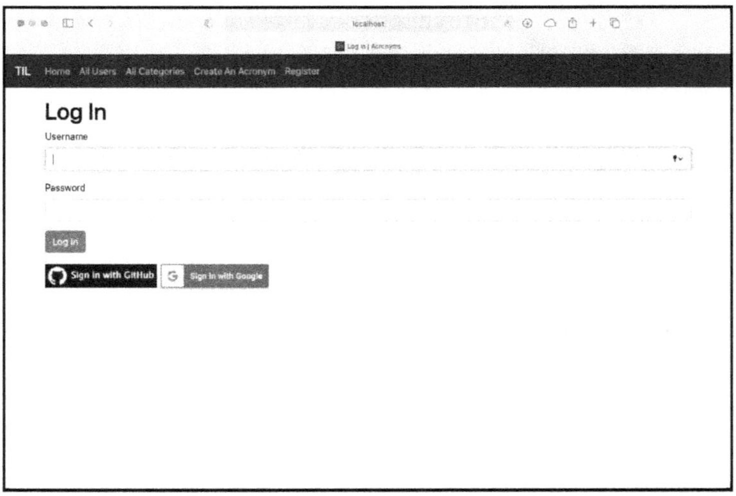

Click the new button and the application takes you to a GitHub page to allow the TIL application access to your information:

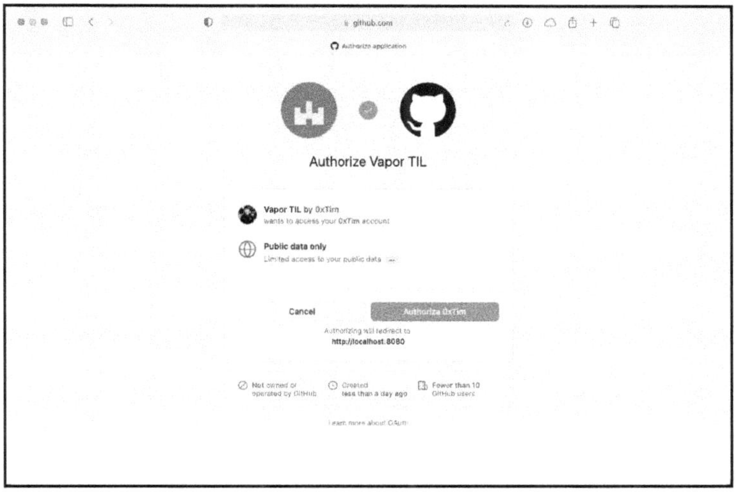

Click the **Authorize** button you see there and the application redirects you back to the home page. Go to the **All Users** screen and you'll see your new user account. If you create an acronym, the application also uses that new user.

Integrating with iOS

Just like signing in with Google, you should offer the ability to sign in with GitHub on iOS as well. You've already done most of this work in the previous chapter :]

Below `iOSGoogleLogin(_:)`, create a new route handler for logging in on iOS with GitHub:

```
func iOSGitHubLogin(_ req: Request) -> Response {
  // 1
  req.session.data["oauth_login"] = "iOS"
  // 2
  return req.redirect(to: "/login-github")
}
```

This new route handler does two things:

1. Sets a flag in the request's session to mark this as an iOS log in attempt.
2. Redirect to **/login-github** to trigger the OAuth flow with GitHub.

Register the new route at the bottom of `boot(routes:)`:

```
routes.get("iOS", "login-github", use: iOSGitHubLogin)
```

This routes a **GET** request to **/iOS/login-github** to `iosGitHubLogin(_:)`. That's all you need to do in TILApp to support iOS log in with GitHub! Build and run the project and open the iOS starter project for this chapter.

The iOS starter project for the chapter contains a new button on the log in page for GitHub. There's a corresponding method in **LoginTableViewController.swift** to invoke when a user taps the new button. Add the following to `signInWithGithubButtonTapped(_:)`:

```
// 1
guard let githubAuthURL =
  URL(string: "http://localhost:8080/iOS/login-github")
else {
  return
}
// 2
let scheme = "tilapp"
// 3
let session = ASWebAuthenticationSession(
  url: githubAuthURL,
  callbackURLScheme: scheme) { callbackURL, error in
  // 4
  guard
    error == nil,
    let callbackURL = callbackURL
  else {
    return
  }

  let queryItems = URLComponents(
    string: callbackURL.absoluteString
  )?.queryItems
  let token = queryItems?.first { $0.name == "token" }?.value
  // 5
  Auth().token = token
  // 6
  DispatchQueue.main.async {
    let appDelegate =
      UIApplication.shared.delegate as? AppDelegate
    appDelegate?.window?.rootViewController =
      UIStoryboard(
        name: "Main",
        bundle: Bundle.main).instantiateInitialViewController()
  }
}
// 7
```

```
session.presentationContextProvider = self
session.start()
```

Here's what the new code does:

1. Create a `URL` for logging in with GitHub. This is the URL you created in TILApp earlier.
2. Set the scheme to **tilapp** — this is the scheme you redirect to. For more information see Chapter 22, "Google Authentication".
3. Create an instance of `ASWebAuthenticationSession` using the scheme and URL.
4. Ensure there's a callback URL and no error. Extract the token from the callback URL.
5. Set the token in the keychain using `Auth`.
6. Finish logging in the user by changing the root view controller to the main navigation view controller.
7. Set `presentationContextProvider` to the `LoginViewController` and start the session.

Build and run the app and log out in the **Users** tab if necessary. On the log in page, you'll see the new **Sign in with GitHub** button:

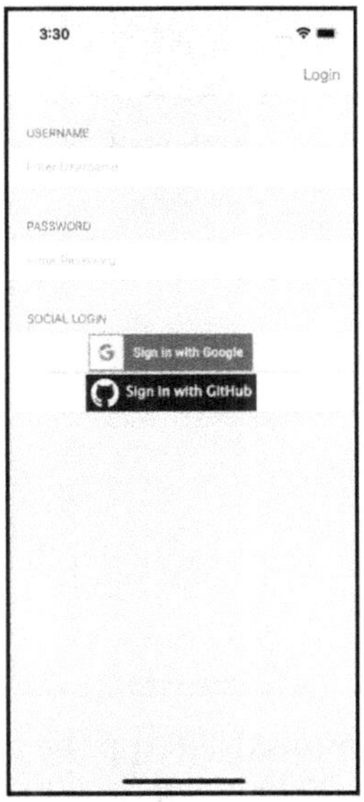

Tap the new button and the app asks you to confirm that you want to use TILApp to log in:

Tap **Continue**. If you're already logged into GitHub on the simulator, the app logs you straight in. Otherwise you'll see the OAuth screen for GitHub to allow access:

Log in to GitHub and if you've approved TILApp the app logs you in. Otherwise GitHub asks you to confirm access for the TIL app, just like the website. Once confirmed, the app logs you in.

Where to go from here?

In this chapter, you learned how to integrate GitHub login into your website using Imperial and OAuth. This complements the Google and first-party sign in experiences and allows your users to choose a range of options for authentication.

In the next chapter, you'll learn how to implement Sign in with Apple, giving your users a third option for using an external authentication service to register with your app.

Chapter 24: Sign in with Apple Authentication

By Tim Condon

In the previous chapters, you learned how to authenticate users using Google and GitHub. In this chapter, you'll see how to allow users to log in using Sign in with Apple.

Sign in with Apple

Apple introduced Sign in with Apple in 2019 as a privacy-centric way of authenticating users in your apps. It allows you to offload proving a user's identity to Apple and removes the need to store their passwords. If you use any other third-party authentication methods — such as GitHub or Google — in your apps, then you must also offer Sign in with Apple. Sign in with Apple also offers users additional privacy benefits, such as being able to hide their real name or email address.

> **Note**: To complete this chapter, you'll need a paid Apple developer account to set up the required identifiers and profiles.

Sign in with Apple on iOS

Here's how authenticating users with Sign in with Apple works on iOS:

1. The iOS app uses `ASAuthorizationAppleIDButton` to show the button and start the sign in flow.
2. When the user completes the Sign in with Apple process, iOS returns an `ASAuthorizationAppleIDCredential` to your app. This contains a JSON Web Token (JWT).
3. The app sends the JWT to the server — the TIL Vapor app in this case. The server then validates the token.
4. If the user is new, the server creates a user account.
5. The server then signs the user in. You'll return a `Token` to the iOS app to complete the sign-in flow.

JWT

JSON Web Tokens, or JWTs, are a way of transmitting information between different parties. Since they contain JSON, you can send any information you want in them. The issuer of the JWT signs the token with a private key or secret. The JWT contains a signature and header. Using these two pieces, you can verify the integrity of the token. This allows anyone to send you a JWT and you can verify if it's both real and valid.

For Sign in with Apple, the server receives the token and then gets Apple's public key from its server to validate the token. Vapor contains helper functions to make this simple.

Sign in with Apple on the web

Sign in with Apple works in a similar way on websites. Apple provide a JavaScript library you integrate to render the button. The button works across platforms. On macOS in Safari, it interacts with the browser directly. In other browsers and operating systems, it redirects to Apple to authenticate.

When a user successfully authenticates, Apple redirects to a URL on your website in a similar way to GitHub and Google. The redirect contains the JWT, which you can then send to your server and validate as before.

Integrating Sign in with Apple on iOS

Open the TILApp project in Xcode and open **Package.swift**. Replace:

```
.package(
  url: "https://github.com/vapor-community/Imperial.git",
  from: "1.0.0")
```

with the following:

```
.package(
  url: "https://github.com/vapor-community/Imperial.git",
  from: "1.0.0"),
.package(
  url: "https://github.com/vapor/jwt.git",
  from: "4.0.0")
```

This adds Vapor's JWT library as a dependency. Next, replace:

```
.product(name: "ImperialGitHub", package: "Imperial")
```

with the following:

```
.product(name: "ImperialGitHub", package: "Imperial"),
.product(name: "JWT", package: "jwt")
```

This adds the JWT library as a dependency to your **App** target. Next, open **User.swift** and add the following property below `var acronyms: [Acronym]`:

```
@OptionalField(key: "siwaIdentifier")
var siwaIdentifier: String?
```

This adds a new field to `User` to store the identifier returned by Sign in with Apple. This allows you to identify users across devices and sessions. Note the use of `@OptionalField` because the property is optional. You **must** use `@OptionalField` with any optional properties. Otherwise, you may encounter issues when saving and retrieving models from the database. Next, replace the initializer to account for the new property with the following:

```
init(
  id: UUID? = nil,
  name: String,
  username: String,
  password: String,
  siwaIdentifier: String? = nil
) {
```

```
    self.name = name
    self.username = username
    self.password = password
    self.siwaIdentifier = siwaIdentifier
  }
```

Using a default property means you don't need to update any code. Open **CreateUser.swift** and add the following:

```
.field("siwaIdentifier", .string)
```

below `.field("password", .string, .required)` to account for the new property:

Since the field is optional, you don't need to mark it with `.required`. Next, open **UsersController.swift**. At the top of the file, below `import Vapor`, import the new dependency:

```
import JWT
import Fluent
```

You need Fluent, as well, for querying the database. Next, at the bottom of the file, create a new type for the data you need to sign in with Apple:

```
struct SignInWithAppleToken: Content {
  let token: String
  let name: String?
}
```

The type contains the JWT from iOS as well as an optional name for you to use when registering. Next, create a new route below `loginHandler(_:)` for signing in with Apple:

```
func signInWithApple(_ req: Request)
  throws -> EventLoopFuture<Token> {
    // 1
    let data = try req.content.decode(SignInWithAppleToken.self)
    // 2
    guard let appIdentifier =
      Environment.get("IOS_APPLICATION_IDENTIFIER") else {
      throw Abort(.internalServerError)
    }
    // 3
    return req.jwt
      .apple
      .verify(data.token, applicationIdentifier: appIdentifier)
      .flatMap { siwaToken -> EventLoopFuture<Token> in
        // 4
```

```
        User.query(on: req.db)
          .filter(\.$siwaIdentifier == siwaToken.subject.value)
          .first()
          .flatMap { user in
            let userFuture: EventLoopFuture<User>
            if let user = user {
              userFuture = req.eventLoop.future(user)
            } else {
              // 5
              guard
                let email = siwaToken.email,
                let name = data.name
              else {
                return req.eventLoop
                  .future(error: Abort(.badRequest))
              }
              let user = User(
                name: name,
                username: email,
                password: UUID().uuidString,
                siwaIdentifier: siwaToken.subject.value)
              userFuture = user.save(on: req.db).map { user }
            }
            // 6
            return userFuture.flatMap { user in
              let token: Token
              do {
                // 7
                token = try Token.generate(for: user)
              } catch {
                return req.eventLoop.future(error: error)
              }
              // 8
              return token.save(on: req.db).map { token }
            }
        }
    }
}
```

Here's what the new method does:

1. Decode the request body to the `SignInWithAppleToken` type created earlier.
2. Get the application identifier from the environment variables. If it doesn't exist, throw an internal server error.
3. Use Vapor's helper method to verify the JWT with Apple. This gets Apple's public key to check the signature and payload.
4. Search the database for an existing user with the Sign in with Apple identifier.
5. If there's no existing user, get the email from the token and name from the request body. Create a new `User`, using a dummy password, and save it in the database.
6. Resolve the user future. This is either the user returned from the database or the recently saved user. This allows you to write the code for generating a token once.
7. Generate a token for the user.
8. Save the token and return it as a response.

Finally, register the route in `boot(routes:)` below `usersRoute.get(":userID", "acronyms", use: getAcronymsHandler)`:

```
usersRoute.post("siwa", use: signInWithApple)
```

This routes a **POST** request to **/api/users/siwa** to `signInWithApple(_:)`. Build the app to make sure everything works.

Setting up the iOS app

Open the iOS app in Xcode and navigate to the **TILiOS** target. Click **+ Capability** and select **Sign in with Apple**. Next, open **LoginTableViewController.swift**. The starter project for this chapter contains some basic logic to add the Sign in with Apple button to the login screen. The button triggers `handleSignInWithApple()` when pressed.

To start, make `LoginTableViewController` conform to the necessary protocols. At the bottom of the file add the following extension:

```
extension LoginTableViewController:
  ASAuthorizationControllerPresentationContextProviding {
    func presentationAnchor(
      for controller: ASAuthorizationController
```

```
    ) -> ASPresentationAnchor {
      guard let window = view.window else {
        fatalError("No window found in view")
      }
      return window
    }
}
```

This conforms `LoginTableViewController` to `ASAuthorizationControllerPresentationContextProviding` to provide a window to present the sign in dialog on. Next, at the bottom of the file, add the following extension:

```
// 1
extension LoginTableViewController:
  ASAuthorizationControllerDelegate {
    // 2
    func authorizationController(
      controller: ASAuthorizationController,
      didCompleteWithAuthorization
        authorization: ASAuthorization
    ) {
    }

    // 3
    func authorizationController(
      controller: ASAuthorizationController,
      didCompleteWithError error: Error
    ) {
      print("Error signing in with Apple - \(error)")
    }
}
```

Here's what the extension does:

1. Conforms `LoginTableViewController` to `ASAuthorizationControllerDelegate`. This handles success and failure cases for signing in with Apple.

2. Implement `authorizationController(controller:didCompleteWithAuthorization:)` as required by the protocol. The app calls this when the device authenticates the user.

3. Implement `authorizationController(controller:didCompleteWithError:)` to handle the case when signing in with Apple fails. For now, just print the error to the console.

Next, add the following implementation to `handleSignInWithApple()`:

```
// 1
let request = ASAuthorizationAppleIDProvider().createRequest()
request.requestedScopes = [.fullName, .email]
// 2
let authorizationController =
  ASAuthorizationController(authorizationRequests: [request])
// 3
authorizationController.delegate = self
authorizationController.presentationContextProvider = self
// 4
authorizationController.performRequests()
```

Here's what the new code does:

1. Create an `ASAuthorizationAppleIDRequest` with the scopes for a user's full name and email.
2. Create an `ASAuthorizationController` with the request created in step 1.
3. Set the delegate and `presentationContextProvider` to the current instance of `LoginViewController`.
4. Start the Sign in with Apple request.

Next, in `authorizationController(controller:didCompleteWithAuthorization:)` add the following:

```
// 1
if let credential = authorization.credential
  as? ASAuthorizationAppleIDCredential {
  // 2
  guard
    let identityToken = credential.identityToken,
    let tokenString = String(
      data: identityToken,
      encoding: .utf8)
  else {
    print("Failed to get token from credential")
    return
  }
  // 3
  let name: String?
  if let nameProvided = credential.fullName {
    let firstName = nameProvided.givenName ?? ""
    let lastName = nameProvided.familyName ?? ""
    name = "\(firstName) \(lastName)"
  } else {
```

```
      name = nil
    }
    // 4
    let requestData =
      SignInWithAppleToken(token: tokenString, name: name)
    do {
      // 5
      try Auth().login(
        signInWithAppleInformation: requestData
      ) { result in
        switch result {
        // 6
        case .success:
          DispatchQueue.main.async {
            let appDelegate =
              UIApplication.shared.delegate as? AppDelegate
            appDelegate?.window?.rootViewController =
              UIStoryboard(name: "Main", bundle: Bundle.main)
                .instantiateInitialViewController()
          }
        // 7
        case .failure:
          let message = "Could not Sign in with Apple."
          ErrorPresenter.showError(message: message, on: self)
        }
      }
    // 8
    } catch {
      let message = "Could not login - \(error)"
      ErrorPresenter.showError(message: message, on: self)
    }
  }
```

Here's what's going on:

1. Try to cast the credential to an `ASAuthorizationAppleIDCredential`. You may handle other credential types so don't return an error if the cast fails.
2. Get the identity token and convert it to a string to send to the API.
3. Get the name from the credentials. You won't receive the name if the user has already signed in with Apple for the app.
4. Create `SignInWithAppleToken` to send to the server.
5. Use `login(signInWithAppleInformation:completion:)` to send the JWT to the server and get a token back.
6. If the login succeeds, change the root view controller to the main screen as before.

7. If log in fails, show an error message.
8. Catch any decoding errors thrown and show an error message.

That's everything you need to do to implement Sign in with Apple!

Finally, in the Project navigator, select the **TILiOS** target and open **Signing & Capabilities**. Select your development team and choose a unique bundle identifier:

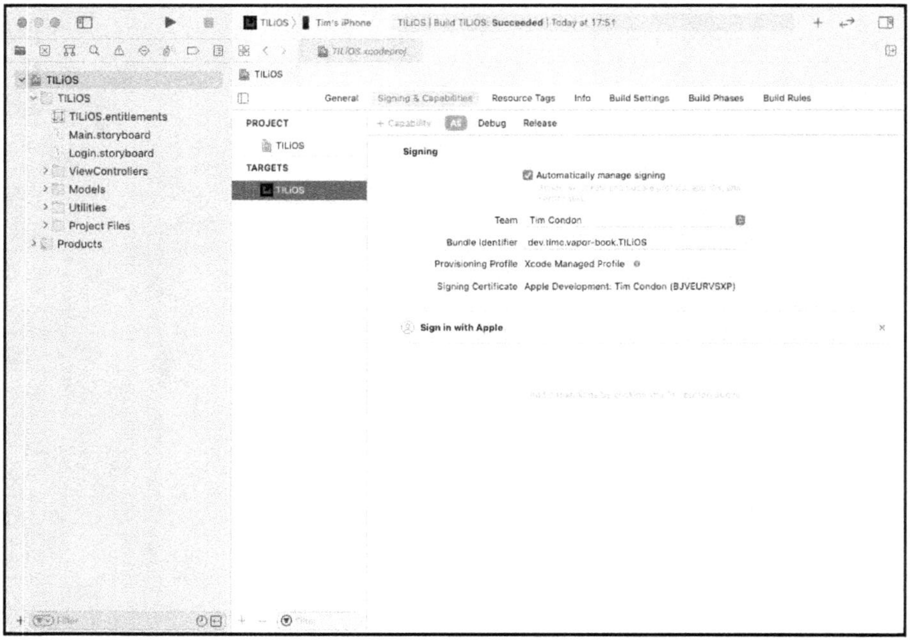

> **Important**: Sign in with Apple does not work reliably on the simulator, so the steps below require you to run the app on an iOS device.

In **TILApp**, open **.env** and add the following at the bottom of the file:

```
IOS_APPLICATION_IDENTIFIER=<YOUR_BUNDLE_ID>
```

Then, in Terminal, reset the database to accommodate the new field on `User`:

```
docker rm -f postgres
docker run --name postgres \
  -e POSTGRES_DB=vapor_database \
  -e POSTGRES_USER=vapor_username \
  -e POSTGRES_PASSWORD=vapor_password \
  -p 5432:5432 -d postgres
```

Build and run the Vapor app. When the firewall asks if you want to accept external connections, click **Allow**.

> The Vapor starter project allows external connections. You set `app.http.server.configuration.hostname = "0.0.0.0"` in **configure.swift**. This allows connections from any IP address.

Finally, in TILiOS, open **ResourceRequest.swift** and replace `let apiHostname = "http://localhost:8080"` to use the IP address of your machine. E.g.

```
let apiHostname = "http://192.168.1.70:8080"
```

Build and run the app on your device. You'll see the Sign in with Apple button on the log in screen:

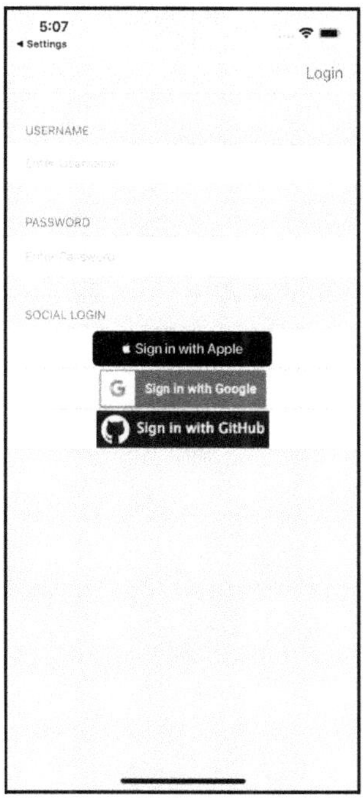

Tap **Sign in with Apple**. You'll see the Sign in with Apple sheet appear:

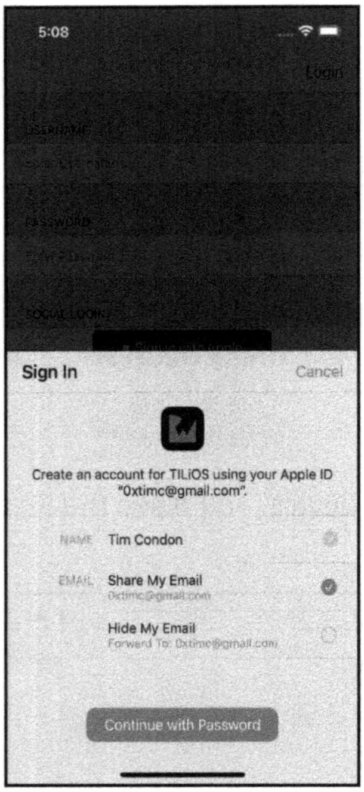

Tap **Share My Email** and then **Continue** or **Continue with Password**. Enter your password or allow Face ID to complete and the app logs you in!

> **Note**: Which option you see in the final step above is a function of which device you're testing on.

> **Pro Tip**: If you need to reset the state of Sign in with Apple for an app you're testing, see https://support.apple.com/en-us/HT210426 for instructions.

Integrating Sign in with Apple on the web

Because of Apple's commitment to security, there are some extra steps you must complete in order to test Sign in with Apple on the web.

Setting up ngrok

Sign in with Apple on the web only works with HTTPS connections, and Apple will only redirect to an HTTPS address. This is fine for deploying, but makes testing locally harder. `ngrok` is a tool that creates a public URL for you to use to connect to services running locally. In your browser, visit https://ngrok.com and download the client and create an account.

> **Note**: You can also install `ngrok` with Homebrew.

Next, head to https://dashboard.ngrok.com/ and get your auth token. Then, in Terminal, type:

```
/Applications/ngrok authtoken <YOUR_TOKEN>
```

This sets up the client with your account. Then, in Terminal, enter:

```
/Applications/ngrok http 8080
```

This creates an HTTP tunnel to your Vapor app. You'll see the URL listed in Terminal:

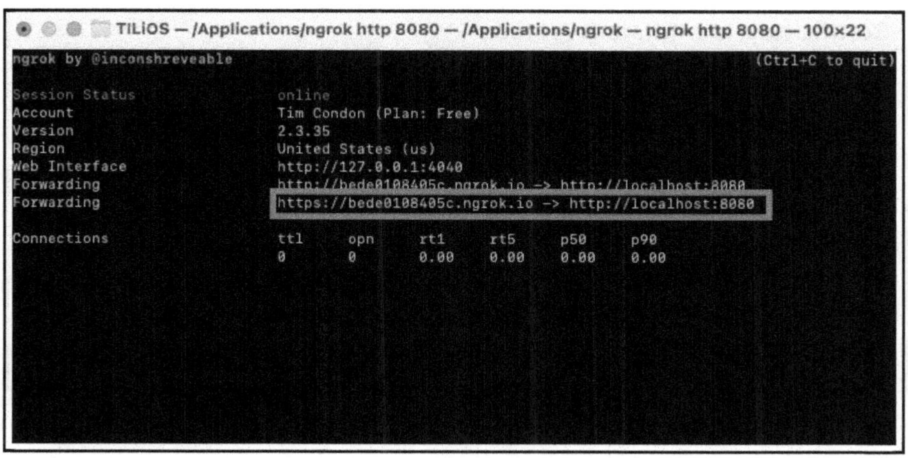

If you visit this URL in your browser, you'll see your TIL website!

Setting up the web app

Sign in with Apple on the web requires you to configure a service ID with Apple. Go to https://developer.apple.com/account/ and click **Certificates, Identifiers & Profiles.** Click **Identifiers** and click + to create a new identifier. Under the identifier type, choose **Services ID** and click **Continue**:

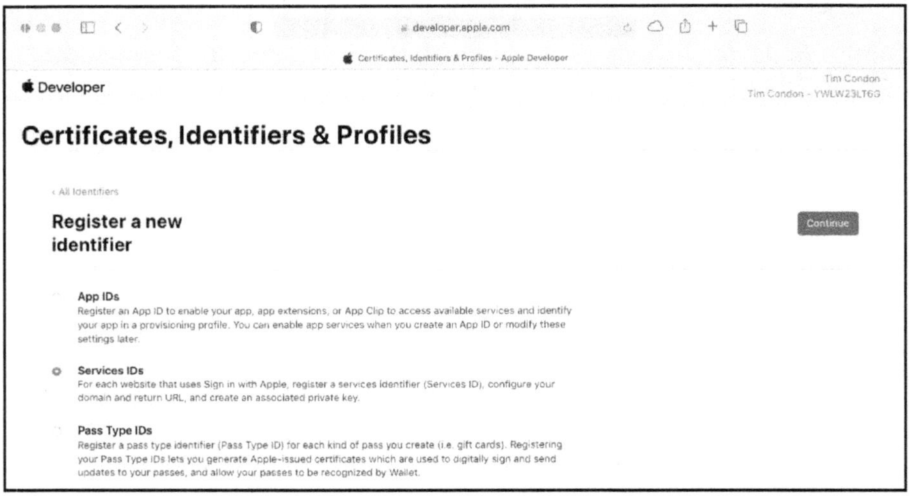

Enter a description and then choose a unique identifier for your website, similar to the bundle identifier for the app. Click **Continue** and then **Register**:

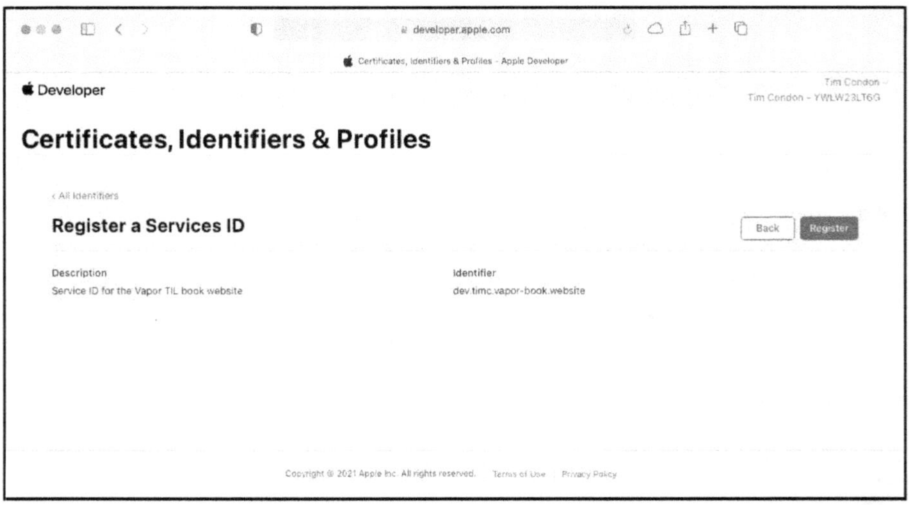

Click your new identifier to configure it. Click the checkbox next to **Sign In with Apple** and click **Configure**:

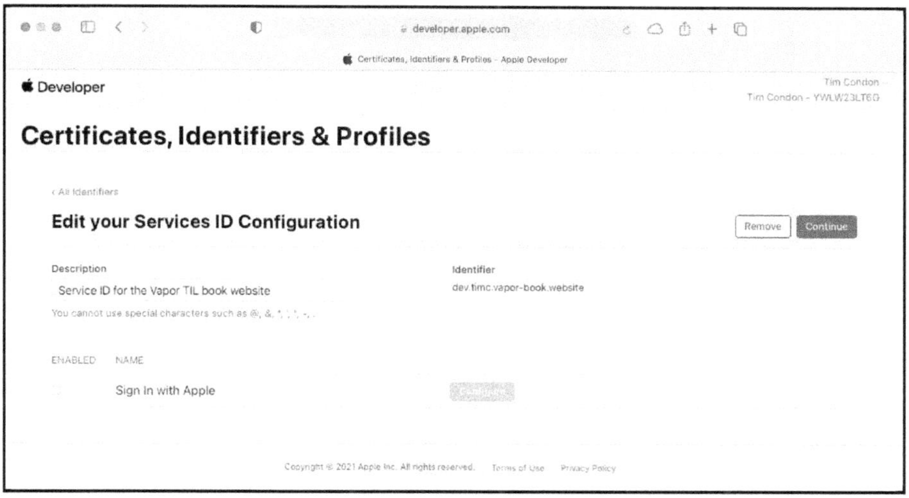

Under **Primary App ID**, select the application identifier for the TILiOS app. Under **Domains and Subdomains**, add the domain of your ngrok listener, e.g. **bede0108405c.ngrok.io**. Then, under **Return URLs**, add **https://<YOUR_NGROK_DOMAIN>/login/siwa/callback**. This is the URL Apple will redirect to when Sign in with Apple is complete:

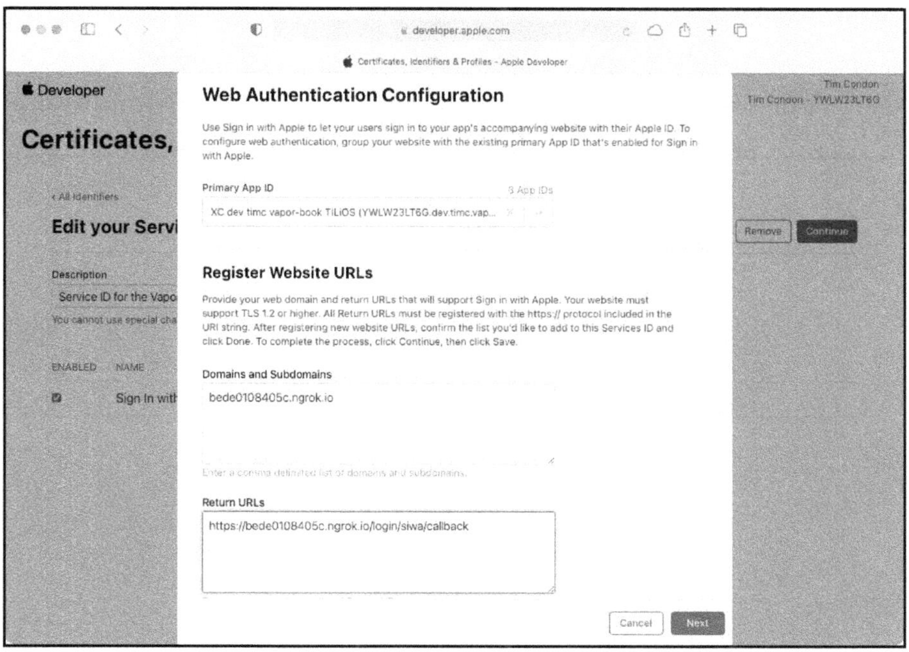

Click **Next** and then **Done**. Back on the **Edit your Services ID Configuration** page, click **Continue** and then **Save**.

Setting up Vapor

Return to the Vapor TILApp project in Xcode and open **WebsiteController.swift**. At the bottom of the file, add the following:

```
struct AppleAuthorizationResponse: Decodable {
  struct User: Decodable {
    struct Name: Decodable {
      let firstName: String?
      let lastName: String?
    }
    let email: String
    let name: Name?
  }

  let code: String
  let state: String
  let idToken: String
  let user: User?

  enum CodingKeys: String, CodingKey {
    case code
    case state
    case idToken = "id_token"
    case user
  }

  init(from decoder: Decoder) throws {
    let values = try decoder.container(keyedBy: CodingKeys.self)
    code = try values.decode(String.self, forKey: .code)
    state = try values.decode(String.self, forKey: .state)
    idToken =
      try values.decode(String.self, forKey: .idToken)

    if let jsonString =
      try values.decodeIfPresent(String.self, forKey: .user),
       let jsonData = jsonString.data(using: .utf8) {
      self.user =
        try JSONDecoder().decode(User.self, from: jsonData)
    } else {
      user = nil
    }
  }
}
```

This `Decodable` type matches the response sent by Apple in the callback. It contains some optional data for the user, the JWT and a state property. Next, at the bottom of the file, create a new context to pass to Leaf after the callback:

```
struct SIWAHandleContext: Encodable {
  let token: String
  let email: String?
  let firstName: String?
  let lastName: String?
}
```

This contains the data from `AppleAuthorizationResponse` in a simpler format for Leaf to use. Next, create a new route handler below `registerPostHandler(_:)` for handling the redirect from Apple:

```
func appleAuthCallbackHandler(_ req: Request)
  throws -> EventLoopFuture<View> {
    // 1
    let siwaData =
      try req.content.decode(AppleAuthorizationResponse.self)
    // 2
    guard
      let sessionState = req.cookies["SIWA_STATE"]?.string,
      !sessionState.isEmpty,
      sessionState == siwaData.state
    else {
      req.logger
        .warning("SIWA does not exist or does not match")
      throw Abort(.unauthorized)
    }
    // 3
    let context = SIWAHandleContext(
      token: siwaData.idToken,
      email: siwaData.user?.email,
      firstName: siwaData.user?.name?.firstName,
      lastName: siwaData.user?.name?.lastName)
    // 4
    return req.view.render("siwaHandler", context)
}
```

1. Decode the request body to `AppleAuthorizationResponse`.
2. Get the session state from a cookie named `SIWA_STATE`. Ensure it matches the state from `AppleAuthorizationResponse`. If it doesn't match, return a **401 Unauthorized** error.
3. Create the context for Leaf.
4. Render the `siwaHandler` template using the provided context.

Register the route in `boot(routes:)` below `authSessionsRoutes.post("register", use: registerPostHandler)` add the following:

```
authSessionsRoutes.post(
  "login",
  "siwa",
  "callback",
  use: appleAuthCallbackHandler)
```

This routes a **POST** request to **/login/siwa/callback** — the URL you registered with Apple — to `appleAuthCallbackHandler(_:)`.

Create a new file in **Resources/Views** called **siwaHandler.leaf** for the Leaf template. Open the new file and insert the following:

```
<!-- 1 -->
<!doctype html>
<html lang="en" class="h-100">
  <head>
    <meta charset="utf-8">
    <meta name="viewport"
     content="width=device-width, initial-scale=1">
    <title>Sign In With Apple</title>
    <!-- 2 -->
    <script>
      // 3
      function handleCallback() {
        // 4
        const form = document.getElementById("siwaRedirectForm")
        // 5
        form.style.display = 'none';
        // 6
        form.submit();
      }
      // 7
      window.onload = handleCallback;
    </script>
  </head>
  <body class="d-flex flex-column h-100">
```

```
    <!-- 8 -->
    <form action="/login/siwa/handle" method="POST"
     id="siwaRedirectForm">
      <!-- 9 -->
      <input type="hidden" name="token" value="#(token)">
      <input type="hidden" name="email" value="#(email)">
      <input type="hidden" name="firstName"
       value="#(firstName)">
      <input type="hidden" name="lastName"
       value="#(lastName)">
      <!-- 10 -->
      <input type="submit"
       value="If nothing happens click here">
    </form>
  </body>
</html>
```

This file doesn't use **base.leaf** like the other files since the user won't see the content. Here's what the template does:

1. Create a basic HTML 5 page for the redirect.
2. Embed some JavaScript code into the page.
3. Define a JavaScript function `handleCallback()`.
4. Get the form from the page using the identifier `siwaRedirectForm`.
5. Set the display for the form to `none` — this hides the form so it's not visible.
6. Submit the form automatically.
7. When the page loads, trigger `handleCallback()`.
8. Define a form the sends a **POST** request to **/login/siwa/handle**. Set the form ID to `siwaRedirectForm` so the JavaScript code can find it.
9. Add a number of hidden fields that contain the data from the callback.
10. Add a submit button. This allows users to manually submit the form if the JavaScript fails to load.

You may be wondering - why bother with the redirect? After all, this code redirects to **/login/siwa/handle**. That's where you then need to register or log in the user? Why not do this here?

Modern browsers use a flag in cookies called **SameSite**. A browser will not send cookies to the server on a POST request from a different domain unless you set the cookie's **SameSite** flag to **none**. This means that you can't access any session data from the callback handler as the request came from Apple's domain. You can't log in a user without this. You workaround this by setting a special cookie on a special page that the browser will send to the server. You can then redirect to the real log in page. Since this redirect comes from the same domain, the browser will send the session cookie, allowing you to complete log in.

In Xcode, at the bottom of **WebsiteController.swift**, add a new type to represent the data sent by the new form:

```
struct SIWARedirectData: Content {
  let token: String
  let email: String?
  let firstName: String?
  let lastName: String?
}
```

Then, at the top of the file below `import Vapor`, add:

```
import Fluent
```

This allows you to use Fluent's queries. Next, create a new route handler below `appleAuthCallbackHandler(_:)` for the redirect:

```
func appleAuthRedirectHandler(_ req: Request)
  throws -> EventLoopFuture<Response> {
    // 1
    let data = try req.content.decode(SIWARedirectData.self)
    // 2
    guard let appIdentifier =
      Environment.get("WEBSITE_APPLICATION_IDENTIFIER") else {
      throw Abort(.internalServerError)
    }
    return req.jwt
      .apple
      .verify(data.token, applicationIdentifier: appIdentifier)
      .flatMap { siwaToken in
        User.query(on: req.db)
          .filter(\.$siwaIdentifier == siwaToken.subject.value)
          .first()
          .flatMap { user in
            let userFuture: EventLoopFuture<User>
```

```
          if let user = user {
            userFuture = req.eventLoop.future(user)
          } else {
            // 3
            guard
              let email = data.email,
              let firstName = data.firstName,
              let lastName = data.lastName
            else {
              return req.eventLoop
                .future(error: Abort(.badRequest))
            }
            // 4
            let user = User(
              name: "\(firstName) \(lastName)",
              username: email,
              password: UUID().uuidString,
              siwaIdentifier: siwaToken.subject.value)
            userFuture = user.save(on: req.db).map { user }
          }
          // 5
          return userFuture.map { user in
            // 6
            req.auth.login(user)
            // 7
            return req.redirect(to: "/")
          }
      }
    }
}
```

This method is similar to `signInWithApple(_:)` for the iOS app. The differences are:

1. Decode the request body to `SIWARedirectData`.
2. Get the application identifier from the environment variables. This is a *different* application identifier from the iOS app.
3. The request body contains the user's first name and last name as separate components. Ensure the request data contains both components for a new user.
4. Create a new `User` from the request data. Combine `firstName` and `lastName` to create the `name`.

5. Get the resolved user from the future. This uses `map(_:)` instead of `flatMap(_:)` since the closure returns a non-future.
6. Log the user in to the website for future requests.
7. Redirect to the homepage.

Register the new route in `boot(routes:)` under `authSessionsRoutes.post("login", "siwa", "callback", use: appleAuthCallbackHandler)`:

```
authSessionsRoutes.post(
  "login",
  "siwa",
  "handle",
  use: appleAuthRedirectHandler)
```

This routes a **POST** request to **/login/siwa/handler** — the URL the form redirects to — to `appleAuthRedirectHandler(_:)`.

Finally, you need to display the Sign in with Apple button on the log in and register pages. At the bottom of the file, add a new type for the data required for Sign in with Apple:

```
struct SIWAContext: Encodable {
  let clientID: String
  let scopes: String
  let redirectURI: String
  let state: String
}
```

This has the required properties for creating the Sign in with Apple button. Next, replace `LoginContext` with the following:

```
struct LoginContext: Encodable {
  let title = "Log In"
  let loginError: Bool
  let siwaContext: SIWAContext

  init(loginError: Bool = false, siwaContext: SIWAContext) {
    self.loginError = loginError
    self.siwaContext = siwaContext
  }
}
```

This adds the new context to `LoginContext`. Next, below `appleAuthRedirectHandler(_:)`, add a new method to create `SIWAContext`:

```
private func buildSIWAContext(on req: Request)
  throws -> SIWAContext {
  // 1
  let state = [UInt8].random(count: 32).base64
  // 2
  let scopes = "name email"
  // 3
  guard let clientID =
    Environment.get("WEBSITE_APPLICATION_IDENTIFIER") else {
      req.logger.error("WEBSITE_APPLICATION_IDENTIFIER not set")
      throw Abort(.internalServerError)
  }
  // 4
  guard let redirectURI =
    Environment.get("SIWA_REDIRECT_URL") else {
      req.logger.error("SIWA_REDIRECT_URL not set")
      throw Abort(.internalServerError)
  }
  // 5
  let siwa = SIWAContext(
    clientID: clientID,
    scopes: scopes,
    redirectURI: redirectURI,
    state: state)
  return siwa
}
```

Here's what the new function does:

1. Create a random state, similar to creating a new token value.
2. Define the scopes required for your app. You need both the name and email.
3. Get the client ID from the environment variables, otherwise throw a **500 Internal Server Error**. This is the same as your website application identifier.
4. Get the redirect URL from the environment variables, otherwise throw a **500 Internal Server Error**.
5. Create `SIWAContext` and return it.

Next, change the return type of `loginHandler(_:)` to:

```
func loginHandler(_ req: Request)
  throws -> EventLoopFuture<Response> {
```

You need to convert `View` to `Response` in order to set the special cookie. You also need to throw errors with the new code. Next, replace the body of `loginHandler(_:)` with the following:

```
let context: LoginContext
// 1
let siwaContext = try buildSIWAContext(on: req)
if let error = req.query[Bool.self, at: "error"], error {
  context = LoginContext(
    loginError: true,
    siwaContext: siwaContext)
} else {
  context = LoginContext(siwaContext: siwaContext)
}
// 2
return req.view
  .render("login", context)
  .encodeResponse(for: req)
  .map { response in
    // 3
    let expiryDate = Date().addingTimeInterval(300)
    // 4
    let cookie = HTTPCookies.Value(
      string: siwaContext.state,
      expires: expiryDate,
      maxAge: 300,
      isHTTPOnly: true,
      sameSite: HTTPCookies.SameSitePolicy.none)
    // 5
    response.cookies["SIWA_STATE"] = cookie
    // 6
    return response
}
```

Here's what the new code does:

1. Build `SIWAContext` from the request and pass it to `LoginContext`.
2. Convert the `EventLoopFuture<View>` to an `EventLoopFuture<Response>` using `encodeResponse(for:)`.
3. Create an expiry date of 5 minutes into the future.
4. Create a new cookie with the state created in `buildSIWAContext(on:)`. Note that `sameSite` is set to `.none` so the server sends the cookie during the redirect.
5. Set the cookie in the response using **SIWA_STATE** as the name. This is the same name you look for in `appleAuthCallbackHandler(_:)`.
6. Return the response.

Next, change the signature of `loginPostHandler(_:)` to allow you to throw errors:

```
func loginPostHandler(_ req: Request)
  throws -> EventLoopFuture<Response> {
```

Next, replace the `else` block in `loginPostHandler(_:)` with the following:

```
let siwaContext = try buildSIWAContext(on: req)
let context = LoginContext(
  loginError: true,
  siwaContext: siwaContext)
return req.view
  .render("login", context)
  .encodeResponse(for: req)
  .map { response in
    let expiryDate = Date().addingTimeInterval(300)
    let cookie = HTTPCookies.Value(
      string: siwaContext.state,
      expires: expiryDate,
      maxAge: 300,
      isHTTPOnly: true,
      sameSite: HTTPCookies.SameSitePolicy.none)
    response.cookies["SIWA_STATE"] = cookie
    return response
}
```

This is the same code as used in `loginHandler(_:)`. It encodes the necessary properties in `LoginContext` and sets the cookie if log in fails.

Next, replace `RegisterContext` with the following:

```
struct RegisterContext: Encodable {
  let title = "Register"
  let message: String?
  let siwaContext: SIWAContext

  init(message: String? = nil, siwaContext: SIWAContext) {
    self.message = message
    self.siwaContext = siwaContext
  }
}
```

This adds `SIWAContext` as a property in `RegisterContext` so you can display the Sign in with Apple button on the register page. Next, replace the signature of `registerHandler(_:)` with the following:

```
func registerHandler(_ req: Request)
  throws -> EventLoopFuture<Response> {
```

This changes the return type to `EventLoopFuture<Response>` so you can set the cookie and throw errors. Next, replace the body of `registerHandler(_:)` with:

```
let siwaContext = try buildSIWAContext(on: req)
let context: RegisterContext
if let message = req.query[String.self, at: "message"] {
  context = RegisterContext(
    message: message,
    siwaContext: siwaContext)
} else {
  context = RegisterContext(siwaContext: siwaContext)
}
return req.view
  .render("register", context)
  .encodeResponse(for: req)
  .map { response in
    let expiryDate = Date().addingTimeInterval(300)
    let cookie = HTTPCookies.Value(
      string: siwaContext.state,
      expires: expiryDate,
      maxAge: 300,
      isHTTPOnly: true,
      sameSite: HTTPCookies.SameSitePolicy.none)
    response.cookies["SIWA_STATE"] = cookie
    return response
}
```

The changes are identical to the changes made in `loginHandler(_:)`. They ensure you pass everything you need to Leaf to show the Sign in with Apple button on the register page.

Open **Resources/Views/login.leaf**. At the bottom of the `content` block, above `#endexport`, add the following:

```
<!-- 1 -->
<div id="appleid-signin" class="signin-button"
 data-color="black" data-border="true"
 data-type="sign in"></div>
<!-- 2 -->
<script type="text/javascript"
 src="https://appleid.cdn-apple.com/appleauth/static/jsapi/
appleid/1/en_US/appleid.auth.js"></script>
<!-- 3 -->
<script type="text/javascript">
  AppleID.auth.init({
    clientId : '#(siwaContext.clientID)',
    scope : '#(siwaContext.scopes)',
    redirectURI : '#(siwaContext.redirectURI)',
    state : '#(siwaContext.state)',
    usePopup : false
  });
</script>
```

Here's what the new code does:

1. Define a `<div>` to contain the Sign in with Apple button.
2. Import the Sign in with Apple JavaScript file from Apple. This handles all the logic for you on the web page.
3. Initialize `AppleID.auth` to create a Sign in with Apple button. This uses the values from `SIWAContext`.

Next, open **Resources/Views/register.leaf** and add the same code below `</form>`:

```
<!-- 1 -->
<div id="appleid-signin" class="signin-button"
 data-color="black" data-border="true"
 data-type="sign in"></div>
<!-- 2 -->
<script type="text/javascript"
 src="https://appleid.cdn-apple.com/appleauth/static/jsapi/
appleid/1/en_US/appleid.auth.js"></script>
<!-- 3 -->
<script type="text/javascript">
  AppleID.auth.init({
    clientId : '#(siwaContext.clientID)',
    scope : '#(siwaContext.scopes)',
    redirectURI : '#(siwaContext.redirectURI)',
    state : '#(siwaContext.state)',
    usePopup : false
  });
```

```
</script>
```

Finally, open **Public/styles/style.css** and add the following to the bottom of the file:

```
#appleid-signin {
  width: 240px;
  height: 40px;
  margin-top: 10px;
}
#appleid-signin:hover {
  cursor: pointer;
}
#appleid-signin > div {
  outline: none;
}
```

This adds some styling to the button to make it look nice on the page.

Open **.env** in a text editor and add the following variables at the end of the file:

```
WEBSITE_APPLICATION_IDENTIFIER=<YOUR_WEBSITE_IDENTIFIER>
SIWA_REDIRECT_URL=https://<YOUR_NGROK_DOMAIN>/login/siwa/
callback
```

These match the values you provided when you created the service ID in Apple's developer portal. Build and run the app and go to **https://<YOUR_NGROK_DOMAIN>**. Click **Register** and you'll see the new Sign in with Apple button!

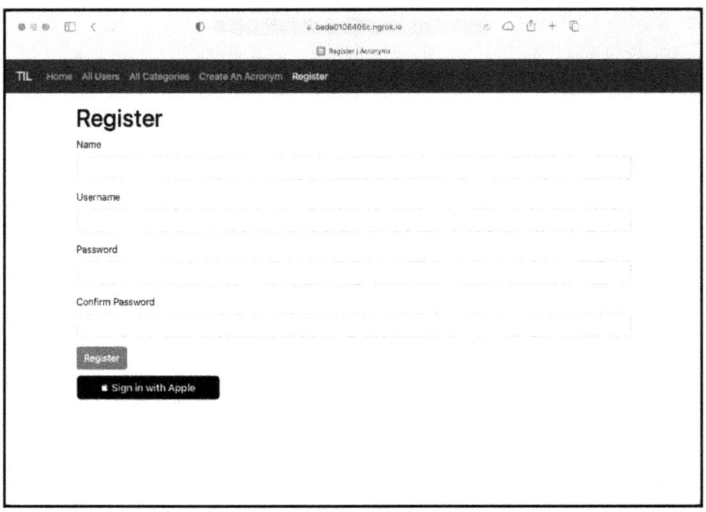

> **Note**: You must use the ngrok URL instead of localhost, otherwise the redirect won't work correctly.

The button also appears on the log in page. Click the **Sign in with Apple** button. On Safari, the browser will prompt you to enter your system password — the one you use to log in on your Mac — to authorize Sign in with Apple:

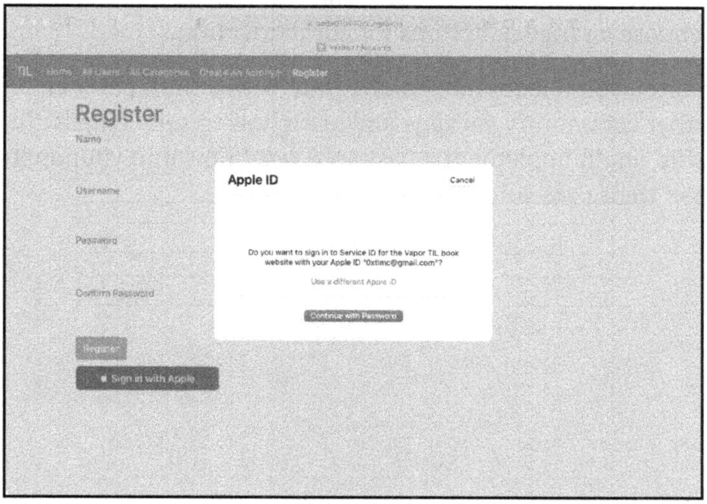

On Chrome, the app will redirect you to sign in to your Apple ID on Apple's website to sign in:

Complete the log in process for your chosen browser and the app will log you in with your Apple ID!

Where to go from here?

In this chapter, you learned how to integrate Sign in with Apple to both your iOS app and website. This complements first-party and external sign in experiences. It allows your users to choose a range of options for authentication.

In the next chapter, you'll learn how to integrate with a third party email provider. You'll use another community package and learn how to send emails. To demonstrate this, you'll implement a password reset flow into your application in case users forget their password.

Section IV: Advanced Server-Side Swift

This section covers a number of different topics you may need to consider when developing server-side applications. These chapters will provide you the necessary building blocks to continue on your Vapor adventure and build even more complex and wonderful applications.

The chapters in this section deal with more advanced topics for Vapor and were written by the Vapor Core Team members. These include the use of Caching, Middleware and how to version your database / api including performing migrations.

Chapter 25: Password Reset & Emails

By Tim Condon

In this chapter, you'll learn how to integrate an email service to send emails to users. Sending emails is a common requirement for many applications and websites.

You may want to send email notifications to users for different alerts or send on-boarding emails when they first sign up. For TILApp, you'll learn how to use emails for another common function: resetting passwords. First, you'll change the TIL `User` to include an email address. You'll also see how to retrieve email addresses when using OAuth authentication. Next, you'll integrate a community package to send emails via SendGrid. Finally, you'll learn how to set up a password reset flow in the website.

User email addresses

To send emails to users, you need a way to store their addresses! In Xcode, open **User.swift** and after `var siwaIdentifier: String?` add the following:

```
@Field(key: "email")
var email: String
```

This adds a new property to the `User` model to store an email address. Next, replace the initializer with the following, to account for the new property:

```
init(
  id: UUID? = nil,
  name: String,
  username: String,
  password: String,
```

```
    siwaIdentifier: String? = nil,
    email: String
  ) {
    self.name = name
    self.username = username
    self.password = password
    self.siwaIdentifier = siwaIdentifier
    self.email = email
  }
```

Next, open **CreateUser.swift**. In `prepare(on:)`, add the following below `.field("siwaIdentifier", .string)`:

```
.field("email", .string, .required)
.unique(on: "email")
```

This adds the field to the database and creates a unique key constraint on the email field. In **CreateAdminUser.swift**, replace `let user = User(...)` with the following:

```
let user = User(
  name: "Admin",
  username: "admin",
  password: passwordHash,
  email: "admin@localhost.local")
```

This adds an email to the default admin user as it's now required when creating a user. Provide a known email address if you wish.

> Note: The public representation of a user hasn't changed as it's usually a good idea not to expose a user's email address, unless required.

Web registration

One method of creating users in the TIL app is registering through the website. Open **WebsiteController.swift** and add the following property to the bottom of `RegisterData`:

```
let emailAddress: String
```

This is the email address a user provides when registering. In the extension conforming `RegisterData` to `Validatable`, add the following:

```
validations.add("emailAddress", as: String.self, is: .email)
```

after:

```
validations.add(
  "zipCode",
  as: String.self,
  is: .zipCode,
  required: false)
```

This ensures the email address provided at registration is valid. In `registerPostHandler(_:data:)`, replace `let user = ...` with the following:

```
let user = User(
  name: data.name,
  username: data.username,
  password: password,
  email: data.emailAddress)
```

This uses the email the user provides at registration to create the new user model. Open **register.leaf** and add the following under the `form-group` for **Username**:

```
<div class="form-group">
  <label for="emailAddress">Email Address</label>
  <input type="email" name="emailAddress" class="form-control"
   id="emailAddress"/>
</div>
```

This adds the new, required email field to the registration form.

Social media login

Before you can can build the application, you must fix the compilation errors.

Fixing Sign in with Apple

Getting the user's email address for a Sign in with Apple login is simple; Apple provides it in the JWT used for logging in! Open **WebsiteController.swift**, find `appleAuthRedirectHandler(_:)` and replace `let user = ...` with the following:

```
let user = User(
  name: "\(firstName) \(lastName)",
  username: email,
  password: UUID().uuidString,
  siwaIdentifier: siwaToken.subject.value,
  email: email)
```

Next, open **UsersController.swift**. In `signInWithApple(_:)`, replace `let user = ...` with the following:

```
let user = User(
  name: name,
  username: email,
  password: UUID().uuidString,
  siwaIdentifier: siwaToken.subject.value,
  email: email)
```

Both of these use the email taken from the JWT and pass it to the initializer. That's Sign in with Apple done.

Fixing Google

Getting the user's email address for a Google login is also simple; Google provides it when you request the user's information! Open **ImperialController.swift** and, in `processGoogleLogin(request:token:)`, replace `let user = ...` with the following:

```
let user = User(
  name: userInfo.name,
  username: userInfo.email,
  password: UUID().uuidString,
  email: userInfo.email)
```

This takes the user information you receive when the user signs in with Google and adds the email address to the initializer. For Google sign-ins, there's nothing more to do.

Fixing GitHub

Getting the email address for a GitHub user is more complicated. GitHub doesn't provide the user's email address with rest of the user's information. You must get the email address in a second request.

First, in **ImperialController.swift** in `boot(routes:)`, replace `try routes.oAuth(from: GitHub.self, ...)` with the following:

```
try routes.oAuth(
  from: GitHub.self,
  authenticate: "login-github",
  callback: githubCallbackURL,
  scope: ["user:email"],
  completion: processGitHubLogin)
```

This requests the `user:email` scope when requesting access to a user's account. Next, add the following below `GitHubUserInfo`:

```
struct GitHubEmailInfo: Content {
  let email: String
}
```

This represents the data received from GitHub's API when requesting a user's email. Next, add the following below `getUser(on:)`, in the `GitHub` extension:

```
// 1
static func getEmails(on request: Request) throws
  -> EventLoopFuture<[GitHubEmailInfo]> {
    // 2
    var headers = HTTPHeaders()
    try headers.add(
      name: .authorization,
      value: "token \(request.accessToken())")
    headers.add(name: .userAgent, value: "vapor")

    // 3
    let githubUserAPIURL: URI =
      "https://api.github.com/user/emails"
    return request.client
      .get(githubUserAPIURL, headers: headers)
      .flatMapThrowing { response in
        // 4
        guard response.status == .ok else {
          // 5
          if response.status == .unauthorized {
            throw Abort.redirect(to: "/login-github")
          } else {
            throw Abort(.internalServerError)
          }
        }
        // 6
        return try response.content
          .decode([GitHubEmailInfo].self)
    }
}
```

Here's what this does:

1. Declare a new method for getting a user's emails from GitHub. The method returns `[GitHubEmailInfo]` since the API returns all emails the user has associated with the account.
2. Set the bearer authorization token to the user's access token.
3. Make a request to the GitHub API to retrieve the user's emails. Unwrap the returned future.
4. Ensure the response from the API was **200 OK**.
5. If the response was **401 Unauthorized**, redirect to the GitHub login OAuth flow. This assumes the token is expired. Otherwise, return a **500 Internal Server Error**.
6. Decode the response to `[GitHubUserInfo]`.

Finally, replace `processGitHubLogin(request:token)` with the following:

```
func processGitHubLogin(request: Request, token: String) throws
  -> EventLoopFuture<ResponseEncodable> {
    // 1
    return try GitHub.getUser(on: request)
      .and(GitHub.getEmails(on: request))
      .flatMap { userInfo, emailInfo in
        return User.query(on: request.db)
          .filter(\.$username == userInfo.login)
          .first()
          .flatMap { foundUser in
            guard let existingUser = foundUser else {
              // 2
              let user = User(
                name: userInfo.name,
                username: userInfo.login,
                password: UUID().uuidString,
                email: emailInfo[0].email)
              return user.save(on: request.db).flatMap {
                request.session.authenticate(user)
                return generateRedirect(on: request, for: user)
              }
            }
            request.session.authenticate(existingUser)
            return generateRedirect(
              on: request,
              for: existingUser)
        }
    }
}
```

Here's what changed:

1. Send a request to get the user's emails at the same time as getting user's information.
2. Use the returned email information to create a new `User` object.

Fixing the tests

The main target now compiles. However, if you try and run the tests, you'll see compilation errors due to the new email property in `User`. Open **Models+Testable.swift** and, in `create(name:username:on:)`, replace `let user = ...` with the following:

```
let user = User(
  name: name,
  username: createUsername,
  password: password,
  email: "\(createUsername)@test.com")
```

This creates a new user with an email based on the username to avoid any conflicts. Since the email isn't exposed in the API, you don't need to test the response with a defined email.

Next, open **Application+Testable.swift**. In `test(_:_:headers:body:loggedInRequest:loggedInUser:file:line:beforeRequest:afterRequest)`, replace `userToLogin = ...` with:

```
userToLogin = User(
  name: "Admin",
  username: "admin",
  password: "password",
  email: "admin@localhost.local")
```

This uses the email from `CreateAdminUser` log the admin user in.

Next, open **UserTests.swift** and, in `testUserCanBeSavedWithAPI()`, replace `let user = ...` with the following:

```
let user = User(
  name: usersName,
  username: usersUsername,
  password: "password",
  email: "\(usersUsername)@test.com")
```

This creates the user with the required email parameter, using `usersUsername` to generate the email address.

Make sure you have your **.env** file that you built over the past three chapters and that you have set a custom working directory in Xcode. Then, run the tests and they should all pass.

> **Note**: You must have the test database in Docker running for the tests to work. See Chapter 11, "Testing", for details on how to set this up.

Running the app

The application should now compile. Before you can run the app, however, you must reset the database due to the new email property. In Terminal, type:

```
docker rm -f postgres
docker run --name postgres \
  -e POSTGRES_DB=vapor_database \
  -e POSTGRES_USER=vapor_username \
  -e POSTGRES_PASSWORD=vapor_password \
  -p 5432:5432 -d postgres
```

These are the same commands you've used in previous chapters to reset the database.

Finally, build and run. In your browser, go to **http://localhost:8080/** and click **Register**. The register screen now requires that you provide an email address:

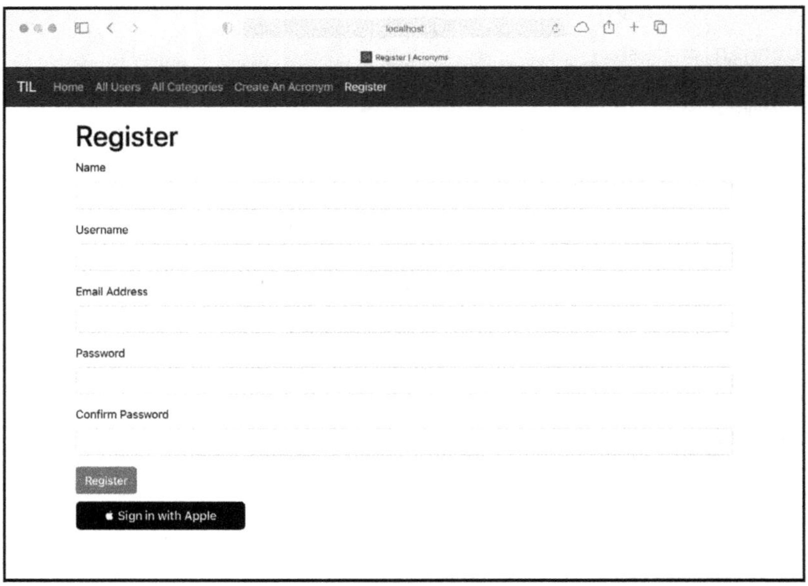

You can also log in with your Google or GitHub account without any issues. Note that when you log in to your GitHub account, GitHub prompts you to allow the app additional access to your account.

This is because you're now requesting the `user:email` scope:

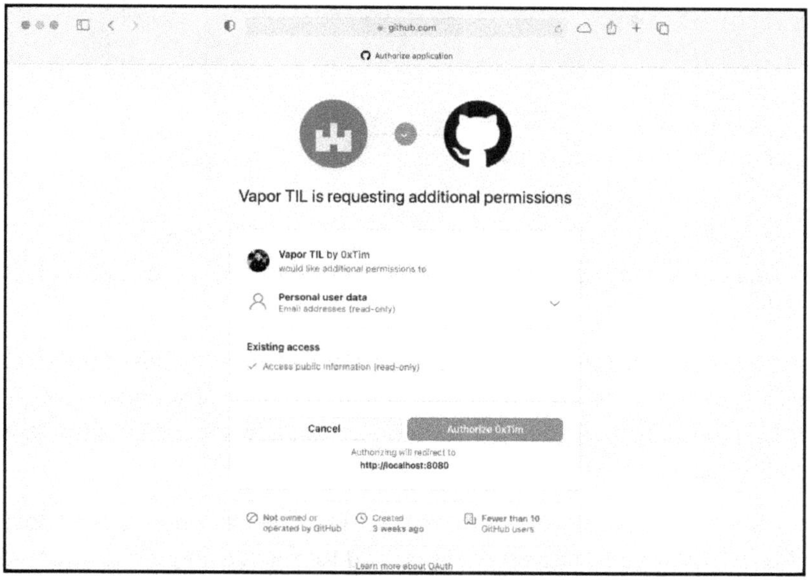

iOS app registration

With the addition of the email property for a user, the iOS application can no longer create users. Open the iOS project in Xcode and open **CreateUserData.swift**. Add a new property to `CreateUserData` below `var password: String?`:

```
var email: String
```

This stores the user's email when sending the new user to the API. Next, replace the initializer with the following:

```
init(
  name: String,
  username: String,
  password: String,
  email: String
) {
  self.name = name
  self.username = username
  self.password = password
  self.email = email
}
```

This adds `email` as a parameter to the initializer and initializes `email` with the provided value.

Next, open **Main.storyboard** and find the **Create User** scene. Select the **Create User** table view and, in the Attributes inspector, set the number of sections to **4**. In the Document Outline, select the new table view section and set the **Header** to **Email Address** in the Attributes inspector.

Next, select the new text field in the Document Outline and change the **Placeholder** to **User's Email**. Change the **Content Type** and **Keyboard Type** to **Email Address** to show the email keyboard when the user selects the field. Uncheck **Secure Text Entry** if it's checked.

Open **CreateUserTableViewController.swift** in the Assistant editor. Create an `IBOutlet` for the user's email text field below `@IBOutlet weak var passwordTextField: UITextField!` by **Control-dragging** to `CreateUserTableViewController`. Name the outlet **emailTextField**.

In `save(_:)`, add the following above `let user = ...`:

```
guard
  let email = emailTextField.text,
  !email.isEmpty
else {
  ErrorPresenter
    .showError(message: "You must specify an email", on: self)
  return
}
```

This ensures the user provides an email address before trying to create a user. Finally, replace `let user = ...` with the following:

```
let user = CreateUserData(
  name: name,
  username: username,
  password: password,
  email: email)
```

This provides an email address to `CreateUserData` from the text field you created above. Run TILApp in another Xcode window. Then, build and run the iOS app and log in with the admin credentials. Tap the **Users** tab and the + icon. Fill in the form, including the new email field, and tap **Save**. The new user will appear in the users list.

Integrating SendGrid

Finally, you've added an email address to the user model! Now it's time to learn how to send emails. This chapter uses SendGrid for that purpose. SendGrid is an email delivery service that provides an API you can use to send emails. It has a free tier allowing you to send 100 emails a day at no cost. There's also a community package — https://github.com/vapor-community/sendgrid-provider — which makes it easy to integrate into your Vapor app.

While it's possible to send emails directly using SwiftNIO, it's not advisable in most cases. On consumer ISPs, the ports to send emails are frequently blocked to combat spam. If you're hosting your application on something like AWS, the IP addresses of the servers are usually blacklisted, again to combat spam. Therefore, it's usually a good idea to use a service to send the emails for you.

Adding the dependency

In the TIL app, open **Package.swift** and replace `.package(url: "https://github.com/vapor/jwt.git", from: "4.0.0"),` with the following:

```
.package(
  url: "https://github.com/vapor/jwt.git",
  from: "4.0.0"),
.package(
  url: "https://github.com/vapor-community/sendgrid.git",
  from: "4.0.0")
```

Next, add the dependency to your App target's dependency array. Replace `.product(name: "JWT", package: "jwt"),` with:

```
.product(name: "JWT", package: "jwt"),
.product(name: "SendGrid", package: "sendgrid")
```

Signing up for SendGrid and getting a token

To use SendGrid, you must create an account. Visit https://signup.sendgrid.com and fill out the form to sign up:

Once you're in the dashboard, click **Settings** to expand the menu and click **API Keys**:

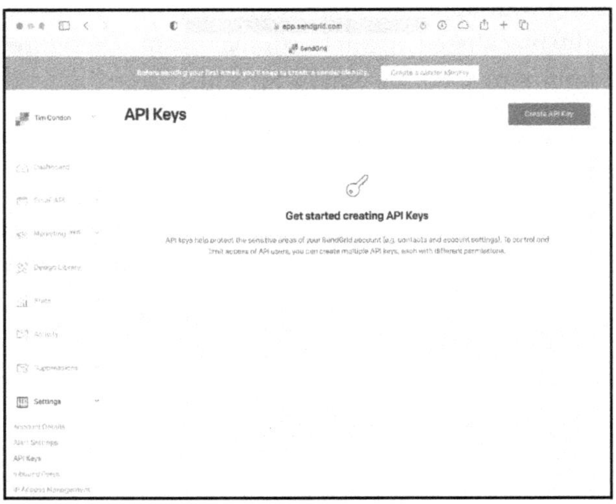

Click **Create API Key** and provide a name for the key — for example, **Vapor TIL**.

Select **Restricted Access**:

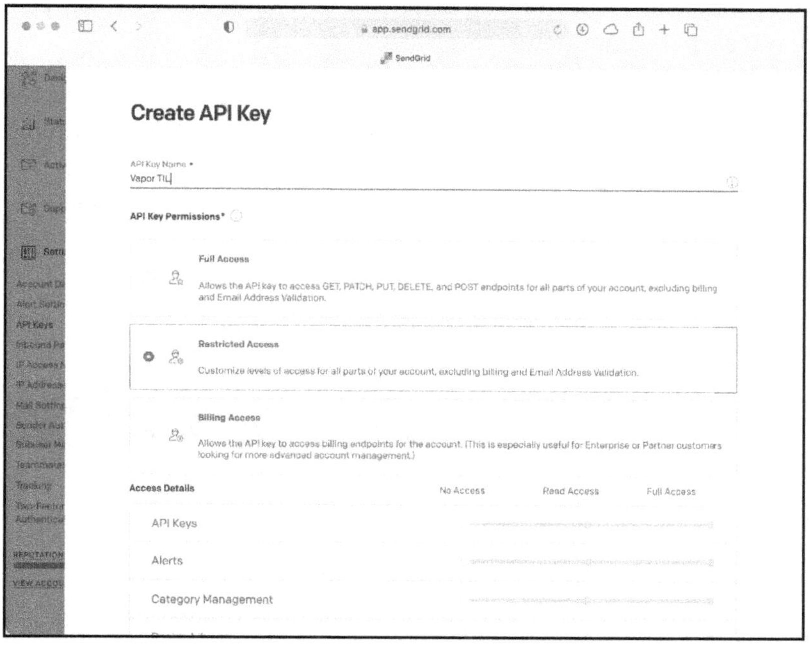

Scroll down and enable the **Mail Send** permission. This gives your API key permission to send emails but no access to other parts of the SendGrid API. Click **Create & View**. and SendGrid will show you your API key:

Like the OAuth client secrets, you *must* keep the API key safe and secure and not check the key into source control. You will not be able to retrieve the key again so make sure you save it somewhere!

Finally, you need to set up a sender identity before sending emails. At the top of the dashboard, click **Create a sender identity**. You can choose two different options, but for now, click **Create a Single Sender**:

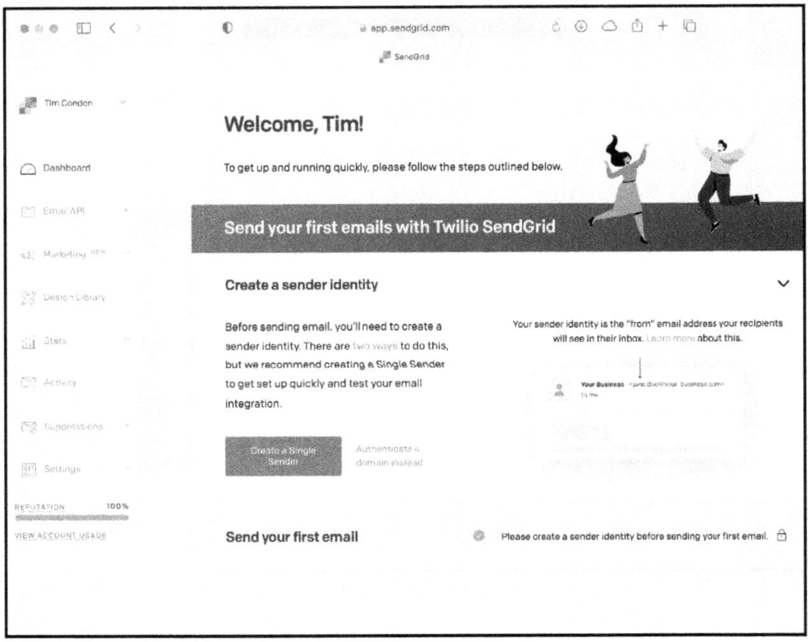

Fill out the form to create a sender identity and click **Create**. You'll receive an email to verify your address, so click **Verify Single Sender** when you receive it.

Integrating with Vapor

With your API key created, go back to the TIL app in Xcode. Open **configure.swift** and add the following below `import Leaf`:

```
import SendGrid
```

Next, add the following below `try routes(app)`:

```
app.sendgrid.initialize()
```

This initializes the SendGrid service and ensures you've configured it correctly. In a text editor, open **.env** and add the following to the bottom of the file:

```
SENDGRID_API_KEY=<YOUR_API_KEY>
```

This adds the API key you created earlier to the app's environment variables. SendGrid looks for **SENDGRID_API_KEY** when interacting with the SendGrid API.

You're now ready to send emails with SendGrid!

Setting up a password reset flow

To build a good experience for your app's users, you must provide a way for them to reset a forgotten password. You'll implement that now.

Forgotten password page

The first part of the password reset flow consists of two actions:

- Presenting a form to the user which asks for the registered email address.
- Handling the POST request the form sends.

Open **WebsiteController.swift** and, below buildSIWAContext(_:), add the following:

```
// 1
func forgottenPasswordHandler(_ req: Request)
  -> EventLoopFuture<View> {
  // 2
  req.view.render(
    "forgottenPassword",
    ["title": "Reset Your Password"])
}
```

Here's what this does:

1. Define a route handler, forgottenPasswordHandler(_:), that returns EventLoopFuture<View>.
2. Return the rendered result of the forgottenPassword template. This template only requires a single property in the context, the title. Instead of creating a new context type to pass to the template, this code code passes the title in a dictionary. This helps reduce the amount of code you need to write.

Register the route in `boot(routes:)` above `authSessionsRoutes.get(use: indexHandler)`:

```
authSessionsRoutes.get(
  "forgottenPassword",
  use: forgottenPasswordHandler)
```

This maps a **GET** request to **/forgottenPassword** to `forgottenPasswordHandler(_:)`. In **Resources/Views**, create the new template file and name it **forgottenPassword.leaf**. Open the new file and insert the following:

```
<!-- 1 -->
#extend("base"):
  <!-- 2 -->
  #export("content"):
    <!-- 3 -->
    <h1>#(title)</h1>

    <!-- 4 -->
    <form method="post">
      <div class="form-group">
        <label for="email">Email</label>
        <!-- 5 -->
        <input type="email" name="email" class="form-control"
        id="email"/>
      </div>

      <!-- 6 -->
      <button type="submit" class="btn btn-primary">
        Reset Password
      </button>
    </form>
  #endexport
#endextend
```

Here's what the new template does:

1. Extend the base template as you have with the rest of the templates.
2. Export the `content` property used by the base template.
3. Display the title of the page using the parameter passed in via the context.
4. Define a form with the POST method. This sends a POST request to the same URL when the user submits the form.
5. Define a single input in the form for the email address.
6. Set a submit button with the title **Reset Password**.

Finally, open **login.leaf** and, below the script for Sign in with Apple, add the following:

```
<br />
<a href="/forgottenPassword">Forgotten your password?</a>
```

This adds a link to the new route with a line break to put the link below the social media login buttons. Build and run the app. Go to **http://localhost:8080/login** in the browser.

You'll see the new link for forgotten password:

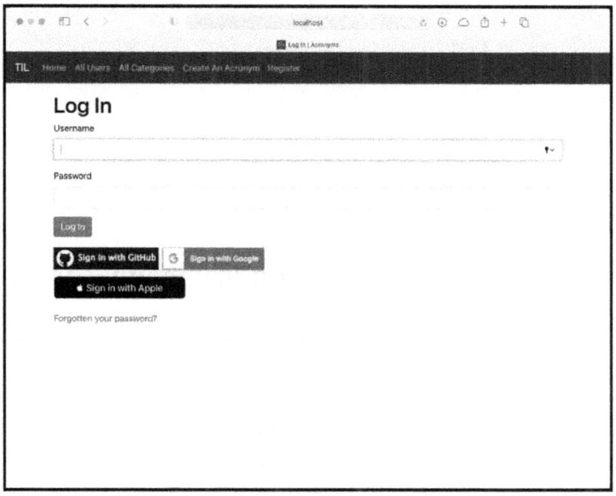

Click the link to see the new forgotten password form:

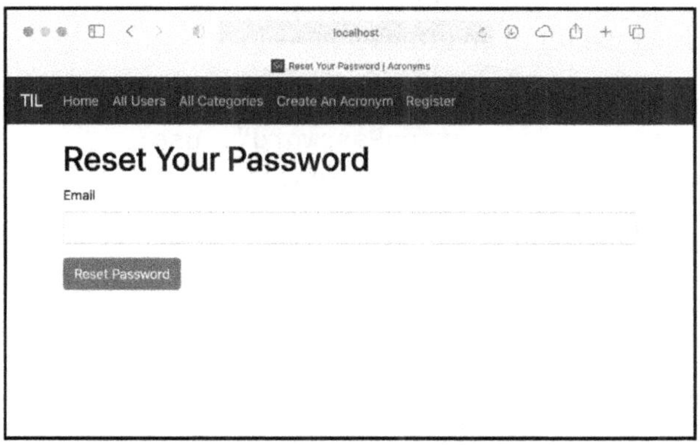

Back in Xcode, open **WebsiteController.swift**. Create a new route below `forgottenPasswordHandler(_:)` to handle the POST request from the form:

```
// 1
func forgottenPasswordPostHandler(_ req: Request)
  throws -> EventLoopFuture<View> {
    // 2
    let email =
      try req.content.get(String.self, at: "email")
    // 3
    return User.query(on: req.db)
      .filter(\.$email == email)
      .first()
      .flatMap { user in
        // 4
        req.view
          .render("forgottenPasswordConfirmed")
    }
}
```

Here's what this route handler does:

1. Define a route handler for the **POST** request that returns a view.
2. Get the email from the request's body. Since there's only one parameter you're interested in, you can use `get(_:at:)` instead of creating a new `Content` type.
3. Get the user from the database by creating a query with a filter for the email provided. Since the emails are unique, you'll either get one result or none.
4. Return a view rendered from a new `forgottenPasswordConfirmed` template. You want to return the same response whether the email exists or not to avoid revealing anything useful to an attacker.

Register the new route by adding the following below `authSessionsRoutes.get("forgottenPassword", use: forgottenPasswordHandler)` in `boot(routes:)`:

```
authSessionsRoutes.post(
  "forgottenPassword",
  use: forgottenPasswordPostHandler)
```

This maps a **POST** request to **/forgottenPassword** to `forgottenPasswordPostHandler(_:)`.

Next, in **Resources/Views**, create the new template file: **forgottenPasswordConfirmed.leaf**. Open the new file in an editor and add the following:

```
#extend("base"):
  #export("content"):
    <h1>#(title)</h1>

    <p>Instructions to reset your password have
     been emailed to you.</p>
  #endexport
#endextend
```

Like the other templates file, this uses **base.leaf** for the majority of the content. The page displays a message indicating the site has sent an email to the user.

To secure a password reset request, you should create a random token and send it to the user. Create a new file called **ResetPasswordToken.swift** in **Sources/App/Models** and insert the following:

```
import Fluent
import Vapor

final class ResetPasswordToken: Model, Content {
  static let schema = "resetPasswordTokens"

  @ID
  var id: UUID?

  @Field(key: "token")
  var token: String

  @Parent(key: "userID")
  var user: User

  init() {}

  init(id: UUID? = nil, token: String, userID: User.IDValue) {
    self.id = id
    self.token = token
    self.$user.id = userID
  }
}
```

Here's what the new model code does:

This defines a new class, `ResetPasswordToken`, that contains a `UUID` for the ID, a `String` for the actual token and the user's ID as a `@Parent` property.

Next, create a new file in **Sources/App/Migrations** called **CreateResetPasswordToken.swift** and add the following:

```
import Fluent

struct CreateResetPasswordToken: Migration {
  func prepare(on database: Database) -> EventLoopFuture<Void> {
    database.schema("resetPasswordTokens")
      .id()
      .field("token", .string, .required)
      .field(
        "userID",
        .uuid,
        .required,
        .references("users", "id"))
      .unique(on: "token")
      .create()
  }

  func revert(on database: Database) -> EventLoopFuture<Void> {
    database.schema("resetPasswordTokens").delete()
  }
}
```

This creates the migration for `ResetPasswordToken`. It links `userID` to the `User`'s table and marks `token` as unique.

Open **configure.swift** and, below `app.migrations.add(CreateAdminUser())`, add the following:

```
app.migrations.add(CreateResetPasswordToken())
```

This adds the new model to the list of migrations so the app creates the table the next time the it runs.

Sending emails

Return to **WebsiteController.swift**. At the top of the file, insert the following below `import Fluent`:

```
import SendGrid
```

Then, in `forgottenPasswordPostHandler(_:)`, replace `req.view.render("forgottenPasswordConfirmed")` with the following:

```
// 1
guard let user = user else {
```

```
    return req.view.render(
      "forgottenPasswordConfirmed",
      ["title": "Password Reset Email Sent"])
  }
  // 2
  let resetTokenString =
    Data([UInt8].random(count: 32)).base32EncodedString()
  // 3
  let resetToken: ResetPasswordToken
  do {
    resetToken = try ResetPasswordToken(
      token: resetTokenString,
      userID: user.requireID())
  } catch {
    return req.eventLoop.future(error: error)
  }
  // 4
  return resetToken.save(on: req.db).flatMap {
    // 5
    let emailContent = """
    <p>You've requested to reset your password. <a
    href="http://localhost:8080/resetPassword?\
    token=\(resetTokenString)">
    Click here</a> to reset your password.</p>
    """
    // 6
    let emailAddress = EmailAddress(
      email: user.email,
      name: user.name)
    let fromEmail = EmailAddress(
      email: "<SENDGRID SENDER EMAIL>",
      name: "Vapor TIL")
    // 7
    let emailConfig = Personalization(
      to: [emailAddress],
      subject: "Reset Your Password")
    // 8
    let email = SendGridEmail(
      personalizations: [emailConfig],
      from: fromEmail,
      content: [
        ["type": "text/html",
        "value": emailContent]
      ])
    // 9
    let emailSend: EventLoopFuture<Void>
    do {
      emailSend =
        try req.application
          .sendgrid
          .client
          .send(email: email, on: req.eventLoop)
    } catch {
```

```
      return req.eventLoop.future(error: error)
    }
    return emailSend.flatMap {
      // 10
      return req.view.render(
        "forgottenPasswordConfirmed",
        ["title": "Password Reset Email Sent"]
      )
    }
  }
```

Here's what the new code does:

1. Ensure there's a user associated with the email address. Otherwise, return the rendered `forgottenPasswordConfirmed` template. Notice how the title is set with a dictionary again.
2. Generate a token string using `CryptoRandom`. Note that this is Base32 encoded to avoid adding characters that break URLs.
3. Create a `ResetPasswordToken` object with the token string and the user's ID.
4. Save the token in the database and unwrap the returned future.
5. Create the email body. This contains a link to use the token to reset the password. You could even use Leaf to generate a full HTML email, if desired.
6. Create `EmailAddress` instances for the addressee and the sender.
7. Create a SendGrid `Personalization` to set the addressee and subject of the email.
8. Create the email using the configuration and email addresses. Set the content type to `text/html` to indicate this is an HTML email. SendGrid requires you to provide `type` and `value` values.
9. Send the email using the `SendGridClient` from `Application` and catch and return any errors as failed futures.
10. Return the rendered `forgottenPasswordConfirmed` template.

Replace `<SENDGRID SENDER EMAIL>` under `// 8` with the email address you verified with SendGrid.

At the bottom of the file, create a new context for the new page sent in the email:

```
struct ResetPasswordContext: Encodable {
  let title = "Reset Password"
  let error: Bool?

  init(error: Bool? = false) {
    self.error = error
  }
}
```

This context contains a static title and allows you to set an error flag. Next, underneath `forgottenPasswordPostHandler(_:)`, create a route handler to handle the link from the email:

```
func resetPasswordHandler(_ req: Request)
  -> EventLoopFuture<View> {
    // 1
    guard let token =
      try? req.query.get(String.self, at: "token") else {
        return req.view.render(
          "resetPassword",
          ResetPasswordContext(error: true)
        )
    }
    // 2
    return ResetPasswordToken.query(on: req.db)
      .filter(\.$token == token)
      .first()
      // 3
      .unwrap(or: Abort.redirect(to: "/"))
      .flatMap { token in
        // 4
        token.$user.get(on: req.db).flatMap { user in
          do {
            try req.session.set("ResetPasswordUser", to: user)
          } catch {
            return req.eventLoop.future(error: error)
          }
          // 5
          return token.delete(on: req.db)
        }
      }.flatMap {
        // 6
        req.view.render(
          "resetPassword",
          ResetPasswordContext()
        )
      }
}
```

Here's what the new route does:

1. Ensure the request contains a token as a query parameter. Otherwise, render the `resetPassword` template with the error flag set.
2. Query the `ResetPasswordToken` table to find the provided token and unwrap the resulting future.
3. Ensure the token provided is valid, otherwise redirect to the home page.
4. Get the token's user and save it in the session as `ResetPasswordUser`.
5. Delete the token as you've now used it.
6. Render the `resetPassword` template, using the default `ResetPasswordContext` and return the result.

In `boot(routes:)`, below `authSessionsRoutes.post("forgottenPassword", use: forgottenPasswordPostHandler)`, register the new route:

```
authSessionsRoutes.get(
  "resetPassword",
  use: resetPasswordHandler)
```

This maps a **GET** request to **/resetPassword** to `resetPasswordHandler(_:)`.

In **Resources/Views**, create a file called **resetPassword.leaf**. This is the new template used by `resetPasswordHandler(_:)`. Open the file in an editor and add the following:

```
#extend("base"):
  #export("content"):
    <h1>#(title)</h1>

    <!-- 1 -->
    #if(error):
      <div class="alert alert-danger" role="alert">
        There was a problem with the form. Ensure you clicked on
        the full link with the token and your passwords match.
      </div>
    #endif

    <!-- 2 -->
    <form method="post">
      <!-- 3 -->
      <div class="form-group">
        <label for="password">Password</label>
        <input type="password" name="password"
        class="form-control" id="password"/>
```

```
      </div>

      <!-- 4 -->
      <div class="form-group">
        <label for="confirmPassword">Confirm Password</label>
        <input type="password" name="confirmPassword"
        class="form-control" id="confirmPassword"/>
      </div>

      <!-- 5 -->
      <button type="submit" class="btn btn-primary">
        Reset
      </button>
    </form>
  #endexport
#endextend
```

This is similar to the other templates, setting `content` and using **base.leaf**. Here's what's different:

1. If `error` is set, display an error message. This template uses the same error property for passwords not matching and no token.
2. Show a form with the **POST** action. This submits the form back to the same URL, **/resetPassword**, as a **POST** request.
3. Add an input for the new password.
4. Add an input to confirm the new password.
5. Add a button to submit the form, labeled **Reset**.

At the bottom of **WebsiteController.swift**, create a `Content` type to decode the data from the form:

```
struct ResetPasswordData: Content {
  let password: String
  let confirmPassword: String
}
```

This type contains a property for each of the inputs in the form. Below `resetPasswordHandler(_:)` create a route handler to handle the **POST** request from the form:

```
func resetPasswordPostHandler(_ req: Request)
  throws -> EventLoopFuture<Response> {
    // 1
    let data = try req.content.decode(ResetPasswordData.self)
    // 2
```

```
    guard data.password == data.confirmPassword else {
      return req.view.render(
        "resetPassword",
        ResetPasswordContext(error: true))
        .encodeResponse(for: req)
    }
    // 3
    let resetPasswordUser = try req.session
      .get("ResetPasswordUser", as: User.self)
    req.session.data["ResetPasswordUser"] = nil
    // 4
    let newPassword = try Bcrypt.hash(data.password)
    // 5
    return try User.query(on: req.db)
      .filter(\.$id == resetPasswordUser.requireID())
      .set(\.$password, to: newPassword)
      .update()
      .transform(to: req.redirect(to: "/login"))
}
```

Here's what the new route handler does:

1. Decode the request body to `ResetPasswordData`.
2. Ensure the passwords match, otherwise show the form again with the error message.
3. Get the user saved in the session. You set this user in the **GET** route above. Once retrieved, clear the user from the session.
4. Hash the user's new password.
5. Perform a query to update the user's password to the new hashed password. This sets the `password` field for all users in the database with a matching ID. Since ID is unique, it only updates a single user. This is analogous to an `UPDATE` SQL query.

Finally, register the route in `boot(routes:)` below `authSessionsRoutes.get("resetPassword", use: resetPasswordHandler)`:

```
authSessionsRoutes.post(
  "resetPassword",
  use: resetPasswordPostHandler)
```

This maps a **POST** request to **/resetPassword** to `resetPasswordPostHandler(_:data:)`. Build and run the app. If necessary, register a new user using your email address and then log out. Head to **http://localhost:8080/login** in your browser and click **Forgotten your password?**. Enter the email address for your user and click **Reset Password**.

You'll see the confirmation screen:

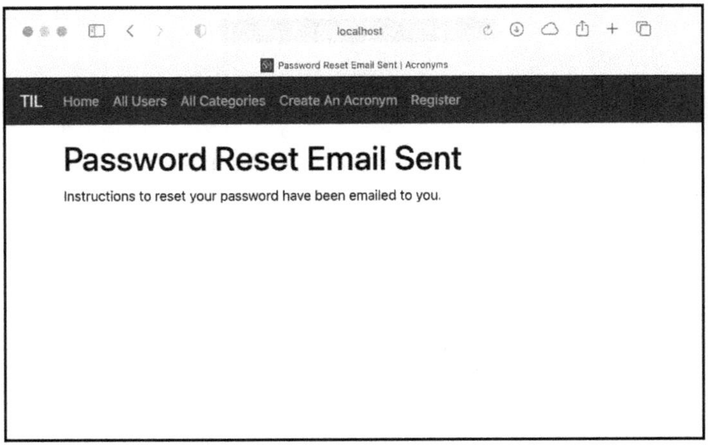

Within a minute or so, you should receive an email. Note that the email may be in your Junk mail folder depending upon your email provider and client:

Click the link in the email. The application presents you with a form to enter a new password:

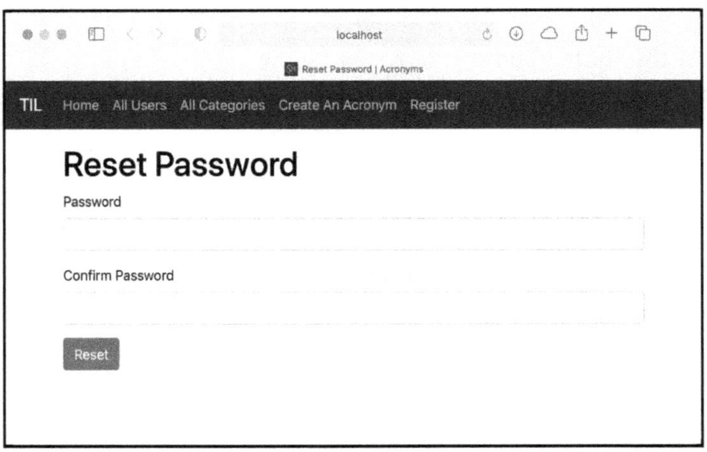

Enter a new password in both fields and click **Reset**. The application redirects you to the login page. Enter your username and your new password and the app will log you in.

Where to go from here?

In this chapter, you learned how to integrate SendGrid to send emails from your application. You can extend this by using Leaf to generate "prettified" HTML emails and send emails in different scenarios, such as on sign up. This chapter also introduced a method to reset a user's password. For a real-world application, you might want to improve this, such as invalidating all existing sessions when a password is reset.

The next chapter will show you how to handle file uploads in Vapor to allow users to upload a profile picture.

Chapter 26: Adding Profile Pictures

By Tim Condon

In previous chapters, you learned how to send data to your Vapor application in POST requests. You used JSON bodies and forms to transmit the data, but the data was always simple text. In this chapter, you'll learn how to send files in requests and handle that in your Vapor application. You'll use this knowledge to allow users to upload profile pictures in the web application.

> **Note**: This chapter teaches you how to upload files to the server where your Vapor application runs. For a real application, you should consider forwarding the file to a storage service, such as AWS S3. Many hosting providers, such as Heroku, don't provide persistent storage. This means that you'll lose your uploaded files when redeploying the application. You'll also lose files if the hosting provider restarts your application. Additionally, uploading the files to the same server means you can't scale your application to more than one instance because the files won't exist across all application instances.

Adding a picture to the model

As in previous chapters, you need to change the model so you can associate an image with a `User`. Open the Vapor TIL application in Xcode and open **User.swift**. Add the following below `var email: String`:

```
@OptionalField(key: "profilePicture")
var profilePicture: String?
```

This stores an optional `String` for the image. It will contain the filename of the user's profile picture on disk. The filename is optional as you're not enforcing that a user has a profile picture — and they won't have one when they register. Replace the initializer to account for the new property with the following:

```
init(
  name: String,
  username: String,
  password: String,
  siwaIdentifier: String? = nil,
  email: String,
  profilePicture: String? = nil
) {
  self.name = name
  self.username = username
  self.password = password
  self.siwaIdentifier = siwaIdentifier
  self.email = email
  self.profilePicture = profilePicture
}
```

Providing a default value of `nil` for `profilePicture` allows your app to continue to compile and operate without further source changes.

> **Note**: You could use the user APIs from Google and GitHub to get a URL to the user's profile picture. This would allow you to download the image and store it along side regular users' pictures or save the link. However, this is left as an exercise for the reader.

You could make uploading a profile picture part of the registration experience, but this chapter does it in a separate step. Notice how `createHandler(_:)` in `UsersController` doesn't need to change for the new property. This is because the route handler uses `Codable` and sets the property to `nil` if the data isn't present in the POST request.

Next, open **CreateUser.swift** and below:

```
.field("email", .string, .required)`:
```

add the following:

```
.field("profilePicture", .string)
```

This adds a new column in the database for the profile picture. Note that you haven't added the `.required` constraint as the property is optional.

Reset the database

As in the past, since you've added a property to `User`, you must reset the database. In Terminal, run:

```
docker rm -f postgres
docker rm -f postgres-test
docker run --name postgres -e POSTGRES_DB=vapor_database \
  -e POSTGRES_USER=vapor_username \
  -e POSTGRES_PASSWORD=vapor_password \
  -p 5432:5432 -d postgres
docker run --name postgres-test -e POSTGRES_DB=vapor-test \
  -e POSTGRES_USER=vapor_username \
  -e POSTGRES_PASSWORD=vapor_password \
  -p 5433:5432 -d postgres
```

Like before, this deletes the existing container named **postgres** and recreates it. It also resets the database used for testing. Ensure both containers are running. In Terminal, type:

```
docker ps -a
```

You should see both your main database container, **postgres**, and the test database container, **postgres-test**. Both should have a status similar to **Up about a minute**:

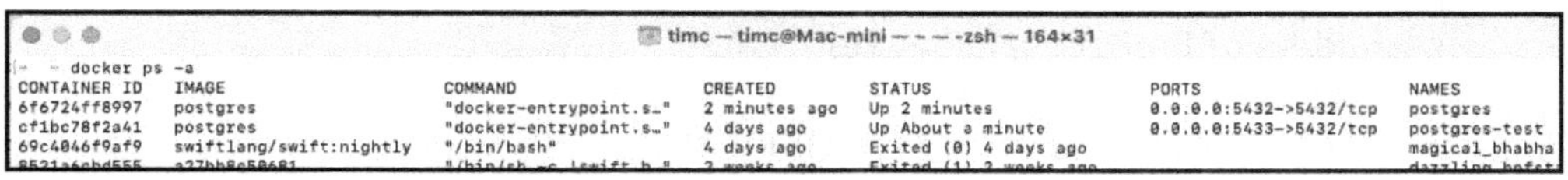

Verify the tests

In Xcode, type **Command+U** to run all the tests. They should all pass.

> **Note**: Xcode uses the existing environment variables from **.env**. If you're using the starter project from the chapter instead of an existing project, you should ensure you set these variables correctly. You also need to set the custom working directory so Vapor knows where to find the file. See Chapters 22–25 for details on setting these up. Each of those four chapters contributes necessary environment variables.

Creating the form

With the model changed, you can now create a page to allow users to submit a picture. In Xcode, open **WebsiteController.swift**. Next, add the following below `resetPasswordPostHandler(_:data:)`:

```
func addProfilePictureHandler(_ req: Request)
  -> EventLoopFuture<View> {
    User.find(req.parameters.get("userID"), on: req.db)
      .unwrap(or: Abort(.notFound)).flatMap { user in
        req.view.render(
          "addProfilePicture",
          [
            "title": "Add Profile Picture",
            "username": user.name
          ]
        )
    }
}
```

This defines a new route handler that renders **addProfilePicture.leaf**. The route handler also passes the title and the user's name to the template as a dictionary. Next, add the following to the end of `boot(routes:)`, to register the new route handler:

```
protectedRoutes.get(
  "users",
  ":userID",
  "addProfilePicture",
  use: addProfilePictureHandler)
```

This connects a **GET** request to **/users/<USER_ID>/addProfilePicture** to `addProfilePictureHandler(_:)`. Note that the route is also a protected route — users must be logged in to add profiles pictures to users.

The TIL application also allows users to upload profile pictures for any user, not just their own.

In **Resources/Views**, create the new template, **addProfilePicture.leaf**. Open the new file in any text editor and insert the following:

```
<!-- 1 -->
#extend("base"):
  <!-- 2 -->
  #export("content"):
    <!-- 3 -->
    <h1>#(title)</h1>
```

```
    <!-- 4 -->
    <form method="post" enctype="multipart/form-data">
      <!-- 5 -->
      <div class="form-group">
        <label for="picture">
            Select Picture for #(username)
        </label>
        <input type="file" name="picture"
        class="form-control-file" id="picture"/>
      </div>

      <!-- 6 -->
      <button type="submit" class="btn btn-primary">
        Upload
      </button>
    </form>
  #endexport
#endextend
```

Here's what the new template does:

1. Extend **base.leaf** to include the main template.
2. Export `content` as required by **base.leaf**.
3. Use the title passed to the template as the title for the page.
4. Create a form and set the method to **POST**. When you submit the form, the browser sends the form as a **POST** request to the same URL. Notice the encoding type of `multipart/form-data`. This allows you to send files to the server from the browser.
5. Create a form group with an input type of `file`. This presents a file browser in your web browser. Bootstrap uses `form-control-file` to help style the input.
6. Add a submit button to allow users to submit the form.

Next, you need a link for users to be able to access the new form. Open **WebsiteController.swift**, add a new property at the bottom of `UserContext`:

```
let authenticatedUser: User?
```

This stores the authenticated user for that request, if one exists. In `userHandler(_:)`, replace `let context = ...` with the following:

```
// 1
let loggedInUser = req.auth.get(User.self)
// 2
```

```
let context = UserContext(
  title: user.name,
  user: user,
  acronyms: acronyms,
  authenticatedUser: loggedInUser)
```

Here's what you changed:

1. Get the authenticated user from `Request`'s authentication cache. This returns `User?` as there may be no authenticated user.
2. Pass the optional, authenticated user to the context.

Finally, open **user.leaf**. Add the following before `#extend("acronymsTable")`:

```
#if(authenticatedUser):
  <a href="/users/#(user.id)/addProfilePicture">
    #if(user.profilePicture):
      Update
    #else:
      Add
    #endif
    Profile Picture
  </a>
#endif
```

This adds a link to the new add profile picture page if the user is logged in. The link will display **Update Profile Picture** if a user already has a profile picture, otherwise the link displays **Add Profile Picture**.

In Xcode, build and run the application. In the browser, visit **http://localhost:8080/login** and log in as the admin user. Once logged in, click **All Users** and select the **admin** user.

There's a new link to the add profile picture page. Click **Add Profile Picture** and you'll see the new form to add a profile picture:

Accepting file uploads

Next, implement the necessary code to handle the **POST** request from the form. In Terminal, enter the following in the **TILApp** directory:

```
# 1
mkdir ProfilePictures
# 2
touch ProfilePictures/.keep
```

Here's what these commands do:

1. Create the directory to store the users' profile pictures.
2. Add an empty file so the directory is added to source control. This helps with deploying applications to ensure the directory exists.

Next, in Xcode, open **WebsiteController.swift**. At the bottom of the file, add the following:

```
struct ImageUploadData: Content {
  var picture: Data
}
```

This new type represents the data sent by the form. `picture` matches the name of the input specified in the HTML form.

Since the form uploads a file, you'll decode the picture into `Data`.

Next, add a new property at the top of `WebsiteController`, above `boot(routes:)`:

```
let imageFolder = "ProfilePictures/"
```

This defines the folder where you'll store the images. Next, below `addProfilePictureHandler(_:)` add a request handler for the **POST** request:

```
func addProfilePicturePostHandler(_ req: Request)
  throws -> EventLoopFuture<Response> {
    // 1
    let data = try req.content.decode(ImageUploadData.self)
    // 2
    return User.find(req.parameters.get("userID"), on: req.db)
      .unwrap(or: Abort(.notFound))
      .flatMap { user in
        // 3
        let userID: UUID
        do {
```

```
        userID = try user.requireID()
      } catch {
        return req.eventLoop.future(error: error)
      }
      // 4
      let name = "\(userID)-\(UUID()).jpg"
      // 5
      let path =
        req.application.directory.workingDirectory +
          imageFolder + name
      // 6
      return req.fileio
        .writeFile(.init(data: data.picture), at: path)
        .flatMap {
          // 7
          user.profilePicture = name
          // 8
          let redirect = req.redirect(to: "/users/\(userID)")
          return user.save(on: req.db).transform(to: redirect)
      }
    }
}
```

Here's what the new request handler does:

1. Decode the request body to `ImageUploadData`.
2. Get the user from the parameters.
3. Get the user ID and catch any errors thrown.
4. Create a unique name for the profile picture.
5. Set up the path of the file to save using the app's working directory, the image folder and the name.
6. Save the file on disk using the path and the image data. This uses NIO's file functionality to avoid blocking any threads while waiting for the write to complete.
7. Update the user with the profile picture filename.
8. Save the updated user and return a redirect to the user's page.

Finally, register the route at the bottom of `boot(routes:)`:

```
protectedRoutes.on(
  .POST,
  "users",
  ":userID",
```

```
    "addProfilePicture",
    body: .collect(maxSize: "10mb"),
    use: addProfilePicturePostHandler)
```

This is a little different from all other route registrations. This still connects a **POST** request to **/users/<USER_ID>/addProfilePicture** to `addProfilePicturePostHandler(_:)`. However, by default, Vapor limits streaming body collection to 16KB to conserve memory consumption. You can change this either globally or on a per-route basis. This route registration changes the maximum allowed size of the body to 10 MB for this route only.

Displaying the picture

Now that a user can upload a profile picture, you need to be able to serve the image back to the browser. Normally, you would use the `FileMiddleware`. However, as you're storing the images in a different directory, this chapter teaches you how to serve them manually.

In **WebsiteController.swift**, add a new route handler below `addProfilePicturePostHandler(_:)`:

```
func getUsersProfilePictureHandler(_ req: Request)
  -> EventLoopFuture<Response> {
    // 1
    User.find(req.parameters.get("userID"), on: req.db)
      .unwrap(or: Abort(.notFound))
      .flatMapThrowing { user in
      // 2
      guard let filename = user.profilePicture else {
        throw Abort(.notFound)
      }
      // 3
      let path = req.application.directory
        .workingDirectory + imageFolder + filename
      // 4
      return req.fileio.streamFile(at: path)
    }
}
```

Here's what the new route handler does:

1. Get the user from the request's parameters.
2. Ensure the user has a saved profile picture, otherwise throw a **404 Not Found** error.
3. Construct the path of the user's profile picture.
4. Use Vapor's `FileIO` method to return the file as a `Response`. This handles reading the file and returning the correct information to the browser.

Next, register the new route in `boot(routes:)` below `authSessionsRoutes.get("categories", ":categoryID", use: categoryHandler)`:

```
authSessionsRoutes.get(
  "users",
  ":userID",
  "profilePicture",
  use: getUsersProfilePictureHandler)
```

This connects a **GET** request to **/users/<USER_ID>/profilePicture** to `getUsersProfilePictureHandler(_:)`. Finally, open **user.leaf**. Before `<h1>#(user.name)</h1>` add the following:

```
#if(user.profilePicture):
  <img src="/users/#(user.id)/profilePicture"
   alt="#(user.name)">
#endif
```

This checks if the user passed to the template's context has a profile picture. If so, Leaf adds the image to the page.

Build and run the application and go to **http://localhost:8080/login** in your browser. Log in as the default admin user then navigate to the admin user's profile page. Click **Add Profile Picture** and in the form click **Choose File**. Select an image to upload then click **Upload**.

The website will redirect you to the user's profile page, where you'll see the uploaded image:

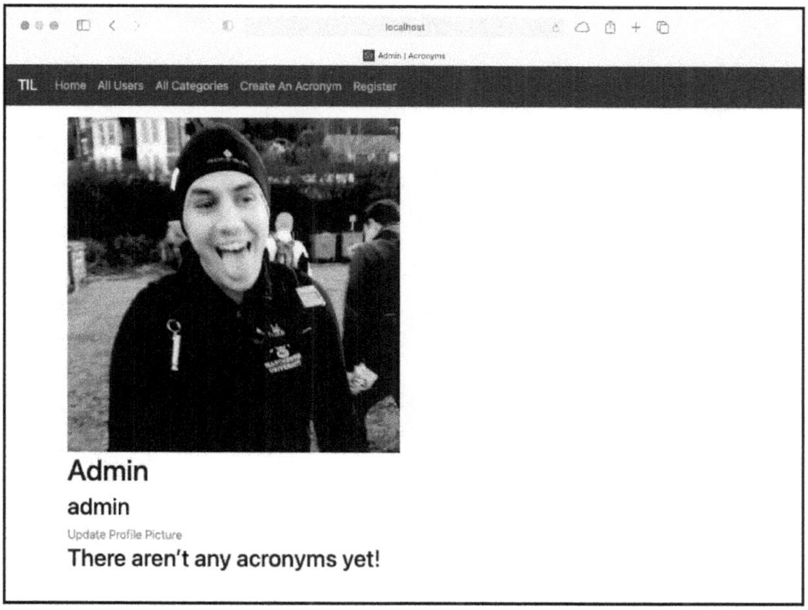

Where to go from here?

In this chapter, you learned how to deal with files in Vapor. You saw how to handle file uploads and save them to disk. You also learned how to serve files from disk in a route handler.

You've now built a fully-featured API that demonstrates many of the capabilities of Vapor. You've built an iOS application to consume the API, as well as a front-end website using Leaf. You've also learned how to test your application.

These sections have given you all the knowledge you need to build the back ends and web sites for your own applications! The next chapters cover more advanced topics that you may need, such as database migrations and caching. You'll also learn how to deploy your application to the internet.

Chapter 27: Database/API Versioning & Migration

By Tim Condon

In the first three sections of the book, whenever you made a change to your model, you had to delete your database and start over. That's no problem when you don't have any data. Once you have data, or move your project to the production stage, you can no longer delete your database. What you want to do instead is modify your database, which in Vapor, is done using **migrations**.

In this chapter, you'll make two modifications to the TILApp using migrations. First, you'll add a new field to `User` to contain a Twitter handle. Second, you'll ensure that categories are unique. Finally, you're going to modify the app so it creates the admin user only when your app runs in development or testing mode.

> **Note**: The starter project for this chapter is based on the TIL application from the end of chapter 21. The starter project contains extra code, so you should use the starter project from this chapter. This project relies on a PostgreSQL database running locally.

How migrations works

When Fluent runs for the first time, it creates a special table in the database. Fluent uses this table to track all migrations it has run and it runs migrations in the order you add them. When your application starts, Fluent checks the list of migrations to run. If it has run a migration, it will move on to the next one. If it hasn't run the migration before, Fluent executes it.

Fluent will never run migrations more than once. Doing so would cause conflicts with the existing data in the database. For example, imagine you have a migration that creates a table for your users. The first time Fluent runs the migration, it creates the table. It it tries to run it again a table with the name would already exist, causing an error.

It's important to remember this. If you change an existing migration, Fluent **will not** execute it. You need to reset your database as you did in the earlier chapters.

Modifying tables

Modifying an existing database is always a risky business. You already have data you don't want to lose, so deleting the whole database is not a viable solution. At the same time, you can't simply add or remove a property in an existing table since all the data is entangled in one big web of connections and relations.

Instead, you introduce your modifications using Vapor's `Migration` protocol. This allows you to cautiously introduce your modifications while still having a revert option should they not work as expected.

> Modifying your production database is always a delicate procedure. You must make sure to test any modifications properly before rolling them out in production. If you have a lot of important data, it's a good idea to take a backup before modifying your database.

To keep your code clean and make it easy to view the changes in chronological order, each migration should have its own file. For file names, use a consistent and helpful naming scheme, for example: **YY-MM-DD-FriendlyName.swift**. This allows you to see the versions of your database at a glance.

Writing migrations

A `Migration` is generally written as a `struct` when it's used to update an existing model. This `struct` must, of course, conform to `Migration`. `Migration` requires you to provide two things:

```
func prepare(on database: Database) -> EventLoopFuture<Void>

func revert(on database: Database) -> EventLoopFuture<Void>
```

Prepare method

Migrations require a database connection to work correctly as they must be able to query the `MigrationLog` model. If the `MigrationLog` is not accessible, the migration will fail and, in the worst case, break your application. `prepare(on:)` contains the migration's changes to the database. It's usually one of two options:

- Creating a new table
- Modifying an existing table by adding a new property.

Here's an example that adds a new model to the database:

```
func prepare(on database: Database) -> EventLoopFuture<Void> {
  // 1
  database.schema("testUsers")
    // 2
    .id()
    .field("name", .string, .required)
    // 3
    .create()
}
```

1. You specify the schema — or table name — to run the migration on.
2. You specify the modifications to perform on the table. You can specify actions for constraints, fields and foreign keys. This includes marking fields as unique. For fields, you specify the field name, type and any constraints.
3. You specify the action to perform and the model to use. If you're adding a new table to the database, such as creating a new `Model`, you use `create()`. If you're adding a field to an existing `Model` type, you use `update()`. This example uses `create()` to create a new model with the fields `id` and `name`.

Revert method

`revert(on:)` is the opposite of `prepare(on:)`. Its job is to undo whatever `prepare(on:)` did. If you use `create()` in `prepare(on:)`, you use `delete()` in `revert(on:)`. If you use `update()` to add a field, you also use it in `revert(on:)` to remove the field with `deleteField(_:)`.

Here's an example that pairs with the `prepare(on:)` you saw earlier:

```
func revert(on database: Database) -> EventLoopFuture<Void> {
  database.schema("testUsers").delete()
}
```

Again, you specify the schema to revert and the action to perform. Since you used `create()` to add the model, you use `delete()` here.

This method executes when you boot your app with the `--revert` option.

> **Note:** Fluent will delete *only* the previous batch of migrations to avoid causing conflicts with old data. When changing a database, including removing fields that you previously added, you should try and "fix forward". This means creating a new migration to remove the field you added in a previous migration.

FieldKeys

In Vapor 3, Fluent inferred most of the table information for you. This included the column types and the names of the columns. This worked well for small apps such as the TIL app. However, as projects grow, they make more and more changes. Removing fields and changing names of columns was difficult because the columns no longer matched the model. Fluent 4 makes migrations a lot more flexible by requiring you to provide the names of fields and schemas.

However, this means you end up duplicating strings throughout your app, a technique which is prone to mistakes. You can define your own `FieldKeys` to work around this. In Xcode, open **CreateAcronym.swift** and add the following at the bottom of the file:

```
extension Acronym {
  // 1
  enum v20210114 {
    // 2
    static let schemaName = "acronyms"
    // 3
    static let id = FieldKey(stringLiteral: "id")
    static let short = FieldKey(stringLiteral: "short")
    static let long = FieldKey(stringLiteral: "long")
    static let userID = FieldKey(stringLiteral: "userID")
  }
}
```

Here's what this new code does:

1. Define an enum in an extension for `Acronym`. You name the enum with the date you created the extension. This makes it easy to see when you defined columns and when things changed.
2. Define a static property for the name of the schema. This is useful in case you change the table name in the future.
3. Define a `FieldKey` for each of the columns in the table. You use these in your `Migration` and `Model`.

Next, replace the body of `CreateAcronym` with the following:

```
func prepare(on database: Database) -> EventLoopFuture<Void> {
  database.schema(Acronym.v20210114.schemaName)
    .id()
    .field(Acronym.v20210114.short, .string, .required)
    .field(Acronym.v20210114.long, .string, .required)
    .field(
      Acronym.v20210114.userID,
      .uuid,
      .required,
      .references(User.v20210113.schemaName, User.v20210113.id))
    .create()
}

func revert(on database: Database) -> EventLoopFuture<Void> {
  database.schema(Acronym.v20210114.schemaName).delete()
}
```

This replaces all the strings in your migration with the keys defined earlier. The reference to `User` also uses keys from the `User` migration already defined in the starter project.

Next, open **Acronym.swift** and replace.

```
static let schema = "acronyms"
```

with the following:

```
static let schema = Acronym.v20210114.schemaName
```

Next, replace the properties and property wrappers for `short`, `long` and `user` with the following:

```
@Field(key: Acronym.v20210114.short)
var short: String
```

```
@Field(key: Acronym.v20210114.long)
var long: String

@Parent(key: Acronym.v20210114.userID)
var user: User
```

This replaces the keys for the property wrappers with the `FieldKeys` you defined in **CreateAcronym.swift**.

Finally, open **CreateAcronymCategoryPivot.swift**. Replace:

```
.field(
  AcronymCategoryPivot.v20210113.acronymID,
  .uuid,
  .required,
  .references("acronyms", "id", onDelete: .cascade))
```

with the following:

```
.field(
  AcronymCategoryPivot.v20210113.acronymID,
  .uuid,
  .required,
  .references(
    Acronym.v20210114.schemaName,
    Acronym.v20210114.id,
    onDelete: .cascade))
```

This replaces the strings with the `FieldKey` and `schemaName` you defined earlier. Now you have no more strings in your migration or model! This provides type safety to your migrations and makes it simple to change and update fields.

Adding users' Twitter handles

To demonstrate the migration process for an existing database, you're going to add support for collecting and storing users' Twitter handles. In Xcode, create a new file called **21-01-14-AddTwitterToUser.swift** in **Sources/App/Migrations**. This new file will hold the `AddTwitterToUser` migration.

Next, open **CreateUser.swift**. In the extension for `User`, add the following below `v20210113`:

```
enum v20210114 {
  static let twitterURL = FieldKey(stringLiteral: "twitterURL")
}
```

This adds a new `FieldKey` for the new property. Next, open **User.swift** and add the following property to `User` below `var acronyms: [Acronym]`:

```
@OptionalField(key: User.v20210114.twitterURL)
var twitterURL: String?
```

This adds the property of type `String?` to the model. You declare it as an optional string since your existing users don't have the property and future users don't necessarily have a Twitter account. You annotate the property with `@OptionalField` to tell Fluent the property is an optional field in the database.

Finally, replace the initializer with the following:

```
init(
  id: UUID? = nil,
  name: String,
  username: String,
  password: String,
  twitterURL: String? = nil
) {
  self.name = name
  self.username = username
  self.password = password
  self.twitterURL = twitterURL
}
```

This adds the `twitterURL` parameter to the initializer and provides a default `nil` value if it's not provided.

Creating the migration

Open **21-01-14-AddTwitterToUser.swift** and add the following to create a migration that adds the new `twitterURL` field to the model:

```
import Fluent

// 1
struct AddTwitterURLToUser: Migration {
  // 2
  func prepare(on database: Database) -> EventLoopFuture<Void> {
    // 3
    database.schema(User.v20210113.schemaName)
      // 4
      .field(User.v20210114.twitterURL, .string)
      // 5
      .update()
  }
```

```
  // 6
  func revert(on database: Database) -> EventLoopFuture<Void> {
    // 7
    database.schema(User.v20210113.schemaName)
      // 8
      .deleteField(User.v20210114.twitterURL)
      // 9
      .update()
  }
}
```

Here's what this does:

1. Define a new type, `AddTwitterURLToUser`, that conforms to `Migration`.
2. Define the required `prepare(on:)`.
3. Select the `User` table using the schema defined.
4. Add the new field with `field(_:_)` using the `FieldKey` defined earlier. Set the type to `string`.
5. Call `update()` to execute the migration and update the table.
6. Define the required `revert(on:)`.
7. Select the `User` table using the schema defined.
8. Delete the field defined by the `FieldKey` earlier.
9. Call `update()` to execute the migration and remove the field.

Now open **configure.swift** and register `AddTwitterURLToUser` as one of the migrations.

Since Fluent executes migrations in order, it must be after the existing migrations in the list. However, since `CreateAdminUser` creates a new user you must add the migration before. Otherwise, when using a fresh database, `CreateAdminUser` fails. Add the following **before** `app.migrations.add(CreateAdminUser())`:

```
app.migrations.add(AddTwitterURLToUser())
```

The next time you launch the app, Fluent adds the new property to `User`. Build and run your application; you'll see the new property in your table.

On your development machine, you can see the table's properties by entering the following in Terminal:

```
docker exec -it postgres psql -U vapor_username vapor_database
\d "users"
\q
```

Versioning the API

You've changed the model to include the user's Twitter handle, but you haven't altered the existing API. While you could simply update the API to include the Twitter handle, this might break existing consumers of your API. Instead, you can create a new API version to return users with their Twitter handles.

To do this, first open **User.swift** and add following definition after `Public`:

```
final class PublicV2: Content {
  var id: UUID?
  var name: String
  var username: String
  var twitterURL: String?

  init(id: UUID?,
       name: String,
       username: String,
       twitterURL: String? = nil) {
    self.id = id
    self.name = name
    self.username = username
    self.twitterURL = twitterURL
  }
}
```

This creates a new `PublicV2` class that includes the `twitterURL`. Next, create the four convert methods for the version 2 API. Add the following to the `extension` for `User` after `convertToPublic()`:

```
func convertToPublicV2() -> User.PublicV2 {
  return User.PublicV2(
    id: id,
    name: name,
    username: username,
    twitterURL: twitterURL)
}
```

Now, add the following to the `extension` for `EventLoopFuture where Value: User` after `convertToPublic()`:

```
func convertToPublicV2() -> EventLoopFuture<User.PublicV2> {
  return self.map { user in
    return user.convertToPublicV2()
  }
}
```

Then, add the following to the `extension` for `Collection` after `convertToPublic()`:

```
func convertToPublicV2() -> [User.PublicV2] {
  return self.map { $0.convertToPublicV2() }
}
```

Finally, add the following to the `extension` for `EventLoopFuture where Value == Array<User>` after `convertToPublic()`:

```
func convertToPublicV2() -> EventLoopFuture<[User.PublicV2]> {
  return self.map { $0.convertToPublicV2() }
}
```

This allows you to convert your Fluent model to `PublicV2` in all the instances you may want to. Open **UsersController.swift** and add the following after `getHandler(_:)`:

```
// 1
func getV2Handler(_ req: Request)
    -> EventLoopFuture<User.PublicV2> {
  // 2
  User.find(req.parameters.get("userID"), on: req.db)
    .unwrap(or: Abort(.notFound))
    .convertToPublicV2()
}
```

This method is just like `getHandler(_:)` with two changes:

1. Return a `User.PublicV2`.

2. Call `convertToPublicV2()` to produce the correct return item.

Finally, add the following at the end of `boot(routes:)`:

```
// API Version 2 Routes
// 1
let usersV2Route = routes.grouped("api", "v2", "users")
// 2
usersV2Route.get(":userID", use: getV2Handler)
```

Here's what this does:

1. Add a new API group that will resolve on **/api/v2/users**.
2. Connect GET requests for **/api/v2/users/<USER_ID>** to `getV2Handler()`.

Now you have a new endpoint to get a user, with a **v2** in the API, that returns the `twitterURL`.

> **Note**: For a more complicated API revision, you should create new controllers to handle the new API version. This will simplify how you reason about the code and make it easier to maintain.

Updating the web site

Your app now has all it needs to store a user's Twitter handle and the API is complete. You need to update the web site to allow a new user to provide a Twitter address during the registration process.

Open **register.leaf** and add the following after the form group for **name**:

```
<div class="form-group">
  <label for="twitterURL">Twitter handle</label>
  <input type="text" name="twitterURL" class="form-control"
   id="twitterURL"/>
</div>
```

This adds a field for the Twitter handle on the registration form. Next, open **user.leaf** and replace `<h2>#(user.username)</h2>` with the following:

```
<h2>#(user.username)
  #if(user.twitterURL):
  - @#(user.twitterURL)
  #endif
</h2>
```

This shows the Twitter handle, if it exists, on the user information page. Finally, open **WebsiteController.swift** and add the following to the end of `RegisterData`:

```
let twitterURL: String?
```

This allows your form handler to access the Twitter information sent from the browser. In `registerPostHandler(_:data:)`, replace

```
let user = User(
  name: data.name,
  username: data.username,
  password: password)
```

With:

```
var twitterURL: String?
if let twitter = data.twitterURL,
    !twitter.isEmpty {
     twitterURL = twitter
}
let user = User(
  name: data.name,
  username: data.username,
  password: password,
  twitterURL: twitterURL)
```

If the user doesn't provide a Twitter handle, you want to store `nil` rather than an empty string in the database.

Build and run. Visit **http://localhost:8080/** in your browser and register a new user, providing a Twitter handle. Visit the user's information page to see the results of your handiwork!

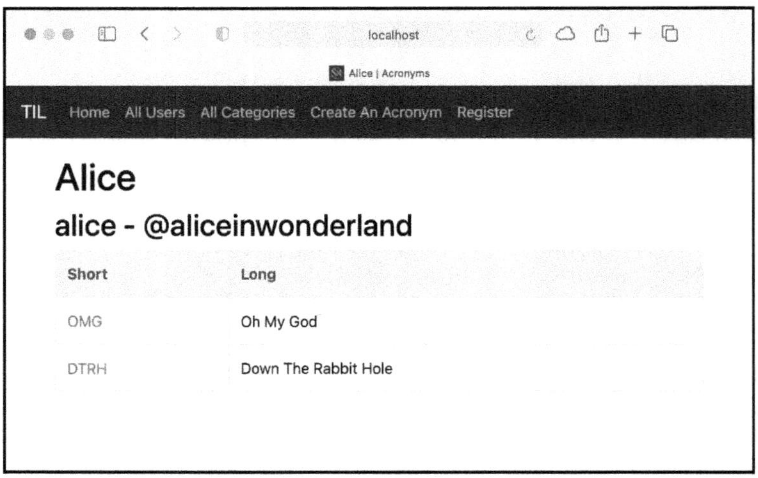

Making categories unique

Just as you've required usernames to be unique, you really want category names to be unique as well. Everything you've done so far to implement categories has made it impossible to create duplicates, but you'd like that enforced in the database as well. It's time to create a `Migration` that guarantees duplicate category names can't be inserted in the database.

First, create a new file inside the **Migrations** directory called **21-01-14-MakeCategoriesUnique.swift**. Open the new file and enter the following:

```
import Fluent

// 1
struct MakeCategoriesUnique: Migration {
  // 2
  func prepare(on database: Database) -> EventLoopFuture<Void> {
    // 3
    database.schema(Category.v20210113.schemaName)
      // 4
      .unique(on: Category.v20210113.name)
      // 5
      .update()
  }

  // 6
  func revert(on database: Database) -> EventLoopFuture<Void> {
    // 7
    database.schema(Category.v20210113.schemaName)
      // 8
      .deleteUnique(on: Category.v20210113.name)
      // 9
      .update()
  }
}
```

1. Define a new type, `MakeCategoriesUnique`, that conforms to `Migration`.
2. Define the required `prepare(on:)`.
3. Select the `Category` schema to tell Fluent to change the table for categories.
4. Use `unique(on:)` to add a new unique index corresponding to the key for `name`.
5. Since `Category` already exists in your database, use `update()` to modify the database.
6. Define the required `revert(on:)`.
7. Select the `Category` schema to tell Fluent to change the table for categories.
8. Use `deleteUnique(on:)` to remove the index corresponding to the key for `name`.
9. Since `Category` already exists in your database, use `update()` to modify the database.

Finally, open **configure.swift** and register `MakeCategoriesUnique` as one of the migrations. Add the following after `app.migrations.add(CreateAdminUser())`:

```
app.migrations.add(MakeCategoriesUnique())
```

Build and run; observe the new migration in the console:

```
[database-id: psql] (PostgresNIO/PostgresDatabase+Query.swift:124)
[ DEBUG ] ALTER TABLE "categories" ADD CONSTRAINT "uq:categories.name" UNIQUE
    ("name") [] [database-id: psql] (PostgresNIO/PostgresDatabase+Query.swift:124)
[ DEBUG ] query create _fluent_migrations input=[[id:
    6D00DFC7-CBC2-4980-A288-0FA964DCFB14, name: "App.MakeCategoriesUnique",
    created_at: 2021-01-14 21:16:22 +0000, batch: 3, updated_at: 2021-01-14
    21:16:22 +0000]] [database-id: psql]
    (FluentKit/Query/Builder/QueryBuilder.swift:297)
[ DEBUG ] INSERT INTO "_fluent_migrations" ("id", "name", "created_at", "batch",
    "updated_at") VALUES ($1, $2, $3, $4, $5) RETURNING "id"
    [6D00DFC7-CBC2-4980-A288-0FA964DCFB14, "App.MakeCategoriesUnique", 2021-01-14
    21:16:22 +0000, 3, 2021-01-14 21:16:22 +0000] [database-id: psql]
    (PostgresNIO/PostgresDatabase+Query.swift:124)
```

Seeding based on environment

In Chapter 18, "API Authentication, Part 1," you seeded an admin user in your database. As mentioned there, you should never use "password" as your admin password. But, it's easier when you're still developing and just need a dummy account for testing locally. One way to ensure you don't add this user in production is to detect your environment before adding the migration. In **configure.swift** replace:

```
app.migrations.add(CreateAdminUser())
```

With the following:

```
switch app.environment {
case .development, .testing:
  app.migrations.add(CreateAdminUser())
default:
  break
}
```

Now the **AdminUser** is only added to the migrations if the application is in either the development (the default) or testing environment. If the environment is production, the migration won't happen. Of course, you still want to have an admin in your production environment that has a random password. In that case, you can switch on the environment inside **AdminUser** or you can create two versions, one for development and one for production.

Where to go from here?

In this chapter, you learned how to modify your database, after your app enters production, using migrations. You saw how to add an extra property — `twitterUrl` — to `User`, how to revert this update and how to enforce uniqueness of category names. Finally, you saw how to switch on your environment in **configure.swift**, allowing you to exclude migrations from the production environment.

You can learn more about migrations in the Vapor documentation at https://docs.vapor.codes/4.0/fluent/migration/.

Chapter 28: Caching

By Tanner Nelson

Whether you're creating a JSON API, building an iOS app or even designing the circuitry of a CPU, you'll eventually need a cache. Caches — pronounced *cashes* — are a method of speeding up slow processes and, without them, the Internet would be a terribly slow place. The philosophy behind caching is simple: Store the result of a slow process so you only have to run it once. Some examples of slow processes you may encounter while building a web app are:

- Large database queries
- Requests to external services, e.g., other APIs
- Complex computation, e.g., parsing a large document

By caching the results of these slow processes, you can make your app feel snappier and more responsive.

Cache storage

Vapor defines the protocol `Cache`. This protocol creates a common interface for different cache storage methods. The protocol itself is quite simple; take a look:

```
public protocol Cache {
  // 1
  func get<T>(_ key: String, as type: T.Type) ->
EventLoopFuture<T?>
    where T: Decodable

  // 2
  func set<T>(_ key: String, to value: T?) ->
EventLoopFuture<Void>
    where T: Encodable
}
```

Here's what each method does:

1. `get(_:as:)` fetches stored data from the cache for a given key. If no data exists for that key, it returns `nil`.

2. `set(_:to:)` stores data in the cache at the supplied key. If a value existed previously, it's replaced. If `nil`, the key is cleared.

Each method returns a future since interaction with the cache may happen asynchronously.

Now that you understand the concept of caching and the `Cache` protocol, it's time to take a look at some of the actual caching implementations available with Vapor.

In-memory caches

Vapor comes with an in-memory cache: `.memory`. This cache stores its data in your program's running memory. This makes it great for development and testing because it has no external dependencies. However, it may not be perfect for all uses as the storage is cleared when the application restarts and can't be shared between multiple instances of your application. Most likely though, this memory volatility won't affect a well thought out caching design.

Thread-safety

The contents of the in-memory cache are shared across all your application's event loops. This means once something is stored in the cache, all future requests will see that same item regardless of which event loop they are assigned to. To achieve this cross-loop sharing, the in-memory cache uses an application-wide lock to synchronize access.

Database caches

Vapor's cache protocol supports using a configured database as your cache storage. This includes all of Vapor's Fluent mappings (PostgreSQL, MySQL, SQLite, MongoDB, etc.).

If you want your cached data to persist between restarts and be shareable between multiple instances of your application, storing it in a database is a great choice. If you already have a database configured for your application, it's easy to set up.

You can use your application's main database for caching or you can use a separate, specialized database.

Redis

Redis is an open-source, cache storage service. It's used commonly as a cache database for web applications and is supported by most deployment services like Heroku. Redis databases are usually very easy to configure and they allow you to persist your cached data between application restarts and share the cache between multiple instances of your application. Redis is a great, fast and feature-rich alternative to in-memory caches and it only takes a little bit more work to configure.

Now that you know about the available caching implementations in Vapor, it's time to add caching to an application.

Example: Pokédex

When building a web app, making requests to other APIs can introduce delays. If the API you're communicating with is slow, it can make your API feel slow. Additionally, external APIs may enforce rate limits on the number of requests you can make to them in a given time period.

Fortunately, with caching, you can store the results of these external API queries locally and make your API feel much faster.

You're going to use a cache to improve the performance of **Pokédex**, an API for storing and listing all Pokémon you've captured.

You've already learned how to create a basic CRUD API and how to make external HTTP requests. As a result, this chapter's starter project already has the basics implemented.

In Terminal, change to the starter project's directory and use the following command to generate and open an Xcode project to work in:

```
open Package.swift
```

Overview

This simple Pokédex API has two routes:

- **GET /pokemon**: Returns a list of all captured Pokémon.
- **POST /pokemon**: Stores a captured Pokémon in the Pokédex.

When you store a new Pokémon, the Pokédex API makes a call to the external API pokeapi.co to verify that the Pokémon name you've entered is real. While this check works, the pokeapi.co API can be pretty slow to respond, thereby making your app feel slow.

Normal request

A typical Vapor requests takes only a couple of milliseconds to respond, when working locally. In the screenshot that follows, you can see the **GET /pokemon** route has a total response time of about 40ms.

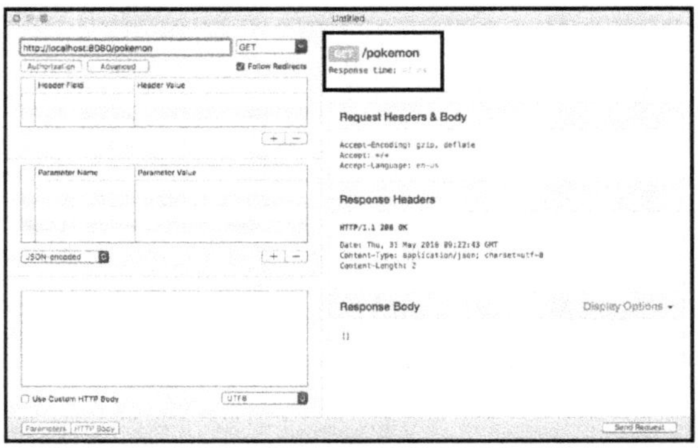

PokeAPI dependent request

In the screenshot below, you can see that the **POST /pokemon** route is 25 times slower at around 1,500ms. This is because the **pokeapi.co** API can be slow to respond to the query.

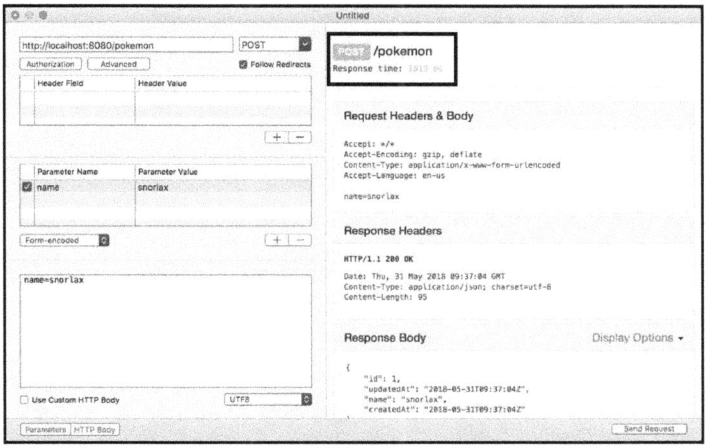

Now you're ready to take a look at the code to better understand what's making this route slow and how a cache can fix it.

Verifying the name

In Xcode, open **PokeAPI.swift** and look at `verify(name:)`.

This class is a simple wrapper around an HTTP client and makes querying the PokeAPI more convenient. It verifies the legitimacy of a supplied Pokémon name using `verify(name:)`. If the name is real, the method returns `true`, wrapped in a future.

Now look at `fetchPokemon(named:)`. This method sends the request to the external pokeapi.co and returns the Pokémon's data. If a Pokémon with the supplied name doesn't exist, the API — and, therefore, this method — returns a **404 Not Found** response.

`fetchPokemon(named:)` is the cause of the slow response time on the **POST / pokemon** route. A cache is just what the doctor ordered!

Creating a cache

The first task is to create a cache for the PokeAPI wrapper. In **PokeAPI.swift**, add a new property to store the cache below let client: Client:

```
/// Cache to check before calling API.
let cache: Cache
```

Next, replace the implementation of init to account for the new property:

```
public init(client: Client, cache: Cache) {
  self.client = client
  self.cache = cache
}
```

Finally, fix the remaining compiler error by replacing the Request extension at the top of the file with:

```
extension Request {
  public var pokeAPI: PokeAPI {
    .init(client: self.client, cache: self.cache)
  }
}
```

By default, Vapor is configured to use the built-in memory cache.

Fetch and Store

Now that the PokeAPI wrapper has access to a working Cache, you can use the cache to store responses from the pokeapi.co API and subsequently fetch them much more quickly.

Open **PokeAPI.swift** and rename verify(name:) to uncachedVerify(name:). Next, add the following method to replace the uncached implementation:

```
public func verify(name: String) -> EventLoopFuture<Bool> {
  // 1
  let name = name
    .lowercased()
    .trimmingCharacters(in: .whitespacesAndNewlines)

  // 2
  return cache.get(name, as: Bool.self).flatMap { verified in
    // 3
    if let verified = verified {
      return self.client.eventLoop.makeSucceededFuture(verified)
    } else {
```

```
        return self.uncachedVerify(name: name).flatMap {
          verified in
          // 4
          return self.cache.set(name, to: verified)
            .transform(to: verified)
        }
      }
    }
  }
```

Here's what this does:

1. Create a consistent cache key by lowercasing the name. This ensures that both "Pikachu" and "pikachu" share the same cache result.
2. Query the cache to see if it contains the desired result.
3. If a cached result exists, return that result. This means that calls to `verify(name:)` will never invoke `fetchPokemon(named:)` a second time for a given name. This is the key step that will improve performance.
4. When `fetchPokemon(named:)` completes, store the result of the API query in the cache.

Build and run, then create a new request in RESTed. Configure the request as follows:

- **URL**: http://localhost:8080/pokemon
- **method**: POST
- **Parameter encoding**: JSON-encoded

Add one parameter with name and value:

- **name**: Test

Take note of the response time for the first request. It'll likely be a couple of seconds. Now, make a second request and note the time; it should be much faster!

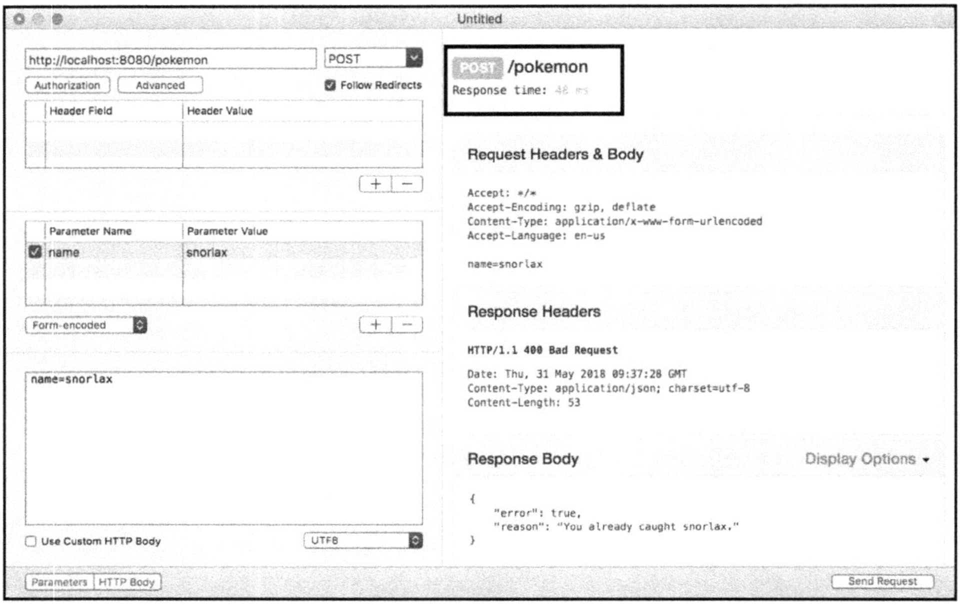

Fluent

Once you have configured your app to use Vapor's cache interface, it's easy to swap out the underlying implementation. Since this app already uses SQLite to store caught Pokémon, you can easily enable Fluent as a cache. Unlike in-memory caching, Fluent caches are shared between multiple instances of your application and are persisted between restarts.

To switch Vapor's cache implementation to use Fluent, open **configure.swift** and add the following:

```
app.caches.use(.fluent)
```

just above the line:

```
try routes(app)
```

Finally, since Fluent is currently configured to use a SQL database (SQLite), it needs to be prepared to store cache values. Still inside **configure.swift**, find:

```
app.migrations.add(CreatePokemon())
```

and add the following migration just below it:

```
app.migrations.add(CacheEntry.migration)
```

You should now notice that cached values are persisted between application restarts. Nice!

Where to go from here?

Caching is an important concept in Computer Science and understanding how to use it will help make your web applications feel fast and responsive. There are several methods for storing your cache data for web applications: in-memory, Fluent database, Redis and more. Each has distinct benefits over the other.

You can check out the different types of algorithms available for caching such as Least Recently Used (LRU), Random Replacement (RR) or Last In First Out (LIFO). Each of these has pros and cons depending on the type of application you're writing and the type of data you're caching within it.

In this chapter, you learned how to configure a Fluent database cache. Using the cache to save the results of a request to an external API, you significantly increased the responsiveness of your app.

If you'd like a challenge, try configuring your app to use a Redis cache. But remember, you gotta cache 'em all!

Chapter 29: Middleware

By Tanner Nelson

In the course of building your application, you'll often find it necessary to integrate your own steps into the request pipeline. The most common mechanism for accomplishing this is to use one or more pieces of middleware. They allow you to do things like:

- Log incoming requests.
- Catch errors and display messages.
- Rate-limit traffic to particular routes.

Middleware instances sit between your router and the client connected to your server. This allows them to view, and potentially mutate, incoming requests before they reach your controllers. A middleware instance may choose to return early by generating its own response, or it can forward the request to the next responder in the chain. The final responder is always your router. When the response from the next responder is generated, the middleware can make any modifications it deems necessary, or choose to forward it back to the client as is. This means each middleware instance has control over both incoming requests *and* outgoing responses.

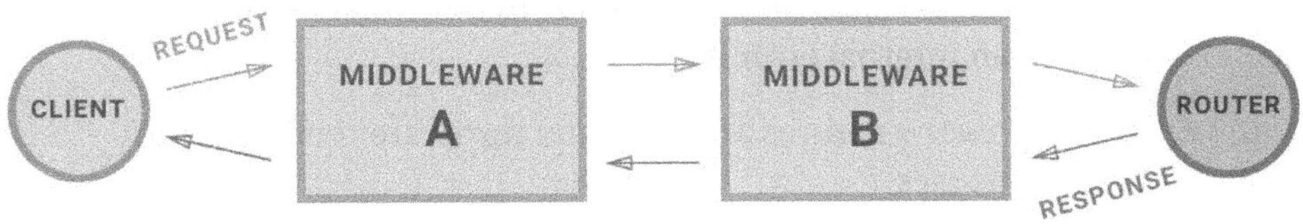

As you can see in the diagram above, the first middleware instance in your application — Middleware A — receives incoming requests from the client first. The first middleware may then choose to pass this request on to the next middleware — Middleware B — and so on.

Eventually, some component generates a response, which then traverses back through the middleware in the opposite direction. Take note that this means the first middleware receives responses *last*.

The protocol for `Middleware` is fairly simple and should help you better understand the previous diagram:

```
public protocol Middleware {
  func respond(
    to request: Request,
    chainingTo next: Responder
  ) -> EventLoopFuture<Response>
}
```

In the case of Middleware A, `request` is the incoming data from the client, while `next` is Middleware B. The asynchronous response returned by Middleware A goes directly to the client.

For Middleware B, `request` is the request passed on from Middleware A. `next` is the router. The future response returned by Middleware B goes to Middleware A.

Vapor's middleware

Vapor includes some middleware out of the box. This section introduces you to the available options to give you an idea of what middleware is commonly used for.

Error middleware

The most commonly used middleware in Vapor is `ErrorMiddleware`. It's responsible for converting both synchronous and asynchronous Swift errors into HTTP responses. Uncaught errors cause the HTTP server to immediately close the connection and print an internal error log.

Using the `ErrorMiddleware` ensures all errors you throw are rendered into appropriate HTTP responses.

In production mode, `ErrorMiddleware` converts all errors into opaque **500 Internal Server Error** responses. This is important for keeping your application secure, as errors may contain sensitive information.

You can opt into providing different error responses by conforming your error types to `AbortError`, allowing you to specify the HTTP status code and error message. You may also use `Abort`, a concrete error type that conforms to `AbortError`. For example:

```
throw Abort(.badRequest, "Something's not quite right.")
```

File middleware

Another common type of middleware is `FileMiddleware`. This middleware serves files from the **Public** folder in your application directory. This is useful when you're using Vapor to create a front-end website that may require static files like images or style sheets.

Other Middleware

Vapor also provides a `SessionsMiddleware`, responsible for tracking sessions with connected clients. Other packages may provide middleware to help them integrate into your application. For example, Vapor's Authentication package contains middleware for protecting your routes using basic passwords, simple bearer tokens, and even JWTs (JSON Web Tokens).

Example: Todo API

Now that you have an understanding of how various types of middleware function, you're ready to learn how to configure them and how to create your own custom middleware types.

To do this, you'll implement a basic Todo list API. This API has three routes:

```
$ swift run Run routes
+--------+---------------+
| GET    | /todos        |
+--------+---------------+
| POST   | /todos        |
+--------+---------------+
| DELETE | /todos/:todo  |
+--------+---------------+
```

You'll create and configure two different middleware types for this project:

1. `LogMiddleware`: Logs response times for incoming requests.
2. `SecretMiddleware`: Protects private routes from being accessed without permission by requiring a secret key.

Log middleware

The first middleware you'll create will log incoming requests. It will display the following information for each request:

- Request method
- Request path
- Response status
- How long it took to generate the response

Open the starter project directory in Terminal and generate an Xcode project for it by entering:

```
open Package.swift
```

Once Xcode opens, navigate to **Middleware/LogMiddleware.swift**. There you'll find an empty `LogMiddleware` class.

Ignore the `TimeInterval` extension for now; you'll use that later.

Start by conforming `LogMiddleware` to the `Middleware` protocol. Only one method is required: `respond(to:chainingTo:)`.

For now, the middleware will just log the incoming request's description. Replace `LogMiddleware` with the following:

```
final class LogMiddleware: Middleware {
  // 1
  func respond(
    to req: Request,
    chainingTo next: Responder
  ) -> EventLoopFuture<Response> {
    // 2
    req.logger.info("\(req)")
    // 3
    return next.respond(to: req)
  }
}
```

Here's a breakdown of the code you just added:

1. Implement the `Middleware` protocol requirement.
2. Send the request's description to the Logger as an informational log.
3. Forward the incoming request to the next responder.

Now that you've created a custom middleware, you need to add it to your application. Open **configure.swift** and add the following line at the beginning of `configure(_:)`:

```
app.middleware.use(LogMiddleware())
```

This enables `LogMiddleware` globally. The ordering is important here since, `Middleware` are run in the order they are added.

Finally, build and run your application, then make a request to **GET /todos** using `curl`:

```
curl localhost:8080/todos
```

Take a look at the log output from your running application. You'll see something similar to the following:

```
[ INFO ] GET /todos HTTP/1.1
Host: localhost:8080
User-Agent: curl/7.64.1
Accept: */*
 [request-id: 4D528CE6-8C10-443A-A5BB-9A6F2BB3A6E7]
```

This is a great start! But you can improve `LogMiddleware` to provide more useful, readable output. Open **LogMiddleware.swift** and replace the implementation of `respond(to:chainingTo:)` with the following methods:

```
func respond(
  to req: Request,
  chainingTo next: Responder
) -> EventLoopFuture<Response> {
  // 1
  let start = Date()
  return next.respond(to: req).map { res in
    // 2
    self.log(res, start: start, for: req)
    return res
  }
}
```

```
// 3
func log(_ res: Response, start: Date, for req: Request) {
  let reqInfo = "\(req.method.string) \(req.url.path)"
  let resInfo = "\(res.status.code) " +
    "\(res.status.reasonPhrase)"
  // 4
  let time = Date()
    .timeIntervalSince(start)
    .readableMilliseconds
  // 5
  req.logger.info("\(reqInfo) -> \(resInfo) [\(time)]")
}
```

Here's a breakdown of how the new methods work:

1. First, create a start time. Do this before doing any additional work to get the most accurate response time measurement.
2. Instead of returning the response directly, map the future result so that you can access the `Response` object. Pass this to `log(_:start:for:)`.
3. This method logs the response for an incoming request using the response start date.
4. Generate a readable time using `timeIntervalSince(_:)` and the extension on `TimeInterval` at the bottom of the file.
5. Log the information string.

Now that you've updated `LogMiddleware`, build and run and curl **GET /todos** again.

```
curl localhost:8080/todos
```

If you check the output of your application, you'll see a new, more concise output format.

```
[ INFO ] GET /todos -> 200 OK [1.7ms] [request-id: ...]
```

Secret middleware

Now that you've learned how to create middleware and apply it globally, you'll learn how to apply middleware to specific routes.

Two of the Todo List APIs routes can make changes to the database:

- **POST /todos**
- **DELETE /todos/:id**

If this were a public API, you'd want to protect these routes with a secret key using middleware. That's exactly what `SecretMiddleware` will do.

Open **Middleware/SecretMiddleware.swift** and replace the class definition of `SecretMiddleware` with the following code:

```
final class SecretMiddleware: Middleware {
  // 1
  let secret: String

  init(secret: String) {
    self.secret = secret
  }

  // 2
  func respond(
    to request: Request,
    chainingTo next: Responder
  ) -> EventLoopFuture<Response> {
    // 3
    guard
      request.headers.first(name: .xSecret) == secret
    else {
      // 4
      return request.eventLoop.makeFailedFuture(
        Abort(
          .unauthorized,
          reason: "Incorrect X-Secret header."))
    }
    // 5
    return next.respond(to: request)
  }
}
```

Here's a breakdown of how `SecretMiddleware` works:

1. Create a stored property to hold the secret key.
2. Implement the `Middleware` protocol requirement.
3. Check the **X-Secret** header in the incoming request against the configured secret key.
4. If the header value does not match, throw an error with `unauthorized` HTTP status.
5. If the header matches, chain to the next middleware normally.

Now you just need to add a method for creating this middleware so that it can be used as a service in your application.

Add the following code after the `SecretMiddleware` implementation.

```
extension SecretMiddleware {
  // 1
  static func detect() throws -> Self {
    // 2
    guard let secret = Environment.get("SECRET") else {
      // 3
      throw Abort(
        .internalServerError,
        reason: """
          No SECRET set on environment. \
          Use export SECRET=<secret>
          """)
    }
    // 4
    return .init(secret: secret)
  }
}
```

Here's a breakdown of how this code works:

1. Add a static, throwing method to SecretMiddleware.
2. Fetch value for `SECRET` from the environment, if it exists.
3. If the environment variable doesn't exist, throw a helpful error.
4. Initialize an instance of `SecretMiddleware` using the configured secret.

Time to use the new middleware. Open **routes.swift** and replace the **POST** and **DELETE** routes with the following code:

```
// 1
try app.group(SecretMiddleware.detect()) { secretGroup in
  // 2
  secretGroup.post("todos", use: todoController.create)
  secretGroup.delete(
    "todos",
    ":id",
    use: todoController.delete)
}
```

Here's what this does:

1. Create a new route group wrapped by `SecretMiddleware`.
2. Register the **POST** and **DELETE** routes in the newly created route group instead of the global router.

Before you use your new middleware, you need to set the secret. Create a new file called **.env** in your project directory and insert the following:

```
SECRET=foo
```

This creates the secret required for `SecretMiddleware`. Vapor reads **.env** files when the app starts and this is one way to inject environment variables into your app. Finally, you must set the custom working directory so Vapor knows where to find the **.env** file. As you have in earlier chapters, edit the scheme for **TodoAPI**. Under the **Run** action, in **Options**, check **Use custom working directory**. Set the path to your project directory:

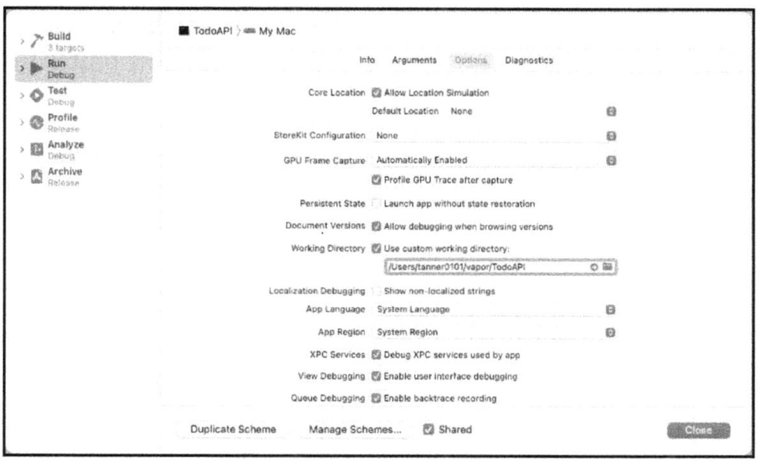

Build and run the application, then create a new request in RESTed. Configure the request as follows:

- **URL**: http://localhost:8080/todos
- **method**: POST

Add a parameter with name and value:

- **title**: This is a test TODO!

Click **Send Request** and notice the response:

```
{
    "error": true,
    "reason": "Incorrect X-Secret header."
}
```

The middleware is protecting the routes! If you try querying **GET /todos** you'll notice it still works.

Add **X-Secret: foo** to the headers section in RESTed and send the request again. Now you'll notice that the response has changed. The middleware is allowing this request through to the controller now it has the appropriate header.

Where to go from here?

Middleware is extremely useful for creating large web applications. It allows you to apply restrictions and transformations globally or to just a few routes using discrete, re-usable components. In this chapter, you learned how to create a global `LogMiddleware` that displayed information about all incoming requests to your app. You then created `SecretMiddleware`, which could protect select routes from public access.

For more information about using middleware, be sure to check out Vapor's API Docs at https://api.vapor.codes/vapor/master/Vapor/Middleware/.

Chapter 30: WebSockets

By Logan Wright

WebSockets, like HTTP, define a protocol used for communication between two devices. Unlike HTTP, the WebSocket protocol is designed for real-time communication. WebSockets can be a great option for things like chat or other features that require real-time behavior. Vapor provides a succinct API to create a WebSocket server or client. This chapter focuses on building a basic server.

In this chapter, you'll build a simple client-server application that allows users to share a touch with other users and view in real-time other user's touches on their own device.

Tools

Testing WebSockets can be a bit tricky since they can send/receive multiple messages. This makes using a simple CURL request or a browser difficult. Fortunately, there's a great WebSocket client tool you can use to test your server at: https://www.websocketking.com. It's important to note that, as of writing this, connections to localhost are only supported in Chrome.

A basic server

Now that your tools are ready, it's time to set up a very basic WebSocket server. Copy this chapter's starter project to your favorite location and open a Terminal window in that directory.

Enter the following commands:

```
cd share-touch-server
open Package.swift
```

This navigates into the **share-touch-server** directory and opens the project in Xcode.

Echo server

Open **WebSockets.swift** and add the following to the end of `sockets(_:)` to create an echo endpoint:

```
// 1
app.webSocket("echo") { req, ws in
  // 2
  print("ws connected")
  // 3
  ws.onText { ws, text in
    // 4
    print("ws received: \(text)")
    // 5
    ws.send("echo: " + text)
  }
}
```

Here's what this does:

1. Create a WebSocket route handler for the **echo** endpoint.
2. Log a message to the console when a client connects.
3. Create a listener that fires each time the endpoint receives text.
4. Log the received text to the console.
5. Echo the received text back to the sender after prepending **echo: **.

In Xcode's scheme selector, choose the **ShareTouchServer** scheme and **My Mac** as the destination. Build and run. In your browser, open **https://websocketking.com** and enter **ws://localhost:8080/echo** in the URL field, then press **Connect**. You should see in the logs something like:

```
Connected to ws://localhost:8080/echo
Connecting to ws://localhost:8080/echo
```

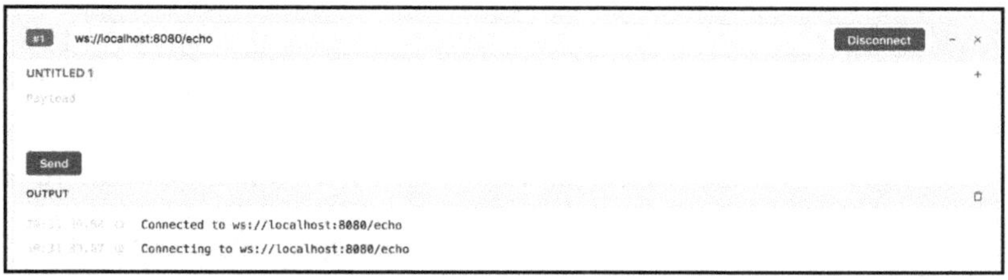

Check the Xcode console and you'll see **ws connected**.

```
[ NOTICE ] Server starting on http://127.0.0.1:8080
[ INFO ] GET /echo [request-id: A95BBB23-21DE-4BAC-8316-E0E63EA7AD4A]
ws connected
```

Enter a message in WebSocketKing, and you'll see your server respond with an appropriate echo.

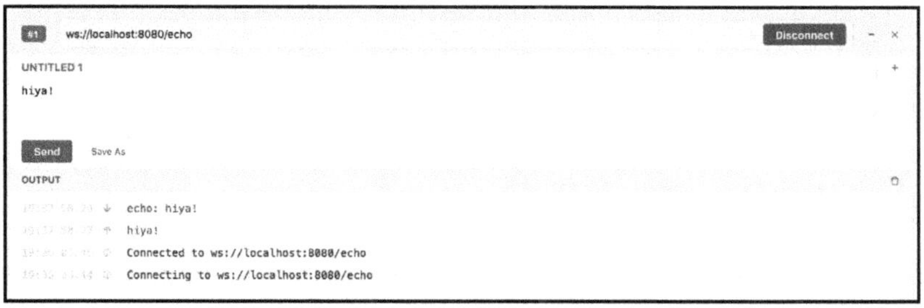

Sessions

Now that you've verified you can communicate with your server, it's time to add more capabilities to it. For the basic application, you'll use a single WebSocket endpoint at **/session**.

You'll be using an in-memory manager. This means if your application were to scale up to multiple servers, you'd need a more complex management system that assigns various users to various servers. For now, you can assume a single session for all your users and a single server is enough.

Here's the basic architecture you'll use:

Client -> Server

The connection from the client to the server can be in one of three states: joined, moved and left.

Joined

A new participant will open a WebSocket using the **/session** endpoint. In the opening request, you'll include two bits of information from the user: the color to use — represented as r,g,b,a — and a starting point — represented using a relative point.

For your purposes, a relative point uses a 0-1.0 scale representing the visible area of a screen. This allows you to translate touches between various screen sizes.

Moved

To keep things simple, after a client opens a new session, the only thing it will send the server is new relative points as the user drags the circle.

Left

This server will interpret any closure on the client's side as leaving the room. This keeps things succinct.

Server -> Client

The server sends three different types of messages to clients: joined, moved and left.

Joined

When the server sends a **joined** message, it includes in the message an ID, a Color and the last known point for that participant.

Upon a client's successful connection, the server will immediately notify that client of all current participants by sending a joined message.

Moved

Any time a participant moves, the server notifies the clients. These notifications include only an ID and a new relative point.

Left

Any time a participant disconnects from the session, the server notifies all other participants and removes that user from associated views.

Now that you understand the states and messages used by the app, it's time to begin implementing.

Setting up "Join"

Open **WebSockets.swift** and add the following to the end of `sockets(_:)`

```
// 1
app.webSocket("session") { req, ws in
  // 2
  ws.onText { ws, text in
    print("got message: \(text)")
  }
}
```

Here's what your new code does:

1. Add a WebSocket endpoint for /**session**.
2. When you receive text, print it to the console.

Run your server application and leave it running. Then, open the iOS project.

iOS project

The materials for this chapter include a complete iOS app. You can change the URL you'd like to use in **ShareTouchApp.swift**. For now, it should be set to `ws://localhost:8080/session`. Build and run the app in the simulator. Select a color and press **BEGIN**, then drag the circle around the screen. You should see logs in your server application that look similar to the following:

```
got message: {"x":0.62031250000000004,"y":0.60037878787878785}
got message: {"x":0.61250000000000004,"y":0.59469696969696972}
got message: {"x":0.60781249999999998,"y":0.59185606060606055}
got message: {"x":0.59999999999999998,"y":0.59469696969696972}
```

Awesome! Your server is communicating with the iOS app via a WebSocket!

This is good! It means your app is sending data successfully to the server, and the server is successfully receiving it. Return to the server application to build out more of the session management logic.

> **Note**: If you try to run the iOS app on a device, you'll need to change the URL in **ShareTouchApp.swift** to locate your computer's IP address over WiFi. If you're looking to test remote devices and tunnel them to your computer's server, checkout ngrok! It's a great tool and makes it easy to setup domains that forward to your computer's server.

Finishing "Join"

As described earlier, the client will include a color and a starting position in the web socket connection request. WebSocket requests are treated as an upgraded GET request, so you'll include the data in the query of the request. In **WebSockets.swift**, replace the code you added earlier for `app.webSocket("session")` with the following:

```
app.webSocket("session") { req, ws in
  // 1
  let color: ColorComponents
  let position: RelativePoint

  do {
    color = try req.query.decode(ColorComponents.self)
    position = try req.query.decode(RelativePoint.self)
  } catch {
    // 2
    _ = ws.close(code: .unacceptableData)
    return
  }
  // 3
  print("new user joined with: \(color) at \(position)")
}
```

This is what your new code does:

1. Get the color and position from the request's query.
2. If you can't decode the color or position, close the WebSocket with an "unacceptable data" status.
3. Print the color and position to the console.

Build and run and then return to the iOS simulator and press **BEGIN**. You should see the server logging the color you selected. Select a different color and notice how the components are changed.

Next, you need to set the user up with `TouchSessionManager`. Still in **WebSockets.swift**, find:

```
print("new user joined with: \(color) at \(position)")
```

and add the following below it:

```
let newId = UUID().uuidString
TouchSessionManager.default
  .insert(id: newId, color: color, at: position, on: ws)
```

This creates a new ID for the user, using `UUID`, and inserts the user into `TouchSessionManager` using the color and position from earlier.

Handling "Moved"

Next, you need to listen to messages from the client. For now, you'll only expect to receive a stream of **RelativePoint** objects. In this case, you'll use `onText(_:)`. Using `onText(_:)` is perhaps slightly less performant than using `onBinary(_:)` and receiving data directly. However, it makes debugging easier and you can change it later.

Below `TouchSessionManager.default.insert(id: newId, color: color, at: position, on: ws)` add the following:

```
// 1
ws.onText { ws, text in
  do {
    // 2
    let pt = try JSONDecoder()
      .decode(RelativePoint.self, from: Data(text.utf8))
    // 3
    TouchSessionManager.default.update(id: newId, to: pt)
  } catch {
    // 4
    ws.send("unsupported update: \(text)")
  }
}
```

This code does the following:

1. Create an `onText(_:)` listener to run when the WebSocket receives some text.
2. Decode the received text to `RelativePoint` from JSON.
3. Update the user in `TouchSessionManager` with the user's new point.
4. If the decoding fails, return a message to the client.

Implementing "Left"

Finally, you need to implement the code for a WebSocket close. You'll consider any disconnect or cancellation that leaves the socket unable to send messages as a close. Below `ws.onText(_:)`, add:

```
// 1
_ = ws.onClose.always { result in
  // 2
  TouchSessionManager.default.remove(id: newId)
}
```

Here's what the final part does:

1. Register a `onClose` handler for the WebSocket. `always(_:)` triggers the closure on any WebSocket close event.
2. Remove the user from `TouchSessionManager` using the ID created earlier.

Build and run the server and return to the simulator to start a new session. Drag the circle around and notice the logs on the server. You should see logs from the TrackingSessionManager, but it's not yet implemented.

Implementing TouchSessionManager: Joined

At this point, you can successfully dispatch WebSocket events to their associated architecture event in the TouchSessionManager. Next, you need to implement the management logic. Open **TouchSessionManager.swift** and replace the body of `insert(id:color:at:on:)` with the following:

```
// 1
```

```
let start = SharedTouch(
  id: id,
  color: color,
  position: pt)
let msg = Message(
  participant: id,
  update: .joined(start))
// 2
send(msg)

// 3
participants.values.map {
  Message(
    participant: $0.touch.participant,
    update: .joined($0.touch))
} .forEach { ws.send($0) }

/// store new session
// 4
let session = ActiveSession(touch: start, ws: ws)
participants[id] = session
```

Here's what the new code does:

1. Create a `SharedTouch` and `Message` from the new user's details.
2. Send the message to all existing users.
3. Loop through each current user and create a new join `Message`. Send the messages to the new user, which allows tracking all existing users.
4. Store the new user's session to respond to future events.

Implementing TouchSessionManager: Moved

Next, to handle "moved" messages, replace the body of `update(id:to:)` with the following code:

```
// 1
participants[id]?.touch.position = pt
// 2
let msg = Message(participant: id, update: .moved(pt))
// 3
send(msg)
```

This new code does the following:

1. Update the position of the participant using the provided `position`.
2. Create a new `Message` with the user's ID and updated point.
3. Send the message to all active sessions.

Implementing TouchSessionManager: Left

Finally, you need to handle closes and cancellations. Replace the body of `remove(id:)` with the following:

```
// 1
participants[id] = nil
// 2
let msg = Message(participant: id, update: .left)
// 3
send(msg)
```

Here's what this does:

1. Remove the associated reference from the backing dictionary.
2. Create a new `Message` for the user to remove. Use `.left` to notify other users this user has left.
3. Send the message to all the remaining active sessions.

Build and run the server, leave it running, then return to the ShareApp iOS Xcode project. Run the project on any two simulators. Xcode can only host one debugging session at a time. However, if you open the second simulator and select the ShareTouch app, you can run two sessions.

Select a color on each simulator and drag the circles around to see the updates. You can even run a third simulator (or more, if your computer can handle it).

Where to go from here?

You've done it. Your iOS Application communicates in real-time via WebSockets with your Swift server. Many different kinds of apps can benefit from the instantaneous communications made possible by WebSockets, including things such as chat applications, games, airplane trackers and so much more. If the app you imagine needs to respond in real time, WebSockets may be your answer!

Challenges

For more practice with WebSockets, try these challenges:

- Upgrade the server and client to transmit raw binary data as opposed to text for a bit of a performance boost.
- Add a way for users to see more information about active sessions, such as how many sessions are active and how long they've been active.
- Maintain some sort of historical record from touch to lift and recreate movements
- Try hosting your basic application on a remote server. Make sure to update `shareSessionURL` in **ShareTouchApp.swift** in the iOS project.

Chapter 31: Advanced Fluent

By Tim Condon

In the previous sections of this book, you learned how to use Fluent to perform queries against a database. You also learned how to perform CRUD operations on models. In this chapter, you'll learn about some of Fluent's more advanced features. You'll see how to save models with `enums` and use Fluent's soft delete and timestamp features. You'll also learn how to use raw SQL and joins, as well as seeing how to "eager load" relationships.

Getting started

The starter project for this chapter is based on the TIL application from the end of chapter 21. You can either use your code from that project or use the starter project included in the book materials for this chapter. This project relies on a PostgreSQL database running locally.

Clearing the existing database

If you've followed along from the previous chapters, you need to delete the existing database. This chapter contains model changes which require either reverting your database or deleting it. In Terminal, type:

```
docker rm -f postgres
```

This stops the Docker container named **postgres** if it's running and deletes it.

Creating a new database

Create a new database in Docker for the TIL application to use. In Terminal, type:

```
docker run --name postgres \
  -e POSTGRES_DB=vapor_database \
  -e POSTGRES_USER=vapor_username \
  -e POSTGRES_PASSWORD=vapor_password \
  -p 5432:5432 -d postgres
```

Here's what this does:

- Run a new container named **postgres**.
- Specify the database name, username and password through environment variables.
- Allow applications to connect to the PostgreSQL server on the default port: 5432.
- Run the server in the background as a daemon.
- Use the Docker image named **postgres** for this container. If the image isn't present on your machine, Docker automatically downloads it.

For more information on how to configure the database in the project, see Chapter 6, "Configuring a Database".

Soft delete

In Chapter 7, "CRUD Database Operations", you learned how to delete models from the database. However, while you may want models to appear deleted to users, you might not want to actually delete them. You could also have legal or company requirements which enforce retention of data. Fluent provides soft delete functionality to allow you to do this. Open the TIL app in Xcode and go to **User.swift**. Look for:

```
var acronyms: [Acronym]
```

and add the following definition below:

```
@Timestamp(key: "deleted_at", on: .delete)
var deletedAt: Date?
```

This adds a new property for Fluent to store the date you performed a soft delete on the model. You annotate the property with `@Timestamp`. Fluent checks for this property wrapper when you call `delete(on:)`. If the property exists for the `.delete` action, Fluent sets the current date on the property and saves the updated model. Otherwise, it deletes the model from the database. That's all that's required to implement soft delete in Fluent!

Next, open **CreateUser.swift**. In `prepare(on:)`, before `.unique(on: "username")` add:

```
.field("deleted_at", .datetime)
```

This adds a field to the migration so Fluent creates the correct column for the new property.

Open **UsersController.swift** and create a route to use the new functionality. Below `loginHandler(_:)`, add the following:

```
func deleteHandler(_ req: Request)
  -> EventLoopFuture<HTTPStatus> {
    User.find(req.parameters.get("userID"), on: req.db)
      .unwrap(or: Abort(.notFound)).flatMap { user in
        user.delete(on: req.db).transform(to: .noContent)
    }
}
```

This deletes the user passed as a parameter and returns a **204 No Content** response. Finally, you need to register the route. Add the following to the end of `boot(routes:)`:

```
tokenAuthGroup.delete(":userID", use: deleteHandler)
```

This routes a **DELETE** request to **/api/users/<USER_ID>** to `deleteHandler(_:)`. Build and run the Vapor application. In RESTed, using the pre-defined **admin** user, send a request to **http://localhost:8080/api/users/login** with the correct HTTP Basic Authentication credentials to get a token. See Chapter 18, "API Authentication, Part 1" for a refresher on how to do this.

Next, create a new request and configure it as follows:

- **URL**: http://localhost:8080/api/users
- **method**: POST
- **Parameter encoding**: JSON-encoded
- **header**: Authorization: Bearer

Add three parameters with names and values:

- **username**: a username of your choice
- **name**: a name of your choice
- **password**: a password of your choice

Click **Send Request**. This creates a user in the application:

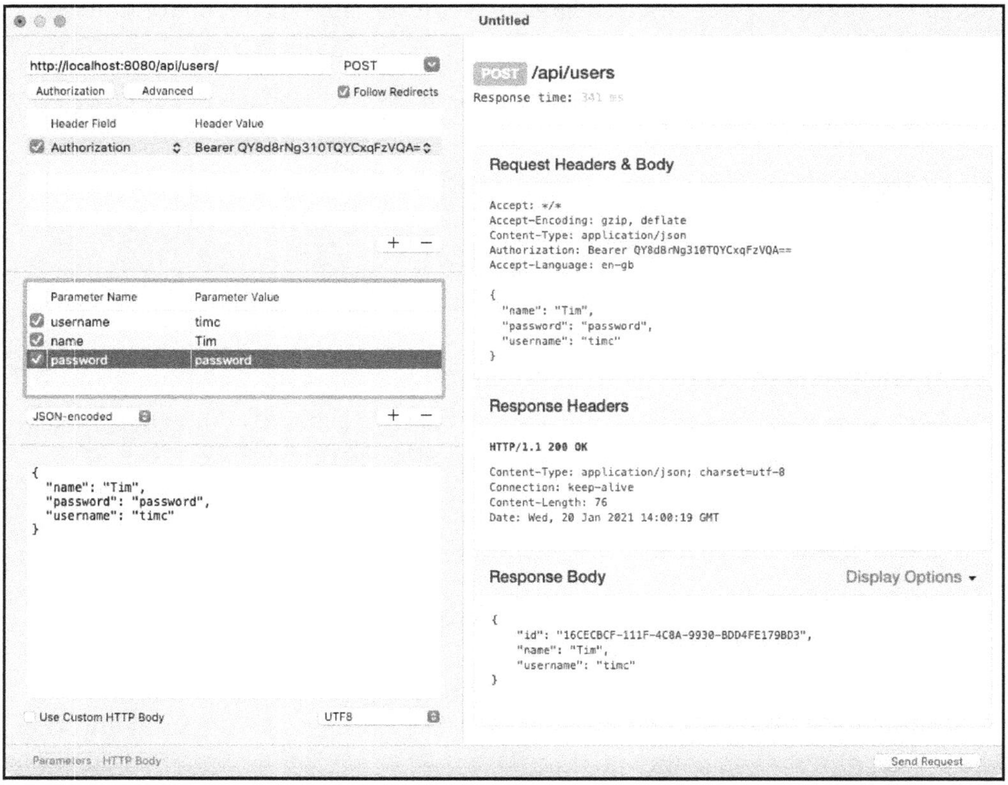

Next, send a request to delete the new user. Configure the request as follows:

- **URL**: http://localhost:8080/api/users/<USER_ID>
- **method**: DELETE
- **header**: Authorization: Bearer

Click **Send Request.** You should see a **204 No Content** response, indicating you successfully performed a soft delete of the user. Finally, configure a request to get all the users:

- **URL**: http://localhost:8080/api/users/
- **method**: GET

Click **Send Request** . You'll note that even though you only soft deleted the user, it doesn't appear in the list of all users:

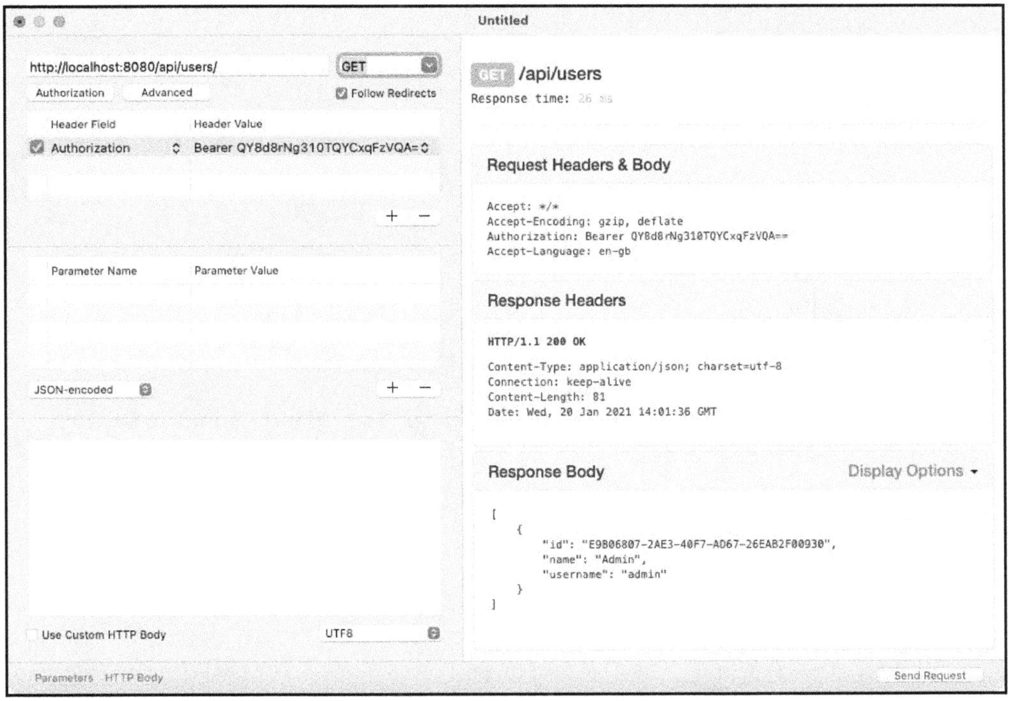

Restoring Users

Even though the application now allows you to soft delete users, you may want to restore them at a future date. First, add the following below `import Vapor` at the top of **UsersController.swift**:

```
import Fluent
```

This allows you to use Fluent's filter functions. Next, create a new route handler below `deleteHandler(_:)` to restore a user:

```
func restoreHandler(_ req: Request)
  throws -> EventLoopFuture<HTTPStatus> {
    // 1
    let userID =
      try req.parameters.require("userID", as: UUID.self)
    // 2
    return User.query(on: req.db)
      .withDeleted()
      .filter(\.$id == userID)
      .first()
      .unwrap(or: Abort(.notFound))
      .flatMap { user in
        // 3
        user.restore(on: req.db).transform(to: .ok)
    }
}
```

Here's what's going on:

1. Get the user's ID as a UUID from the request's parameters.
2. Perform a query to find the user with that ID. `withDeleted()` tells Fluent to include soft-deleted models.
3. Call `restore(on:)` on the user to restore that user. Transform the response to **200 OK**.

Finally, register the route handler. Add the following to the end of `boot(routes:)`:

```
tokenAuthGroup.post(":userID", "restore", use: restoreHandler)
```

This maps a **POST** request to **/api/users/<UUID>/restore** to `restoreHandler(_:)`. Build and run the application and open RESTed. Configure a request as follows, using the UUID of the user you deleted above:

- **URL**: http://localhost:8080/api/users/<USER_ID>/restore
- **method**: POST
- **header**: Authorization: Bearer

Click **Send Request**. You'll receive a **200 OK** response, indicating you've restored the user.

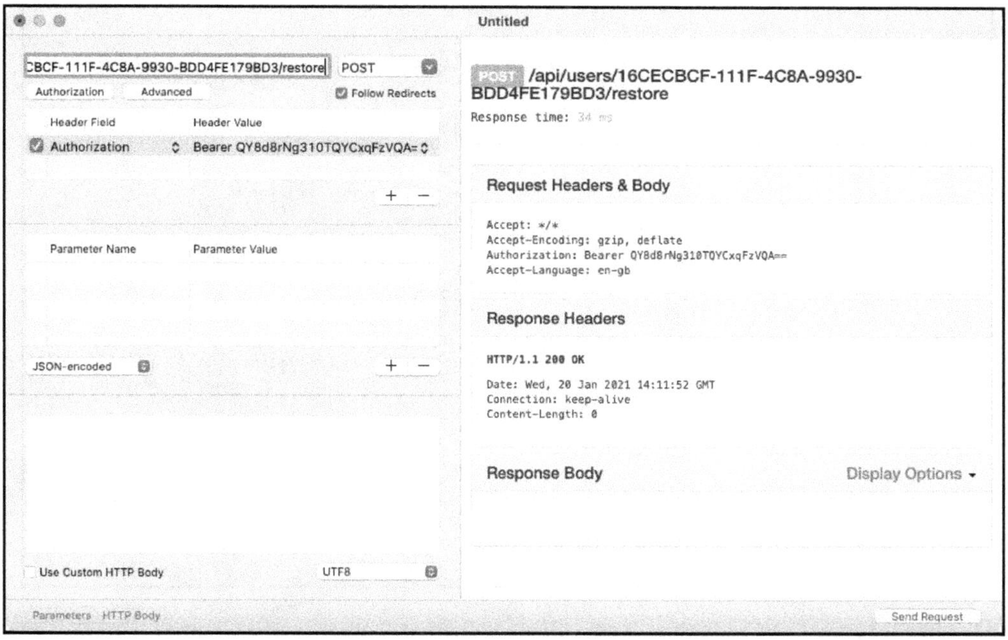

> If you no longer have the UUID of the user, you can retrieve it using the following magic in Terminal:

```
docker exec -it postgres psql -U vapor_username vapor_database
select id from "users" where username = '<your username>';
\q
```

Configure a final request as follows:

- **URL**: http://localhost:8080/api/users/
- **method**: GET

Click **Send Request**. The restored user now appears in the list of users:

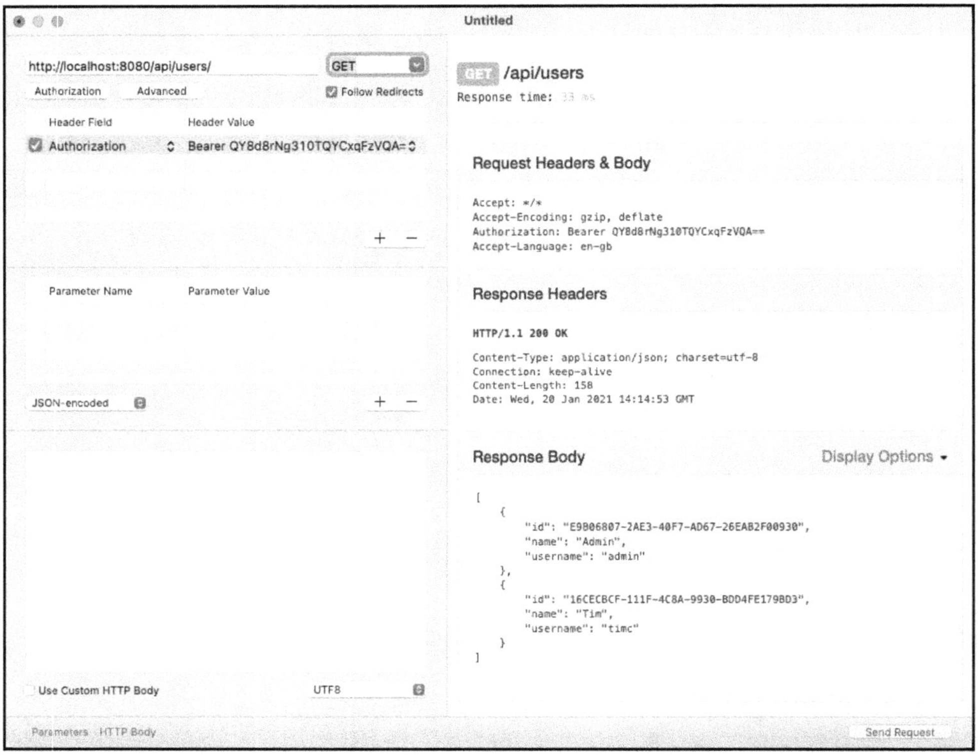

Force delete

Now that you can soft delete and restore users, you may want to add the ability to properly delete a user. You use force delete for this. Back in Xcode, still in **UsersController.swift**, create a new route to do this. Add the following below `restoreHandler(_:)`:

```
func forceDeleteHandler(_ req: Request)
  -> EventLoopFuture<HTTPStatus> {
    User.find(req.parameters.get("userID"), on: req.db)
      .unwrap(or: Abort(.notFound))
      .flatMap { user in
        user.delete(force: true, on: req.db)
```

```
            .transform(to: .noContent)
    }
}
```

Your code is similar to `deleteHandler(_:)`. However, this time you call `delete(force:on:)` on the model. Setting `force` to `true` bypasses the soft delete and removes the model from the database.

Finally, register the route handler. Add the following to the end of `boot(routes:)`:

```
tokenAuthGroup.delete(
  ":userID",
  "force",
  use: forceDeleteHandler)
```

This routes a **DELETE** request to **/api/users/<USER_ID>/force** to `forceDeleteHandler(_:)`. Build and run the application and go back to RESTed. Configure a new request as follows:

- **URL**: http://localhost:8080/api/users/<USER_ID>/force
- **method**: DELETE
- **header**: Authorization: Bearer

Click **Send Request** and you'll receive a **204 No Content** response. Configure a final request as follows:

- **URL**: http://localhost:8080/api/users/<USER_ID>/restore
- **method**: POST
- **header**: Authorization: Bearer

Click **Send Request**.

You'll receive a **404 Not Found** error as the model no longer exists in the database to be restored:

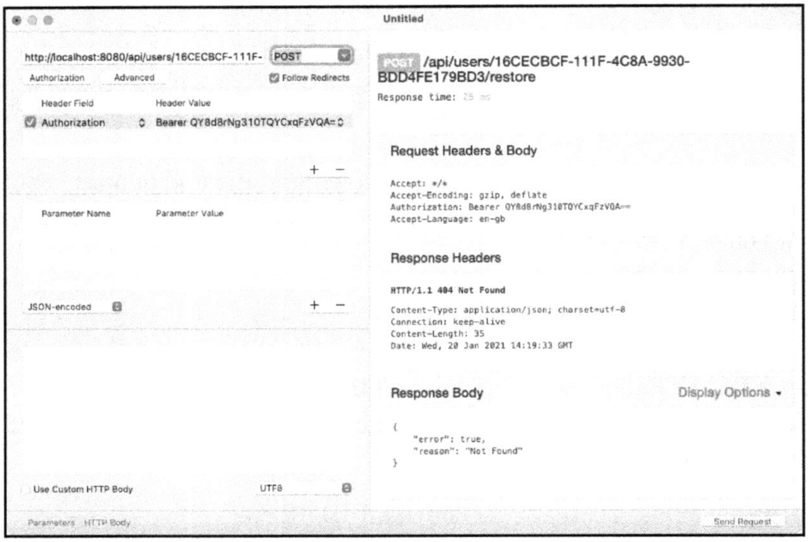

Timestamps

Fluent has built-in functionality for timestamps for a model's creation time and update time. In fact, you used one above to implement soft-delete functionality. If you configure these, Fluent automatically sets and updates the times. To enable this, open **Acronym.swift** in Xcode. Below `var categories: [Category]` add two new properties for the dates:

```
@Timestamp(key: "created_at", on: .create)
var createdAt: Date?

@Timestamp(key: "updated_at", on: .update)
var updatedAt: Date?
```

Just like soft deletes, Fluent looks for these timestamps when creating and updating models. If they exist, Fluent sets the dates. Now, open **CreateAcronym.swift**. In `prepare(on:)`, before `.create()` add the following:

```
.field("created_at", .datetime)
.field("updated_at", .datetime)
```

This adds the two new fields to the migration so Fluent creates the columns in the database. That's all that's required! Create a new route handler to use the functionality.

Open **AcronymsController.swift** and add the following below `removeCategoriesHandler(_:)`:

```
func getMostRecentAcronyms(_ req: Request)
  -> EventLoopFuture<[Acronym]> {
    Acronym.query(on: req.db)
      .sort(\.$updatedAt, .descending)
      .all()
}
```

This route returns all acronyms, sorted by `updatedAt`. The sort uses a descending order to ensure the most recent appear first. For more information on how to use `sort(_:)`, see Chapter 7, "CRUD Database Operations". Fluent sets `createdAt` when you create the model. Fluent also sets `updatedAt` when you create the model *and* any time you update it. Register this route in `boot(routes:)` below `acronymsRoutes.get(":acronymID", "categories", use: getCategoriesHandler)` with the following:

```
acronymsRoutes.get("mostRecent", use: getMostRecentAcronyms)
```

This routes a **GET** request to **/api/acronyms/mostRecent** to `getMostRecentAcronyms(_:)`. Before you run the application, you must either update or reset the database to add the new fields in for `Acronym`. For the sake of time, this chapter resets the Docker database. To change the table using a migration, see Chapter 27, "Database/API Versioning & Migration". In Terminal, run the following commands:

```
docker rm -f postgres
docker run --name postgres \
  -e POSTGRES_DB=vapor_database \
  -e POSTGRES_USER=vapor_username \
  -e POSTGRES_PASSWORD=vapor_password \
  -p 5432:5432 -d postgres
```

These commands stop, delete and recreate the PostgreSQL database in Docker, as described at the start of this chapter. Finally, build and run the application and open RESTed. Create a few acronyms, remembering you need to log in first, as described in Chapter 18, "API Authentication, Part 1".

> **Hint**: You might find it simpler to use the Web interface to add the acronyms by visiting **http://localhost:8080** in your browser.

Next, configure a new request in RESTed as follows:

- **URL**: http://localhost:8080/api/acronyms/<ID_OF_FIRST_ACRONYM>
- **method**: PUT
- **header**: Authorization: Bearer

This updates the first acronym created. Add two parameters with names and values:

- **short**: the same short as the original acronym, e.g. OMG
- **long**: an updated meaning for the acronym, e.g. Oh My Gosh

Click **Send Request** to update the acronym. Finally, configure a new request in RESTed as follows:

- **URL**: http://localhost:8080/api/acronyms/mostRecent
- **method**: GET

Click **Send Request** to get the list of all acronyms, sorted by most recently updated. You'll see the first acronym appears first in the list, since you updated it last:

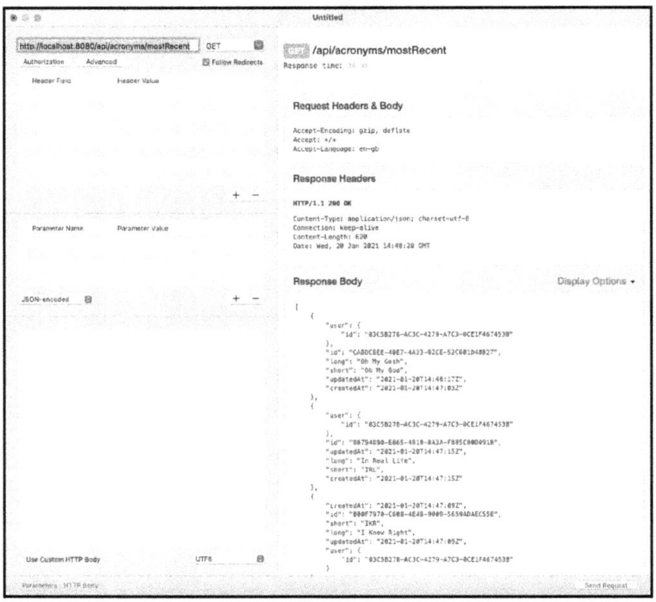

Enums

A common requirement for database columns is to restrict the values to a pre-defined set. Both FluentPostgreSQL and FluentMySQL support enums for this. To demonstrate this, you'll add a type to the user to define basic user access levels. In Xcode, create a new file called **UserType.swift** in **Sources/App/Models**. Open the new file and add the following:

```
import Foundation

// 1
enum UserType: String, Codable {
  // 2
  case admin
  case standard
  case restricted
}
```

Here's what the new code does:

1. Create a new `String` enum type, `UserType` that conforms to `Codable`. The type must be a `String` enum to conform to `Codable`.
2. Define three types of user access for use in the Vapor application.

Next, open **User.swift** and add a new property below `var deletedAt: Date?` to store the user's type:

```
@Enum(key: "userType")
var userType: UserType
```

This adds a new property for `User`. You annotate the property with `@Enum`. This is a special type of `Field` property wrapper used to store native database enums. Change the initializer to support the new property:

```
init(
  id: UUID? = nil,
  name: String,
  username: String,
  password: String,
  userType: UserType = .standard
) {
  self.name = name
  self.username = username
  self.password = password
  self.userType = userType
}
```

This defaults the user type to a newly created user to a standard user. Finally, in **CreateAdminUser.swift**, change `let user = User(...)` to the following:

```
let user = User(
  name: "Admin",
  username: "admin",
  password: passwordHash,
  userType: .admin)
```

This makes the admin user an `admin` type. Then, open **CreateUser.swift**. Replace the body of `prepare(on:)` with the following:

```
// 1
database.enum("userType")
  // 2
  .case("admin")
  .case("standard")
  .case("restricted")
  // 3
  .create()
  .flatMap { userType in
    database.schema("users")
      .id()
      .field("name", .string, .required)
      .field("username", .string, .required)
      .field("password", .string, .required)
      .field("deleted_at", .datetime)
      // 4
      .field("userType", userType, .required)
      .unique(on: "username")
      .create()
}
```

Here's what the new code does:

1. Set up a database enum using `enum(_:)`. This is similar to setting up a table using `schema(_:_)`.
2. Define the different cases for your enum.
3. Call `create()` to create the enum in the database. Wait for the create to complete using `flatMap(_:)`. The closure for `flatMap(_:)` receives the enum type created.
4. Use the enum type to define a new field in the **users** table for the new property.

Next, open **UsersController.swift** to make use of this new property. Replace the function signature of `deleteHandler(_:)` with the following:

```
func deleteHandler(_ req: Request)
  throws -> EventLoopFuture<HTTPStatus> {
```

This allows you to throw errors in the function body. Next, replace the body of `deleteHandler(_:)` with the following:

```
// 1
let requestUser = try req.auth.require(User.self)
// 2
guard requestUser.userType == .admin else {
  throw Abort(.forbidden)
}
// 3
return User.find(req.parameters.get("userID"), on: req.db)
  .unwrap(or: Abort(.notFound))
  .flatMap { user in
    user.delete(on: req.db)
      .transform(to: .noContent)
}
```

The changes made were:

1. Get the authenticated user from the request.
2. Ensure the authenticated user is an admin. This ensures that only admins can delete other users. Otherwise, throw a **403 Forbidden** response.
3. Delete the user specified in the request's parameters, as before.

Reset the database using the commands from earlier, then build and run the application. Open RESTed and log in as the admin user to get a token. Configure a new request as follows:

- **URL**: http://localhost:8080/api/users
- **method**: POST
- **Parameter encoding**: JSON-encoded
- **header**: Authorization: Bearer

Add four parameters with names and values:

- **username**: a username of your choice
- **name**: a name of your choice
- **password**: a password of your choice

- **userType**: standard

Click **Send Request** to create the user. Change the values to create another user to delete and click **Send Request**. Take a note of the second user's ID. Log in as the first user you created and configure another request as follows:

- **URL**: http://localhost:8080/api/users/<FINAL_USER_ID>
- **method**: DELETE
- **Parameter encoding**: JSON-encoded
- **header**: Authorization: Bearer

Click **Send Request**, and you'll receive a **403 Forbidden** response:

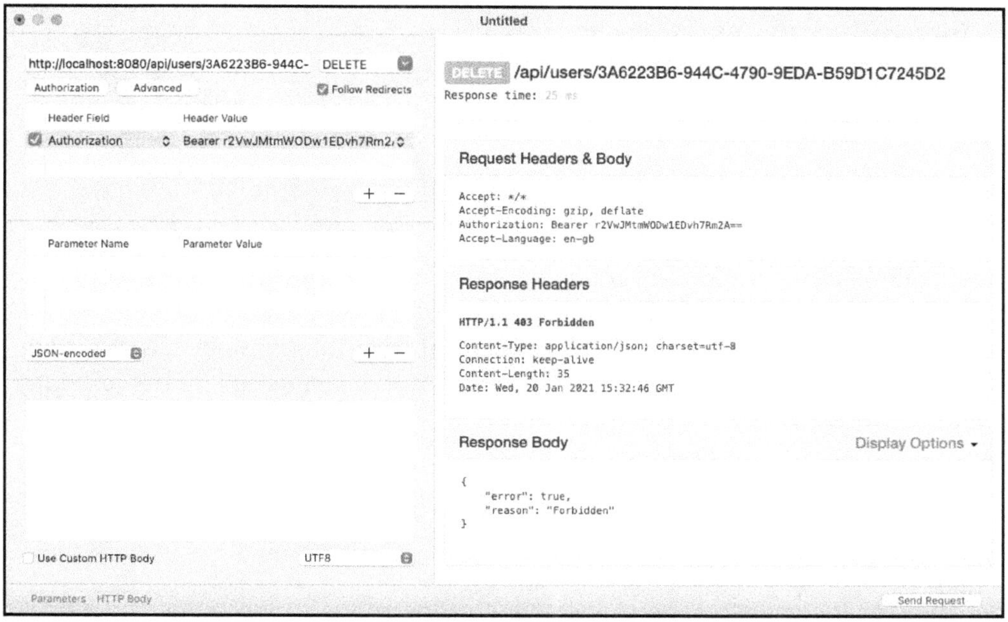

Change the **Authorization** header to use the token from the admin user and click **Send Request** again. This time the request succeeds, and you'll receive a **204 No Content** response:

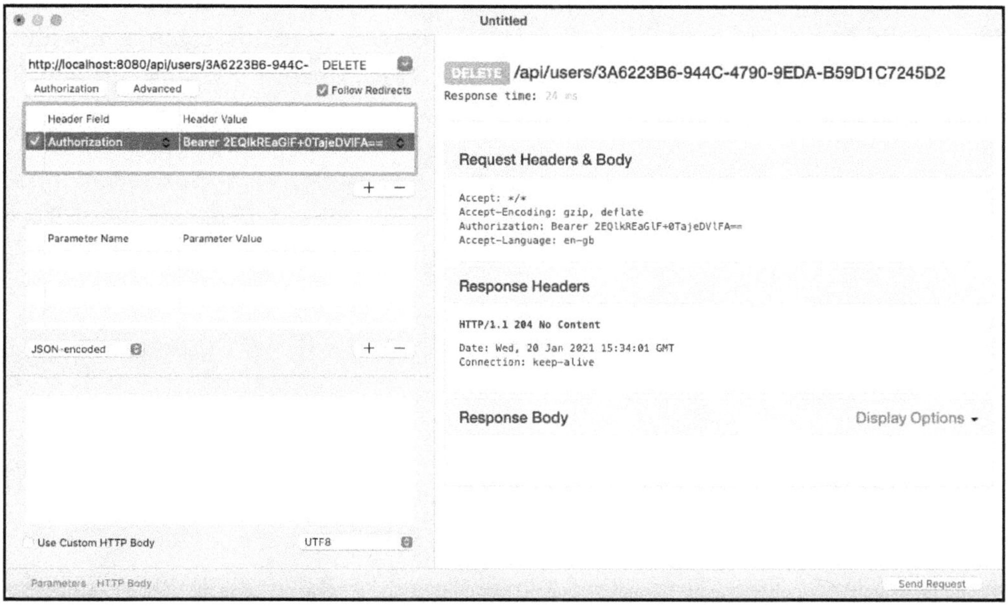

> **Note**: To be more complete, you should make the same changes to `forceDeleteHandler(_:)` and `restoreHandler(_:)`. This is left as an exercise for the reader.

Lifecycle hooks

Fluent allows you to hook into various aspects of a model's lifecycle using model middleware. These work in a similar way to other middleware and allow you to execute code before and after different events. For more information on middleware, see Chapter 29, "Middleware". Fluent allows you to add middleware for the following events:

- **create**: called when Fluent creates a model.
- **update**: called when Fluent updates a model.
- **delete**: called when Fluent deletes a model.
- **softDelete**: called when Fluent soft deletes a model.
- **restore**: called when Fluent restores a model.

These hooks allow you to add additional checks to your models, populate or remove fields or add extra steps such as log messages. To demonstrate this, create a new file in **Sources/App/Models** called **UserMiddleware.swift**. Open the new file and add the following:

```
import Fluent
import Vapor

// 1
struct UserMiddleware: ModelMiddleware {
  // 2
  func create(
    model: User,
    on db: Database,
    next: AnyModelResponder) -> EventLoopFuture<Void> {
    // 3
    User.query(on: db)
      .filter(\.$username == model.username)
      .count()
      .flatMap { count in
        // 4
        guard count == 0 else {
```

```
          let error =
            Abort(
              .badRequest,
              reason: "Username already exists")
          return db.eventLoop.future(error: error)
        }
        // 5
        return next.create(model, on: db).map {
          // 6
          let errorMessage: Logger.Message =
            "Created user with username \(model.username)"
          db.logger.debug(errorMessage)
        }
    }
  }
}
```

Here's what the new code does:

1. Create a new type that conforms to `ModelMiddleware`.
2. Implement `create(model:on:next:)` to perform additional checks before you create a user.
3. Query the database to get the number of users with the new user's username.
4. Ensure there are no users with that username, otherwise return a failed future with an `AbortError` and reason. This returns a better error message to the client than the database constraint violation message. Returning a failed future cancels the save. You should still use the database constraint to assert that a username is unique in case two users try and register with the same username at the exact same time.
5. Chain the next responder to allow other middleware to run.
6. Log a message to the console once the save completes. You can run additional code after Fluent has saved the model here.

It's useful to validate unique usernames using a `ModelMiddleware` as you only have to do it in one place. The TIL app contains two places to create users — the API and the website. By using a `ModelMiddleware`, you don't need to duplicate the logic to ensure usernames are unique.

Finally, open **configure.swift** to register the middleware. Below `app.migrations.add(CreateAdminUser())` add the following:

```
app.databases.middleware.use(UserMiddleware(), on: .psql)
```

This registers `UserMiddleware` to `psql` to ensure it runs whenever you create a `User`.

Build and run the application and log in to get a token, if you don't already have one. In RESTed, configure a new request as follows:

- **URL**: http://localhost:8080/api/users
- **method**: POST
- **Parameter encoding**: JSON-encoded
- **header**: Authorization: Bearer

Add four parameters with names and values:

- **username**: admin
- **name**: Admin
- **password**: password
- **userType**: admin

Click **Send Request**, and you'll see the error message returned since the admin username already exists:

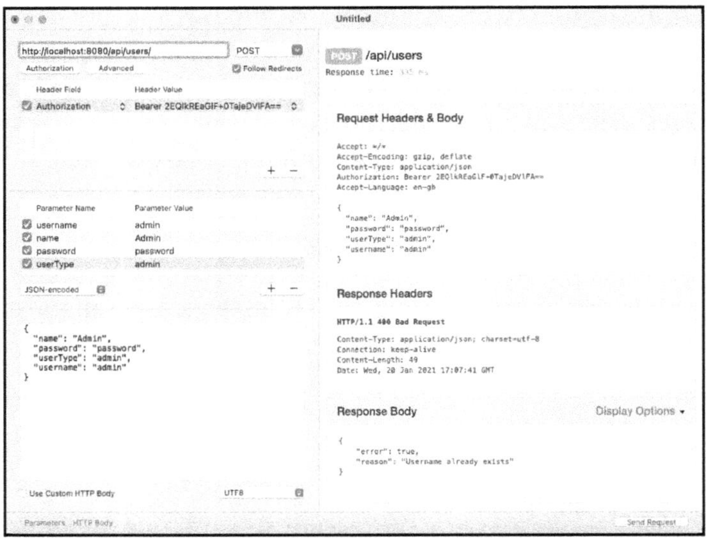

Eager loading and nested models

If you follow a strict REST API, you should retrieve a model's children in a separate request. However, this isn't alway ideal, and you may want the ability to send a single request to get all models with all their children. For example, in the TIL application, you may want a route that returns all categories with all their acronyms. You may even want to return all categories with all their acronyms with all their users. This is commonly referred to as the N+1 problem and Fluent makes this easy with eager loading. Open **CategoriesController.swift** and add the following at the bottom of the file:

```
struct AcronymWithUser: Content {
  let id: UUID?
  let short: String
  let long: String
  let user: User.Public
}

struct CategoryWithAcronyms: Content {
  let id: UUID?
  let name: String
  let acronyms: [AcronymWithUser]
}
```

This defines two new types to use when returning all the categories with their acronyms and the acronyms' users. Below `getAcronymsHandler(_:)`, add the code to perform the query:

```
func getAllCategoriesWithAcronymsAndUsers(_ req: Request)
  -> EventLoopFuture<[CategoryWithAcronyms]> {
    // 1
    Category.query(on: req.db)
      // 2
      .with(\.$acronyms) { acronyms in
        // 3
        acronyms.with(\.$user)
      // 4
      }.all().map { categories in
        // 5
        categories.map { category in
          // 6
          let categoryAcronyms = category.acronyms.map {
            AcronymWithUser(
              id: $0.id,
              short: $0.short,
              long: $0.long,
              user: $0.user.convertToPublic())
          }
```

```
        // 7
        return CategoryWithAcronyms(
          id: category.id,
          name: category.name,
          acronyms: categoryAcronyms)
      }
    }
}
```

Here's what the new route handler does:

1. Perform a query on `Category` to get all the categories.
2. Eager load the categories' acronyms using `with(_:)`. `with(_:)` accepts a key path to the relationship to eager load — in this case, `$acronyms`.
3. `with(_:)` also accepts an optional closure allowing you to nest eager loads. This allows you to eager load `$user` on `Acronym` at the same time. Fluent works out the queries it needs to perform for you.
4. Use `all()` to finish the query and get all the results.
5. Loop through all the returned categories to convert them to `CategoryWithAcronyms`.
6. Convert all the category's acronyms to `AcronymWithUser`. When you eager load a model's relationships, you can access the property directly. You don't need to go through the property wrapper like previous chapters. Be warned: If you do this without eager loading the relationship, you'll get a fatal error.
7. Return the category converted to `CategoryWithAcronyms`.

Finally, register the route in `boot(routes:)` below `categoriesRoute.get(":categoryID", "acronyms", use: getAcronymsHandler)`:

```
categoriesRoute.get(
  "acronyms",
  use: getAllCategoriesWithAcronymsAndUsers)
```

The routes a **GET** request to **/api/categories/acronyms** to `getAllCategoriesWithAcronymsAndUsers(_:)`. Build and run the application and create some users and acronyms and categories. In RESTed, configure a new request as follows:

- **URL**: http://localhost:8080/api/categories/acronyms
- **method**: GET

Click **Send Request** and you'll see all the categories with their acronyms and the acronyms have their users:

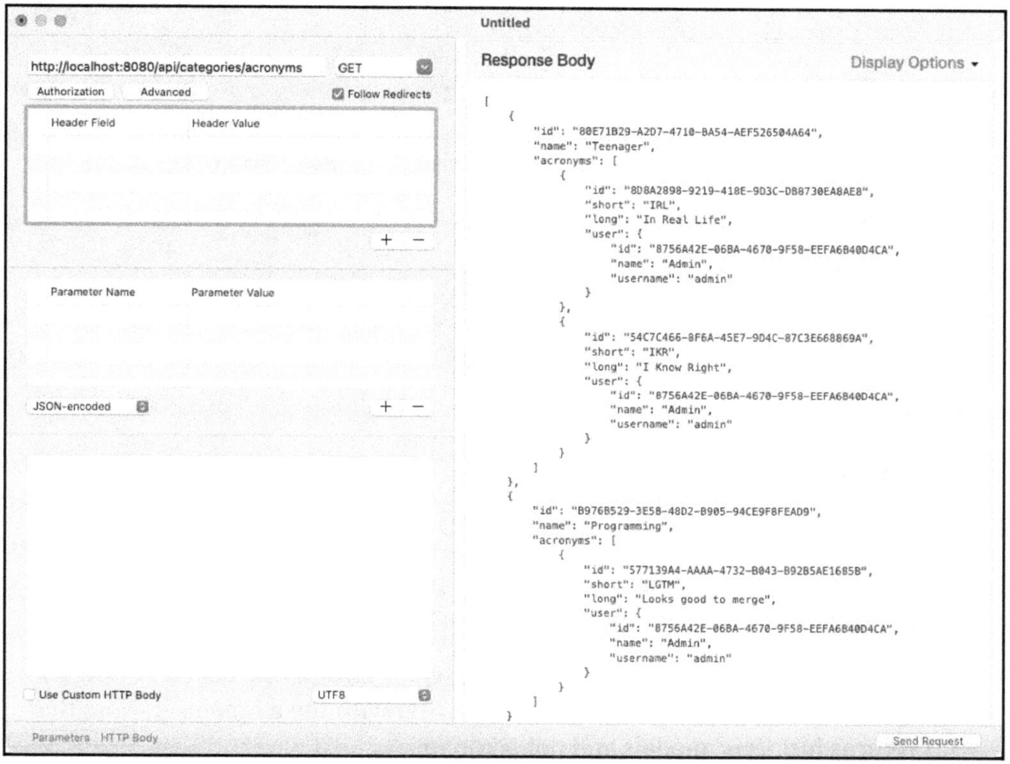

Joins

Sometimes, you want to query other tables when retrieving information. For example, you might want to get the user who created the most recent acronym. You could do this with eager loading and Swift. You'd do this by getting all the users and eager load their acronyms. You can then sort the acronyms by their created date to get the most recent and return its user. However, this means loading all users and their acronyms into memory, even if you don't want them, which is inefficient. Joins allow you to combine columns from one table with columns from another table by specifying the common values. For example, you can combine the acronyms table with the users table using the users' IDs. You can then sort, or even filter, across the different tables.

Open **UsersController.swift** and add a route handler below `forceDeleteHandler(_:)` to get users who have created acronyms recently:

```
func getUserWithMostRecentAcronym(_ req: Request)
  -> EventLoopFuture<User.Public> {
    // 1
    User.query(on: req.db)
      // 2
      .join(Acronym.self, on: \Acronym.$user.$id == \User.$id)
      // 3
      .sort(Acronym.self, \Acronym.$createdAt, .descending)
      // 4
      .first()
      .unwrap(or: Abort(.internalServerError))
      .convertToPublic()
}
```

Here's what the new code does:

1. Perform a query on `User`.
2. Join `User` to `Acronym` by linking the user's ID to the acronym's user's `$id` value.
3. Sort on `Acronym` and sort on the `createdAt` property to get the most recent acronyms. You can use sort and filters with a join.
4. Return the first user and return an internal server error if one doesn't exist. The database should always contain at least one user with the admin user. Note that this returns just `User` models and not acronyms.

Register the route in `boot(routes:)` under `usersRoute.get(":userID", "acronyms", use: getAcronymsHandler)`:

```
usersRoute.get(
  "mostRecentAcronym",
  use: getUserWithMostRecentAcronym)
```

This routes a **GET** request to **/api/users/mostRecentAcronym** to `getUserWithMostRecentAcronym(_:)`. Build and run the application and launch RESTed. Configure a new request as follows:

- **URL**: http://localhost:8080/api/users/mostRecentAcronym
- **method**: GET

Click **Send Request** and you'll see the user who created the most recent acronym:

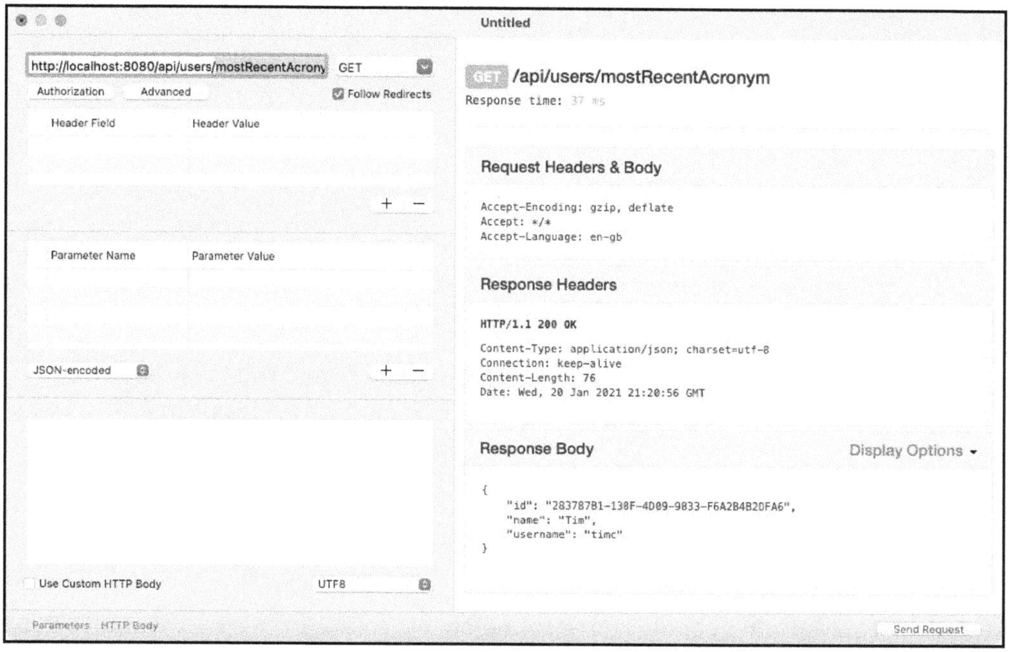

Raw SQL

Whilst Fluent provides tools to allow you to build lots of different behaviors, there are some advanced features it doesn't offer. Fluent doesn't support querying different schemas or aggregate functions. In a complex application, you may find that there are scenarios where Fluent doesn't provide the functionality you need. In these cases, you can use raw SQL queries to interact with the database directly. This allows you to perform any type of query the database supports.

In **AcronymsController.swift**, add the following add the top of the file below `import Fluent`:

```
import SQLKit
```

This allows you to see the necessary methods for raw queries. Next, below `getMostRecentAcronyms(_:)`, add:

```
func getAllAcronymsRaw(_ req: Request)
  throws -> EventLoopFuture<[Acronym]> {
    // 1
```

```
    guard let sql = req.db as? SQLDatabase else {
      throw Abort(.internalServerError)
    }
    // 2
    return sql.raw("SELECT * FROM acronyms")
      // 3
      .all(decoding: Acronym.self)
}
```

Here's what the code does:

1. Cast the database on `Request` to `SQLDatabase` to allow you to perform raw queries. If the cast fails, return a **500 Internal Server Error**.
2. Use `raw(_:)` to create a raw query on the database. **Note**: You must be careful and sanitize any input into your query to avoid injection attacks. `raw(_:)` supports parameter binding if necessary.
3. Get all the results and decode the rows to `Acronym`. Even though this uses a raw query, you still use `Codable` to convert the data from the database, thereby providing type safety.

Register the new route in `boot(routes:)` below `acronymsRoutes.get("mostRecent", use: getMostRecentAcronyms)` with the following:

```
acronymsRoutes.get("raw", use: getAllAcronymsRaw)
```

This routes a **GET** request to **/api/acronyms/raw** to `getAllAcronymsRaw(_:)`. Build and run your application and head to RESTed. Configure a final request as follows:

- **URL**: http://localhost:8080/api/acronyms/raw
- **method**: GET

Click **Send Request** and you'll see all acronyms returned:

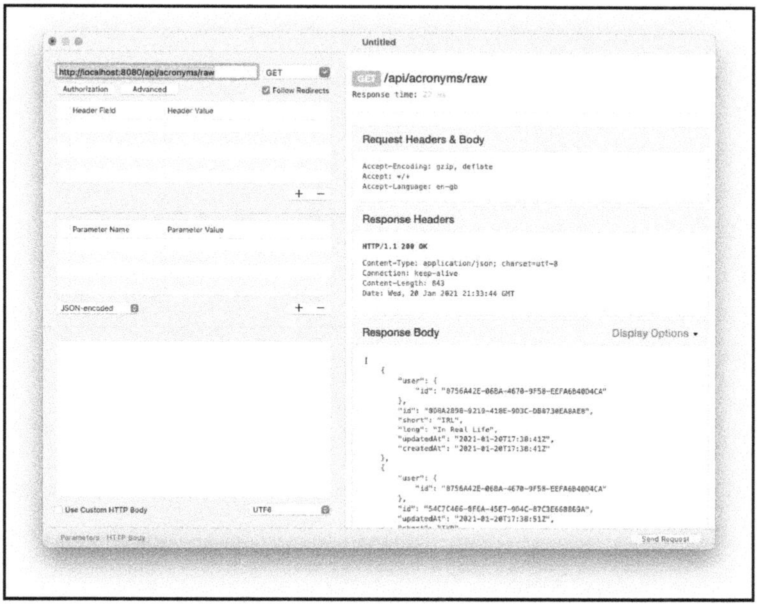

Where to go from here?

In this chapter, you learned how to use some of the advanced features Fluent provides to perform complex queries. You also saw how to send raw SQL queries if Fluent can't do what you need.

With the knowledge of advanced features, you should now be able to build anything with Vapor and Fluent!

Section V: Production & External Deployment

This section shows you how to deploy your Vapor application to external Cloud-based providers to offload the job of hosting your application. You'll learn how to upload to Heroku, a popular platform for deploying applications as well as deploying to AWS or Docker.

The chapters in this section deal with hosting and production concerns when deploying your Vapor application and how to split your application into multiple services (microservices) to balance the load on your application.

Chapter 32: Deploying with Heroku

By Logan Wright

Heroku is a popular hosting solution that simplifies deployment of web and cloud applications. It supports a number of popular languages and database options. In this chapter, you'll learn how to deploy a Vapor web app with a PostgreSQL database on Heroku.

Setting up Heroku

If you don't already have a Heroku account, sign up for one now. Heroku offers free options and setting up an account is painless. Simply visit https://signup.heroku.com/ and follow the instructions to create an account.

Installing CLI

Now that you have your Heroku account, install the Heroku CLI tool. The easiest way to install on macOS is through Homebrew. In Terminal, enter:

```
brew install heroku/brew/heroku
```

If you don't wish to use Homebrew, or are running on Linux, there are other installation options available at https://devcenter.heroku.com/articles/heroku-cli#download-and-install.

Logging in

With the Heroku CLI installed, you need to log in to your account. In Terminal, enter:

```
heroku login
```

Follow the prompts, entering your email and password. Once you've logged in, you can verify success by checking `whoami` to ensure it outputs the correct email. Use the following command:

```
heroku auth:whoami
```

That's it; Heroku is all set up on your system. Now it's time to create your first project.

Create an application

Visit heroku.com in your browser to create a new application. Heroku.com should redirect you to dashboard.heroku.com. If it doesn't, make sure you're logged in and try again. Once at the dashboard, in the upper right hand corner, there's a button that says **New**. Click it and select **Create new app**.

Enter application name

At the next screen, choose the deployment region and a unique app name. If you don't want to choose your app's name, leave the field blank and Heroku automatically generates a unique slug to identify the application for you. Whether you create a name, or Heroku assigns you one, make note of it; you'll use it later when configuring your app.

Click **Create app**.

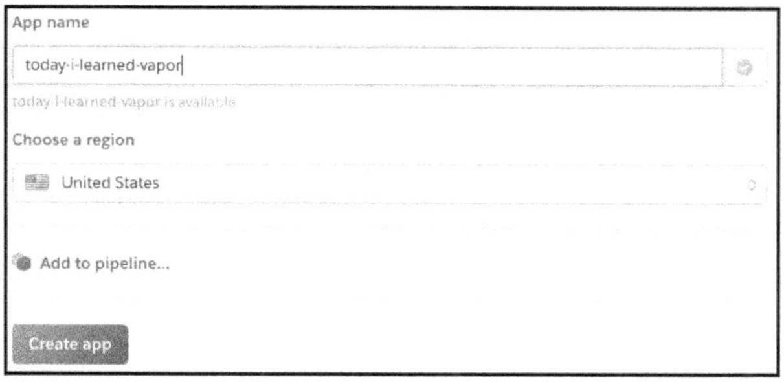

Add PostgreSQL database

After creating your application, Heroku redirects you to your application's page. Near the top, under your application's name, there is a row of tabs. Select **Resources**.

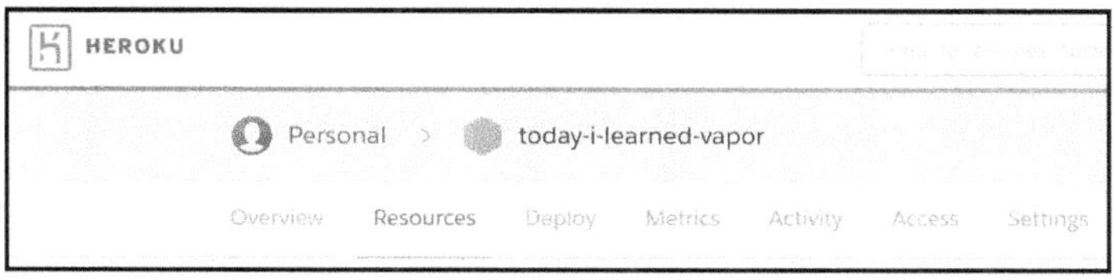

Under the section titled **Add-ons**, enter **postgres** and you'll see an option for **Heroku Postgres**. Select this option.

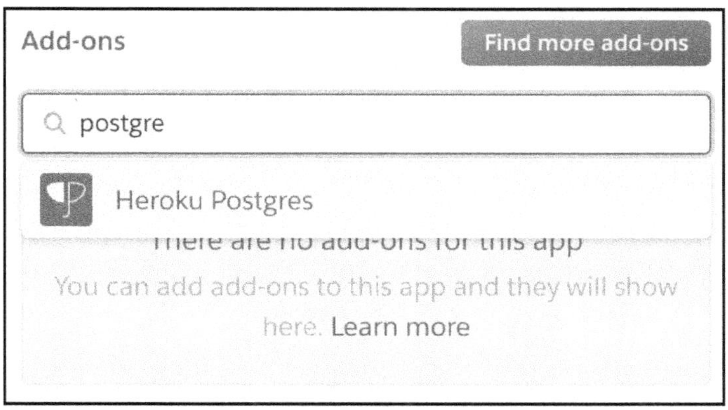

This takes you to one more screen which asks what type of database to provision. For now, provision a **Hobby Dev** - **Free** version to use.

Click **Submit Order Form** and Heroku does the rest.

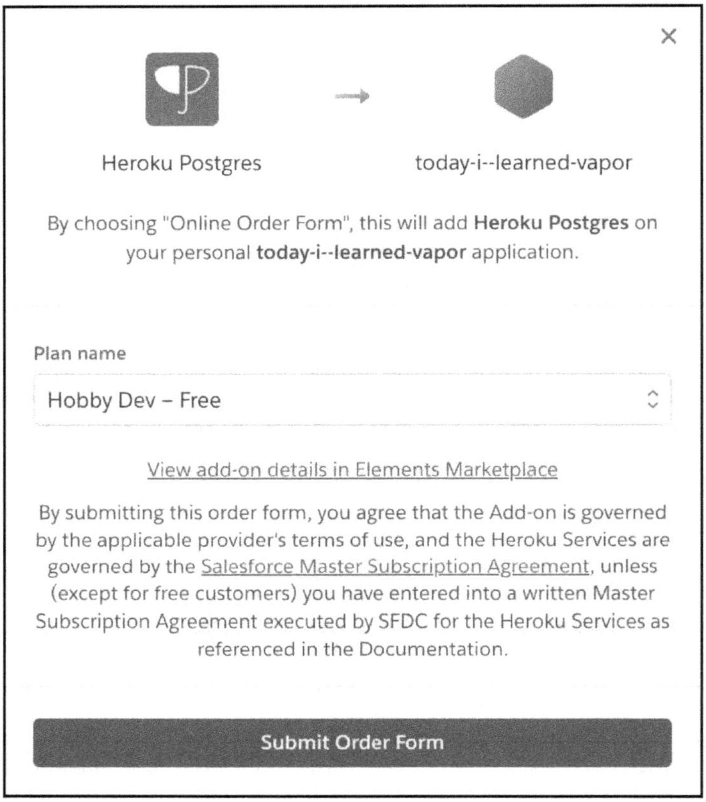

Once you finish, you'll see the database appears under the **Resources** tab.

Setting up your Vapor app locally

Your application is now setup with Heroku; the next step is to configure the Vapor app locally. Download and open the project associated with this chapter. If you've been following along with the book, it should look like the TIL project you've been working on. You're free to use your own project instead.

Git

Heroku uses Git to deploy your app, so you'll need to put your project into a Git repository, if it isn't already.

First, determine whether your application already has a Git repository. To do this, enter the following command in Terminal:

```
git rev-parse --is-inside-work-tree
```

It should output **true**. If it doesn't, then you must initialize a Git repository. Otherwise, skip the next section.

Initialize Git

If you need to add Git to your project, enter the following command in Terminal:

```
git init
git add .
git commit -m "Initial commit"
```

These commands create a local Git repository within your project and create an initial commit of your project in that repository.

Branch

Heroku deploys the **main** branch. Make sure you are on this branch and have merged any changes you wish to deploy.

To see your current branch, enter the following in Terminal:

```
git branch
```

The output will look similar to the following. The branch with the asterisk next to it is the current branch:

```
* main
```

```
  commander
  other-branches
```

If you're not currently on **main**, navigate there by entering:

```
git checkout main
```

Git may have automatically created a `master` branch for you instead of `main`. If this is the case, navigate to `master` by entering the following:

```
git checkout master
```

Subsequently, you can rename this branch by using the following command:

```
git branch -m main
```

The rest of this chapter assumes you have a `main` branch as your default branch. If you create a branch named `main` in addition to a `master` branch, it may cause issues.

Commit changes

Make sure all changes are in your main branch and committed. You can verify by entering the following command. If you see any output, it means you have uncommitted changes.

```
git status --porcelain
```

If you have uncommitted changes, enter the following commands to commit them:

```
git add .
git commit -m "a description of the changes I made"
```

This ensures your project is committed to your local repository.

Connect with Heroku

Heroku needs to configure another remote on your Git repository. Enter the following command in Terminal, substituting your app's Heroku name:

```
heroku git:remote -a your-apps-name-here
```

You can confirm the format of this command by clicking the **Deploy** tab on the Heroku dashboard in your browser and looking at the command under **Existing Git repository**.

Set Buildpack

Heroku uses something called a Buildpack to provide the recipe for building your app when you deploy it. The Vapor Community currently provides a Buildpack designed for Vapor apps. To set the Buildpack for your application, enter the following in Terminal:

```
heroku buildpacks:set \
  https://github.com/vapor-community/heroku-buildpack
```

Enable Test Discovery

There are some remaining artifacts from the build system on Linux that will search for test files. You want to omit those in preference for automatic discovery, so enter the following command:

```
heroku config:set SWIFT_BUILD_FLAGS="--enable-test-discovery"
```

Swift version file

Now that your Buildpack is set, Heroku needs a couple of configuration files. The first of these is **.swift-version**. This is used by the Buildpack to determine which version of Swift to install for the project. Enter the following command in Terminal:

```
echo "5.3" > .swift-version
```

This creates **.swift-version** with `5.3` as its contents. It's important to note that files with a leading `.` are hidden by default on macOS, so you may not see this file in finder.

Procfile

Once the app is built on Heroku, Heroku needs to know what type of process to run and how to run it. To determine this, it utilizes a special file named **Procfile**. Enter the following command to create your Procfile:

```
echo "web: Run serve --env production" \
  "--hostname 0.0.0.0 --port \$PORT" > Procfile
```

This gives Heroku the needed command to run your app. If you don't include the \ before $PORT, then it will interpret this entry as a bash command and will not run properly. Your completed Procfile should match these contents exactly:

```
web: Run serve --env production --hostname 0.0.0.0 --port $PORT
```

Commit changes

As mentioned earlier, Heroku uses Git and the main branch to deploy applications. Since you configured Git earlier, you've added two files: **Procfile** and **.swift-version**. These need to be committed before deploying or Heroku won't be able to properly build the application. Enter the following commands in Terminal:

```
git add .
git commit -m "adding heroku build files"
```

Configure the database

There's one more thing to do before you deploy your app: You must configure the database within your app. Start by listing the configuration variables for your app.

In Terminal, enter:

```
heroku config
```

You should see output similar to the following. It provides you with information about the database you provisioned for this project.

```
=== today-i-learned-vapor Config Vars
DATABASE_URL: postgres://cybntsgadydqzm:
2d9dc7f6d964f4750da1518ad71hag2ba729cd4527d4a18c70e024b11cfa8f4b
@ec2-54-221-192-231.compute-1.amazonaws.com:5432/dfr89mvoo550b4
```

There are two parts to this output; the first is **DATABASE_URL**. This represents the name of the environment variable. The second component will be similar to the following:

```
postgres://cybntsgadydqzm:
2d9dc7f6d964f4750da1518ad71hag2ba729cd4527d4a18c70e024b11cfa8f4b
@ec2-54-221-192-231.compute-1.amazonaws.com:5432/dfr89mvoo550b4
```

This component represents the actual value of the environment variable. In this case, it's the direct link to your PostgreSQL database. You can use this direct url for purposes of manually connecting to the database should you need to for some reason. However, it's important that you **NEVER** hard code this value into your application. Not only is it bad practice and unsafe, Heroku specifies that the value of this environment variable could change at any time, rendering the absolute value useless.

The important part is the environment variable's name: **DATABASE_URL**.

Open your Vapor app in Xcode and navigate to **configure.swift**. Find the section that sets up the database configuration. Look for this line:

```
app.databases.use(.postgres(
  hostname: Environment.get("DATABASE_HOST") ?? "localhost",
  port: databasePort,
  username: Environment.get("DATABASE_USERNAME") ??
    "vapor_username",
  password: Environment.get("DATABASE_PASSWORD") ??
    "vapor_password",
  database: Environment.get("DATABASE_NAME") ?? databaseName
), as: .psql)
```

This code works great for the database configurations you've used so far, but Heroku passes the entire URL, so you'll have to make use of that. Replace the line of code above with the following:

```
if var config = Environment.get("DATABASE_URL")
    .flatMap(URL.init)
    .flatMap(PostgresConfiguration.init) {
  config.tlsConfiguration = .forClient(
    certificateVerification: .none)
  app.databases.use(.postgres(
    configuration: config
  ), as: .psql)
} else {
  app.databases.use(
    .postgres(
      hostname: Environment.get("DATABASE_HOST") ??
        "localhost",
      port: databasePort,
      username: Environment.get("DATABASE_USERNAME") ??
        "vapor_username",
      password: Environment.get("DATABASE_PASSWORD") ??
        "vapor_password",
      database: Environment.get("DATABASE_NAME") ??
        databaseName),
    as: .psql)
}
```

This allows the project to retrieve the database URL from the environment if it's running on Heroku. If **DATABASE_URL** is *not* set in the environment, the app continues to use the previous method for determining its database.

Once again, you need to save your changes in Git. Enter the following in Terminal:

```
git add .
git commit -m "configured heroku database"
```

Configure Google environment variables

If you completed Chapter 22, "Google Authentication" and are using that as your project here, you must configure the same Google environment variables you used there.

Enter the following commands in Terminal:

```
heroku config:set \
  GOOGLE_CALLBACK_URL=https://<YOUR_HEROKU_URL>/oauth/google

heroku config:set GOOGLE_CLIENT_ID=<YOUR_CLIENT_ID>

heroku config:set GOOGLE_CLIENT_SECRET=<YOUR_CLIENT_SECRET>
```

You can find your Heroku URL on the **Settings** tab of the Heroku dashboard. This sets the environment variables for **GOOGLE_CALLBACK_URL**, **GOOGLE_CLIENT_ID** and **GOOGLE_CLIENT_SECRET** so they're available at runtime. Remember to visit https://console.developers.google.com to add the Heroku callback URL as an authorized redirect. See Chapter 22, "Google Authentication," if you need a refresher.

Configure GitHub environment variables

If you completed Chapter 23, "GitHub Authentication" and are using that as your project here, you must configure the same GitHub environment variables you used there.

Enter the following commands in Terminal:

```
heroku config:set \
  GITHUB_CALLBACK_URL=https://<YOUR_HEROKU_URL>/oauth/github

heroku config:set GITHUB_CLIENT_ID=<YOUR_CLIENT_ID>

heroku config:set GITHUB_CLIENT_SECRET=<YOUR_CLIENT_SECRET>
```

You can find your Heroku URL on the **Settings** tab of the Heroku dashboard. This sets the environment variables for **GITHUB_CALLBACK_URL**, **GITHUB_CLIENT_ID** and **GITHUB_CLIENT_SECRET** so they're available at runtime. Remember to visit https://github.com/settings/developers to add the Heroku callback URL as an authorized redirect. See Chapter 23, "GitHub Authentication," if you need a refresher.

Deploy to Heroku

You're now ready to deploy your app to Heroku. Push your main branch to your Heroku remote and wait for everything to build. This can take a while, particularly on a large application.

To kick things off, enter the following in Terminal:

```
git push heroku main
```

Once everything deploys, Heroku notifies you of your app's status. Heroku normally starts your app automatically when it finishes building. In the unlikely event it doesn't, enter the following in Terminal to start your app:

```
heroku ps:scale web=1
```

Going forward, pushing the **main** branch to Heroku will redeploy your app. Open your app by visiting the app URL as seen in the **Settings** tab of the Heroku dashboard in your browser. You can also open the site in a browser by entering the following in Terminal:

```
heroku open
```

Where to go from here?

In this chapter, you learned how to set up the app in the Heroku dashboard, configure your Git repository, add the necessary configuration files to your project, and deploy your app. Explore your dashboard and the Heroku Help to learn even more options!

Chapter 33: Deploying with Docker

By Tim Condon

Docker is a popular containerization technology that has made a huge impact in the way applications are deployed. Containers are a way of isolating your applications, allowing you to run multiple applications on the same server.

Using a container, instead of a full-fledged virtual machine, allows your containerized applications to share more of the host machine's resources. In turn, this leaves more resources for your application to use rather than consuming them to support the virtual machine itself.

Docker can run almost anywhere, so it provides a good way to standardize how your application should run, from local testing to production.

> **Note**: If you need a refresher on Docker terminology — concepts such as containers and images — check out our Docker tutorial at https://www.raywenderlich.com/9159-docker-on-macos-getting-started.

Docker Compose

This chapter will also show you how to use Docker Compose. Docker Compose is a way to specify a list of different containers that work together as a single unit. These containers share the same virtual network, making it simple for them cooperate with each other.

For example, with Docker Compose, you can spin up both your Vapor app and a PostgreSQL database instance with just one command. They can communicate with each other but are isolated from other instances running on the same host.

Setting up Vapor and PostgreSQL for Development

Begin by setting up a simple development configuration to test your app in a Linux environment. To facilitate debugging any problems that arise, this will be a much simpler configuration than you'll use in production.

> **Note**: This chapter's sample project is identical to the project at the end of Chapter 21, "Validation". You may use it or you may continue to use your existing project.

In the main directory for your project, create a file named **develop.Dockerfile** and add the following contents:

```
#1
FROM swift:5.3
#2
WORKDIR /app
#3
COPY . .
#4
RUN swift package clean
RUN swift build -c release  --enable-test-discovery
RUN mkdir /app/bin
RUN mv `swift build -c release --show-bin-path` /app/bin
EXPOSE 8080
#5
ENTRYPOINT ./bin/release/Run serve --env local \
  --hostname 0.0.0.0
```

A **Dockerfile** provides the "recipe" for creating a Docker container for your app.

Here's what this one does:

1. Use version 5.3 of the "swift" image from the Docker Hub repository as the starting point.
2. Tell Docker to use **/app** as its working directory.
3. Copy your project to the Docker container.
4. Build your project and move the executable to **/app/bin** within the container. Note the use of `--enable-test-discovery`. Swift requires this to build your project even though you're not running any tests.
5. Tell Docker how to start the Vapor app.

Next, also in your project's main directory, create a file named **docker-compose-develop.yml** and add the following contents:

```
# 1
version: '3'
# 2
services:
  # 3
  til-app:
    # 4
    depends_on:
      - postgres
    # 5
    build:
      context: .
      dockerfile: develop.Dockerfile
    # 6
    ports:
      - "8080:8080"
    environment:
      - DATABASE_HOST=postgres
      - DATABASE_PORT=5432
  # 7
  postgres:
    # 8
    image: "postgres"
    # 9
    environment:
      - POSTGRES_DB=vapor_database
      - POSTGRES_USER=vapor_username
      - POSTGRES_PASSWORD=vapor_password

  # 10
  start_dependencies:
    image: dadarek/wait-for-dependencies
    depends_on:
```

```
      - postgres
    command: postgres:5432
```

A Docker Compose file specifies the "recipe" for your entire app with all of its dependencies. Here's what this one does:

1. Specify the Docker Compose version.
2. Define the services for this application.
3. Define a service for the TIL application.
4. Set a dependency on the `postgres` service so Docker Compose starts the PostgreSQL container first.
5. Build **develop.Dockerfile** in the current directory. This is the **Dockerfile** you created earlier.
6. Make port 8080 accessible on the host system and inject the `DATABASE_HOST` environment variable. Docker Compose has an internal DNS resolver. This allows the `til-app` container to connect to the `postgres` container with the hostname `postgres`. Also set the port for the database. You can specify any other environment variable values your app needs here, such as GitHub OAuth credentials.
7. Define a service for the PostgreSQL database.
8. Use the standard `postgres` image.
9. Set the necessary environment variables.
10. Docker starts all containers at once and PostgreSQL takes several seconds to become ready to accept connections. If TILapp starts before PostgreSQL is ready, TILapp will crash. This service provides a way to ensure the database is running before starting your app.

To bring your app to life, enter the following commands in Terminal:

```
# 1
docker-compose -f docker-compose-develop.yml build
# 2
docker-compose -f docker-compose-develop.yml run --rm
start_dependencies
# 3
docker-compose -f docker-compose-develop.yml up til-app
```

Here's what this does:

1. Build the different Docker images defined in **docker-compose-develop.yml**.
2. Run the `start_dependencies` service from **docker-compose-develop.yml** to ensure that PostgreSQL is running and ready.
3. Start your app.

> If you receive an error stating the **"vapor"** database is not found, follow the clean up steps below and retry the commands above and the application should start successfully. This error might occur if you have previous Docker PostgreSQL images on your system.

In your browser, visit **http://localhost:8080** to verify the app is up and running. When you're ready to move ahead, press **Control-C** to stop everything. Then, clean up your development environment by entering the following in Terminal:

```
docker-compose -f docker-compose-develop.yml down
docker volume prune -f
```

This shuts down any running containers from the compose file. It then removes all containers and network definitions associated with your app. Finally, it cleans up any old Docker storage you can no longer access.

Setting up Vapor and PostgreSQL for Production

There are several changes you can make to your Docker configuration to simplify managing your app in a production environment. In this section, you'll split your app into a "builder" container and a production image. You'll also configure the PostgreSQL container to save its database in your host's file system. This makes your data persist across changes to your app and its configuration.

The Vapor template already contains a Dockerfile suitable for production, named **Dockerfile**. Open the file in a text editor to inspect it's contents. It looks something like this:

```
# 1
FROM swift:5.3-focal as build
```

```
# 2
RUN export DEBIAN_FRONTEND=noninteractive
DEBCONF_NONINTERACTIVE_SEEN=true \
    && apt-get -q update \
    && apt-get -q dist-upgrade -y \
    && rm -rf /var/lib/apt/lists/*

# 3
WORKDIR /build

# 4
COPY ./Package.* ./
RUN swift package resolve

# 5
COPY . .
RUN swift build --enable-test-discovery -c release

# 6
WORKDIR /staging
RUN cp "$(swift build --package-path /build -c release \
    --show-bin-path)/Run" ./
RUN [ -d /build/Public ] && \
    { mv /build/Public ./Public && chmod -R a-w ./Public; } \
    || true
RUN [ -d /build/Resources ] && \
    { mv /build/Resources ./Resources && \
    chmod -R a-w ./Resources; } || true

# 7
FROM swift:5.3-focal-slim

# 8
RUN export DEBIAN_FRONTEND=noninteractive \
    DEBCONF_NONINTERACTIVE_SEEN=true && \
    apt-get -q update && \
    apt-get -q dist-upgrade -y && \
    rm -r /var/lib/apt/lists/*

# 9
RUN useradd --user-group --create-home --system \
    --skel /dev/null --home-dir /app vapor
# 10
WORKDIR /app
# 11
COPY --from=build --chown=vapor:vapor /staging /app
# 12
USER vapor:vapor
# 13
EXPOSE 8080
# 14
ENTRYPOINT ["./Run"]
CMD ["serve", "--env", "production", "--hostname",
```

```
      "0.0.0.0", "--port", "8080"]
```

1. Use version 5.3 of the "swift" image from the Docker Hub repository as the starting point. This container is only for building your app and you may delete it once Docker builds the app.
2. Update the system packages, then clean up the working files. This cleanup is a standard operation when building Docker images based on Linux. It reduces the overall size of the image.
3. Tell Docker to use **/build** as its working directory.
4. Copy **Package.swift** and **Package.resolved** and resolve the app's dependencies. This allows Docker to cache dependencies between builds, if required.
5. Copy your project to the Docker container. Build the project with the release configuration.
6. Create a staging directory and copy the executable and any required libraries into it. Also copy the **Public** directory and **Resources** directory if they exist. You need to do this if you use Leaf, for example.
7. Base your production image on Swift's slim Docker image. This contains only what's necessary to run a Swift executable. This is significantly smaller than the image required to *build* a Swift executable.
8. Update all packages, then clean up the working files.
9. Create a user to run the executable. This avoids running the executable as root, which can be a security risk.
10. Tell Docker to use **/app** as the working directory.
11. Copy files from the builder container.
12. Set the user to the one created in step 9.
13. Expose port 8080 so clients can connect to the Vapor app in the Docker container.
14. Tell Docker how to start the Vapor app.

Next, also in your project's main directory, open **docker-compose.yml** in a text editor. This contains a production ready compose file. The contents looks similar to the following:

```
# 1
version: '3.7'
```

```
# 2
volumes:
  db_data:

# 3
x-shared_environment: &shared_environment
  LOG_LEVEL: ${LOG_LEVEL:-debug}
  DATABASE_HOST: db
  DATABASE_NAME: vapor_database
  DATABASE_USERNAME: vapor_username
  DATABASE_PASSWORD: vapor_password

# 4
services:
  # 5
  app:
    # 6
    image: tilapp:latest
    # 7
    build:
      context: .
    # 8
    environment:
      <<: *shared_environment
    # 9
    depends_on:
      - db
    # 10
    ports:
      - '8080:8080'
    # 11
    command: ["serve", "--env", "production", "--hostname",
              "0.0.0.0", "--port", "8080"]
  # 12
  db:
    # 13
    image: postgres:12-alpine
    # 14
    volumes:
      - db_data:/var/lib/postgresql/data/pgdata
    # 15
    environment:
      PGDATA: /var/lib/postgresql/data/pgdata
      POSTGRES_USER: vapor_username
      POSTGRES_PASSWORD: vapor_password
      POSTGRES_DB: vapor_database
    ports:
      - '5432:5432'
```

The compose file also contains services for `migrate` and `revert` but these aren't included here for brevity. Here's what the compose file does:

1. Specify the Docker Compose version.
2. Specify a list of volumes used by this application.
3. Define a number of shared environment variables, such as database credentials. This allows you to define variables in a single place and share them across different services, such as the main app, migrate and revert. You can specify any variables you require here, such as OAuth Client details.
4. Define the services for this application.
5. Define a service for the TIL application.
6. Specify the image for this service. Docker Compose reuses the images across different services so you don't have to rebuild it different use cases.
7. Specify the build context for the service. By default this uses **Dockerfile** discussed earlier.
8. Specify any environment variables for the service. Include the shared environment variables from step 2.
9. Set a dependency on the `db` service so Docker Compose starts the PostgreSQL container first if not already started.
10. Expose port 8080 to allow you to connect to the app when it's running.
11. Specify the command to use to start the app. Migrate and revert use different commands.
12. Define a service for the PostgreSQL database.
13. Use the Alpine `postgres` image. This is a full PostgreSQL database running in a very lightweight container.
14. Set up a persistent volume from **~/db_data** into the container. This causes the data to live in the host system's file system rather than inside a Docker container and allows it to persist across launches.
15. Set the necessary environment variables.

> **Important**: Docker compose doesn't allow image names to contain capital letters. At the time of writing, the toolbox doesn't account for this so you may need to lowercase the image names manually, as shown above.

First, ensure that you stop any existing PostgreSQL containers from previous chapters:

```
docker stop postgres
```

To bring your app to life, enter the following commands in Terminal:

```
docker-compose build
docker-compose up -d db
docker-compose up app
```

These commands build the different containers, start the database in the background and then start the app.

Where to go from here?

You've seen some basic recipes for how to run your app in a Docker environment. Because Docker is so flexible, these recipes only scratch the surface of the possibilities available to you. For example, you might want to allow your app to save uploaded files in the host's file system. Or, you might want to configure the app to run behind an Nginx proxy server to get secure HTTPS access.

Chapter 34: Deploying with AWS

By Tim Condon

Amazon Web Services (AWS) is by far the largest Cloud provider today. It provides many service offerings which simplify the deployment and maintenance of applications. In this chapter, you'll learn how to use a few of these to deploy a Vapor app.

Before starting

To perform the steps in this chapter, you must have an AWS account. If you don't already have one, follow the instructions at https://aws.amazon.com/premiumsupport/knowledge-center/create-and-activate-aws-account/ to create one.

Setup your AWS instance

Your first step is to start an EC2 instance. EC2 is an AWS Virtual Machine product. This gives you a plain Linux machine you can use to run your Vapor application.

For this example, you'll create an Ubuntu 20.04 instance. 20.04 is the latest LTS (Long Term Service) version from Ubuntu.

First, you must decide which region you want to use. Click the drop-down next to your name and select the region closest to you.

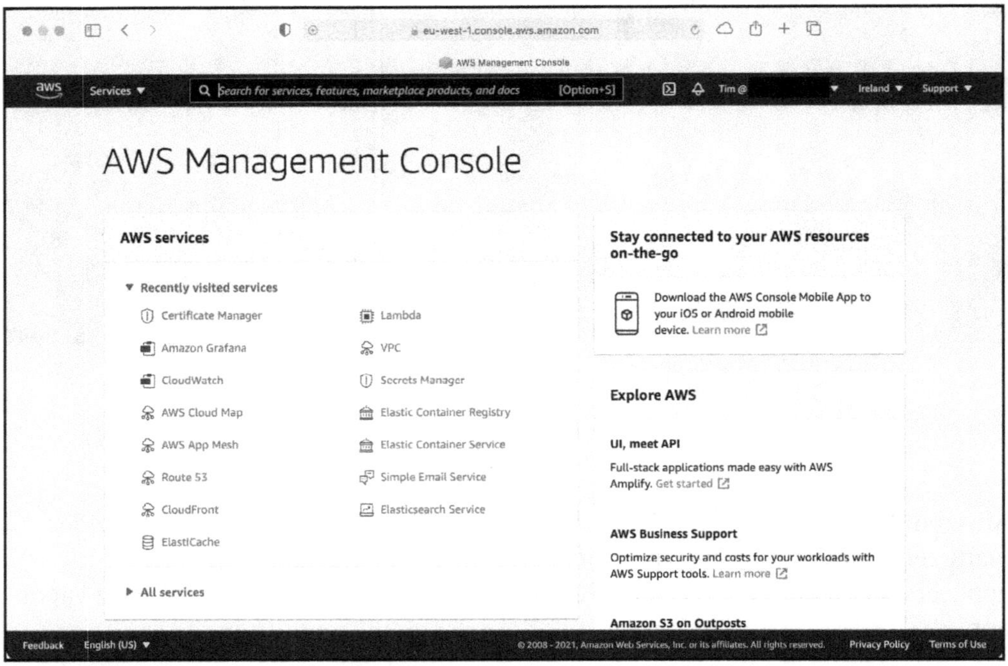

After selecting the region, click **Services** and **EC2**.

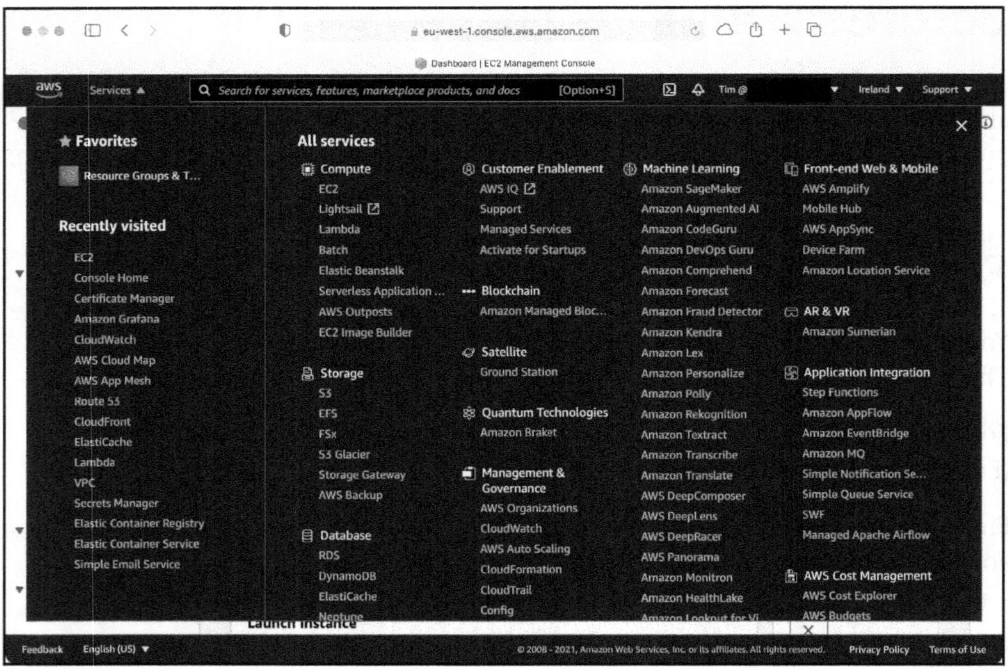

Before you start your instance, you must create a **Security Group**. This is essentially the firewall for your instance, allowing you to specify which ports are open on the server.

Click **Security Groups**, then click **Create Security Group**.

In the resulting dialog, enter a **Security group name** and **Description** that will make it easy for you to associate it with your app. For this example, name your group **vapor-til**.

Under the **Inbound** section, click **Add Rule** to add a new rule. Use the drop-down under **Type** to select **SSH**. Under **Source**, choose **My IP**. Repeat the process for **HTTP** and **HTTPS** but set **Source** to **Anywhere**. Your screen should look similar to the following:

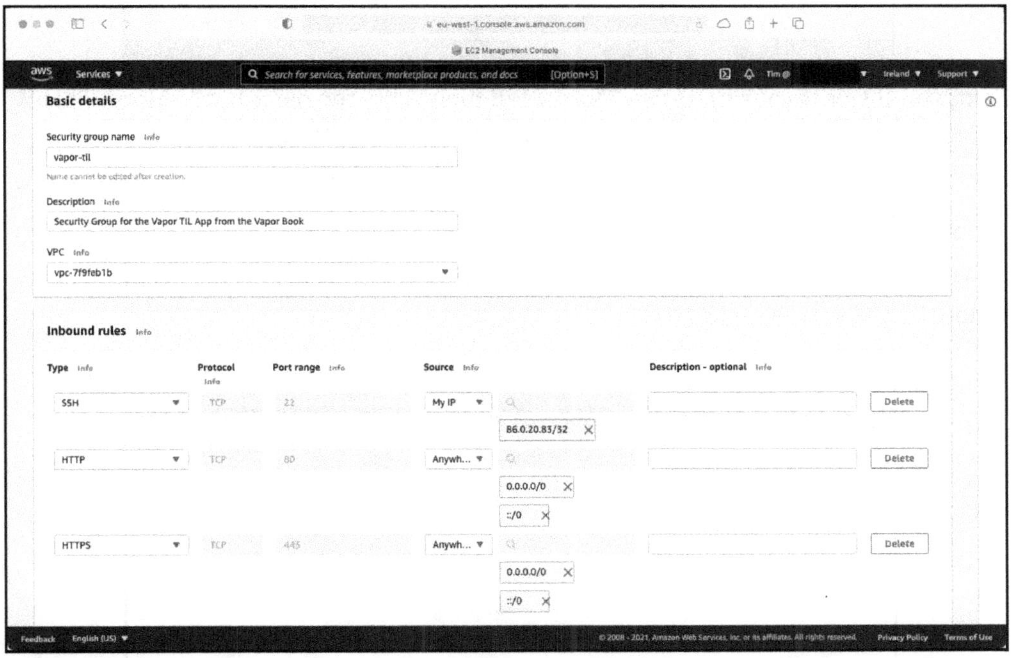

Click **Create security group** at the bottom of the page to create your security group.

You're now ready to create your instance. Click **Instances** and **Launch Instances**. This begins a seven step process to configure and launch an EC2 instance.

First, you must pick an Amazon Machine Image (AMI) as the base for your EC2 instance. To simplify finding the correct AMI, enter **20.04** in the search box and check **Free tier only**. Choose the one called **Ubuntu Server 20.04 LTS** by clicking **Select** in its row.

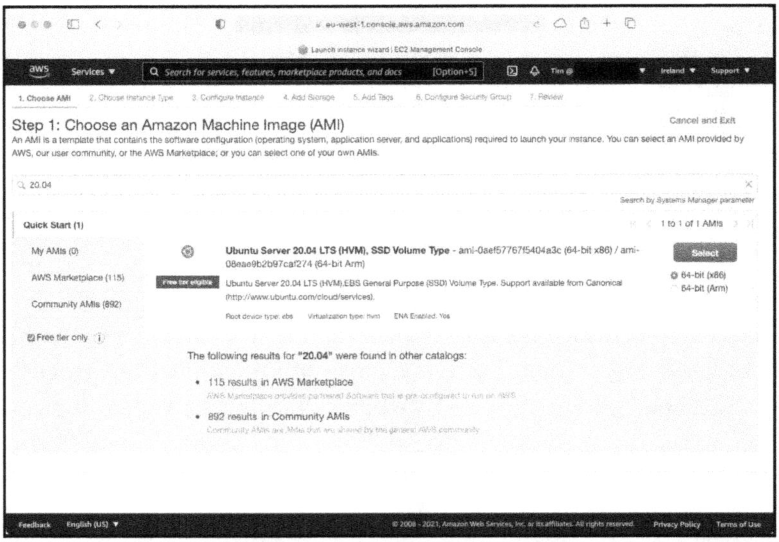

Next, you'll select your **Instance Type**. AWS highlights the default, **t2.micro**. This is **Free tier eligible**, meaning you get 1GB memory and 1vCPU for free for the first 12 months you have your account. You'll stick with this choice.

Click **Next: Configure Instance Details**.

On this page, you can set up various details for your instance. For this example, simply leave everything as it is.

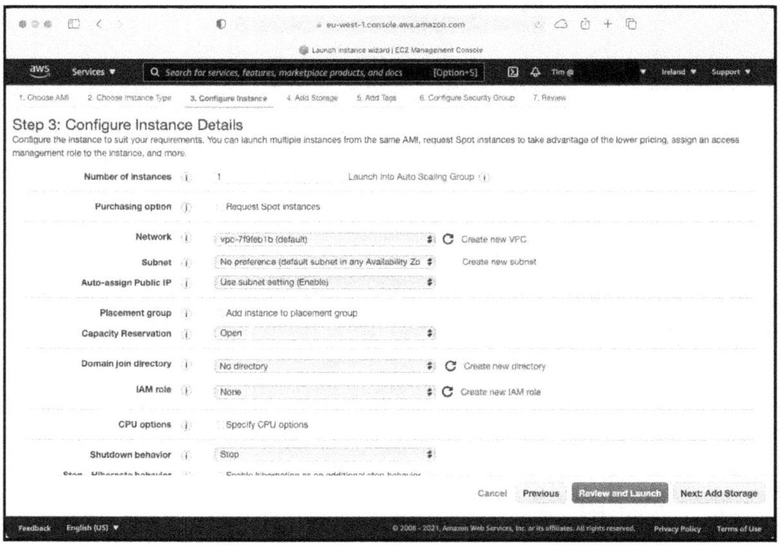

Click **Next: Add Storage**.

On this page, you'll configure the volume for your app. Change **Size** to **20**; this will give you plenty of space for your app.

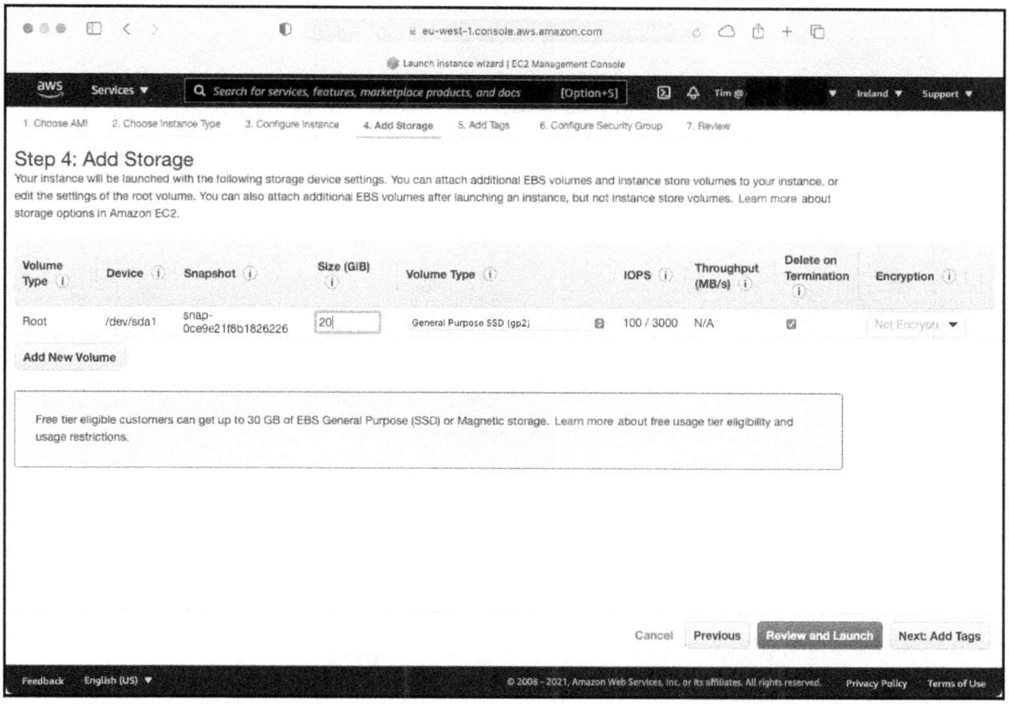

Click **Next: Add Tags.**

This page allows you to add tags to your instance. This step is optional but doing so will simplify managing your AWS resources as your usage grows. Click **Add Tag** and enter the following values:

- **Key**: Name
- **Value**: vapor-til

This gives the instance the name **vapor-til.**

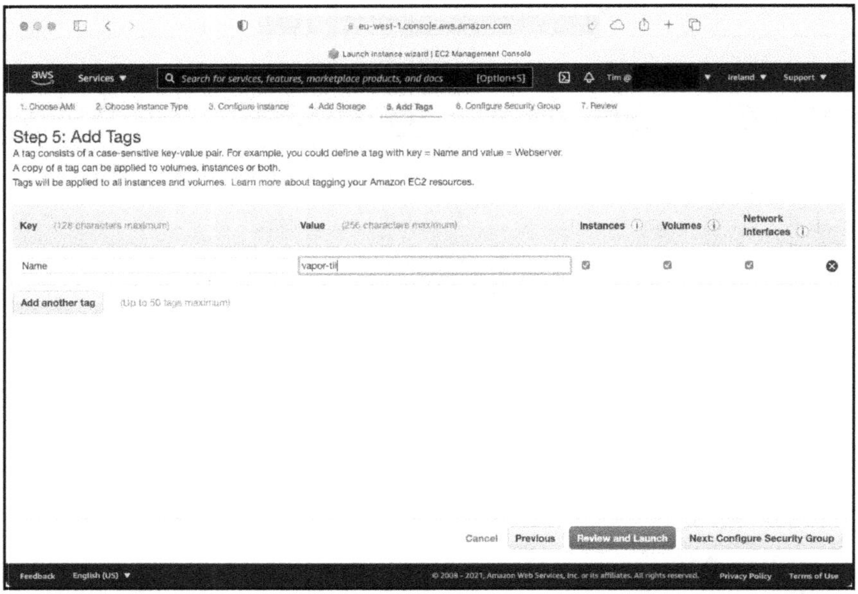

Click **Next: Configure Security Group.**

On this page, you'll attach the security group you created earlier to your instance. Click the **Select an *existing* security group** radio button. Then, select your **vapor-til** group:

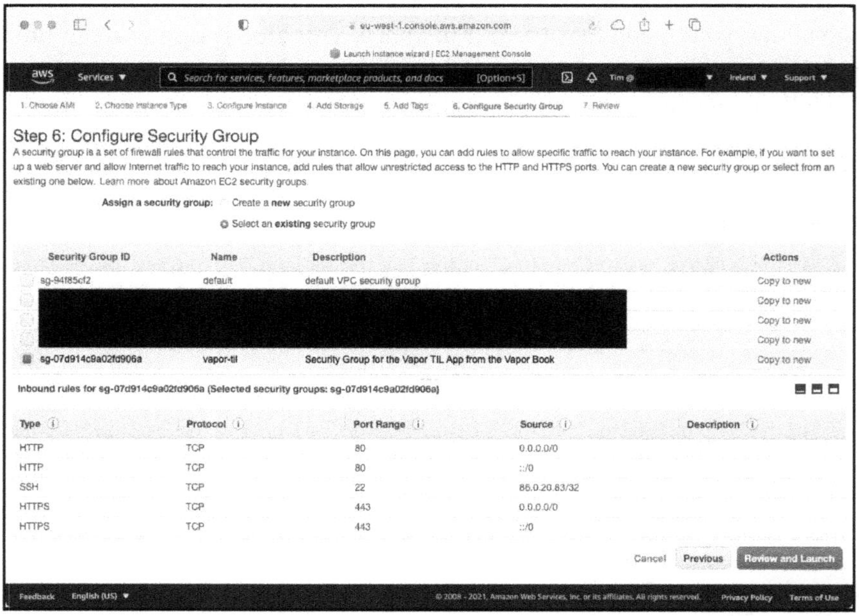

Finally, click **Review and Launch**.

On this page, you can verify the options you chose previously. When you're satisfied, click **Launch**. AWS will prompt you to either select an existing key pair or create a new one. You need a key pair to allow you SSH access to your instance, so don't skip this step. If you create a new key pair, remember to click **Download Key Pair**.

Once you have configured and saved your key pair, click **Launch Instances**.

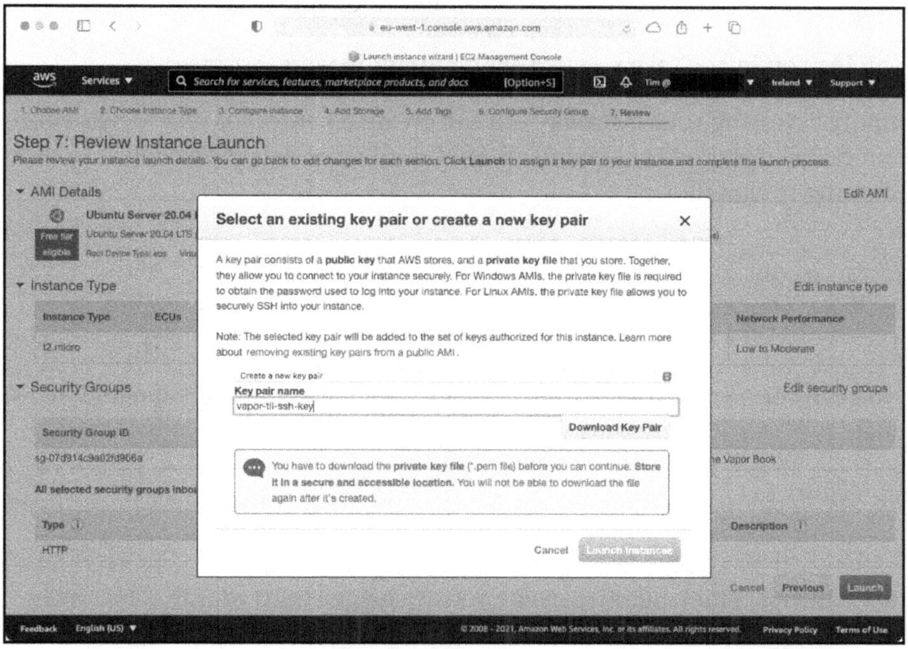

AWS will confirm that it is starting your instance. Click **View Instances** to return to your instance summary page. If you're quick enough, your instance will show an **Instance State** of **Pending** with a yellow indicator. After a little while, it will show as **Running** and have a green indicator.

Copy the **IPv4 Public IP**. You'll use this to login to your instance.

SSH requires that you set your private key as read-only to its owner — that would be you — with no access to anyone else. If the file has any other protection set, SSH will refuse to use it. In Terminal, enter following command set protect your private key:

```
chmod 600 /path/to/your/ssh/key
```

> **Note**: Generally, SSH keys and other related files should be in the hidden directory **~/.ssh**. If you didn't put your key there, please consider doing so before setting its protection.

Now, in Terminal, enter the following command:

```
ssh -i /location/to/your/ssh/key ubuntu@your-aws-ip
```

This will log you in and take you to a shell prompt in your instance.

To simplify accessing your instance, you can create an entry for it in **~/.ssh/config**. Use your favorite text editor — nano, vi, Sublime Text are all good choices — to add the following to that file:

```
Host vapor-til
    HostName <your public IP or public DNS name>
    User ubuntu
    IdentityFile </path/to/your/key/file>
```

Now, you can connect to your instance by entering the following command in Terminal:

```
ssh vapor-til
```

> The following commands all assume you are logged in to your EC2 instance and have root access.

On a new system, it's always a good idea to make sure all packages are up to date. To update your system, enter the following commands:

```
sudo apt-get update
sudo apt-get upgrade -y
```

Install Swift

To build your Vapor app, you must install Swift on your EC2 instance. Swift supports a number of Linux platforms, including Ubuntu and CentOS. Visit https://swift.org/getting-started/ for details on installing for your platform.

First, download the toolchain for your platform. You can find the latest toolchain at https://swift.org/download/#releases. For example, in terminal, run:

```
wget https://swift.org/builds/swift-5.3.2-release/ubuntu2004/
swift-5.3.2-RELEASE/swift-5.3.2-RELEASE-ubuntu20.04.tar.gz
```

This downloads the toolchain for Swift 5.3.2 to your local directory. Next, unzip the downloaded file:

```
tar -xzf swift-5.3.2-RELEASE-ubuntu20.04.tar.gz
```

This extracts the downloaded file into the current working directory.

Next, install the dependencies required for your system. For Ubuntu 20.04, in Terminal, enter:

```
sudo apt-get install binutils git gnupg2 libc6-dev \
  libcurl4 libedit2 libgcc-9-dev libpython2.7 \
  libsqlite3-0 libstdc++-9-dev libxml2 libz3-dev \
  pkg-config tzdata zlib1g-dev -y
```

Finally, add the Swift toolchain to your path so you can use it from the command line. In Terminal, run:

```
echo "export PATH=/home/ubuntu/swift-5.3.2-RELEASE-ubuntu20.04/
usr/bin:${PATH}" >> .profile
source .profile
```

> **Note**: If you download a newer version of the toolchain, be sure to update the path to reflect the new version.

This adds the directory to the Swift binary to your profile and reloads it. **Important:** remember to set the directory to the path where your Swift installation exists.

You can verify your installation by entering:

```
swift --version
```

You should see the correct version returned:

System Memory

The Swift compiler can use a lot of memory. Small cloud instances, such as a **t2.micro**, don't contain enough memory for the Swift compiler to work. You can solve this problem by enabling swap space. In Terminal, enter the following:

```
sudo su -
fallocate -l 2G /swapfile
chmod 600 /swapfile
mkswap /swapfile
swapon /swapfile
exit
```

These commands switch to a super user and create a 2GB swap file. This should be enough to allow the compiler to work.

Setting up your application

To set up your application, you will first clone it from GitHub. To build the TILapp example from the rest of the book, enter the following commands:

```
# 1
git clone https://github.com/raywenderlich/vapor-til.git
# 2
cd vapor-til
# 3
swift build -c release --enable-test-discovery
```

Here's what this does:

1. Clone the vapor-til project from GitHub.
2. Change to the vapor-til folder.
3. Build the project in release mode.

After building the project, you can try to start the app by entering:

```
./.build/release/Run
```

This won't work because you haven't set up a database or the necessary environment variables.

Setting up a PostgreSQL server

For your database, you will use Amazon Relational Database Service (RDS). This AWS database service supports several popular relational database systems, including PostgreSQL.

Before creating your database, you need to configure another security group. Click **Services** at the top of your AWS page and enter **VPC** in the search bar. This will take you to the VPC dashboard. Click **Your VPCs** to show your VPC (Virtual Private Cloud) information. Choose the VPC you chose for the EC2 instance earlier. In the description section, make a note of your **IPv4 CIDR**. It will be something like **172.31.0.0/16**.

Now, in the console click **Security Groups** in the list on the left. The resulting screen should now look familiar. Click **Create Security Group**. Name the group **vapor-til database**.

On the **Inbound** tab, click **Add Rule**. Select **PostgreSQL** from the **Type** drop-down and enter your IPv4 CIDR in the **Source** box.

Your screen should look something like this:

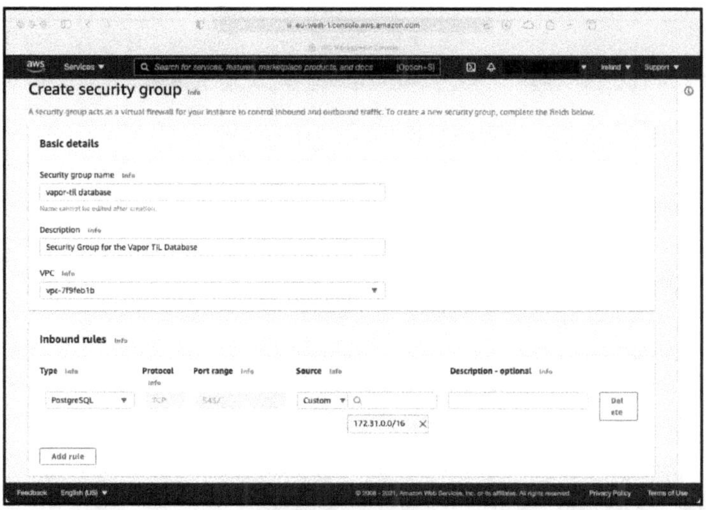

Click **Create security group**.

In the AWS Console, click **Services** and find **RDS**. Click **Create Database**. This will display the **Select engine** page. Choose **PostgreSQL** as your engine.

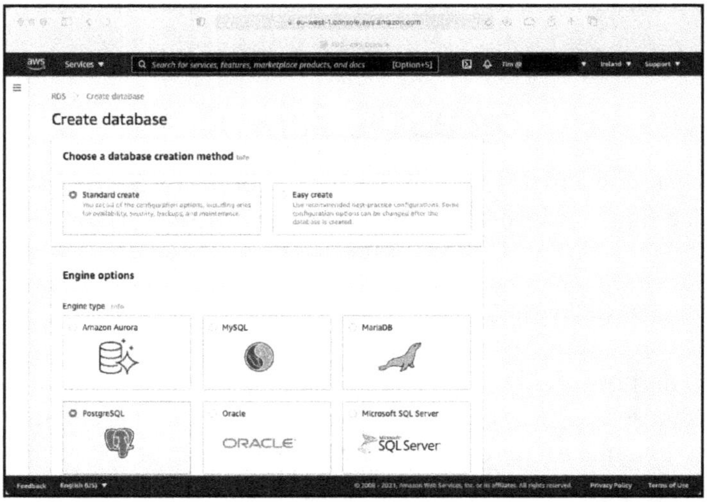

Next, you must choose your use case. For this tutorial, select **Dev/Test**. Below that, you're asked to specify some details about your database. Under **Settings**, enter the following information:

- **DB instance identifier**: vapor-til
- **Master username**: vaportil
- **Master password** and **Confirm password**: your choice

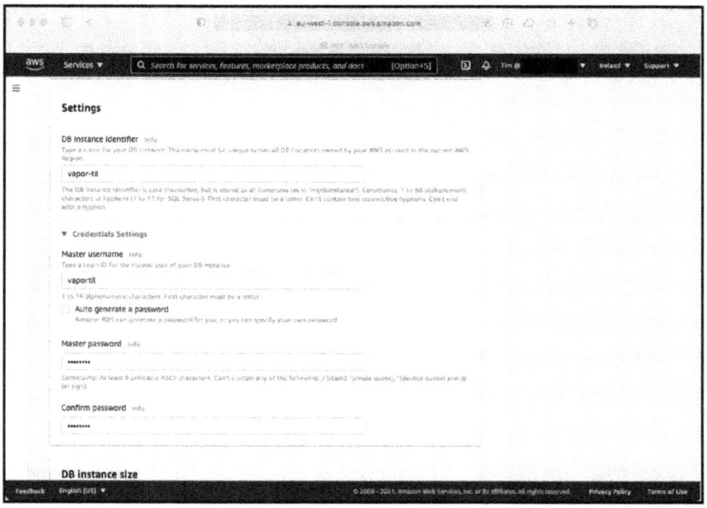

Next, under **DB instance size**, select the **Burstable classes** radio button and choose **db.t3.micro** from the drop-down list.

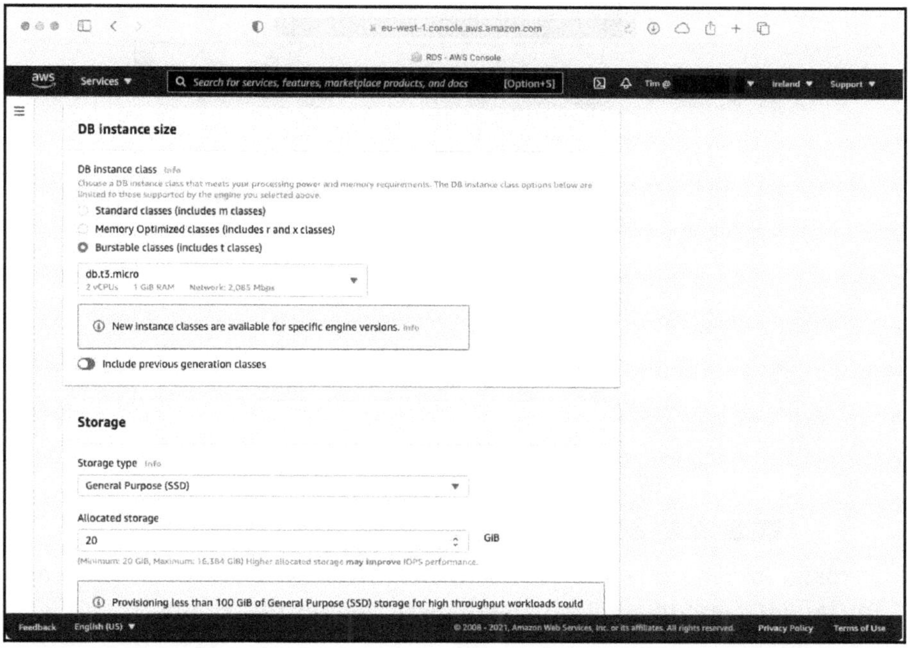

Then, under **Connectivity**, ensure you pick the same VPC as your EC2 instance. Next, set **Public accessibility** to **Yes**. This will allow you to access the database from your local machine, should you so desire.

> **Note**: If you do wish to access your database from your local machine, you'll need to add a rule to your security group to permit the access.

Set **VPC security groups** to **Choose existing VPC security groups**. Click the **X** next to **Default** to remove that group and add **vapor-til database** from the drop-down. Leave the other settings at their defaults.

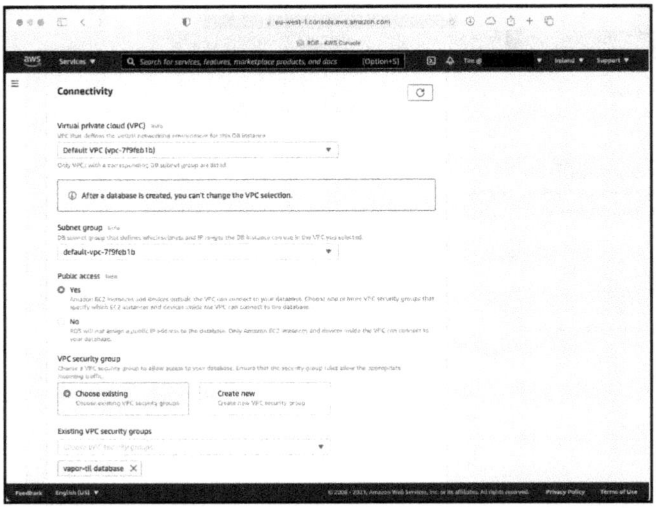

Finally, expand **Additional configuration.** Under **Database options**, enter **vaportil** as the **Initial database name**. Leave all other options as the default.

Scroll to the bottom of the page and click **Create database**. It will take some time for this to complete. Click the database in the database list to view its details. Find the **Endpoint** in the **Connectivity & security** section and make a note of it. You'll need it shortly.

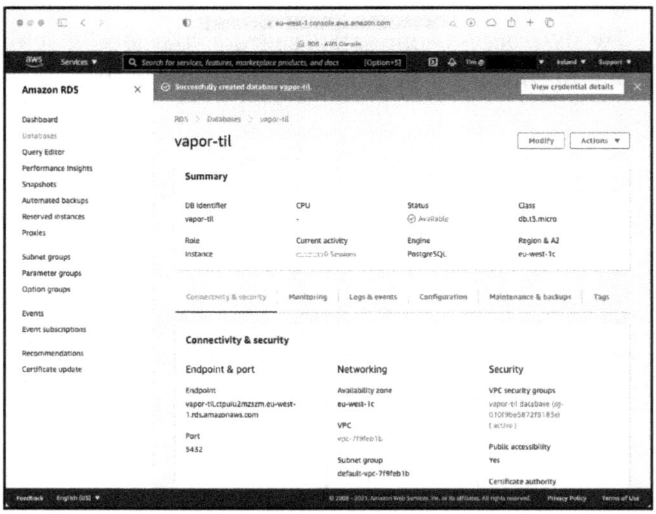

Installing and configuring nginx

`nginx` is a popular web server, typically used as a proxy server in front of other web apps. For Vapor apps, this is useful because it provides additional features such as compression, caching, HTTP/2 support, TLS (HTTPS) and more.

The example here is very simple and just gets you going. However, it's easy to customize to allow for more features.

Begin by installing nginx on your EC2 instance. SSH into your EC2 instance and enter the following commands:

```
sudo su -
apt-get install nginx -y
```

This switches to the super user and install nginx from the APT repository. For setting up nginx config, create a file in **/etc/nginx/sites-available** called **vapor-til** and add the following content to it with your favorite editor:

```
server {
  listen 80;

  root /home/ubuntu/vapor-til/Public;
  try_files $uri @proxy;

  location @proxy {
    proxy_pass http://localhost:8080;
    proxy_pass_header Server;
    proxy_set_header Host $host;
    proxy_set_header X-Real-IP $remote_addr;
    proxy_set_header X-Forwarded-For $proxy_add_x_forwarded_for;
    proxy_connect_timeout 3s;
    proxy_read_timeout 10s;
  }
}
```

Then run the following commands

```
# 1
rm /etc/nginx/sites-enabled/default
# 2
ln -s /etc/nginx/sites-available/vapor-til \
  /etc/nginx/sites-enabled/vapor-til
# 3
systemctl reload nginx
```

Here's what this does:

1. Disable the default site.
2. Enable your vapor-til site.
3. Reload nginx to activate your changes.

Before you can test all of this, you need a way to start your app.

Running your app as a system service

You want your app to run when your instance boots and to restart if it crashes due to a critical error. The easiest way to accomplish this is to integrate it as a system service. Most versions of Linux that Swift — and, therefore, Vapor — support use a service called `systemd` to accomplish this.

You'll need to add two files to your running system. One which contains all the environment variables your app needs and one which defines your app's service.

> **Note**: You can do it all in one file but this division makes it simpler to adjust environment variables should that become necessary.

First, SSH to your EC2 instance and become root again, if you aren't already. In Terminal, enter:

```
sudo su -
```

Next, use your favorite editor to create **/etc/vapor-til.conf** and add the following to it:

```
DATABASE_HOST='<your AWS RDS endpoint>'
DATABASE_USERNAME='vaportil'
DATABASE_NAME='vaportil'
DATABASE_PASSWORD='<your chosen password>'
SENDGRID_API_KEY='test'
GOOGLE_CALLBACK_URL='test'
GOOGLE_CLIENT_ID='test'
GOOGLE_CLIENT_SECRET='test'
GITHUB_CALLBACK_URL='test'
GITHUB_CLIENT_ID='test'
GITHUB_CLIENT_SECRET='test'
SIWA_REDIRECT_URL='test'
IOS_APPLICATION_IDENTIFIER='test'
WEBSITE_APPLICATION_IDENTIFIER='test'
```

This sets the environment variables the TILapp uses to find its database and to integrate with other services. They are identical to the environment you've been creating in Xcode in other chapters.

> **Note**: To have all of the pieces of TILapp working correctly, you'll need to substitute valid values for all of the SENDGRID, GOOGLE, GITHUB and SIWA values. See chapters 22–26 for how to configure these. For now, any non-empty string will allow the app to run.

Next, use your favorite editor to create **/etc/systemd/system/vapor-til.service** and add the following to it:

```
# 1
[Unit]
Description="Vapor TILapp"
After=network.target

# 2
[Service]
User=ubuntu
EnvironmentFile=/etc/vapor-til.conf
WorkingDirectory=/home/ubuntu/vapor-til

# 3
Restart=always

# 4
ExecStart=/home/ubuntu/vapor-til/.build/release/Run \
  --env production

[Install]
WantedBy=multi-user.target
```

Here's what this does:

1. `systemd` refers to an item it manages as a **unit**. This section defines the unit for your app and specifies that it can't start until after the network is started.
2. Specify the parameters for your app's service. You can have the app run as any valid user. Notice that you use the configuration file you created earlier to describe the environment in this section.
3. Tell `systemd` that it should always attempt to restart your app if it fails.
4. Specify the command `systemd` will execute to start your app. You can add additional arguments here should that be necessary.

After saving the changes to the service definition file, you must tell `systemd` to read it in order to have it recognize the service. Enter the following command:

```
systemctl daemon-reload
```

This will make `vapor-til.service` available as an option. With the following commands, you'll discover that standard keyboard shortcuts, such as tab completion, work with your new service just as they do with existing system services.

To start your app and enable it to start automatically after a reboot, enter the following commands:

```
systemctl start vapor-til.service
systemctl enable vapor-til.service
```

Your app should launch. You can check its status by entering:

```
systemctl status -l vapor-til.service
```

You should see the server starting:

Once your app is running, you should be able to access it by entering your EC2 instance's Public DNS name (the same one you use for SSH) into your browser.

Should you need to restart your app manually, use the following command:

```
systemctl restart vapor-til.service
```

And, if you wish to stop your app, the following command does the trick:

```
systemctl stop vapor-til.service
```

Where to go from here?

You now have the basics of how to set up a Vapor app on AWS. There are many more things AWS allows, such as scaling, IP pooling, automatic backups, replication and so on. You can add load balancers and custom DNS names with TLS certificates. There are also other deployment options, such as running in Docker or even using AWS Lambda. Covering all of AWS would be a whole book in itself! Spend some time with the AWS documentation and tutorials to learn more.

When you're finished with your EC2 instance and RDS database from this chapter, be sure to **Delete** the database instance and **Terminate** the EC2 instance so AWS will delete them and you avoid paying any (additional) charges for them.

Chapter 35: Production Concerns & Redis

By Tim Condon

One of the most exciting parts of programming is sharing what you've created with the world. For web applications, this usually means deploying your project to a server that is accessible via the internet.

Web servers can be dedicated machines in a data center, containers in a cloud or even a Raspberry Pi sitting in your closet. As long as your server can run Swift and has a connection to the internet, you can use it to deploy Vapor applications.

In this chapter, you'll learn the advantages and disadvantages of some common deployment methods for Vapor. You'll also learn how to properly optimize, configure and monitor your applications to increase efficiency and uptime.

Using environments

Every instance of `Application` has an associated `Environment`. Each environment has a `String` name. Common environments include: `production`, `development`, and `testing`. You can retrieve the current environment from the `environment` property of `Application`.

```
print(req.application.environment) // "production"
```

For the most part, the environment is there for you to use as you wish while configuring your application.

However, some parts of Vapor will behave differently when running in a release environment. Some differences include hiding debug information in 500 errors and reducing the verbosity of error logs.

Because of this, make sure you are using the `production` environment when running your application in production.

Choosing an environment

Most templates include code to detect the current environment when the application runs. If you open **main.swift** in your project's `Run` module, you'll see something similar to the following:

```
import App
import Vapor

var env = try Environment.detect()
try LoggingSystem.bootstrap(from: &env)
let app = Application(env)
defer { app.shutdown() }
try configure(app)
try app.run()
```

This code calls `Environment.detect()`, which parses the command line arguments passed to your application and returns the environment specified. If you don't specify an environment, Vapor uses `development` by default. You can specify the environment using the `--env` flag followed by the name of the environment.

You can do this when running your application's executable from the command line using `swift run`.

```
swift run Run serve --env development
```

You can also specify the environment when running your application from within Xcode using the scheme editor.

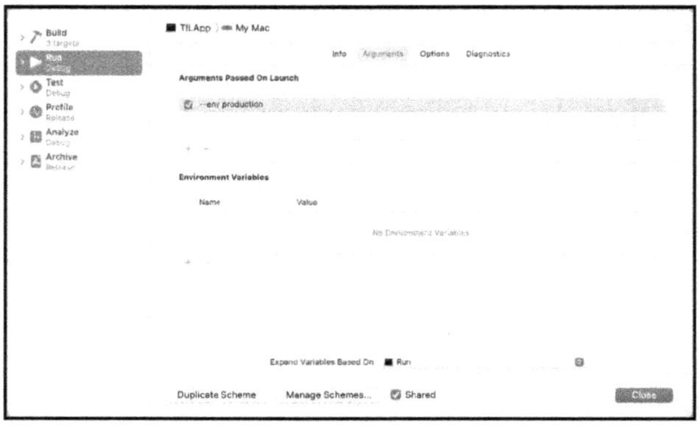

Vapor supports shortcuts like `prod` for `production` and `dev` for `development`. It also supports the `-e` abbreviation for `--env`.

```
$ swift run Run serve -e prod
```

Compiling with optimizations

While developing your application, you'll usually compile code using Swift's debug build mode. Debug build mode is fast and includes useful debug information in the resulting binary. Xcode can use this information later to provide more information about fatal errors and breakpoint debugging.

For production deployments, you should use Swift's release build mode. When building in release mode, Swift spends more time analyzing and optimizing your program. While this increases the overall build time, it's well worth the performance improvements at runtime. Swift also removes debugging information from the resulting binary, making it smaller.

Vapor and Swift NIO may also behave slightly differently in release build mode. A common pattern in these packages is to convert recoverable developer errors into fatal errors while in debug mode. This helps the developer track down common errors quickly during development without compromising stability in production.

This section shows you how to enable release build mode, both in Xcode and directly using SwiftPM. It also shows you how to run your tests in release mode. This can be useful for tests that depend on runtime performance.

Building release in Xcode

You enable release build mode in Xcode using the scheme editor. To build in release mode, edit the scheme for your app's executable target. Then, select **Release** under **Build Configuration**.

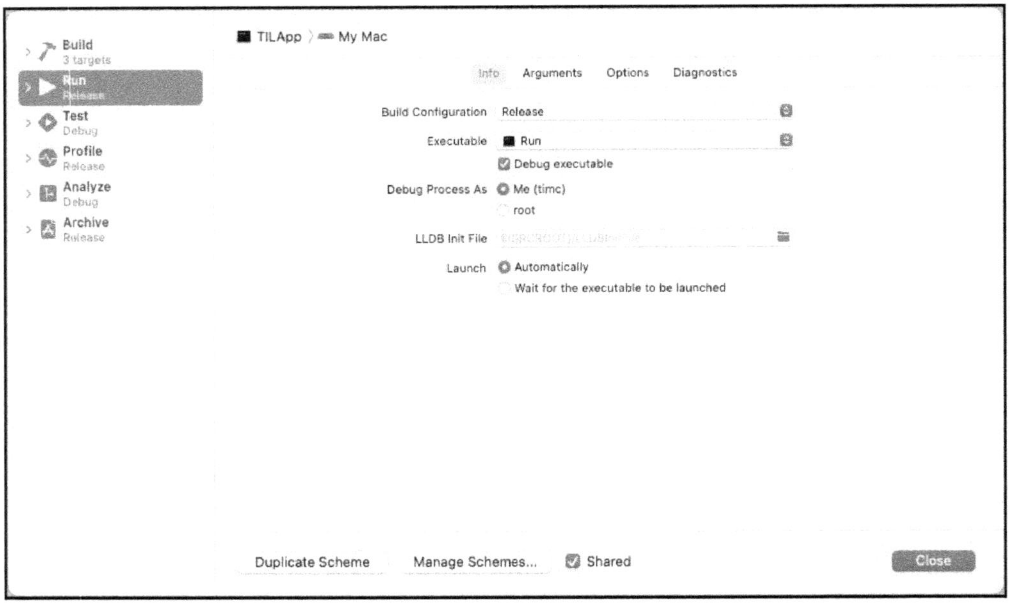

To test in release mode, again edit the scheme for your app's executable target. Then, select **Test** from the left side of the scheme editor and change **Build Configuration** mode to **Release**.

Building release using SwiftPM

When deploying to Linux, you'll need to use SwiftPM to compile release executables since Xcode is not available. By default, SwiftPM compiles in debug build mode. To specify release mode, append **-c release** to your build command.

```
swift build -c release
```

When the build finishes, the compiler prints the path of the resulting executable to the terminal. You can copy and paste that path to run your application.

If you visit the build folder, you may notice additional files exist alongside your executable binary. Among these files are any shared libraries (**.dylib** on macOS and **.so** on Linux) produced by the build process. These shared libraries are required for your executable to run.

You can also run your tests in release mode with SwiftPM.

```
swift test -c release
```

Note that some features, like `@testable import`, may not be available when testing in release mode.

Note on testing

Building and testing your code regularly in production-like environments is important for catching issues early. Some modules you will use, like Foundation, have different implementations depending on the platform. Subtle differences in implementation can cause bugs in your code. Sometimes, an API's implementation may not yet exist for a platform. Container environments like Docker help you address this by making it easy to test your code on platforms different from your host machine, such as testing on Linux while developing on macOS.

Using Docker

Docker is a great tool for testing and deploying your Vapor applications. Deployment steps are coded into a **Dockerfile** you can commit to source control alongside your project. You can execute this **Dockerfile** to build and run instances of your app locally for testing or on your deployment server for production. This has the advantage of making it easy to test deployments, create new ones and track changes to how your deploy your code.

See Chapter 33, "Deploying with Docker," for more information.

Process monitoring

To run a Vapor application, you simply need to launch the executable generated by SwiftPM.

```
swift build -c release
```

```
.build/release/Run serve -e prod
```

While this works great for testing, it has one major problem: What happens if your application crashes? In that case, you would need to log in to your server and restart it manually. Fortunately, process monitors can help remedy this.

Supervisor

Supervisor, also called `supervisord`, is a popular process monitor for Linux. This program allows you to register processes that you would like to start and stop on demand. If one of those processes crashes, Supervisor will automatically restart it for you. It also makes it easy to store the process's `stdout` and `stderr` in `/var/log` for easy access.

Supervisor is usually installed using APT on Ubuntu but may vary depending on your deployment method.

```
apt-get install supervisor
```

Once installed, Supervisor can be started using Ubuntu's `systemctl` command.

```
systemctl restart supervisor
```

Supervisor's configuration files are stored in **/etc/supervisor/conf.d**. Create a new file there to manage your Vapor app called **my-app.conf**.

```
// 1
[program:my-app]
command=/path/to/my-app/.build/release/Run serve -e prod
// 2
autostart=true
autorestart=true
// 3
stderr_logfile=/var/log/my-app.err.log
stdout_logfile=/var/log/my-app.out.log
```

Here's a breakdown of what this configuration file does:

1. Declare a new Supervisor program that launches your application's `Run` executable using the serve command and production environment.

2. Enable auto-start and auto-restart, which ensures your application is always running when the server is on.

3. Configure Supervisor to direct your application's `stderr` and `stdout` to log files.

Now that you've added the configuration file, run the following command to update Supervisor.

```
supervisorctl reread
supervisorctl update
```

Your application should now be running. If the application crashes, Supervisor will notice this and immediately attempt to restart it.

Systemd

Another alternative that doesn't require you to install additional software is called `systemd`. It's a standard part of the Linux versions that Swift supports. For more on how to configure your app using `systemd`, see Chapter 34, "Deploying with AWS".

Reverse Proxies

Regardless of where or how you deploy your Vapor application, it's usually a good idea to host it behind a reverse proxy like nginx. nginx is an extremely fast, battle tested and easy-to-configure HTTP server and proxy. While Vapor supports directly serving HTTP requests, proxying behind nginx can provide increased performance, security, and ease-of-use. nginx, for example, can provide support for TLS (SSL), public file serving and HTTP/2.

Installing Nginx

nginx is usually installed using APT on Ubuntu but may vary depending on your deployment method.

```
apt-get update
apt-get install nginx
```

Once installed, nginx can be started using Ubuntu's `systemctl` command.

```
systemctl start nginx
systemctl restart nginx
systemctl stop nginx
```

Once started, you can create a new site configuration in **/etc/nginx/sites-enabled**. Take a look at the example nginx configuration file below:

```
server {
  ## 1
  server_name hello.com;

  ## 2
  listen 80;

  ## 3
  root /home/vapor/Hello/Public/;
  try_files $uri @proxy;

  ## 4
  location @proxy {
    ## 5
    proxy_pass http://127.0.0.1:8080;

    ## 6
    proxy_set_header Host $host;
    proxy_set_header X-Real-IP $remote_addr;
    proxy_set_header X-Forwarded-For $proxy_add_x_forwarded_for;

    ## 7
    proxy_connect_timeout 3s;
    proxy_read_timeout 10s;
  }
}
```

Here's what each line of the nginx configuration does:

1. Specify this configuration is used for requests to `hello.com`. You can list multiple server names here.
2. Specify this configuration is used for requests to port 80, the default HTTP port.
3. Specify a document root for this server. Any requests to `hello.com/*` which match file names in this folder will be served directly by nginx, bypassing your Vapor application.
4. Specify this server should be a reverse proxy.
5. Pass all requests to the Vapor application bound to `127.0.0.1` port `8080`.
6. Specify special headers to add to the incoming request. These headers help Vapor maintain information about the connected client.
7. Specify connection and read timeouts for your server.

Once you've saved the configuration file, restart nginx to enable the new site. Next, ensure your Vapor server is running at the hostname and port specified in your configuration. You should now be able to access your Vapor server through nginx.

Logging

Using Swift's `print` method for logging is great during development and can even be a suitable option for some production use cases. Programs like Supervisor help aggregate your application's print output into files on your server that you can access as needed.

However, there may be situations where you want to collect your logs in a different way. For example, maybe you would prefer to collect logs and send them to a remote API for storage. You may also want to specify each log's importance, so you know how to treat it. Vapor uses SwiftLog (https://github.com/apple/swift-log) to provide a consistent API for you and all packages you use to build upon.

Using logging is easy; simply `import Vapor` and access a `Logger` from your `Request` or `Application`.

```
app.get("log-test") { req -> HTTPStatus in
    req.logger.info("The route was called")
    return .ok
}
```

The logger has several log level methods available:

- **trace**: Log any and all information. Used to trace specific problems.
- **debug**: Used to debug problems.
- **info**: Indicates an infrequent event has occurred.
- **notice**: Used to notify about specific events or status that should be noted but not treated as an error.
- **warning**: Indicates something should be fixed.
- **error**: Indicates something went wrong.
- **critical**: Fatal errors. Execution must be canceled.

By default, accessing a `Logger` will yield a `ConsoleLogger`, which outputs your logs to the console using terminal colors to specify log level.

However, there are several other implementation for SwiftLog for you to choose, which can be found at https://github.com/apple/swift-log#selecting-a-logging-backend-implementation-applications-only.

Horizontal scalability

Finally, one of the most important concerns in designing a production-ready app is that of scalability. As your application's user base grows and traffic increases, how will you keep up with demand? What will be your bottlenecks? When first starting out, a reasonable solution can be to increase your server's resources as traffic increases — adding RAM, better CPU, more disk space, etc. This is commonly referred to as **scaling vertically**.

Where vertical scaling falls apart is when your application's requirements start to exceed the power of a single server. Eventually, if your application grows large enough, you may need to scale to multiple servers. This is called **horizontal scaling**. However, horizontal scaling is not only useful when you've exhausted your ability to scale vertically. Scaling to multiple cheap servers can be more cost effective than a single expensive server.

Load balancing

Now that you understand some of the benefits of horizontal scaling, you may be wondering how it actually works. The key to this concept is load balancers. Load balancers are light-weight, fast programs that sit in front of your application's servers. When a new request comes in, the load balancer chooses one of your servers to send the request to.

If one of the servers is unhealthy — responding slowly or returning errors — the load balancer can temporarily stop sending requests to that server.

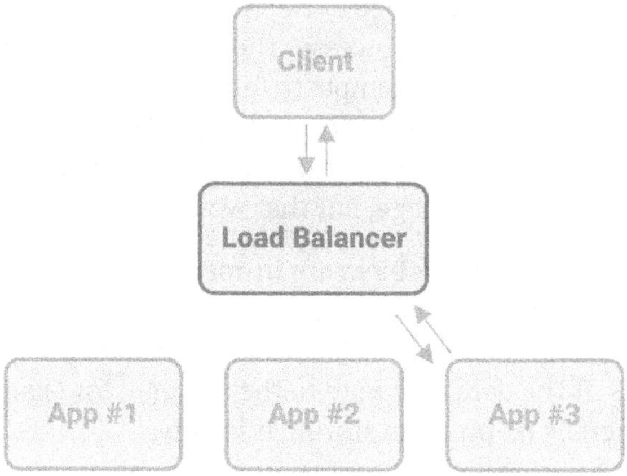

In the diagram above, the load balancer receives a message from the client and decides to forward the request to App #3. The application generates a response for the request, and the load balancer delivers that response back to the client.

While the basics of horizontal scaling are simple, you should understand some common pitfalls that can prevent your application from being scaled this way. Most commonly, these problems relate to storing information locally on the server.

To better understand this, take the following example of a profile picture upload endpoint that saves the image to disk:

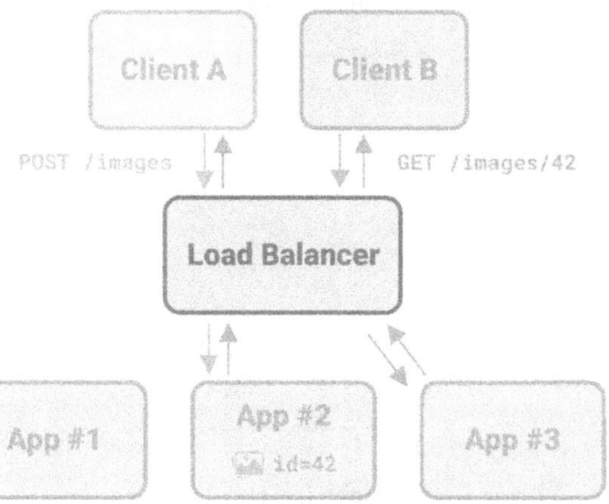

When Client A uploads its profile image to the API, the load balancer directs the request to App #2. This application processes the request and saves the image to the server's disk. Later, when Client B attempts to fetch that image, the load balancer directs the request to App #3. The server running App #3 does not know about that image, so it returns an error. It's possible that Client B could have been directed to App #2 to successfully fetch the image, but that would have been pure luck.

Other common examples of this problem are in-memory session caches and SQLite databases. A general solution to this problem is to use shared storage for your application's *common* data. This means data that any instance of your application might need to access. If the data is private to the server — for example, an API response cache — there is no problem storing it locally.

There are a plethora of tools available for you to make your application scalable. For file upload, there are APIs like Amazon Web Service's S3 buckets that let you store and fetch files from a single, remote source. You may also be able to configure your servers with a shared drive for file storage, as the following figure shows:

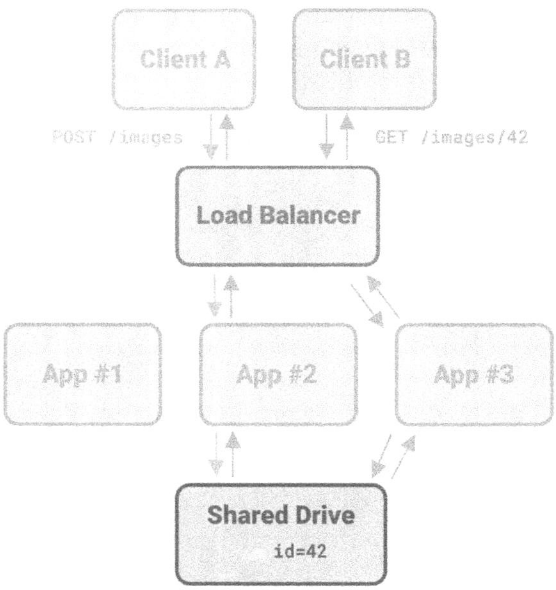

In the example above, Client B's request for the image succeeds since both App #2 and App #3 have access to the same shared drive. For databases and sessions, you can use non-file based databases like Redis, MySQL, PostgreSQL, MongoDB and more. These databases run on a separate server that all of your application instances can access.

If you think your application will need to handle a lot of traffic, or it has the potential to grow quickly, keep horizontal scalability in mind as you design and write code.

Sessions with Redis

To demonstrate how this works in an app, download the starter project for this chapter. The project is based on the TIL app from the first sections of this book. Open the project in Xcode and build the application.

> **Note**: As in previous chapters, you need to set the custom working directory for the project.

When a user logs in to the website, the application stores the user's ID in an associated session. Currently the application stores sessions in memory. This presents a couple of problems:

- When you restart the application, you lose all your sessions. Any logged in users will have to log in again.
- If you scale your application horizontally, the sessions aren't shared. If a user logs in to server #1 and the next request from that user goes to server #2, it doesn't know about the session, so the user can't access any protected routes. Logging into server #2 overwrites the session information for server #1, thereby losing that session. As you scale horizontally, the chance this causes problems increases.

You can solve this by moving the sessions into a database. Redis is a fast, in-memory database that has many uses, and it's a great choice for this use case. If all instances of the application use Redis, they can share sessions.

In Xcode, open **configure.swift**. The starter project already has Redis configured as a dependency in **Package.swift**. Below `import Leaf`, add the following:

```
import Redis
```

This allows you to see Redis functions and types. Next, configure the Redis database in your application. Below `app.databases.use(...)` add the following:

```
// 1
let redisHostname = Environment
  .get("REDIS_HOSTNAME") ?? "localhost"
// 2
```

```
let redisConfig =
  try RedisConfiguration(hostname: redisHostname)
// 3
app.redis.configuration = redisConfig
```

Here's what this does:

1. Set the hostname to the **REDIS_HOSTNAME** environment variable, if it exists. Otherwise, default to **localhost**. This allows you to inject the hostname for hosting solutions.
2. Create a `RedisConfiguration` using the hostname.
3. Set the `RedisConfiguration` on the application's `Redis` service.

Next, add the following after `app.views.use(.leaf)`:

```
app.sessions.use(.redis)
```

This tells the application to use Redis when storing session data.

Finally, move `app.middleware.use(app.sessions.middleware)` to below `app.sessions.use(.redis)`. This ensures that the sessions middleware uses the Redis sessions configuration.

That's all that's required to use Redis with sessions!

In Terminal, enter the following to start the databases:

```
# 1
docker run --name postgres \
  -e POSTGRES_DB=vapor_database \
  -e POSTGRES_USER=vapor_username \
  -e POSTGRES_PASSWORD=vapor_password \
  -p 5432:5432 -d postgres
# 2
docker run --name redis -p 6379:6379 -d redis
```

Here's what this does:

1. Start the PostgreSQL database:

- Run a new container named **postgres**.
- Specify the database name, username and password through environment variables.
- Allow applications to connect to the PostgreSQL server on its default port: 5432.
- Run the server in the background as a daemon.
- Use the Docker image named **postgres** for this container. If the image isn't present on your machine, Docker automatically downloads it.

2. Start the Redis database:

- Run a new container named **redis**.
- Allow applications to connect to the Redis server on its default port: 6379.
- Run the server in the background as a daemon.
- Use the Docker image named **redis** for this container. If the image isn't present on your machine, Docker automatically downloads it.

Build and run the application in Xcode. In your browser, navigate to **http://localhost:8080/**. Click **Create An Acronym** and the app redirects you to the log in page. Log in with the username **admin** and the password **password**. Click **Create An Acronym** and you can view the page:

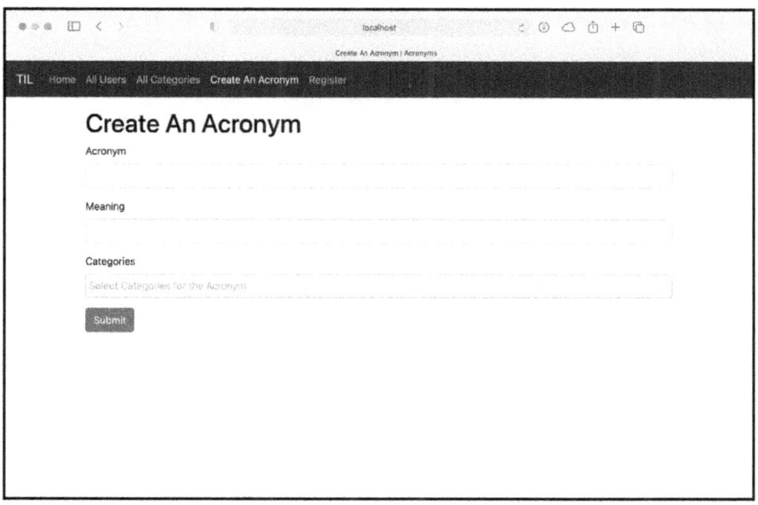

In Xcode, stop and start the app and refresh the page in the browser. The application knows you're still logged in as it stores the session in Redis instead of in-memory.

Where to go from here?

You now understand the common pitfalls to avoid when moving your Swift web application to production. It's time to put the best practices and useful tools listed here to use. Here are some additional resources that should prove invaluable as you continue to hone your skills:

- Swift optimization tips: https://github.com/apple/swift/blob/master/docs/OptimizationTips.rst
- Supervisor documentation: http://supervisord.org
- nginx documentation: https://nginx.org/en/docs/
- Docker documentation: https://docs.docker.com

Chapter 36: Microservices, Part 1

By Tim Condon

In previous chapters, you've built a single Vapor application to run your server code. For large applications, the single monolith becomes difficult to maintain and scale. In this chapter, you'll learn how to leverage microservices to split up your code into different applications. You'll learn the benefits and the downsides of microservices and how to interact with them. Finally, you'll learn how authentication and relationships work in a microservices architecture.

Microservices

Microservices are a design pattern that's become popular in recent years. The aim of microservices is to provide small, independent modules that interact with one another. This is different to a large monolithic application. Such an approach makes the individual services easier to develop and test as they are smaller. Because they're independent, you can develop them individually. This removes the need to use and build all the dependencies for the entire application.

Microservices also allow you to scale your application better. In a monolithic application, you must scale the entire application when under heavy load. This includes parts of the application that receive low traffic. In microservices, you scale only the services that are busy.

Finally, microservices make building and deploying your applications easier. Deploying very large applications is complex and prone to errors. In large applications, you must coordinate with every development team to ensure the application is ready to deploy. Breaking a monolithic application up into smaller services makes deploying each service easier.

Each microservice should be a fully contained application. Each service has its own database, its own cache and, if necessary, its own front end. The only shared part should be the public API to allow other services to interact with that microservice. Typically, they provide an HTTP REST API, although you can use other techniques such as protobuf or remote procedural calls (RPC). Since each microservice interacts with other services only via a public API, each can use different technology stacks. For instance, you could use PostgreSQL for one service that required it, but use MySQL for the main user service. You can even mix languages. This allows different teams to use the languages they prefer.

Swift is an excellent choice for microservices. Swift applications have low memory footprints and can handle large numbers of connections. This allows Swift microservices to fit easily into existing applications without the need for lots of resources.

The TIL microservices

In the first few sections of this book, you developed a single TIL application. You could have used a microservices architecture instead. For instance, you could have one service that deals with users, another that deals with categories and another for acronyms. Throughout this chapter, you'll start to see how to do this.

Download and open the starter project for this chapter. There are two Vapor applications in there:

- **TILAppUsers**: a microservice for users running on port 8081. This services uses a PostgreSQL database to persist the users' information.
- **TILAppAcronyms**: a microservice for the acronyms running on port 8082. This service uses a MySQL database to store the acronyms.

The user microservice

Navigate to the **TILAppUsers** directory in Terminal. Enter the following the start the database:

```
docker run --name postgres -e POSTGRES_DB=vapor_database \
  -e POSTGRES_USER=vapor_username \
  -e POSTGRES_PASSWORD=vapor_password \
  -p 5432:5432 -d postgres
```

Here's what this does:

- Run a new container named **postgres**.
- Specify the database name, username and password through environment variables.
- Allow applications to connect to the PostgreSQL server on its default port: 5432.
- Run the server in the background as a daemon.
- Use the Docker image named **postgres** for this container. If the image isn't present on your machine, Docker automatically downloads it.

Next generate and open the project in Xcode:

```
open Package.swift
```

Once Xcode finishes downloading the dependencies, open **User.swift**. The `User` model for this service is a simplified version from the main TIL application.

Next, open **UsersController.swift**. Again, like the TIL application, this contains routes to create a user, retrieve a user and retrieve all users.

Build and run the application and launch RESTed. Configure a request as follows:

- **URL**: http://localhost:8081/users
- **method**: POST
- **Parameter encoding**: JSON-encoded

Add three parameters with names and values:

- **username**: a username of your choice
- **name**: a name of your choice
- **password**: a password of your choice

Click **Send Request**. This creates a user in the application.

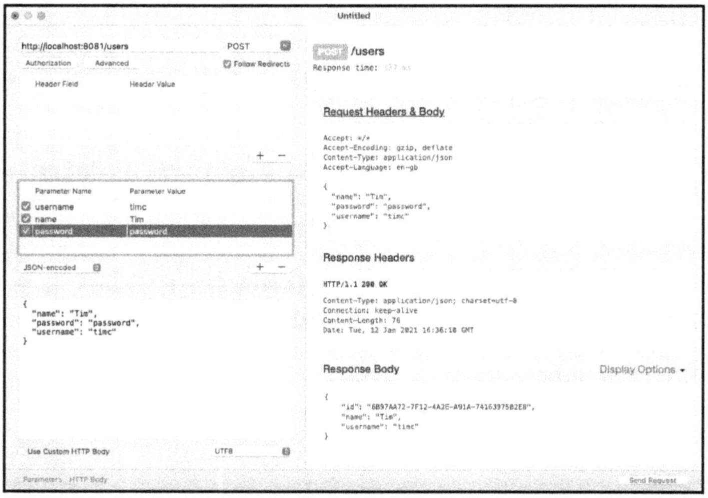

Configure a new request as follows:

- **URL**: http://localhost:8081/users
- **method**: GET

Click **Send Request**. You'll see the user you created:

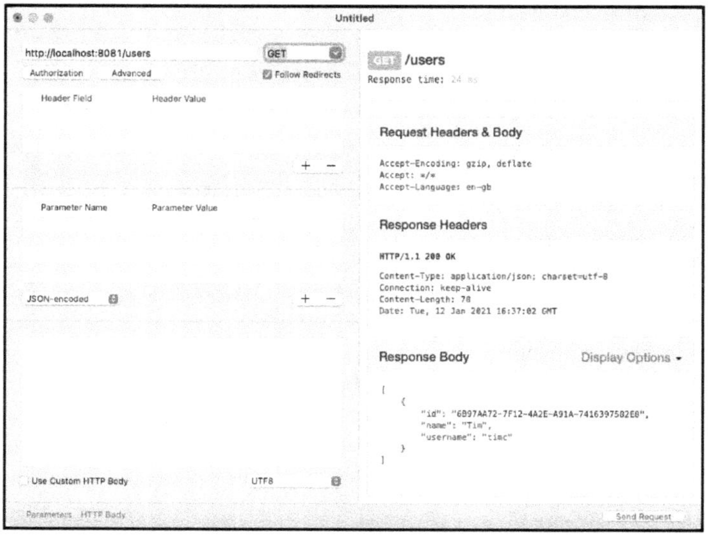

For now, that's as complicated as the user service needs to be!

The acronym microservice

Keep the user service running and navigate to the **TILAppAcronyms** directory in Terminal. Enter the following the start the database:

```
docker run --name mysql -e MYSQL_USER=vapor_username \
  -e MYSQL_PASSWORD=vapor_password \
  -e MYSQL_DATABASE=vapor_database \
  -e MYSQL_RANDOM_ROOT_PASSWORD=yes \
  -p 3306:3306 -d mysql
```

Here's what this does:

- Run a new container named **mysql**.
- Specify the database name, username and password through environment variables.
- Set `MYSQL_RANDOM_ROOT_PASSWORD` which sets the required root password to a random value.
- Allow applications to connect to the MySQL server on its default port: 3306.
- Run the server in the background as a daemon.
- Use the Docker image named **mysql** for this container. If the image is not present on your machine, Docker automatically downloads it.

Next enter the following in Terminal to open the project in Xcode:

```
open Package.swift
```

This service contains the exact same `Acronym` model as the main TIL application. Open **AcronymsController.swift**. You'll see routes for CRUD operations on `Acronym`. When Xcode finishes downloading the dependencies, build and run the service and configure a new request in RESTed as follows:

- **URL**: http://localhost:8082/
- **method**: POST
- **Parameter encoding**: JSON-encoded

Add three parameters with names and values:

- **short**: **OMG**
- **long**: **Oh My God**
- **userID**: The ID of the user created earlier

Click **Send Request**. This creates an acronym in the service:

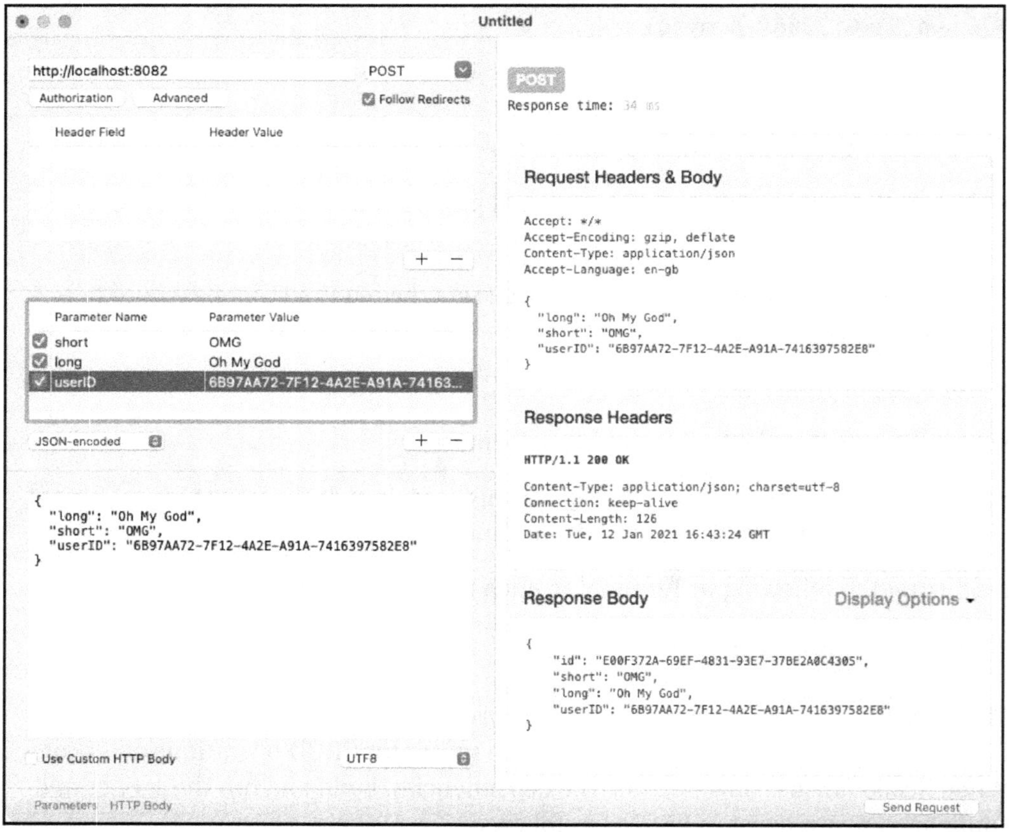

Configure a new request as follows:

- **URL**: http://localhost:8082/
- **method**: GET

Click **Send Request**. You'll see the acronym you created:

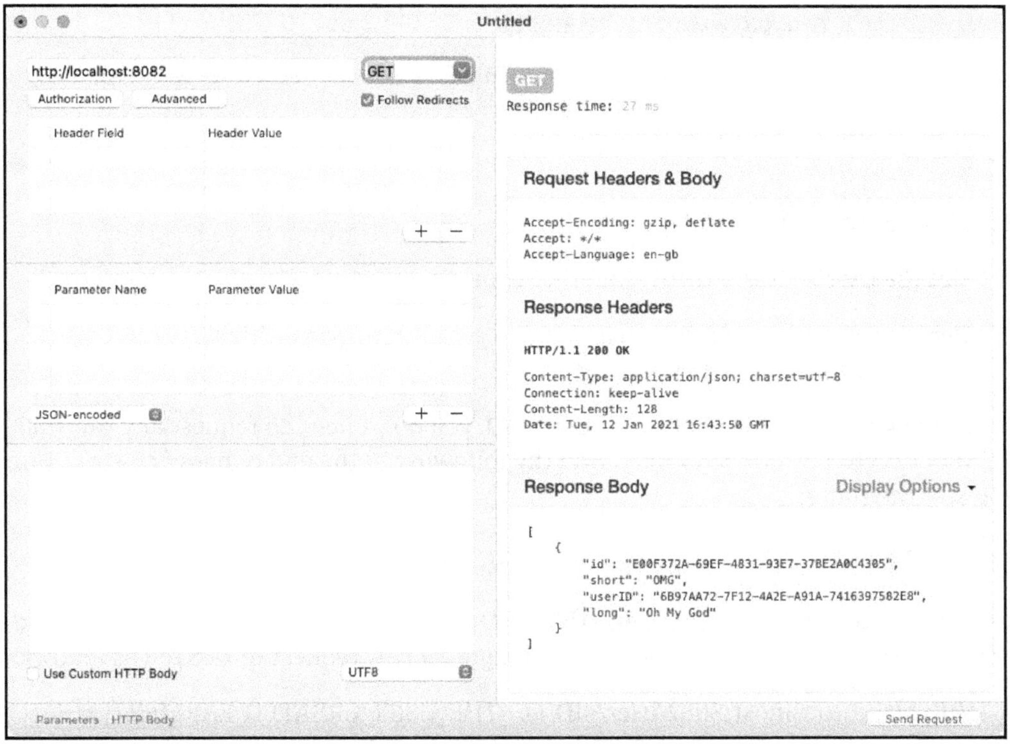

Dealing with relationships

At this point, you can create both users and acronyms in their respective microservices. However, dealing with relationships between different services is more complicated. In Section 1 of this book, you learned how to use Fluent to enable you to query for different relationships between models. With microservices, since the models are in different databases, you must do this manually.

Getting a user's acronyms

In the **TILAppAcronyms** Xcode project, open **AcronymsController.swift**. Below `updateHandler(_:)`, add a new route handler to get the acronyms for a particular user:

```
func getUsersAcronyms(_ req: Request)
  throws -> EventLoopFuture<[Acronym]> {
```

```
    // 1
    let userID =
      try req.parameters.require("userID", as: UUID.self)
    // 2
    return Acronym.query(on: req.db)
      .filter(\.$userID == userID)
      .all()
}
```

Here's what the route handler does:

1. Get the user's ID as a UUID from the request's parameters.
2. Perform a query on the `Acronym` table to get all acronyms with a `userID` that matches the ID passed in.

Since the `Acronym` table contains the user ID, you don't need to request any external information to perform the query. Add the following to the end of `boot(routes:)` to register the route:

```
routes.get("user", ":userID", use: getUsersAcronyms)
```

This routes **GET** requests to **/user/<USER_ID>** to `getUsersAcronyms(_:)`. Build and run the **TILAppAcronyms** service and configure a new request in RESTed as follows:

- **URL**: http://localhost:8082/user/<ID_OF_THE_USER_CREATED_EARLIER>
- **method**: GET

Click **Send request** and you'll see all acronyms created by that user:

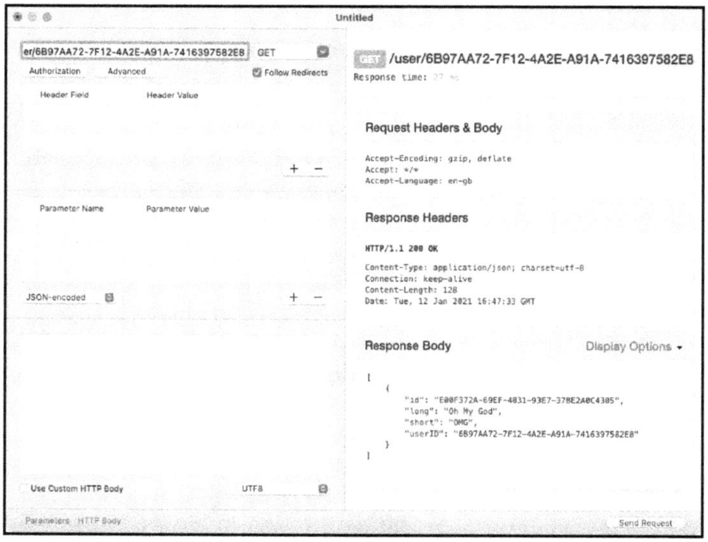

Getting an acronym's user

You can already get an acronym's user with the current projects. You make a request to get the acronym, extract the user's ID from it, then make a request to get the user from the user service. Chapter 37, "Microservices, Part 2" discusses how to simplify this for clients.

Authentication in Microservices

Currently a user can create, edit and delete acronyms with no authentication. Like the TIL app, you should add authentication to microservices as necessary. For this chapter, you'll add authentication to the **TILAppAcronyms** microservice. However, you'll delegate this authentication to the **TILAppUsers** microservice.

In practice, it works like this:

- A user logs in to the **TILAppUsers** microservice and obtains a token.
- When creating an acronym, the user provides the token to the **TILAppAcronyms** service.
- The **TILAppAcronyms** service validates the token with the **TILAppUsers** service.
- If the token is valid, the **TILAppAcronyms** proceeds with the request, otherwise it rejects the request.

Logging in

Open the **TILAppUsers** project in Xcode. The starter project already contains a `Token` type and an empty `AuthContoller`. You could store the tokens in the same database as the user. Since every validation request requires a lookup and you have multiple services, you want this to be as quick as possible. One solution is to store them in memory. However, if you want to scale your microservice, this doesn't work. You need to use something like Redis. Redis is a fast, key-value database, which is ideal for storing session tokens. You can share the database across different servers which allows you to scale without any performance penalties.

In Terminal, type the following to start a Redis database server:

```
docker run --name redis -p 6379:6379 -d redis
```

Here's what this does:

- Run a new container named **redis**.
- Allow applications to connect to the Redis server on its default port: 6379.
- Run the server in the background as a daemon.
- Use the Docker image named **redis** for this container. If the image isn't present on your machine, Docker automatically downloads it.

Back in Xcode, open **configure.swift** for the **TILAppUsers** project. At the top of the file, add the following underneath `import Vapor`:

```
import Redis
```

This allows you to use Redis in your application. The project already has Redis configured as a dependency. Next, below:

```
app.migrations.add(CreateUser())
```

add the following:

```
// 1
let redisHostname: String
if let redisEnvironmentHostname =
  Environment.get("REDIS_HOSTNAME") {
    redisHostname = redisEnvironmentHostname
} else {
  redisHostname = "localhost"
}
// 2
app.redis.configuration =
  try RedisConfiguration(hostname: redisHostname)
```

Here's what the code does:

1. Use the **REDIS_HOSTNAME** environment variable for the Redis server hostname, if it's set. Otherwise, use **localhost**.
2. Configure the app's `Redis` setup to use a `RedisConfiguration`.

You've now configured the **TILAppUsers** project to use Redis. Notice the project now uses two databases — PostgreSQL and Redis. Next, open **AuthController.swift** and create a new route handler below `boot(routes:)` to handle a user logging in:

```
func loginHandler(_ req: Request)
  throws -> EventLoopFuture<Token> {
```

```
    // 1
    let user = try req.auth.require(User.self)
    // 2
    let token = try Token.generate(for: user)
    // 3
    return req.redis
      .set(RedisKey(token.tokenString), toJSON: token)
      .transform(to: token)
}
```

Here's what the new code does:

1. Get the authenticated user from the request. The route will use Basic HTTP Authentication to retrieve the user.
2. Generate a `Token` for the user.
3. Save the token in Redis as a JSON string for the value. Create a `RedisKey` using the token string. Return the `Token` as the response using `transform(to:)`.

Finally, register the route in `boot(routes:)`:

```
// 1
let authGroup = routes.grouped("auth")
// 2
let basicMiddleware = User.authenticator()
// 3
let basicAuthGroup = authGroup.grouped(basicMiddleware)
// 4
basicAuthGroup.post("login", use: loginHandler)
```

Here's what the routing code does:

1. Create a new route group under **/auth** for handling all authentication routes.
2. Create the HTTP Basic Authentication middleware from `User` using `authenticator()`.
3. Create a new route group using the middleware.
4. Route **POST** requests to **/auth/login** to `loginHandler(_:)`.

For more information on HTTP Basic Authentication, see Chapter 18, "API Authentication, Part 1."

Authenticating tokens

Now that users can log in and get a token, you need a way for other microservices to validate that token and retrieve the user information associated with it.

First, create a new type to represent the data sent in token validation requests. At the bottom of **AuthController.swift**, add the following:

```
struct AuthenticateData: Content {
  let token: String
}
```

The request only needs the token to validate the request. Next, create a new route below `loginHandler(_:)` to handle the requests with this data from other microservices:

```
func authenticate(_ req: Request)
  throws -> EventLoopFuture<User.Public> {
    // 1
    let data = try req.content.decode(AuthenticateData.self)
    // 2
    return req.redis
      .get(RedisKey(data.token), asJSON: Token.self)
      .flatMap { token in
      // 3
      guard let token = token else {
        return req.eventLoop.future(error: Abort(.unauthorized))
      }
      // 4
      return User.query(on: req.db)
        .filter(\.$id == token.userID)
        .first()
        .unwrap(or: Abort(.internalServerError))
        .convertToPublic()
    }
}
```

Here's what the route handler does:

1. Decode the request body to `AuthenticateData`.
2. Retrieve the data in Redis using the token sent in the request as the key. Decode the data to `Token`.
3. Ensure the token exists, otherwise return a **401 Unauthorized** response.
4. Query the user database to get the user with the ID from the `Token`. Ensure the user exists, otherwise throw an internal server error. The application should never store a token in the database with a user ID of a user that doesn't exist. Return the public representation of the user to avoid sending the user's password in the response.

Finally, add the following at the end of `boot(routes:)` to register the route:

```
authGroup.post("authenticate", use: authenticate)
```

This routes a **POST** request to **/auth/authenticate** to `authenticate(_:data:)`. Build and run the application and configure a new request in RESTed as follows:

- **URL**: http://localhost:8081/auth/login
- **method**: POST

Click the **Authorization** button and set **Username** and **Password** to the values for the user you created earlier. Ensure you check **Present Before Authentication Challenge** and click **OK**. Click **Send Request** and you'll see the token returned in the response:

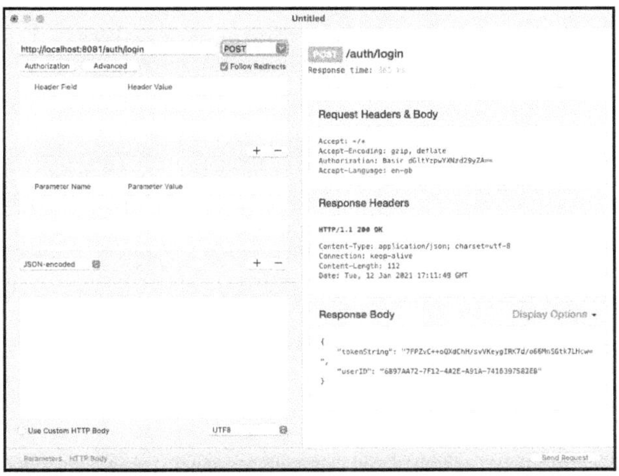

Click **Authorization** again and uncheck the checkbox. This ensures the HTTP Basic Authentication header isn't sent with the next request. Configure a new request as follows:

- **URL**: http://localhost:8081/auth/authenticate
- **method**: POST

Add a single parameter with the name **token** and value of the token returned in the previous request. Click **Send request** and you'll see the user returned in the response:

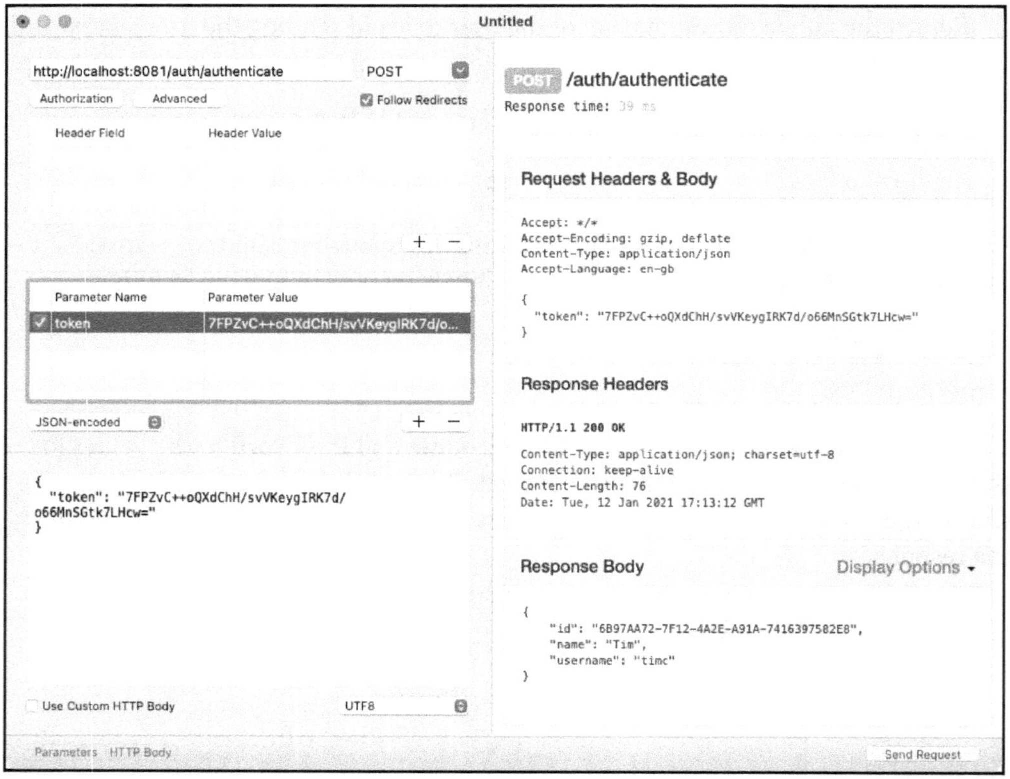

Authenticating with other microservices

Go back to the **TILAppAcronyms** project in Xcode and stop the app. Open **User.swift** and add the following at the bottom of the file:

```
extension User: Authenticatable {}
```

This allows you to add authenticated users to requests, using Vapor's authentication logic. Next, create a new file in **Sources/App/Middlewares/** called **UserAuthMiddleware.swift**. You'll create a middleware to talk to the other microservice. Open the new file and insert the following:

```
import Vapor

struct AuthenticateData: Content {
  let token: String
}
```

This represents the data sent to the **TILAppUsers** microservice to validate tokens. Notice this is the exact same code as used in that microservice. Next, above `AuthenticateData`, add the middleware to authenticate tokens with the **TILAppUsers** microservice:

```
struct UserAuthMiddleware: Middleware {
  // 1
  func respond(to request: Request, chainingTo next: Responder)
    -> EventLoopFuture<Response> {
      // 2
      guard let token =
        request.headers.bearerAuthorization else {
          return request.eventLoop
            .future(error: Abort(.unauthorized))
      }
      // 3
      return request.client.post(
        "http://localhost:8081/auth/authenticate",
        beforeSend: { authRequest in
          // 4
          try authRequest.content
            .encode(AuthenticateData(token: token.token))
      // 5
      }).flatMapThrowing { response in
        // 6
        guard response.status == .ok else {
          if response.status == .unauthorized {
            throw Abort(.unauthorized)
          } else {
            throw Abort(.internalServerError)
```

```
          }
        }
        // 7
        let user = try response.content.decode(User.self)
        // 8
        request.auth.login(user)
      // 9
      }.flatMap {
        // 10
        return next.respond(to: request)
      }
    }
}
```

Here's what the new middleware does:

1. Implement `respond(to:chainingTo:)` as required by `Middleware`.
2. Ensure the request contains a bearer token in the **Authorization** header. Otherwise, return a **401 Unauthorized** response.
3. Send a request to the **TILAppUsers** microservice to validate the token.
4. Encode the token into the request string using the `beforeSend` parameter of `post(_:headers:beforeSend)`.
5. Resolve the future using `flatMapThrowing(_:)`. This allows you to throw errors inside the closure.
6. Ensure the response code is **200 OK**. If not, return a **401 Unauthorized** if the service returned that status, otherwise return a **500 Internal Server Error**.
7. Decode the response body into a `User`.
8. Authenticate the request with the user returned from the **TILAppUsers** service.
9. Use `flatMap(_:)` to chain the result of `flatMapThrowing(_:)` and allow you to return a future.
10. Call the next middleware in the chain.

For more information on middleware, see Chapter 29, "Middleware".

Use the new middleware to protect the routes that mutate the database. Open **AcronymsController.swift** and, add the following at the end of `boot(routes:)`:

```
let authGroup = routes.grouped(UserAuthMiddleware())
authGroup.post(use: createHandler)
authGroup.delete(":acronymID", use: deleteHandler)
```

```
authGroup.put(":acronymID", use: updateHandler)
```

This creates a new route group using `UserAuthMiddleware` and protects the create, update and delete routes. Delete the following routes that are now duplicated:

```
routes.post(use: createHandler)
routes.delete(":acronymID", use: deleteHandler)
routes.put(":acronymID", use: updateHandler)
```

Now that those routes contain an authenticated user, change the route handlers to use that user instead. At the bottom of the file, add a new type for the data required to create an acronym:

```
struct AcronymData: Content {
  let short: String
  let long: String
}
```

Since the user comes from the request, you only need the short and long properties. Next, replace the body of `createHandler(_:)` with the following:

```
// 1
let data = try req.content.decode(AcronymData.self)
// 2
let user = try req.auth.require(User.self)
// 3
let acronym = Acronym(
  short: data.short,
  long: data.long,
  userID: user.id)
return acronym.save(on: req.db).map { acronym }
```

Here's what the new code does:

1. Get the acronym data from the request body using the new type created above.

2. Get the authenticated user from the request.

3. Create an `Acronym` from the user and data and save it.

Next, in `updateHandler(_:)`, replace the type decoded from the request:

```
let updateData = try req.content.decode(AcronymData.self)
```

This uses `AcronymData` instead of `Acronym`. Below the changed line, add:

```
let user = try req.auth.require(User.self)
```

This gets the authenticated user from the request. You do this here as you can throw errors at this level. Finally, replace `acronym.userID = updateData.userID` with the following:

```
acronym.userID = user.id
```

This uses the ID of the request's authenticated user. Build and run the app and configure a new request in RESTed as follows:

- **URL**: http://localhost:8082/
- **method**: POST
- **Parameter encoding**: JSON-encoded

Add two parameters with names and values:

- **short**: **IKR**
- **long**: **I Know Right**

Add a header for **Authorization** with the value **Bearer** . Click **Send Request**. You'll see the new acronym returned in the response:

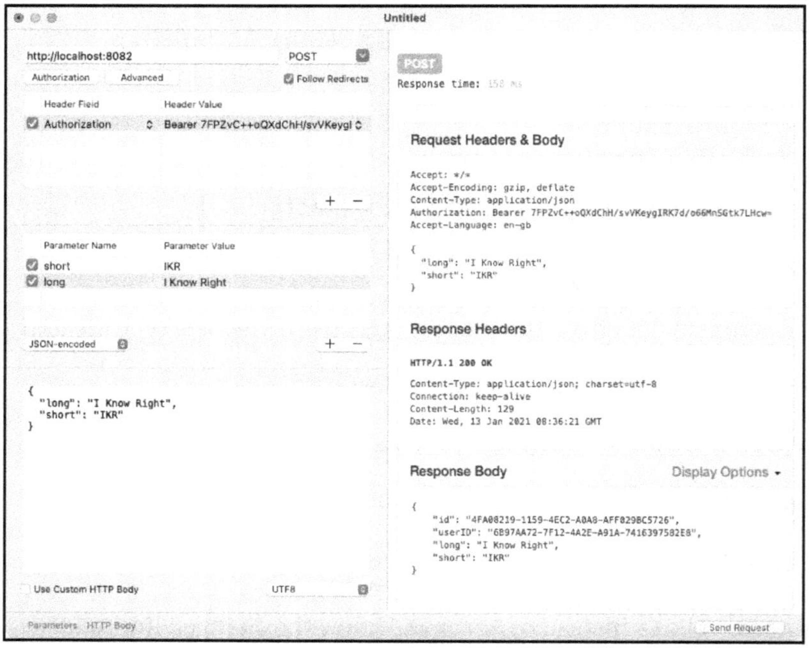

There are a number of options for authenticating requests across microservices. For large applications, you could split the authentication out into another microservice.

You may also want authentication between microservices, even if the original request from the user doesn't need it. Finally, another option is to use JWT (JSON Web Tokens). These are JSON tokens that contain information encoded in them and a signature. They are useful because the signature ensures you can trust the token without needing access to another microservice.

Where to go from here?

In this chapter, you learned how to split the TIL app into different microservices for users and acronyms. You've seen how to handle authentication and relationships across different services.

In the next chapter, you'll build another microservice that acts as a gateway for clients to access the different services. You'll also learn how to build and run the different services together easily on Linux using Docker.

Chapter 37: Microservices, Part 2

By Tim Condon

In the previous chapter, you learned the basics of microservices and how to apply the architecture to the TIL application. In this chapter, you'll learn about API gateways and how to make microservices accessible to clients. Finally, you'll learn how to use Docker and Docker Compose to spin up the whole application.

The API gateway

The previous chapter introduced two microservices for the TIL application, one for acronyms and one for users. In a real application, you may have many more services for all different aspects of your application. It's difficult for clients to integrate with an application made up of such a large number of microservices. Each client needs to know what each microservice does and the URL of each service. The client may even have to use different authentication methods for each service. A microservices architecture makes it hard to split a service into separate services. For example, moving authentication out of the users service in the TIL application would require an update to all clients.

One solution to this problem is the API gateway. An API gateway can aggregate requests from clients and distribute them to all required services. Additionally, an API gateway can retrieve results from multiple services and combine them into a single response.

Most cloud providers offer API gateway solutions to manage large numbers of microservices, but you can easily create your own. In this chapter, you'll do just that.

Download the starter project for this chapter. The **TILAppUsers** and **TILAppAcronyms** projects are the same as the final projects from the previous chapter. There's a new **TILAppAPI** project that contains the skeleton for the API gateway.

Starting the services

In Terminal, open three separate tabs. Ensure the MySQL, PostgreSQL and Redis Docker containers are running from the previous chapter. In Terminal, type the following:

```
docker ps
```

This command displays the currently running containers. You should see the three containers running:

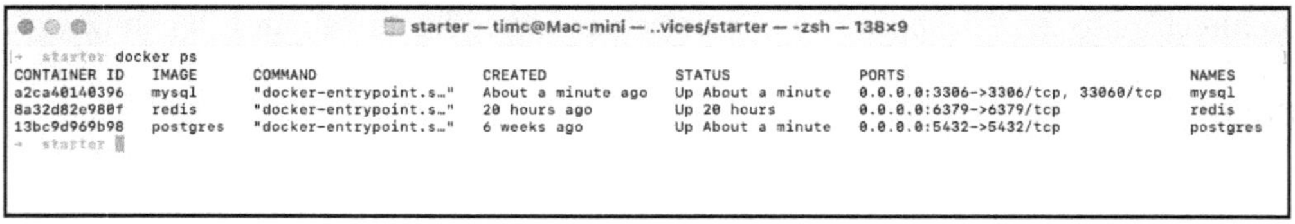

Next, in the first tab, navigate to the **TILAppUsers** directory and run the following command:

```
swift run
```

This starts the **TILAppUsers** service. In the second tab, navigate to the **TILAppAcronyms** and run the following command:

```
swift run
```

This starts the **TILAppAcronyms** service. Finally, in the third tab, navigate to the **TILAppAPI** directory and enter this command:

```
open Package.swift
```

This opens the Xcode project and starts downloading the dependencies.

Forwarding requests

In the **TILAppAPI** Xcode project, open **UsersController.swift**. Below `boot(routes:)` enter the following:

```
// 1
func getAllHandler(_ req: Request)
  -> EventLoopFuture<ClientResponse> {
    return req.client.get("\(userServiceURL)/users")
}

// 2
func getHandler(_ req: Request) throws
  -> EventLoopFuture<ClientResponse> {
    let id = try req.parameters.require("userID", as: UUID.self)
    return req.client.get("\(userServiceURL)/users/\(id)")
}

// 3
func createHandler(_ req: Request)
  -> EventLoopFuture<ClientResponse> {
    return req.client.post("\(userServiceURL)/users") {
      createRequest in
      // 4
      try createRequest.content.encode(
        req.content.decode(CreateUserData.self))
  }
}
```

Here's what happening in the new code:

1. Create a route handler to get all the users. Simply return the response from the / **users** route of the **TILAppUsers** microservice.
2. Create a route handler to get a single user. Get the UUID of the user from the request's parameters and return the response from the **TILAppUsers** microservice for that user.
3. Create a route handler to create a user. Send a POST request to the **users** route of the **TILAppUsers** service and return the response.
4. Before you send the request, encode the data from the request to the API gateway into the request to the **TILAppUsers** service. This is the data required to create a user.

To register the new routes, add the following to the end of `boot(routes:)`:

```
// 1
routeGroup.get(use: getAllHandler)
// 2
routeGroup.get(":userID", use: getHandler)
// 3
routeGroup.post(use: createHandler)
```

Here's what this does:

1. Route a **GET** request to **/api/users/** to `getAllHandler(_:)`.
2. Route a **GET** request to **/api/users/<USER_ID>** to `getHandler(_:)`, using `userID` as the dynamic parameter name.
3. Route a **POST** request to **/api/users/** to `createHandler(_:)`.

These requests don't need any authentication or multiple services. You can forward them directly onto the **TILAppUsers** microservice.

Open **AcronymsController.swift** to do the same for the **GET** requests. Below `boot(routes:)` add the following:

```
// 1
func getAllHandler(_ req: Request)
  -> EventLoopFuture<ClientResponse> {
    return req.client.get("\(acronymsServiceURL)/")
}

// 2
func getHandler(_ req: Request) throws
  -> EventLoopFuture<ClientResponse> {
    let id =
      try req.parameters.require("acronymID", as: UUID.self)
    return req.client.get("\(acronymsServiceURL)/\(id)")
}
```

Here's what the new code does:

1. Create a route handler to get all the acronyms. Simply return the response from the / route of the **TILAppAcronyms** microservice.
2. Create a route handler to get a single acronym. Get the id of the acronym from the request's parameters as a UUID. Return the response from the **TILAppAcronyms** microservice for that acronym.

To register the new routes, add the following to the end of `boot(routes:)`:

```
// 1
acronymsGroup.get(use: getAllHandler)
// 2
acronymsGroup.get(":acronymID", use: getHandler)
```

Here's what this does:

1. Route a **GET** request to **/api/acronyms/** to `getAllHandler(_:)`.
2. Route a **GET** request to **/api/acronyms/<ACRONYM_ID>** to `getHandler(_:)`.

Build and run the application and launch RESTed. Configure a new request as follows:

- **URL**: http://localhost:8080/api/users
- **method**: GET

Click **Send Request** and you'll see all the users in the **TILAppUsers** microservice:

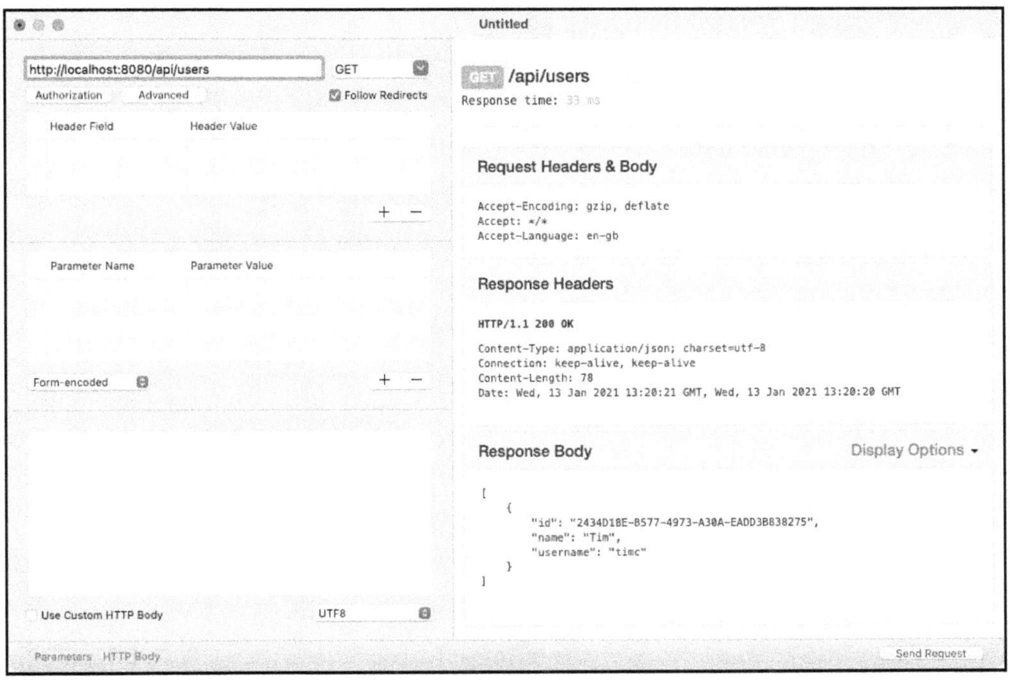

API Authentication

Logging in

Authentication for the API gateway works in exactly the same way as the microservices. First, you must allow a user to log in.

In Xcode, open **UsersController.swift**. Below `createHandler(_:)`, add a new route handler to handle logging in:

```
func loginHandler(_ req: Request)
  -> EventLoopFuture<ClientResponse> {
    // 1
    return req.client.post("\(userServiceURL)/auth/login") {
      loginRequest in
        // 2
        guard let authHeader =
          req.headers[.authorization].first else {
            throw Abort(.unauthorized)
        }
        // 3
        loginRequest.headers.add(
          name: .authorization,
          value: authHeader)
    }
}
```

Here's what the new route handler does:

1. Send a **POST** request to the **TILAppUsers** microservice to log the user in.
2. Ensure the incoming request contains an **Authorization** header. Otherwise, return a **401 Unauthorized** response.
3. Encode the outgoing request with the authorization header from the incoming request. This header contains the HTTP Basic Authentication information for the user.

To register the route, add the following to the end of `boot(routes:)`:

```
routeGroup.post("login", use: loginHandler)
```

This routes a **POST** request to **/api/users/login** to `loginHandler(_:)`. Build and run the application and launch RESTed. Configure a new request as follows:

- **URL**: http://localhost:8080/api/users/login
- **method**: POST

Click **Authorization** and enter the username and password for the user created in the previous chapter. Check **Present Before Authentication Challenge** and click **OK**.

Click **Send Request** and you'll receive a token for that user. Copy the token value:

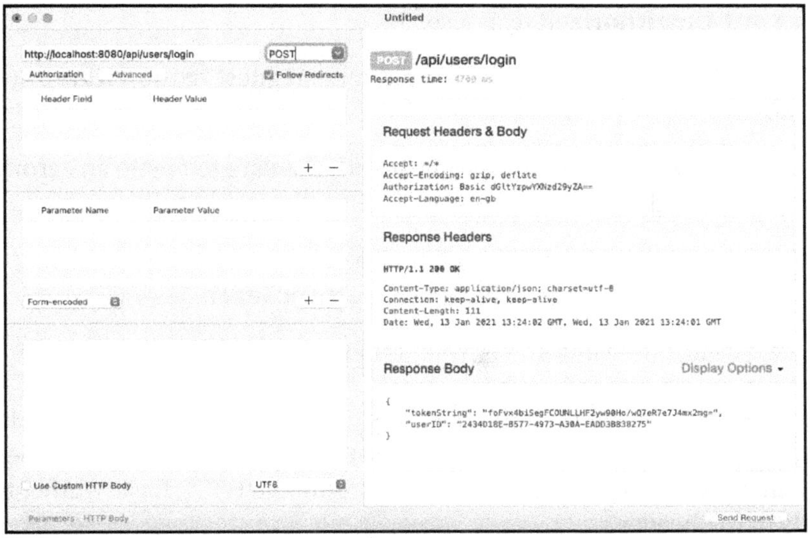

Accessing protected routes

Back in Xcode, open **AcronymsController.swift**. Below `getHandler(_:)`, create a new route handler to create an acronym:

```
func createHandler(_ req: Request)
  -> EventLoopFuture<ClientResponse> {
    // 1
    return req.client.post("\(acronymsServiceURL)/") {
      createRequest in
        // 2
        guard let authHeader =
          req.headers[.authorization].first else {
            throw Abort(.unauthorized)
        }
        // 3
        createRequest.headers.add(
          name: .authorization,
          value: authHeader)
        // 4
        try createRequest.content.encode(
          req.content.decode(CreateAcronymData.self))
    }
}
```

Here's what the code does:

1. Send a **POST** request to the **TILAppAcronyms** microservice to create a new acronym.
2. Ensure the incoming request contains an **Authorization** header, otherwise return a **401 Unauthorized** response.
3. Add the **Authorization** header to the outgoing request to the **TILAppAcronyms** microservice.
4. Encode the body of the outgoing request with the data to create an acronym. The data comes from the incoming request.

Register the route handler in `boot(routes:)` below `acronymsGroup.get(":acronymID", use: getHandler)`:

```
acronymsGroup.post(use: createHandler)
```

This routes a **POST** request to **/api/acronyms** to `createHandler(_:)`. Build and run the app and return to RESTed. Click **Authorization** and uncheck **Present Before Authentication Challenge** to stop RESTed sending the HTTP Basic Authentication credentials in the header.

Then, configure a new request as follows:

- **URL**: http://localhost:8080/api/acronyms/
- **method**: POST
- **Parameter encoding**: JSON-encoded

Add two parameters with names and values:

- **short**: IRL
- **long**: In Real Life

Create a new header field for **Authorization** with the value **Bearer <TOKEN STRING>** using the token string you copied earlier.

Click **Send Request** and you'll see the acronym created in the **TILAppAcronyms** microservice via the API gateway:

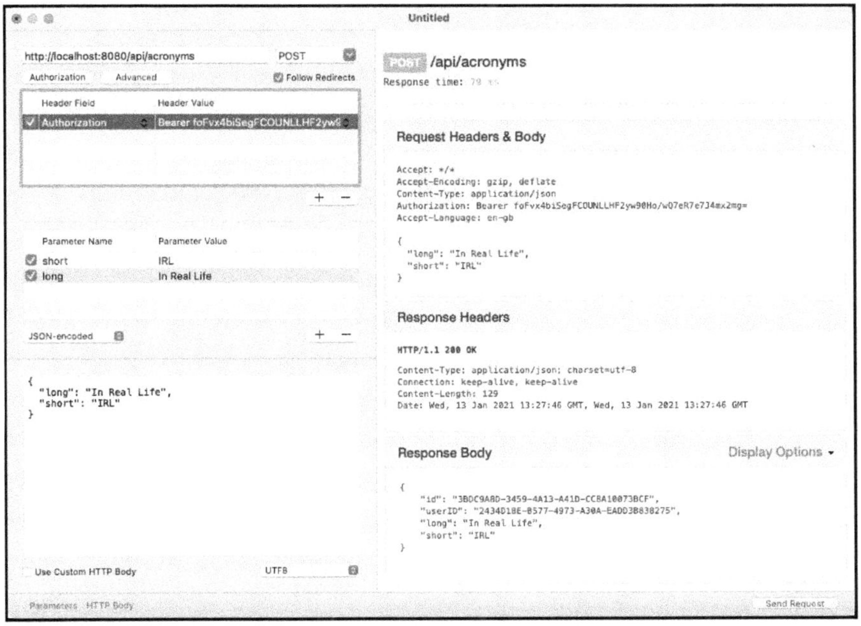

Back in Xcode, create the route handlers for updating and deleting acronyms. Below `createHandler(_:)`, add the following:

```
func updateHandler(_ req: Request) throws
  -> EventLoopFuture<ClientResponse> {
    // 1
    let acronymID =
      try req.parameters.require("acronymID", as: UUID.self)
    // 2
    return req.client
      .put("\(acronymsServiceURL)/\(acronymID)") {
        updateRequest in
          // 3
          guard let authHeader =
            req.headers[.authorization].first else {
              throw Abort(.unauthorized)
          }
          // 4
          updateRequest.headers.add(
            name: .authorization,
            value: authHeader)
          // 5
          try updateRequest.content.encode(
            req.content.decode(CreateAcronymData.self))
    }
```

```
}

func deleteHandler(_ req: Request) throws
  -> EventLoopFuture<ClientResponse> {
    // 6
    let acronymID =
      try req.parameters.require("acronymID", as: UUID.self)
    // 7
    return req.client
      .delete("\(acronymsServiceURL)/\(acronymID)") {
        deleteRequest in
          // 8
          guard let authHeader =
            req.headers[.authorization].first else {
              throw Abort(.unauthorized)
          }
          // 9
          deleteRequest.headers.add(
            name: .authorization,
            value: authHeader)
    }
}
```

Here's what the new code does:

1. Get the ID of the acronym from the request's parameters.
2. Send a request to the **TILAppAcronyms** microservice to update that acronym. Return the response.
3. Ensure the incoming request contains an **Authorization** header before you send the request. If not, return a **401 Unauthorized** response.
4. Add the **Authorization** header to the outgoing request.
5. Encode the body of the outgoing request with the data to update the acronym. The data comes from the incoming request.
6. Get the ID of the acronym from the request's parameters.
7. Send a request to the **TILAppAcronyms** microservice delete that acronym. Return the response.
8. Ensure the incoming request contains an **Authorization** header before you send the request. If not, return a **401 Unauthorized** response.
9. Add the **Authorization** header to the outgoing request.

Finally, to register the new routes, add the following to the end of `boot(routes:)`:

```
// 1
acronymsGroup.put(":acronymID", use: updateHandler)
// 2
acronymsGroup.delete(":acronymID", use: deleteHandler)
```

Here's what this does:

1. Route a **PUT** request to **/api/acronyms/<ID>** to `updateHandler(_:)`.
2. Route a **DELETE** request to **/api/acronyms/<ID>** to `deleteHandler(_:)`.

Handling relationships

In the previous chapter, you saw how relationships work with microservices. Getting relationships for different models is difficult for clients in an microservices architecture. You can use the API gateway to help simplify this.

Getting a user's acronyms

In Xcode, open **UsersController.swift**. Below `loginHandler(_:)`, add a new route handler to get a user's acronyms:

```
func getAcronyms(_ req: Request) throws
  -> EventLoopFuture<ClientResponse> {
    // 1
    let userID =
      try req.parameters.require("userID", as: UUID.self)
    // 2
    return req.client
      .get("\(acronymsServiceURL)/user/\(userID)")
}
```

Here's what's going on:

1. Get the ID of the user from the request's parameters.
2. Send a request to the **TILAppAcronyms** microservice to get all the acronyms for that user and return the response.

To register the new route, add the following to the end of `boot(routes:)`:

```
routeGroup.get(":userID", "acronyms", use: getAcronyms)
```

This routes a **GET** request to **/api/users/<USER_ID>/acronyms** to `getAcronyms(_:)`.

Getting an acronym's user

Getting a user's acronyms looks the same as other requests in the microservice as the client knows the user's ID. Getting the user for a particular acronym is more complicated. Open **AcronymsController.swift** and add a new route handler to do this below `deleteHandler(_:)`:

```
func getUserHandler(_ req: Request) throws
  -> EventLoopFuture<ClientResponse> {
    // 1
    let acronymID =
      try req.parameters.require("acronymID", as: UUID.self)
    // 2
    return req
      .client
      .get("\(acronymsServiceURL)/\(acronymID)")
      .flatMapThrowing { response in
        // 3
        return try response.content.decode(Acronym.self)
      // 4
      }.flatMap { acronym in
        // 5
        return req
          .client
          .get("\(userServiceURL)/users/\(acronym.userID)")
    }
}
```

Here's what the new route handler does:

1. Get the ID of the acronym from the request's parameters.
2. Make a request to **TILAppAcronyms** to get the details for that acronym.
3. Decode the response to an `Acronym` and return the result.
4. Use `flatMap(_:)` to get the `Acronym` from the previous future chain and pass it into another chain. Chaining the futures allows you to avoid wrapping any `trys` in catch statements.
5. Make a request to **TILAppUsers** using the user ID from the acronym.

This route handler requires a request to both microservices. The API gateway makes this a simple request to make for clients, much like the monolithic TIL application. Register the route in `boot(routes:)` below `acronymsGroup.delete(":acronymID", use: deleteHandler)`:

```
acronymsGroup.get(":acronymID", "user", use: getUserHandler)
```

This routes a **GET** request to **/api/acronyms/<ACRONYM_ID>/user** to `getUserHandler(_:)`. Build and run the app and launch RESTed. Configure a new request as follows:

- **URL**: http://localhost:8080/api/acronyms/<ID_OF_ACRONYM_YOU_CREATED>/user
- **method**: GET

Click **Send Request**. The API gateway makes the necessary requests to all the microservices to get the user for the acronym with that ID. You'll see the user information returned:

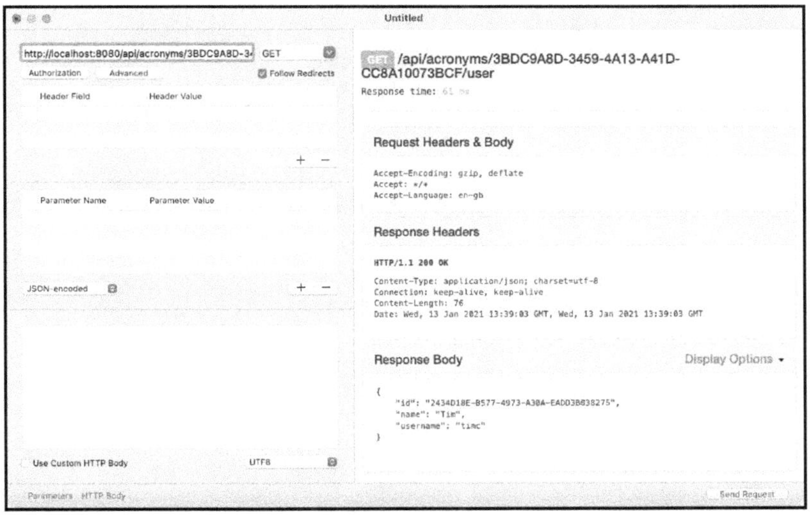

Finally, stop the **TILAppAPI** application in Xcode.

Running everything in Docker

You now have three microservices that make up your TIL application. These microservices also require another three databases to work. If you're developing a client application, or another microservice, there's a lot to run to get started. You may also want to run everything in Linux to check your services deploy correctly. Like in Chapter 11, "Testing", you're going to use Docker Compose to run everything.

Injecting in service URLs

Currently the application hard codes the URLs for the different microservices to **localhost**. You must change this to run them in Docker Compose. Back in Xcode in **TILAppAPI**, open **AcronymsController.swift**. Replace the definitions of `userServiceURL` and `acronymsServiceURL` with the following:

```
let acronymsServiceURL: String
let userServiceURL: String

init(
  acronymsServiceHostname: String,
  userServiceHostname: String) {
    acronymsServiceURL =
      "http://\(acronymsServiceHostname):8082"
    userServiceURL = "http://\(userServiceHostname):8081"
}
```

This allows you to inject in the host names for the different services. Open **UsersController.swift** and, again, replace the definitions of `userServiceURL` and `acronymsServiceURL` with the following:

```
let userServiceURL: String
let acronymsServiceURL: String

init(
  userServiceHostname: String,
  acronymsServiceHostname: String) {
    userServiceURL = "http://\(userServiceHostname):8081"
    acronymsServiceURL =
      "http://\(acronymsServiceHostname):8082"
}
```

Finally, open **routes.swift** and replace the body of `routes(_:)` with the following:

```
let usersHostname: String
let acronymsHostname: String

// 1
if let users = Environment.get("USERS_HOSTNAME") {
  usersHostname = users
} else {
  usersHostname = "localhost"
}

// 2
if let acronyms = Environment.get("ACRONYMS_HOSTNAME") {
  acronymsHostname = acronyms
} else {
```

```
  acronymsHostname = "localhost"
}

// 3
try app.register(collection: UsersController(
  userServiceHostname: usersHostname,
  acronymsServiceHostname: acronymsHostname))
try app.register(collection: AcronymsController(
  acronymsServiceHostname: acronymsHostname,
  userServiceHostname: usersHostname))
```

Here's what changed:

1. Use `USERS_HOSTNAME` for the users microservice host name, if the environment variable exists. Otherwise, default to `localhost`.
2. Use `ACRONYMS_HOSTNAME` for the acronyms microservice host name, if the environment variable exists. Otherwise, default to `localhost`.
3. Register `UsersController` and `AcronymsController` as `RouteCollections`, injecting in the host names.

Build the project to ensure everything compiles and close Xcode. Now, open the tab with **TILAppUsers** and stop the app with **Control-C** since you no longer need a standalone instance running.

Next, open the tab with **TILAppAcronyms** and stop the app with **Control-C**. Open the project in Xcode and open **UserAuthMiddleware.swift**. Before `respond(to:chainingTo:)` add the following:

```
let authHostname: String

init(authHostname: String) {
  self.authHostname = authHostname
}
```

This allows you to pass in the hostname for the **TILAppUsers** microservice. Next, replace the URL that the middleware makes a request to — `http://localhost:8081/auth/authenticate` — with the following:

```
"http://\(authHostname):8081/auth/authenticate"
```

This uses the hostname passed in to make the request. Finally, open **AcronymsController.swift** and, inside `boot(routes:)`, replace `let authGroup = routes.grouped(UserAuthMiddleware())` with the following:

```
let authHostname: String
```

```
// 1
if let host = Environment.get("AUTH_HOSTNAME") {
  authHostname = host
} else {
  authHostname = "localhost"
}
// 2
let authGroup = routes.grouped(
  UserAuthMiddleware(authHostname: authHostname))
```

Here's what the new code does:

1. Check for an `AUTH_HOSTNAME` environment variable and use the value for `authHostname`. Default to `localhost` if the environment variable doesn't exist.
2. Create a route group using `UserAuthMiddleware` and pass in `authHostname`.

Build the project to ensure the code compiles.

The Docker Compose file

In the root directory containing all three projects, create a new file called **docker-compose.yml** and open it in an editor of your choice. Add the following to define the version and database services:

```
# 1
version: '3'
services:
  # 2
  postgres:
    image: "postgres"
    environment:
      - POSTGRES_DB=vapor_database
      - POSTGRES_USER=vapor_username
      - POSTGRES_PASSWORD=vapor_password
  # 3
  mysql:
    image: "mysql"
    environment:
      - MYSQL_USER=vapor_username
      - MYSQL_PASSWORD=vapor_password
      - MYSQL_DATABASE=vapor_database
      - MYSQL_RANDOM_ROOT_PASSWORD=yes
  # 4
  redis:
    image: "redis"
```

Here's what's happening:

1. Set the version number for the Docker Compose file.
2. Define a service for the PostgreSQL database. Use the **postgres** image and the same environment variables as your local Docker container.
3. Define a service for the MySQL database. Use the **mysql** image and the same environment variables as your local Docker container.
4. Define a service for the Redis database. Use the **redis** image.

At the end of the file, add the following for the **TILAppUsers** microservice:

```
  # 1
  til-users:
    # 2
    depends_on:
      - postgres
      - redis
    # 3
    build:
      context: ./TILAppUsers
      dockerfile: Dockerfile
    # 4
    environment:
      - DATABASE_HOST=postgres
      - REDIS_HOSTNAME=redis
      - PORT=8081
      - ENVIRONMENT=production
```

Note: The indentation must match the other services defined.

Here's what the new code does:

1. Define a service for **TILAppUsers**.
2. Tell Docker Compose this service depends on the **postgres** and **redis** containers. Docker Compose will start those services before **TILAppUsers**.
3. Tell Docker Compose the working directory for the service and the Dockerfile to use. The default Vapor template contains a compatible Dockerfile.
4. Set the necessary environment variables for the service. These define the variables required for the databases and the environment and port.

You may notice this service does not expose any ports outside of Docker Compose. Since you're routing everything via the API gateway, there's no need to expose the other microservices.

At the end of the file, add the specification for **TILAppAcronyms**:

```
# 1
til-acronyms:
  # 2
  depends_on:
    - mysql
    - til-users
  # 3
  build:
    context: ./TILAppAcronyms
    dockerfile: Dockerfile
  # 4
  environment:
    - DATABASE_HOST=mysql
    - PORT=8082
    - ENVIRONMENT=production
    - AUTH_HOSTNAME=til-users
```

Here's what the new specification does:

1. Define a service for **TILAppAcronyms**.
2. Tell Docker Compose this service depends on the **mysql** and **til-users** containers. Docker Compose will start those services before **TILAppAcronyms**.
3. Tell Docker Compose the working directory for the service and the Dockerfile to use. The default Vapor template contains a compatible Dockerfile.
4. Set the necessary environment variables for the service. These define the variables required for the database and the environment and port. This also sets the **AUTH_HOSTNAME** environment variable so this service can send requests to **TILAppUsers**.

Finally, at the end of the file, add the specification for **TILAppAPI**:

```
# 1
til-api:
  # 2
  depends_on:
    - til-users
    - til-acronyms
  # 3
  ports:
    - "8080:8080"
  # 4
  build:
    context: ./TILAppAPI
    dockerfile: Dockerfile
  # 5
```

```
    environment:
      - USERS_HOSTNAME=til-users
      - ACRONYMS_HOSTNAME=til-acronyms
      - PORT=8080
      - ENVIRONMENT=production
```

Here's what the new specification does:

1. Define a service for **TILAppAPI**.
2. Tell Docker Compose this service depends on the **til-users** and **til-acronyms** containers. Docker Compose will start those services before **TILAppAcronyms**.
3. Expose the container's 8080 port to your local machine on port 8080. This allows you to connect to the container.
4. Tell Docker Compose the working directory for the service and the Dockerfile to use. The default Vapor template contains a compatible Dockerfile.
5. Set the necessary environment variables for the service. This defines the environment and port. This also sets the **USERS_HOSTNAME** and **ACRONYMS_HOSTNAME** environment variables so this service can send requests to **TILAppUsers** and **TILAppAcronyms**.

Modifying Dockerfiles

Before you can run everything, you must change the Dockerfiles. Docker Compose starts the different containers in the requested order but won't wait for them to be ready to accept connections. This causes issues if your Vapor application tries to connect to a database before the database is ready. In **TILAppAcronyms**, open **Dockerfile** and replace:

```
ENTRYPOINT ["./Run"]
CMD ["serve", "--env", "production", "--hostname", "0.0.0.0",
"--port", "8080"]
```

With the following:

```
ENTRYPOINT sleep 20 && \
  ./Run serve --env $ENVIRONMENT --hostname 0.0.0.0 --port $PORT
```

This tells the container to wait for 20 seconds before starting the Vapor application. This should give the databases enough time to start up. In a real application, you may want to consider putting this in a script and testing the database before starting the Vapor app. You can also see Chapter 33, "Deploying with Docker", for a more robust solution.

In **TILAppUsers**, open **Dockerfile** and make the same change you made above.

Running everything

You're now ready to spin up your application in Docker Compose. In `Terminal`, in the directory containing **docker-compose.yml**, enter the following:

```
docker-compose up
```

This will download and build all the containers specified in **docker-compose.yml** and start them up. Note that it can take some time to build all the microservices.

When everything is up and running you'll see something like:

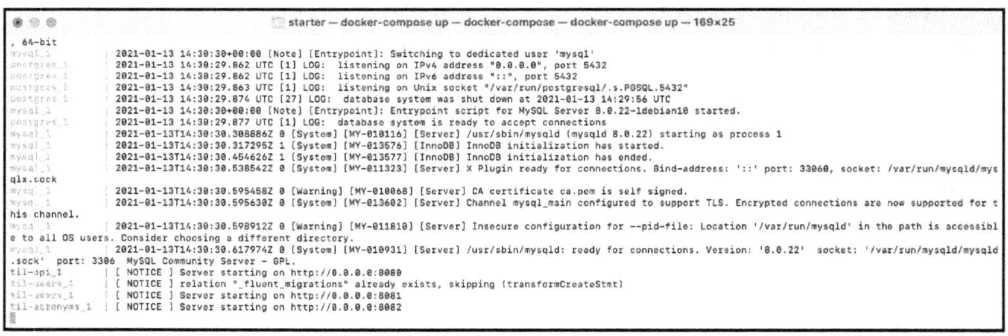

You can then open RESTed and make requests like before.

Where to go from here?

In this chapter, you learned how to use Vapor to create an API gateway. This makes it simple for clients to interact with your different microservices. You learned how to send requests between different microservices and return single responses. You also learned how to use Docker Compose to build and start all the microservices and link them together.

You now have the basic knowledge required to write powerful microservices. You can enhance this further with message queues, protocol buffers and remote procedural calls. There's no limit to the applications you can now build!

38 Conclusion

Throughout this book, you've learned how to build complex server applications using the Vapor framework. The book covers everything you need to know to build the applications to support your apps and front-end websites. All the basic building blocks for any application are in the book as well, as more complex use cases. You've learned everything from the basics of routing in Vapor to creating large templates for generating HTML. There should be nothing stopping you from taking Vapor and your new found knowledge and using it wherever you need.

We hope this book provides an awesome reference as you use Vapor throughout your projects and as server-side Swift becomes ever more popular.

If you have any questions or comments as you work through this book, please stop by our forums at http://forums.raywenderlich.com and look for the particular forum category for this book.

Thank you again for purchasing this book. Your continued support is what makes the tutorials, books, videos, conferences and other things we do at raywenderlich.com possible, and we truly appreciate it!

Wishing you all the best in your continued adventures with server-side Swift,

– Tim, Logan, Tanner, Richard and Darren

The *Server-Side Swift with Vapor* team